★ ★ ★ ★ ★ ★ ★ ★ ★ ★ ★

America Is A Democracy
- Not A Theocracy -

The Proposition For

A Constitutional Amendment
For Abortion and Defining Life
Guaranteeing Reproductive Liberty

LARRY S. MILNER
MD, JD, MLS

★ ★ ★ ★ ★ ★ ★ ★ ★ ★ ★

Don't judge a man
until you walk in his shoes.

Native American wisdom,
specifically the Cherokee people

~ ~ ~

Don't judge a pregnant woman
until you walk in her shoes.

The Society for
the Prevention of Infanticide

America Is A Democracy, Not A Theocracy

ISBN 978-1-956381-92-4

Copyright © 2025 by Larry S. Milner
infanticide@ameritech.net

Published by
The Society for the Prevention of Infanticide
infanticide@ameritech.net

54321

Contents

About The Author

Dr. Larry S. Milner, MD, JD, MLS is a board-certified physician in Internal Medicine, Hematology and Oncology, as well as an attorney. He received his medical training at the University of Illinois, Massachusetts General Hospital, University of Pennsylvania Hospital, and the National Institutes of Health. He trained at Loyola Law School in Chicago, and has a Master of Liberal Studies degree from Lake Forest College.

In 2025, Dr. Milner was chosen for inclusion in *Marquis Who's Who* listing of the nation's top professionals, a distinction granted to individuals who have demonstrated noteworthy leadership and impact in their profession.

Dr. Milner is the founder of The Society for the Prevention of Infanticide.

In addition to being the author of *Hardness of Heart, Hardness of Life: the Stain of Human Infanticide,* for which he is an expert in the field of infanticide, Dr. Milner is also a recognized historian with expertise in Hebraic, Greek, and Egyptian cultures.

He is the author of *Shattered Faith: The Life of Abraham; Shattered Trust: The Life of Moses; Moses' And Muhammad's Contribution To Monotheism; Hebraic Influences On Greek Philosophy And Mysticism: The Legacy Of Isaiah's Anointing Of King Cyrus II Of Persia; Hebraic Influences On Greek Civilization: Was Achilles a Jew?*; *Legacy Of The Burning Bush: A Kabbalistic Interpretation of the Hebrew Exodus; Tainted Hands: An Encounter With The Mosaic Code*; *Your Name Is Achilles: Son Of Daniel; The Sun Shone Only In Goshen: The Effect Of The Exodus On Akhenaten In Egypt* and *Shattered Dreams.*

Dr. Milner and his wife, Marlene, divide their time between Lincolnshire, Illinois and Boynton Beach, Florida. They have three daughters, Kimberly Seiden, Wendy LaVarre, and Jodi Morton, and wonderful grandchildren.

Preface

The United States Constitution today is generally considered to be the most hallowed document of the most fair Democracy that has ever existed on earth. The United States has been referred to as both a Republic and a Democracy, but there is a difference between these two words. I want to point out the distinction at the very start of this book, because to understand why I am introducing a new amendment to the Constitution, you must realize why three United States Supreme Courts over the past fifty years interpreted the same Constitution in opposite ways, with two of them, *Roe v. Wade, 410 U.S. 113 (1973)* and *Planned Parenthood of Southeastern Pennsylvania v. Casey, 505 U.S. 833 (1992),* holding abortion to be a protected personal right in the Constitution, and one, *Dobbs v. Jackson Women's Health Organization 597 U.S. 215 (2022)*, then overturning both of these cases, declaring them to be unconstitutional.

Dobbs determined that because the word "abortion" never appeared in the Constitution, it could not be considered a personal right, and would have to be made a legal constitutional right by the passage of an amendment, and not a judicial decision. This was America acting as a Republic, where the government is run by elected and appointed officials, rather than by the people directly. In a Democracy, the power of the government is invested in the people, who may either directly manage governmental function, or let their elected representatives make decisions on their behalf.[1] In America, we are usually governed as a Republic because our population size makes it difficult to govern with a popular vote on all matters. We do act as a Democracy, however, when our governmental officials are elected, for that tally is by popular vote, and we also act as a Democracy in 49 states when state amendments are put to a popular vote, the one exception being Delaware, where the legislature decides the amendment by a 2/3 vote in both chambers, separated by 90-120 days, rather than the general public.

It is the amendments that modify the words of our Constitution. Because we can alter what the Constitution says by popular vote,

---

1   Microsoft CoPilot (6/1/2025). Personal communication; Coby, <u>The Constitutional Convention of 1787: Constructing the American Republic</u>, 31.

we remain both a Democracy and a Republic. Although *Dobbs* was correct in making this statement, they were wrong to overturn the prior decisions because their reasoning was reached by making a new law regarding the definition of when life begins to determine what was meant by a "person" in the Constitution. The Supreme Court cannot make a new law; it can only determine what the law is, and that is common law, which both prior Supreme Courts determined was defined by "quickening," and not conception.

Many well-known scholars don't always realize the distinction between a Republic and a Democracy, in my opinion, as evidenced by Laurence H. Tribe, a Professor at Harvard Law School, and an acknowledged constitutional law scholar, who has claimed that "ours is a republican form of government, in which the votes of citizens are used primarily to select legislatures and executives, which themselves select judges," an opinion that totally ignores the process of approving amendments.[2] I'm not excited about taking on a pillar of constitutional law like Laurence H. Tribe, but I disagree with his conclusion that we are a "republican form of government," and I still demand that we are primarily a Democracy, for when push comes to shove, our Founding Fathers were intelligent enough to devise the amendment process to maintain the control of the American population over their government, which I contend is a must-always sign of remaining a Democracy, and not a Republic, or even worse, a Theocracy. Yes, we still are at the mercy of our executive and legislative branches of government in how our country is run on a daily basis, but in the end, the people in the country are the ones in control, and not the elected and appointed officials.

The Founding Fathers couldn't detail every personal right the citizens were entitled to when they wrote the Constitution, so they provided an amendment process to update the Constitution when necessary. This brilliant technique is used today by almost every country in the world. It was the incredible foresight of our Founding Fathers who perfected the system of Democracy. Although they decided that the Supreme Court had the ultimate power of interpreting the Constitution, they included a way in which Democracy could modify the interpretation of the Supreme Court when it erred in its judgment, as when they ruled that slavery, and the right of women

---

2 Tribe, "Finding Abortion Rights in the Constitution," 474.

to vote, was a State, rather than a Federal constitutional concern. Amendments were able to be passed to change the meaning of the Constitution, as determined by the Supreme Court, and we are in that predicament today because the *Dobbs* Court overturned the decisions of *Roe v. Wade* and *Casey*, both of whom found a constitutional right for women to have an abortion of an unwanted, nonviable fetus, but did it by first changing the common law of our country, which they cannot do. *Dobbs* ruled that it was a matter for the States to decide whether abortion is a right of all citizens, and it would require an amendment to the Constitution to specifically state that abortion was a guaranteed right. Even though they were wrong to make this judgment, they said it, so I will do it. Like my love of food, however, if it's not fresh, I won't like it, but I'll eat it.

I emphasize this point because our two major political parties have today taken on the same image of violent disputation over the issue of abortion as took place during the Constitutional Convention, when delegates were chosen from the thirteen colonies at the end of the Revolutionary War to write the Constitution that continues to be revered across the world today. It took place at the Pennsylvania State House in Philadelphia from May 25, 1787-September 17, 1787, known today as Independence Hall, and George Washington, who headed the Revolutionary War army, was elected President of the Convention, and later President of the United States on February 4, 1789, by the Electoral College.

Although Philadelphia at the time was the largest American city, it only had forty thousand inhabitants closely packed in an eight-block stretch, and at the time was also home to two thousand free blacks, so the issue of slavery was fresh in their mind.[3] Fifty-five delegates from twelve states were chosen to write the document, with Rhode Island refusing to attend because it was opposed to a strong central government, although they would later sign the Constitution. Amy Coney Barrett, one of the Supreme Court Justices who I will castigate for voting to overturn *Roe v. Wade*, described them as having "witnessed a decade in which their new country had declared independence, defeated against all odds the world's most powerful empire, united its states (albeit loosely) under a central government, and began functioning as an independent nation," a just reason for

---

3   Barrett, <u>Listening to the Law: Reflections on the Court and Constitution</u>, 123-124.

us to consider them our Founding Fathers, but her to be a traitor to our cause.[4] The delegates quickly realized, however, that there were going to be difficulties getting the two sides to agree on many vital issues, and decided that they should first agree on the structure of the Federal Government in the Constitution itself, and then return at a later date to decide what civil liberties would exist on the federal level to all citizens, and what rights would be determined by the individual states. The delegates were separated into two relatively equal factions from the start, with one group called the Federalists, who were in favor of a shared governmental authority, but desired a strong federal authority, led by Alexander Hamilton (1755-1804) from New York,[5] James Madison (1751-1836) from Virginia,[6] and John Jay (1745-1829) from New York.[7]

They were opposed by the Anti-Federalists, who were concerned that the federal government could become too powerful, especially on the issue of personal rights, and favored more authority being left to the states, like Patrick Henry (1736-1799) from Virginia, George Mason (1725-1792) from Virginia, and Samuel Adams (1722-1803) from Massachusetts. Their attitude had shown up during the Revolutionary War when George Washington asked a group of New Jersey militiamen to pledge an oath to the United States, and they refused, insisting that their country was New Jersey.[8] This was the reason that Rhode Island did not attend the Convention, because they were ardent Anti-Federalists, but they did eventually sign the agreed-upon Constitution, and join the Union. The Federalists kept their identities secret to minimize partisan bickering, and signed each

---

4   Ibid., 121.

5   Hamilton was a voracious reader in the law and economics, and a military commander in the War for Independence. He later became the first Secretary of the Treasury.

6   Madison is considered the Father of the Constitution and the Bill of Rights and later became the fifth Secretary of State, and the fourth President of the United States, leading the U.S. through the War of 1812.

7   Jay served twice as a delegate to Congress, as well as Ambassador to Spain, Secretary of Foreign Affairs, and President of Congress during the war.

8   Barrett, Listening to the Law: Reflections on the Court and Constitution, 122.

essay they wrote with the pen name "Publius," from Publius Valerius Poplicola (d. 503 BCE), who was one of the leaders of the Roman revolution who set up a republic in Rome.[9] Patrick Henry at that time made his personal view as an Anti-Federalist famous when he declared: "Give me liberty or give me death," and his intensity was accepted by every one of the Founders, although they bitterly disagreed on what exactly that term "liberty" was intended to mean, a sign that their task was going to be difficult.

The Federalists wanted a strong central government, like those known as Democrats today want, and the Anti-Federalists wanted more control given to each of the thirteen colonies, which today are the states, and the politicians who believe in this call themselves Republicans. It is odd that our political parties have remained basically the same over our entire history of 250 years, but I am not partial to either party, and I have voted for Presidents from different political parties all my life, always backing the man or woman I felt most represented the desire for America to remain a Democracy. I am aware that history teaches that the first country to set up a method of rule that was called a Democracy was the ancient Greek city of Athens, when the Greeks refused to be ruled by a king. They never truly reached that status, however, because like our situation when our Constitution was written, slavery was a common practice, and the country was ruled only by men, as women were not allowed to vote. We began in a similar fashion, but unlike ancient Greece, our fledgling country was attempting to form a Democracy with a population that was much larger, and more diverse, than was present in ancient Athens at that time. It is estimated that Athens had a total population of 250-300,000 people, and 30-60,000 were adult citizen males who could vote.[10] At their size of only 926 square miles (2,400 sq. km.), it was possible to have the entire population of men tallied on all important decisions, but when our Constitution was written, the population in America was about 2.5 million, and the Caucasian male population was 200-300,000, spread over an area of 141,276 square miles (366,000 sq. km.), making it impossible for the entire population to vote at the same time, except during general elections,

---

9   Skousen, <u>The Federalist Papers Made Easier: The Complete and Original Text Subdivided and Annotated for Easier Understanding</u>, x.

10 "What was the Population of Ancient Greece," 2, 4.

and when amendments were proposed and voted on.[11] Our Founding Fathers may have wanted our country to be a Democracy, but it was going to be necessary to incorporate both the Republic and Democracy methods of governance to achieve that goal. It would take a lot more time to reach their formidable vision, but the eventual result would be a Constitution that showed how freedom was not a concept easily achieved, but was a goal that could be reached if people were willing to inch their way toward a successful solution.

Because the present Supreme Court was put together by Republican Presidents to reverse the right of women to have a constitutional right to an abortion, I must now turn back to the people – the only source of sovereign authority under our constitutional system of government — and have them pass an amendment ensuring that this essential freedom of abortion of unwanted, nonviable fetuses is constitutionally guaranteed in writing, as they demand. I believe that our Founding Fathers were concerned that every resident who had "sacrificed, fought, and died" in a Revolutionary War to achieve the benefit of living in a country free from being ruled by others by crossing an ocean, and inheriting the land they now owned under the natural law, and they should have liberty, because "all men are created equal; that they are endowed by their Creator with certain inalienable rights; that among these are life, liberty and the pursuit of happiness," as they said in the Declaration of Independence adopted on July 4, 1776.[12] By the time most Americans graduate from grade school, these words are usually burned into their memory, as they should be, although it seems that sometimes our elected and appointed officials forget the responsibility that these words also place upon their actions. We are presently in a state of political uncertainty because all three of these Supreme Court decisions cannot be correct, since at least one of their readings must be wrong, and I am writing this book to propose an amendment that states definitely that women in America have the right to abort unwanted, nonviable pregnancies, and to explain why, in a way that will show why the decision the Supreme Court made in *Dobbs* was wrong.

I realize that in writing this book I will be infuriating a President who does not take to accepting such resistance passively, but I contend that he is trying to change our Democracy into a Theocracy, and I cannot allow that to happen. I proudly retain the view that America

11 Microsoft CoPilot (7/22/2025). Personal Communication.
12 Coby, <u>The Constitutional Convention of 1787: Constructing the American Republic</u>, 32.

must remain a Democracy. I am confident that our country will not submit to *Roe v. Wade* being overturned, and will "throw the bums out of town," as Steve Goodman (1948-1984), my favorite folk singer along with Bob Gibson (1931-1966), said he would do to the Lincoln Park Pirates, who towed cars away in Chicago. The *Dobbs* decision was based on religious faith and not constitutional interpretation, in my opinion, as I will explain in this book, and it was purposely designed by electing devout Catholics who believe that life begins at conception, as Pope Pius IX (1792-1878) declared, rather than at quickening, which is the American common law. I find this action reprehensible, but out of respect for what the President and Supreme Court represents, I won't call them bums, but I will only disagree with their ruling, and show them the errors of their ways by recommending this amendment.

Despite the fact that our Constitution was approved with the words I have quoted as written, it still did not afford equal rights to *all* of its citizens, even when Delaware, the first state to agree to its terms, ratified it on December 7, 1787. It still did not afford equal rights to *everyone* when it was ratified by the ninth state, New Hampshire, on June 21, 1788, making it the Federal Law of the United States. Finally, when the 13th state, Rhode Island, ratified it on May 29, 1790, and made the approval unanimous, after initially refusing to be part of the Constitutional Convention because it feared a strong central governmental authority, the Constitution still did not guarantee rights in writing for *all* of its citizens.[13] Only three states had unanimous votes for approval, including Delaware, New Jersey, and Georgia, and two states had votes that barely approved the document, New York at 30-27, and Rhode Island at 34-32.[14] The citizens with rights did not include slaves or women who could vote on the federal level. Those rights had to await slaves being made citizens by the Fourteenth Amendment in 1868, and women being given the right to vote in the Nineteenth Amendment in 1920, a period of time that took 132 years, 11 months, and 9 days to complete.[15] It was the Amendments that afforded equal rights to everyone who achieved citizenship status, but our task to perfect the system of Democracy for the world had just

---

13 "Constitution of the United States," 4.
14 Barrett, Listening to the Law: Reflections on the Court and Constitution, 134.
15 Microsoft CoPilot (9/7/2025). Personal Communication.

started, and there are still many rights that have never been mentioned with particularity, such as the right to an abortion, and so our goal is still a work in progress, and it is essential that we continue to function in that capacity until we can reach a true Democracy.

The process of writing the United States Constitution began after the Revolutionary War ended on September 3, 1783, with the signing of the Treaty of Paris, and the Constitutional Convention then met in Philadelphia on May 25, 1787, "for the sole and express purpose of revising the Articles of Confederation," which had acted as a temporary Constitution that the thirteen colonies could use as a way to manage their affairs while fighting the Revolutionary War.[16] The writing of the Articles of Confederation were begun by the Confederation Congress, and were ratified in 1781, after the major fighting in the Revolutionary War ended. The document lacked the description of a strong central government, however, and was not a structure that could manage the control of a new nation, now prepared to compete on the world stage as an independent country. It had a unicameral legislature with each state having one vote, and had neither a judicial nor an executive branch, so it's power was minute.[17] The primary goal of the Constitutional Convention was to write a document that would guarantee the liberties of all Americans from that time forward, and show the world how a truly free people could prosper and grow into a world superpower.[18]

We revere our Founding Fathers for their foresight, but we are presently in danger of destroying the Democracy they formulated, and we fought so hard to defend.

To truly become the most fair democracy on earth, a promise was made in the Preamble to the U.S. Constitution, primarily written by Gouverneur Morris (1752-1816), a Pennsylvania delegate to the 1787 Constitutional Convention held in Independence Hall in Philadelphia,

---

16 Dry, "The Debate Over the Ratification of the Constitution: The Federalists v. The Anti-Federalists," 29.

17 Barrett, Listening to the Law: Reflections on the Court and Constitution, 126.

18 One of the important legislative acts of that Congress, however, was also the formation of the Northwest Territory in 1787, which was the land that eventually would become the states of Ohio, Indiana, Illinois, Wisconsin, Michigan, and Minnesota, that was ceded to the United States in the Treaty of Paris, as I will discuss in Chapter II. "Northwest Territory," 1.

that the Constitution would guarantee equal rights to all citizens when it said:

> We the People of the United States, in Order to form a more perfect Union, establish Justice, insure domestic tranquility, provide for the common defence, promote the general Welfare, and secure the Blessings of Liberty to ourselves and our Posterity, do ordain and establish this Constitution for the United States of America.[19]

This bold statement, by a man few people remember today, has been generally accepted as reflecting the aims of the Constitutional Convention to provide for *all* "the People of the United States," that they would attain rights that established "justice" through the passage of amendments which would define the nature of those rights at a later date, so that there would be equal rights for *all* the citizens of the United States, and not just Caucasian males, which is how the Constitution was originally intended to be written by many of the Founding Fathers. The Preamble indicated that the goal was to allow the Constitution time to determine what exactly those rights would be, but to have it apply to all "the People of the United States," because that was what a true Democracy was. They knew that such a goal was never reached by the ancient Greeks who began the concept of Democracy, for back then, as it was when the Constitution was written, slavery was legal, and women could not vote. We have come a long way since then, but full Democracy has not yet been achieved, and we have at least one more amendment that needs to be added, that of abortion, before we can say we're almost there.

This lofty goal that was written into the Preamble would, over the next two years, prove to be more difficult to reach than at first appeared, for the Constitutional Convention that began after the thirteen colonies won their War of Independence from England saw a bitter debate develop at the very start between the two factions of Framers who were hotly divided over the issue of what powers were going to be given to the Federal government, and what powers were to be retained by each individual State, which by now had lived in individual districts, united by their existence in North America, but divided in both their heritage and lifestyle.

---

19 "Preamble to the United States Constitution," 1.

When the representatives, whom I have said were dubbed Federalists and Anti-Federalists, met to decide how to rule their new country independently, their differences showed up in both the manner in which the powers of the governing bodies were going to be designed, and also how the individual rights of the citizens were going to be delineated at the federal and state levels. How the power of the government was going to be spread among the various states, small and large, was a major issue because the thirteen colonies were composed of vastly different numbers of inhabitants, with Virginia the largest colony at 447,016, and Georgia the smallest at 23,375.[20] In addition, Massachusetts had recently been three provinces – Massachusetts Bay, Plymouth, and Maine – but was now united into one state, much larger in size than the rest.[21] How was the variance of the colonies going to be made equitable in the federal format was a question that needed to be answered, but on this issue they quickly found a way to do it by making the legislature bicameral, with a Congress that had Representatives from each state determined by their population number, so the larger states had more Representatives; but the Senators were limited to two per state, so that every state had an equal number of elected delegates providing a compromise that satisfied all concerned.

Deciding how to divide authority turned out not to be very difficult, but the delegates would find that the issues of liberty would be a much greater problem to attain. The fact was that at the time our War of Independence was won, there was still a common belief in many of the colonies that slavery was natural, and in all of them, except New Jersey, that women were intended to be dependent on the control of their husbands, and were not allowed to vote.[22] It was 2,295 years since Athens became a Democracy under the leadership of Cleisthenes (c. 570-508 BCE), but the southern states still had a large number of slaves that were not considered as citizens, and rather were seen as slave "property," which was not accepted by the northern states.[23] It would take many years of amendments, and a Civil War from 1861-

---

20 "Thirteen Colonies," 1-13; Microsoft CoPilot (6/20/2025), Personal Communication.

21 Coby, The Constitutional Convention of 1787: Constructing the American Republic, 7.

22 Microsoft CoPilot (5/20/2025). Personal communication.

23 Dry, "The Debate Over the Ratification of the Constitution: The Federalists v. The Anti-Federalists," 31.

1865, for this problem to be settled, and the Statue of Liberty could then be finally given by the people of France in 1886 to the United States as a way to commemorate the abolition of slavery. The ability to decide on a format to govern themselves may have turned out to be relatively easy for our Founding Fathers, but the issues of freedoms each citizen would have on a federal level were another matter altogether, and equality for women – and for people of color – were still years away from equal recognition.

I mention these often overlooked details about the difference between a Democracy and a Republic to highlight the importance of the Constitution because I am going to claim in this book that an amendment to approve abortion is not only necessary to protect the rights of women to end an unwanted pregnancy before the fetus is viable, but, more importantly, to be sure that our country is guided by the Constitution as a guarantee of our rights as a Democracy.

I want to emphasize here that I am only claiming that there is a right of pregnancies to be aborted in the Constitution that are "unwanted" for a variety of reasons, but all must also be nonviable, meaning they could not survive a premature birth for very long, because I agree that abortion of a viable fetus is equivalent to murder. We are not dealing with "bad" women here; they are not immoral or uncaring because they don't want to carry every pregnancy to completion.

Most women who have an abortion eventually give birth to other children, but I am only writing an amendment to abort unwanted, nonviable fetuses, for I agree that the abortion of a viable fetus that could eventually live independently outside of the uterus would be equivalent with infanticide, which is murder, and would therefore require special constitutional permission, as takes place during declared wars, and legally approved executions for crimes.

"Unwanted" and "nonviable" were both mentioned in the argument made to the Supreme Court in *Roe v. Wade* as a crucial necessity to decide in order to obtain an abortion, and I believe it reflects the view of a majority of Americans as well.[24] Two Supreme Courts, *Roe v. Wade* and *Casey*, both agreed on this issue, and only one, *Dobbs*, did not, which I will explain later in Chapters III and IV, but it is necessary to clarify this issue because there is no question that viable fetuses who have to be aborted is an act of murder that must have special

---

24 "Transcript of First Oral Argument in *Roe v. Wade*, 410 U.S. 113 (1973)," 8.

issues shown, as takes place during times of declared war or corporal punishment for crimes.

As I said, our present government is as functionally bifurcated as the Congress that wrote our Constitution was, meaning we, in essence, have the same system of government as existed when the Constitution was first written, although our politicians today are known as Democrats, who, like the Federalists, favor a strong federal government; and Republicans, who resemble the Anti-Federalists, favor more authority to be given to the state governments.

It is in this current environment that our country has found itself divided on the most pressing issue of our time – the legality of abortion.

I contend that we are now going to have to convince our present population that an amendment should be passed, approving an abortion of unwanted, nonviable pregnancies, because the amendments we now have in place have proven that personal liberties will make our country stronger, and with a more healthy environment for children from unwanted births to live, if the vast number of unwanted births is reduced by elective abortions before the fetus is viable.

Our present government, and two disparate Supreme Court rulings on abortion, have shown that they are not capable of dealing with this situation, and we are going to have to rely on the population-at-large as a Democracy to determine whether we can legalize abortion of nonviable fetuses through the amendment process.

Chapter I

Introduction

The plan of our Founding Fathers to utilize amendments to protect the rights of all citizens in the United States of America has worked wonderfully, but it is now 238 years later, and with over two centuries of improvement embedded in the historical record, we find ourselves knee-deep in an attempt to turn the clock back by a conservative President who has created a conservative Supreme Court, which has agreed to once again try to turn the control of our future welfare back over to the 50 states by limiting the power of the Federal government, and not allowing abortion of unwanted, and nonviable pregnancies as decided by two prior Supreme Court decisions.

Acting like the Anti-Federalists during the Constitutional Convention, President Trump and the Republican Party are now trying to defeat all the gains our country has made by the passage of Twenty-Seven Amendments, and has put us in a true constitutional crisis because their hand-picked Supreme Court, with six of the nine Justices conservative and Catholic, demanded that an amendment be passed to give women the right to an abortion in *Dobbs v. Jackson Women's Health Organization*, as they overturned the opinions of both *Roe v. Wade*, and *Planned Parenthood of Southeastern Pennsylvania v. Casey* in the process. They did this because they believed that their constituents would never agree to such an amendment, given the fact that Donald Trump was reelected as President in 2024, and had proclaimed in his first presidential campaign in 2016, in a debate with Hillary Clinton on October 19, 2016, that he would put Pro-Life Justices on the Supreme Court if elected, and send the issue back to the states.[1]

Despite expecting the verdict delivered in the case, I am still devastated by the *Dobbs* proclamation, but I remain confident that the American public will approve my amendment proposal because the Mississippi legislation which led to the *Dobbs* decision had written

---

1 Biskupic, <u>Nine Black Robes: Inside the Supreme Court's Drive to the Right and Its Historic Consequences</u>, 76-77. He had said in a debate with Hillary Clinton that if he became president, the overturning of *Roe* "would happen automatically." Waldman, <u>The Supermajority: How the Supreme Court Divided America</u>, 131.

a statute that was very similar to the amendment I know propose, and it was one of the states that helped vote Trump into power as President. In order to prevent interference by the Supreme Court again, I also am proposing that we make our present common law part of the amendment by declaring that the definition of "person" in the Constitution includes a fetus who has reached the age of 20-weeks gestation, and not conception as suggested by the *Dobbs* verdict.

The Supreme Court, according to our Constitution, is the judicial power that has the final say about how the Constitution is meant to be interpreted, but in a Democracy, the citizens of the United States actually have the authority to override their judgment by making an amendment clear and concise about the meaning of the amendment, which is what Justice Alito was attempting to do by changing the common law in his verdict. The Supreme Court can interpret the common law, but not change it, and as I will explain in Chapter IV, Justice Alito agreed that the common law was "quickening," but declared that it was no longer valid. Since the last two Supreme Courts both agreed that quickening was the common law, he is clearly wrong in this statement, and my amendment will allow his judgment to be discarded.

My task is still difficult because for an amendment to be approved, 3/4 of the states have to approve the proposal by popular in every state except for the state of Delaware, which requires two consecutive legislatures, approving the amendment by a 2/3 vote. The states vary in their requirements, with ten states needing a simple majority in one session; twenty-five states needing a supermajority in one session (e.g., two-thirds or three-fifths vote); eleven states needing a majority in two consecutive sessions; and four states requiring either a majority in two sessions or a supermajority vote in one session.[2] I believe the citizens of our country will see why my amendment should be approved after reading this book, and will pass my amendment proposal, just like they did to abolish the legality of slavery, and give women the right to vote, both issues which the Supreme Court at the time refused to approve. Once this is done, I hope I can convince the Supreme Court that their attempt to trust what the Catholic Pope declares should not override their swearing to follow what the Founding Fathers intended to say in writing the text of our Constitution, and if future cases reach the

---

2   "Constitutional Amendment Processes in the 50 States," 1-9.

Supreme Court on the subject of abortion, that they promise to recuse themselves if they follow the Catholic Pope's claim that life begins at conception, rather than the common law definition of quickening. They swore an oath to do that, and if they cannot, they must recuse themselves from voting in any case that involves the issue of abortion. I know that Amy Coney Barrett knew that every Supreme Court Justice swears to only follow the Constitution in deciding the law because she said that in her book, *Listening to the Law: Reflections on the Court and Constitution*, but she voted to overturn *Roe v. Wade* because life begins at conception, and that is making the law, and not following the oath to support the Constitution.[3]

Our Founding Fathers wrote a Constitution that truly reflected a Democracy, and our Congress has since then continued to properly define the rights all citizens should legally have through the amendment process. I trust that the American populace today will continue that legacy by validating the rights of women to choose whether they should prevent the birth of unwanted pregnancies before the fetus is viable, as two prior Supreme Court rulings did. The choice to terminate an unwanted pregnancy is, and should be, a woman's right to decide, as long as the fetus is nonviable, because as the common law throughout the world has generally decided that viability of the fetus begins at quickening, and not conception.

We now know that abortion is actually safer than delivering a full-term neonate, and we also know that the long history of infanticide and child abuse of unwanted children throughout our course of civilization is a preventable crime by letting the women make that choice if they do not want to take a pregnancy to full-term. The incidence of both of these crimes has significantly abated since *Roe v. Wade* was passed, with the data showing that the crime of infanticide of unwanted children has dropped from the prior rate of 10-15%, to now below 1%, and although the data on child abuse is still unacceptable, most sociologists agree we are making progress.

Our country had to go through a Civil War, and the passage of Twenty-Seven Amendments, before the Supreme Court gave the right of abortion to women in the *Roe v. Wade* verdict, and for fifty years the advantage of that decision has proven to the world that the benefits of

---

3   Barrett, Listening to the Law: Reflections on the Court and Constitution, 24.

preventing unwanted pregnancies outweighs the false claims that life begins at conception, and any abortion is murder.

If we fail to approve this amendment, there is no question that we will witness a rise in the infanticide rate of unwanted births, and the incidence of child abuse, both of which will be a travesty of justice. Neglect accounts for 59% of the cases of child abuse, with physical abuse, sexual abuse, psychological maltreatment, medical neglect, and other forms of abuse also significant contributors.[4] I am not about to stand aside and let an ultra-Orthodox Supreme Court try to turn the clock back, and erase the many years of polishing our trophy case of personal liberties by failing to appreciate that the Constitution is not only the original document written, but every amendment that was added to it is also a protected liberty that made sure that the original intention of the Founding Fathers was ultimately fulfilled.

We are still today one America, strong and united in our concepts of Justice, and the independence of the individual states that joined to fight the Revolutionary War is no longer the tiny force it once was, functioning without a Constitution to keep the federal government strong.

You can't "Make America Great Again," as Donald Trump's MAGA proponents claim, with a Supreme Court that refuses to accept the rights of all citizens to the same degree, and this includes the right of a woman to choose to not give birth to an unwanted, nonviable pregnancy, as two prior Supreme Courts ruled. A third Court now demands that an amendment be passed to confirm that right, and that is what I am going to do in this book, not because I should have to, but because I cannot let Donald Trump manipulate our Constitution, and threaten the integrity of our country's history.

We must always guarantee to every American citizen, no matter their country of origin or sexual status, no matter what religious belief they may hold, the rights they were promised to have in the Preamble to our Constitution, and we must assure that we keep our integrity alive by following the intention of the Constitution, along with the amendments, which is the product of our willingness to fight two World Wars, and multiple other conflicts, to insure that all people who choose to call themselves American are equal to every other.

America became great in the first place by declaring that our

---

4   Hattery and Smith, <u>The Social Dynamics of Family Violence,</u>" 139.

nation would separate Church and State, and assuring that every resident would be free to follow any religion they choose, as long as that devotion was not harmful to those who disbelieve in their God, or, perhaps, to no God at all. Donald Trump says he wants to "Make America Great Again," but the word "Again" is only necessary because he was the one who caused the problem with the Supreme Court he formed for the sole purpose of making abortion illegal. I want to emphasize this fact because I am going to claim in this book that Justice Samuel A. Alito, Jr., who wrote the opinion in *Dobbs*, made a critical error in his overturning *Roe v. Wade* when he declared that life begins at conception, and not at quickening, when the mother feels the movement of her fetus, which was when Justice Harry Blackmun said in *Roe. v. Wade* life began, and basically is what the state of Mississippi said as well.

The common law has been the standard of justice across the globe for many millennia before the Constitution was written, and it has always identified quickening as a manifestation of the beginning of life because it reflected the ability of the fetus to move. In 1812, a Massachusetts case known as *Commonwealth v. Bangs* confirmed that abortions before quickening were not criminal cases, extending the law to America, which the English jurist William Blackstone (1723-1780), had stated was the principle in England, as I will discuss in Chapters II and III.[5]

The word "religion" may have only appeared in the First Amendment of the Constitution one time, when it read: "Congress shall make no law respecting an establishment of religion, or prohibiting the free exercise thereof," but that line says it all.[6] Catholics can practice their religion freely, and disapprove of abortion if they choose, but Justice Alito must not allow his religious beliefs to prevent other religions from accepting that an nonviable fetus is not yet a "person," and choose to have a legal abortion because under the common law, life does not begin until quickening takes place. I personally believe that future Supreme Courts, whether they are conservative or liberal, will agree with my position, for there are too many children's lives at stake today, and we know the Founding Fathers were adamant that freedom

---

5   Mohr, <u>Abortion in America: The Origins and Evolution of National Policy, 1800-1900</u>, 5.
6   "First Amendment to the United States Constitution," 2.

to practice whatever religion you had faith in was a vital component of what the United States would stand for. We cannot wait for that to happen, however, for the immediate stakes are too high, and it is critical that we legalize abortion of unwanted, nonviable pregnancies as soon as possible.

The importance of separating religion from the function of the government was critical to the Founding Fathers for that to take place, as indicated by Thomas Jefferson's (1743-1826) correspondence which called for "a wall of separation between Church and State," a dictum which was approved by the Supreme Court in *Everson v. Board of Education, 330 U.S. 1 (1947)*.[7]

As Lee C. Bollinger, President Emeritus and Seth Low Professor of Columbia University, said in his "Opening Dialogue" to the book he edited about *Roe v. Dobbs*: "It is vitally important that the Constitution not serve as a contentless charter for justices to implement their personal or political preferences under the guise of doing 'law,'" but that is exactly what Justice Alito did when he read the verdict in *Dobbs v. Jackson Women's Health Organization*.[8]

We don't know precisely what religion every one of our Founding Fathers followed, but Microsoft CoPilot indicates that "most were Protestant Christians," including George Washington (1732-1799), who was head of the army that fought the Revolutionary War, and then was elected to serve as President of that Convention, John Jay, and Edward Rutledge (1749-1800), who were Anglican; Richard Stockton (1730-1781) and John Witherspoon (1723-1794), who were Presbyterian; John Adams (1735-1826) and Samuel Adams, who were Congregationalists; Charles Carroll (1737-1832) and Daniel Carroll (1730-1796) of Maryland, along with Thomas Fitzsimmons (1741-1811) of Pennsylvania, who were Catholic; and Thomas Jefferson and Benjamin Franklin, who leaned toward Deism.[9] Thirty-nine men signed the Constitution on September 17, 1787, representing twelve of the thirteen colonies, with Rhode Island absent. I want to emphasize that only three of those Founding Fathers were known to be Catholic. There is no evidence that any of them would have disputed what Thomas Jefferson said about the importance of separating Church and

---

7   Ibid., 1.
8   Bollinger and Stone, "Opening Dialogue," xxii.
9   Microsoft CoPilot (4/18/2025). Personal communication.

State, however, for when the Constitution was signed, the Catholic Church had not yet decided that life began at conception, and the dominant view was still based on Aristotle's (384-322 BCE) theory of "mediate animation," which held that it was 40 days after conception for males, and 80 days for females, before life could truly be said to begin, so it was then that a fetus became a "person," and not at conception.[10]

The issue of the definition of who is a "person," and who is not, is a critical element in interpreting the meaning of the Constitution, because the word "person," or "persons," appears 52 times in the Constitution, but is never actually defined.[11]   If you are going to believe in Originalism, which is a conservative principle to interpret the Constitution only as it was intended at the time it was written, as I will explain in Chapter IV, you cannot claim that life began at conception for that was not a Papal edict at the time the Constitution was written.   Pope John Paul II (1920-2005), in his *Evangelium Vitae* encyclical letter in 1995, may have declared that life began at conception because even though the soul cannot be ascertained by empirical data, he declared: "how could a living human creature (*vivens creatura humana*) not also (*etiam*) be a human person?" but that was said in the 21st century, not the 18th century.[12]

I respect the Pope, and I agree that Catholics should listen to his pronouncements reverently, but when it comes to the government of the United States of America, a religious opinion should not be the prevailing law unless it is a proven truth.   Justice Alito's answer about the soul qualifying as a "person" may be acceptable as Catholic dogma, but it is not medical or legal proof, and it is not common law. It should not be an opinion given in a Supreme Court decision on what is the definition of personhood, a word which is used to refer to the condition of being a person, but does not appear in the U.S. Constitution. If Justice Alito wants it to be common law, he should submit its proposal as an amendment, in the same way he said the Pro-Choice advocates should do.

Of the nine Judges on the *Dobbs* Supreme Court, there were seven

---

10 Ibid. (5/5/2025).

11 "Full Text of the United States Constitution with All 27 Amendments," 1-24.

12 Ford, "The Human Embryo as Person in Catholic Teaching," 234.

who were Catholic, three of whom went to Catholic High Schools, and three others who went to public schools, but were trained to be devout Catholics from the time they were born by their parents. The one Catholic Justice on the Supreme Court who dissented in the case was Sonia Sotomayor, who was appointed by Barack Obama in 2009 to replace David Souter. The other six all agreed to a determination that life begins at conception in *Dobbs*, and not at quickening, as had been the accepted standard across the world throughout history. In my opinion, they did this because they were following their Catholic upbringing, and not the intention of the Constitution, which they had sworn to follow. They could not have been referring to the views of the Founding Fathers, for that was not the Catholic position at that the time the Constitution was written.

The view that life begins at conception may have been a precept of the Catholic religion they were taught as children, and followed throughout their lives, but it is not a valid medical opinion today, and was not a Catholic opinion when the Constitution was written. When the Catholic Justices were sworn in to their position, they promised to follow the Constitution, as I will detail shortly, and if they did not believe that they could, then they were allowed to recuse themselves from the case, as Justice William Rehnquist (1924-2005) did when he was asked to rule on Richard Nixon's refusal to give up his Watergate tapes. I have not been able to find the exact number of times this has happened in the history of the Supreme Court, but during the 2016 term alone, 180 Justices decided to recuse themselves from cases they didn't believe they could give a fair verdict.[13]

It was not only the *Dobbs* decision that made notice of changes in the interpretation of the separation of Church and State in the First Amendment during the term of this Court, but four other cases redefined "the concepts of neutrality and coercion under the Religion Clauses of the First Amendment," according to Morgan Marietta, Professor of Political Science at the University of Massachusetts Lowell.[14] I will not discuss these cases in detail, but they include *Carson v. Makin, 596 U.S. 767 (2022)*, which dealt with public funding for religious schools; *Kennedy v. Bremerton School District 597 U.S. 507 (2022)*,

---

13 Weiss, "Supreme Court Justices Recused Themselves 180 Times in Most Recent Term," 1.

14 Marietta, "Introduction: The 2021-2022 Term at the Supreme Court," 9.

which dealt with religious expression in schools and the boundaries of the First Amendment; *Ramirez v. Collier 595 U.S. 411 (2022)*, which dealt with religious liberty in the Execution Chamber; and *Shurtleff v. Boston 596 U.S. 243 (2022)*, which dealt with free express and government speech. Each case sought to modify the criteria for separation of Church and State, and I contend that this is a dangerous precedent being put forward by the conservative Catholic Justices on the present Supreme Court in an attempt to modify the principle of Separation of Church and State, and must be shown to be erroneous by passing an amendment to overturn their decision in *Dobbs*.

Morgan Marietta agreed that the Supreme Court was redefining religious neutrality into "'coequal' neutrality, which abandons the view that secularism is the assumption and religion the exception, in favor of a new standard which assumes that both religion and secularism are co-equals present in the public realm."[15] He claimed that the Court's intention was that "mere existence is not endorsement and does not necessarily constitute coercion," but there is no question that in the issue of abortion, the Justices changed the definition of personhood from true life, to mere conception, and that is more than coercion, it is following the opinion of a Catholic Pope.[16] It is also attempting to redefine the common law definition of life beginning at conception, and that can only be done by an amendment, and not a Supreme Court decision, since two prior Supreme Court decisions accepted that quickening was the common law.

I realize that my concern over this issue may look like I am simply against trump's MAGA campaign, but my problem is not with what Trump wants to do, but how he is attempting to do it by promoting a Catholic doctrine as the law of the land. He has many good ideas, but I am against promotion of one religious doctrine over all others to achieve that goal. You can see it in Justice Neil Gorsuch's agreement with the change in these cases, despite him saying that *"the government may never coerce regarding religion, in either direction, toward compelling or suppressing religious expression,"* for in changing the definition of personhood for all United States citizens to conception, that is exactly what *Dobbs* was doing, because a papal decree is

---

15 Ibid.
16 Ibid., 10.

religious doctrine, and not American common law.[17] No other religion except Hinduism and Buddhism makes this claim except Catholicism and certain Protestant sects, and so it is a papal bull, and not a legal fact. Marietta defined this Supreme Court as a "supermajority of six conservative Justices," but failed to point out that these six Judges were also Catholic, and were accepting the Pope's definition of life beginning at conception, and the only Catholic who dissented in the case was Sonia Sotomayor.[18] These are not conservative Justices, these are Catholic Justices following their Catholic training, and paying no attention to what the Constitution intended.

In this book, I will argue that this reinterpretation of the First Amendment is not acceptable, or constitutional, and must be overturned by passing this amendment, just as slavery was overturned in the same manner, and women were given the right to vote.

Let me amplify why I believe Justice Alito made this decision as a religious principle, and not a judicial choice based on the common law and the Constitution. The concept of the soul is how Catholics accept that life's inception is at conception, for when the body dies, the soul is believed to continue to exist eternally, as a separate component of personhood from that of the body. While this belief is intriguing, and may even be true, there is no way to prove the existence of the soul, as its formation is dependent solely on faith, and not on scientific validation, because there is no way to test the actual existence of the soul, either during life, or after death. We can think it is possible that the activity of the functioning brain is as a "soul," but we have no way of knowing that, and it is very unlikely that we will be any closer to knowing in the next 100 years. What we do know now, however, is that when the brain dies, that activity dies as well, unless you can think of some way to prove it doesn't, and with today's knowledge, that is not possible.

The concept of a soul was first derived from the teaching of the Greek philosopher Pythagoras (570-495 BCE), who also explained that the soul was formed at conception, and became a living being at that moment, which is similarly dependent upon faith, and not proof.[19] Upon the death of the body, however, according to Pythagoras the

---

17 Ibid., 11.

18 Ibid., 17.

19 Kapparis, <u>Abortion in the Ancient World</u>, 39.

soul then transmigrated into a new body in a concept known as metempsychosis, which is not followed by Catholicism, since the soul in that religion remains in either Heaven or Hell.[20] Both of these explanations by Pythagoras and the Pope are philosophical beliefs, and you cannot possibly claim that they represent the legal basis of life in the Constitution. I understand that the Gospel of Luke in the New Testament tells how an angel appeared to Zehariah to announce the future birth of John, and that "he shall be filled with the Holy Spirit, even from his mother's womb," which is the essence of the Catholic soul, but we don't know who Luke was, or who wrote the Gospel, and we don't know anything about the Holy Spirit either.[21]

I believe in a monotheistic God, as do the Catholics, but I do not accept that every word in both the Old and New Testament are proof of what that God actually said. In Judaism, Orthodox Jews believe that the Torah was actually written by Moses, but scholars claim that the Torah was instead written during the Babylonian Exile by a variety of rabbinic sources that is known as the Documentary Hypothesis. A Catholic can believe that the Pope speaks valid Catholic doctrine, and a Jew can believe that either Moses or the sources of the Documentary Hypothesis did the same, and that God actually influenced what they wrote, but there is no way that this can become legal doctrine without some proof that the theory is valid.

When it comes to the Constitution, we know who wrote it, and we can dispute on what they intended, but we must point to factual language and debate the validity of prior Supreme Court cases, for it is essential that we separate Church and State when Supreme Court decisions are made. If we do not, we are practicing Theocracy instead of Democracy.

Every religion has a God, or gods, or spirits that represent divine authority, and those divine authorities do not say the same things. It is clear that the disparate views among religions cannot all be factually correct, and this means that we cannot rely on any one method to prove which one is possibly correct. In America, the separation of Church and State in the legal system that runs our country means that you are entitled to believe in whatever God you want, and the government will not overrule your choice. I will continue to demand

---

20 "Pythagoras's Philosophy and Immortality of the Soul," 1-14.
21 Ward, "The Use of the Bible in the Abortion Debate," 248-249.

that all people who swear to protect the Constitution follow that principle, and not allow religion to be the determining factor in any of their legal judgments. This rule should be part of all three parts of our government – Executive, Legislative, and Judiciary – and part of our state and federal mandates. It is the welfare of the country that is the deciding factor, and not the tenets of any one religious belief.

In addition to this principle, if one is going to make a judgment in the Supreme Court, it requires that you find support either by *stare decisis* of prior Supreme Court judgments, or by scientific proof, or common decency and equality, which was the reason slavery was not allowed to be a legal right. The judicial principle of *stare decisis*, which means "let the decision stand," is often followed by most Supreme Court Justices, and has long been held with great respect. Its longer original version is more informative, for it is actually called *stare decisis et quieta non movere*, which means "to stand by the decisions and not to disturb what is settled," but that does not mean that if a Supreme Court decision is wrong, it should not be overturned. Anyone can make a mistake, and if they do in on the Supreme Court, it should be overturned, and this can even extend to more than one case.[22] The problem in the *Dobbs* case is that it is the overturner that needs to be overturned. Supreme Court decisions have only been overturned 232 times since 1810, and few have been as controversial as *Roe v. Wade*.[23] Our country, and our Democracy, must remain free of religious influence by any one religion alone, and this applies to Catholicism, and all other religious beliefs, and this is the reason that Supreme Court Justices swear to abide by our Constitution, and not God. I will show in this book that Justice Alito failed to follow the oath he swore to follow the Constitution when he was appointed as a Supreme Court Justice, and his actions are therefore erroneous despite the fact that as he gave the oath, he swore to God he meant it, as I will detail in Chapter IV.

I am not going to denigrate any religious belief or principle in this book, including Catholicism, because every religious faith has leaders who clarify their belief in God to their devotees, and they are perfectly

---

22 McConnell, "Some Realism about Precedent in the Wake of *Dobbs*," 101.

23 Bomboy, "A Short List of Overturned Supreme Court Landmark Cases," 2.

free to do so, because they are said to be in direct contact with their God. I am, however, going to denigrate Alito specifically, not for his religious beliefs, but for refusing to put those beliefs aside when he acted as a Supreme Court Justice. At that point, he had sworn to follow the Constitution only, and separation of Church and State was an important doctrine that I contend he should have followed in interpreting the meaning of our Constitution.

It is the Founding Fathers the Justices must look to for guidance, and not the person you believe is God's contact on earth, and to do this, you must look to the Amendments that were written to the Constitution, and not just the Founding Fathers' decision alone. This means you have to look to prior Supreme Court decisions on their meaning, as well as to scientific advancements that can support any change you make to the legal precepts you find. In this book I will show why we must approve abortion of unwanted fetuses that are not viable, and for whatever reason they are unwanted, as long as they are nonviable, abortion is not a crime of murder. By doing this, we can eliminate much of the child abuse in our country, and more importantly eliminate the crime of murder in 10-15% of unwanted births.

I will discuss this claim throughout this book, but I also need to clarify certain other issues that are important to understand in the Introduction before I talk about abortion and the manner in which both of these cases were handled.

The colonists who settled in our country first arrived on our shores in 1607 from England, settling in Jamestown, Virginia. They were followed by the Pilgrims, who landed at Plymouth Rock, Massachusetts in 1620, as I will discuss in more detail in the next chapter. The problems all the colonists faced settling in the land were initially restricted, for the most part, to the local Indian residents who saw their land suddenly taken from them by foreigners who began arriving from many lands. Gradually, however, other European immigrants settled throughout North America, and conflicts eventually led to the Seven Years War, from 1756-1763, when other countries began to join the battle to take control of the lands they settled. England eventually emerged as the country who most threatened the independence of the colonists, and this finally led to the Declaration of Independence signed on July 4, 1776, and the Revolutionary War, which ended with a victory by the thirteen colonies over England on September 3, 1783.

It was then that the Constitution was written, but what we must realize today is that since that time, our country has grown from the small size of thirteen colonies to now fifty states, including Hawaii, which is not attached to the mainland, and Alaska, which is noncontiguous, as well as Washington, D.C., which is a federal district, rather than a state. In addition to these fifty United States, we also now have five populated territories, including Puerto Rico, Guam, American Samoa, U.S. Virgin Islands, and the Mariana Islands, which are distant territories that do not have voting rights in the United States, but are represented by non-voting delegates in Congress who are able to convey their desires. This is a vast region, comprising 3.8 million square miles (9.83 million sq. km.), and while the intent of the Founding Fathers is still an important principle for the Supreme Court to follow, the modifications made by the added amendments cannot be forgotten. In addition, the fact that our growth has placed America as the model of Democracy to the whole world, and our strength has helped us win two World Wars, and many other military conflicts, to make sure that Democracy remains available to all who want to move here. It is necessary that we continue to act as the model of Democracy as well. We must respect the rights of others as we fight to maintain our position of strength in the world, but most of all, we must make sure we always respect the rights of our own citizens.

I emphasize this point because most legal scholars who disagree with the ruling of the Supreme Court in *Roe v. Wade, 410 U.S. 113 (1973)* to approve the constitutional right of a woman to choose abortion of a nonviable fetus have claimed that "there is nothing in the constitutional text that even alludes to abortion, and nothing in the history of First, Ninth, Fourteenth or any other amendment indicating that the constitution-makers had the slightest intent to remove it from the legitimate realm of representative lawmaking."[24] This statement by Rex E. Lee (1935-1996), former President of Brigham Young University and Solicitor General of the United States, shows how most conservative scholars interpreting the Constitution emphasize the fact that the word "abortion" does not appear in the text, but fail to appreciate that the Preamble points out how our Constitution is not just a collection of words, but a basic plan that demands that "Justice" applies to all the citizens of the United States of America, and there

---

24 Lee, "Forward," xiv.

are many words that are included in the concept of Justice. Because the Framers of our Constitution did not write the word "abortion" into their product does not mean they didn't intend to include it in their final product before quickening was present. That was why amendments were made an integral part of the Constitution, and why the Supreme Court was entrusted with determining what the words of the Constitution, and the Amendments contained therein, were intended to mean at the time they were written. While the word "abortion" does not appear in the Constitution, many Supreme Court rulings have discussed how birth control and other aspects of pregnancy are covered by both the Ninth and Fourteenth Amendments, and all prior Supreme Court judgments included the concept of abortion in those amendments.

This issue is the very crux of the problem we're faced with today, as our present ultra-Orthodox Supreme Court formed by Donald Trump is attempting to overturn many opinions by the ultra-liberal Warren Court, which led up to the *Roe v. Wade* decision, as I will discuss in Chapters III and IV. The Warren Court expanded their readings of the amendments to include many personal liberties that were not specifically delineated in the Constitution, but which the majority of Supreme Court Justices over time have believed were intended to be included by the Founding Fathers.

Conservative justices today want to interpret the Constitution under a concept of "Originalism," which was first recommended by Robert Bork (1927-2012) in his 1971 law review article, "Neutral Principles and Some First Amendment Problems," published in *The Yale Law Journal*. Bork was the Solicitor General of the United States under Richard Nixon (1913-1994) from 1973-1977, and then was the Acting U.S. Attorney General from October 20, 1973-January 4, 1974, when he agreed to dismiss special prosecutor Archibald Cox (1912-2004) during the Watergate Scandal in 1973, after multiple other qualified politicians refused to perform that task. He would later be appointed as a Judge of the U.S. Court of Appeals for the District of Columbia Circuit by Ronald Reagan (1911-2004) from 1982-1988, and was then nominated to the Supreme Court by Reagan, but was denied by the Senate by a vote of forty-two in favor, and fifty-eight against, because of the role he played in what became known as the *Saturday Night Massacre*, when he fired Cox, as directed by Nixon who did not want to turn over the White House tapes that Cox had been seeking.

Bork has been portrayed by most scholars as a model for all six Catholic Supreme Court Justices who are on the bench today, and appointed by Republican Presidents, and I personally believe he is given that honor to deflect what they know, and won't say with respect to the issue of abortion, and that it is that the present Catholic Supreme Court Justices are not making judicial decisions that are conservative, but rather from being devout followers of the teaching of the Catholic Pope. Bork converted to Catholicism shortly after he wrote his thesis because he, as well, was in favor of a Theocracy, and not a Democracy.

Bork is no longer alive today, having died on December 19, 2012, so it is not likely that I can prove by thesis, but I contend that this is the reason we are in a constitutional crisis today. Our country resembles how Muslim countries around the world are promoting the belief in a Theocracy, and we are in danger of repeating the atmosphere that was present during the Holy War Crusades.

Bork's view of constitutional interpretation was that the Supreme Court should not infer that rights were present unless the right in question was specifically described in the Constitution, or in the Amendments. He was adamant that Justices should not create new rights by supposition alone, which is what the Warren Court was famous for, and what became the basis for the *Roe v. Wade* decision. The word "abortion" did not appear in the text, as Justice Alito said, but that did not mean that such a right was not intended, according to the Warren Court. Over the years, the Warren Supreme Court often interpreted the Amendments as expanding rights not specifically stated in both liberal and conservative Supreme Courts, but Bork's views only became popular once the Orthodox Supreme Court was completed by President Trump during his first term as President. This made *stare decisis* a *non-sequitir* for the conservative *Dobbs* court, so they had no problem declaring both *Roe v. Wade* and *Dobbs* unconstitutional. The problem for me, however, is that their reasoning to make this decision was not based on the Constitution, but on the fact that the modern Catholic Popes have decided that life begins at conception, which means that all abortions are murder.

If we eliminate rights not definitively defined by name in the Constitution, we are left only with the Bill of Rights, which were the ten amendments alone that were passed by the Constitutional Congress, and which the Founding Fathers knew were inadequate.

We don't need the Supreme Court to tell us what the Founding Fathers intended in Originalism, for all we really need in that discipline is a dictionary. That is not what we mean by trying to know what the authors of the Constitution intended the rights of all citizens to be. What is more important to remember is that this process was meant to change with the times, and with the added amendments, which were what the Warren Court, and other Courts as well, interpreted as indicating other protected rights, providing insight into what the intention was at the time the Constitution was written.

Our fate, according to the Founding Fathers was to represent the model of Democracy, and that means we must not be partial to one religion alone, and we must allow immigrants to legally enter our country, but not by illegal means. I agree with Trump on this point, although I do not accept the method he is trying to expel everyone by his authority alone.

Antonin Scalia (1936-2016), who was an Assistant Attorney General under Gerald Ford, and then nominated to the United States Court of Appeals in the District of Columbia by Ronald Reagan in 1982, and to the Supreme Court in 1986, became the first to be a "self-described Originalist" on the Supreme Court, as well as a devout Catholic.[25] When he was nominated to the Supreme Court, the preferred choices were he and Bork, who were both Catholic, but Reagan wanted to appoint the first Italian, and so Scalia won out, since he was an Italian who was born in Trenton, New Jersey to a father from Sommatino, Sicily.[26] Bork would later be nominated to replace Lewis F. Powell Jr. (1907-1998) in 1987, but was rejected, and Reagan then nominated Douglas H. Ginsburg, who withdrew because of marijuana use, and so Anthony Kennedy, who retired in 2018, was

---

25 Cienappo, Against Constitutional Originalism: A Historical Critique, 5. Amy Coney Barrett told how she was a law clerk for Scalia after law school, so it is no surprise where her conservative influence came from. Barrett, Listening to the Law: Reflections on the Court and Constitution, 4. Six of the nine present sitting Justices had also clerked on the Court, including John Roberts, Elena Kagan, Neil Gorsuch, Brett Kavanaugh, Ketanji Brown Jackson, and Amy Coney Barrett. Justice Horace Gray (1882-1902) was the first Justice to hire a law clerk, and Justice Byron White (1917-2002) was the first to have clerked for another Justice. Ibid., 78-79.

26 Toobin, The Nine: Inside the Secret World of the Supreme Court, 22.

chosen. What I find very ironic, is that when Ronald Reagan defeated Jimmy Carter (1924-2024) in 1980, the faculty at Yale Law School went into mourning, for most institutions were liberal, and supported the rulings of both the Warren and Burger Courts, but Steven Calabresi was a Torts Professor there, as was Robert Bork, and they started an organization to advocate conservative ideas in legal thought which they called the Federalist Society.[27] Since I have compared the Federalists who wrote the Constitution more like Democrats today, I found that decision unusual, but it was not a surprise that Justice Alito received his training there as well. The problem is that these Bork enthusiasts, like Bork himself, were illegitimate jurists who tried to claim that Bork was only trying to promote democracy by his expansion of judicial power, for in his book *The Tempting of America* in 1989, Bork said that *Roe v. Wade* was: "the assumption of illegitimate judicial power and usurpation of the democratic authority of the American people."[28] Bork's argument was in reality that his judicial power was legitimate because he was using it, while the decision in *Roe v. Wade* was not to his liking. In typical fashion, Bork was resorting to obfuscation to turn the tables, and attack with the argument that most characterized his own intentions.

I am writing this book because our country has become dangerously divided by a war of words over how to properly interpret the Constitution, and the debate is threatening to erupt into a second Civil War that does not reflect the same intensity of disagreement that was associated with the southern states after the Constitution was written for not giving citizenship to Black slaves. Today the dispute is primarily over the issue of abortion, but it has become a heated religious crusade that has gotten out of control, and left the Supreme Court of the United States to no longer reflect the democracy which allowed America to be portrayed as the Statue of Liberty, welcoming immigrants since its erection on Liberty Island in New York Harbor on October 28, 1886.

The Statue of Liberty was inspired by our Civil War, which reversed the acceptance of slavery, and it was built by Gustave Eiffel (1832-1923). The statue was designed in the image of the Roman goddess of Liberty, *Libertas,* who is shown holding in her right hand

---

27 Ibid., 15.
28 Tribe, "Finding Abortion Rights in the Constitution," 476.

a torch high above her head, and in her left hand, she carried a *tabula ansata*, with the date July 4, 1776, reflecting when the Declaration of Independence was written.[29] Our present governmental dispute has forgotten many of the principles our country was founded upon, and it is time we gather together again as a Union now of 50 states, and not thirteen colonies, and represent to the world-at-large that we accept the recognized right of women to have abortion rights for unwanted, nonviable fetuses, not only because it is a freedom that they should have, but because it has become an accepted right across the world, even allowed in the country of Italy, where the Vatican is a sovereign city-state, which is able to independently not allow abortion to be practiced. The Vatican city-state came into existence on February 11, 1929, when the Lateran treaty was made between the Holy See and the Kingdom of Italy, creating the Vatican, which is ruled by the Pope.[30] The treaty was signed by Cardinal Pietro Gasparri (1852-1934), who served as the Cardinal Secretary of State under Pope Pius XI.

The common law prohibiting abortion was instituted with the papal edict, and the Vatican then passed legislation known as the Canon Law of 1983 which declared: "anyone who procures a completed abortion incurs automatic excommunication (Canon 1398)."[31] Only 23 other countries in the world do not approve abortion out of a total of 195 countries, including the Dominican Republic, Laos, El Salvador, Haiti, Honduras, Iraq, Jamaica, the Philippines, Sierra Leone, and Tonga, even though the procedure has been proven safe, and has allowed infanticide of unwanted children to become a rare occurrence, and helped reduce the frequency of child abuse.[32]

I specifically want to emphasize the fact that the description of fetuses that are approved in my amendment are "unwanted," and not simply "unintended," pregnancies, for throughout history, before there were safe methods of abortion, there has always been much difference in how unwanted children were treated once they were born. Even in our modern era of contraception, 45% of the six million annual pregnancies in the United States are unplanned, but that does not mean they are all unwanted.[33] Throughout our history, when a pregnancy

---

29 "Statute of Liberty," 1.
30 "Vatican City," 1.
31 Microsoft CoPilot (9/12/2025). Personal Communication.
32 "Countries Where Abortion is Illegal, 2025," 3.
33 Peters and Kamitsuka, "Introduction," 3.

was desired, children have generally been well-cared for, because many of them died when they were still young from what today are treatable infections, and the need to replenish families with offspring was a necessary element to success, despite the problems it often caused.

Johann Wolfgang von Goethe (1749-1832), the famous German polymath who greatly affected the development of the modern Western World, was the eldest of seven siblings, but only he and his sister Cornelia lived to celebrate their seventh birthday, and this was not unusual, for only 50% of children in Germany reached the age of fifteen-years-old when he was alive.[34] This high fatality rate of children throughout history was also generally believed to have been present in prehistoric times, when over one-half of children never reached puberty, and in Classical Greece and Rome, when similar statistics were present.[35] This is the primary reason so many children throughout history were often born and raised, knowing that many would succumb to illnesses or fatal accidents before they came adults. But unwanted pregnancies have always been harshly treated, and babies who are born unwanted have been killed 10-15% of the time, so in addition to being nonviable, the pregnancies that are unwanted are usually the ones that are sought to be aborted.

The burden of wasted time spent in having to raise unwanted children through dangerous times, and economic disasters, often resulted in their being killed shortly after birth, or led to an early death because of child abuse and neglect which was why 10-15% of the time, unwanted children were killed by their parents, as I have discussed in my book *Hardness of Heart/Hardness of Life: The Stain of Human Infanticide*.

The problem of child abuse has also often been ignored, as evidenced by the fact that the first Society for the Prevention of Cruelty to Animals (SPCA) was opened in England in 1824, and the first American Society for the Prevention of Cruelty to Animals (ASPCA) opened in 1866, while the first Society for the Prevention of Cruelty to Children (SPCC) was opened in New York in 1874, and this finally inspired the Liverpool Society for the Prevention of Cruelty to

---

34 Harari, <u>Nexus: A Brief History of Information Networks From the Stone Age to AI,</u>, xi.

35 Microsoft CoPilot (4/13/2025). Personal communication.

Children to open on April 19, 1883, and the one in London to open in 1884. The concern of people for the welfare of animals continues to dominate the television airways today, with advertisements for donations for starving animals common place, although, fortunately, donations for starving children far outweighs those for animals.[36]

Statistics for child abuse are not always easy to come by, but according to the Centers for Disease Control and Prevention (CDC) in America, in 2009, more than 5.8 million children in the United States were involved in 3.2 million acts of abuse, and although there is not way of knowing for sure, I am certain that most of those children were unwanted when they were born or adopted.[37] Times have changed, however, because of the effect we know *Roe v. Wade* had on the statistics of unwanted births, even though children today having a better chance of becoming adults because of better medical care and nutritional assistance than in the distant past.

During the two years the first Continental Congress was in operation, only twelve amendments were initially proposed and agreed upon. They were primarily written by James Madison, who would later serve as the fourth president of our country. Madison was mainly a Federalist whose primary interests in being one of the Founding Fathers was to create a strong Federal governing body. When the states only approved 10 of the 12 amendments he was able to get the Congress to approve over a two-year session, he immediately dubbed them as the "Bill of Rights," an assertion that reflected how his goal for the United States was to be a true Democracy, as promised in the Preamble that was approved.

In the two years it took to reach this point, many of the states had begun to pass laws providing what individual civil rights each of their own citizens could have, which the federal Constitution allowed them to do, and the fact that the Congress could only agree on twelve amendments showed that their job was far from over because many of the states did not have the same degree of moral responsibility to apply many freedoms to all people.

Once the Bill of Rights expanded the constitutional "law of the land," it became the responsibility of the Supreme Court to decide

---

36 Microsoft CoPilot (7/20/2025). Personal Communication.
37 Hattery and Smith, The Social Dynamics of Family Violence," 135. This results in the death of 5 children every day. Ibid.

what the intent of the Founding Fathers was in any deliberation of law suits which challenged the rights of the parties contesting the meaning of the law. There were two ways the rights could be expanded from this point forward, and we will see that both options were taken to achieve the desired end.

The first way rights could be added would be if the Supreme Court decided that the intentions of the Founding Fathers who wrote the amendments meant to include a personal liberty under the terminology of one of the Amendments. At first, this was relatively easy to do, for many of the men who wrote the Constitution were still alive, and all the Justices had to do was ask them if the right in question was intended. As time passed, however, the Supreme Court Justices had little personal knowledge of what truly went on before, and it became more difficult to agree on exactly what every personal right that was not specifically mentioned actually was. The writings of the Federalists and Anti-Federalists were preserved, and so for many years, that resource was helpful to use, but one hundred years later, Civil War broke out, and everything changed, except for the population that remained after the war, which was composed of both winners and losers, who remained as Americans, but never totally accepted that the war was truly over.

It is a permanent part of being an American that there will always be a difference of opinion on how the country should be run, and I don't expect that fact to change. What I do expect, however, is that we can agree on a rational expectance that our personal liberties which are guaranteed by our Amendments are those of every American citizen, Black or White, male and female, and naturally-born or naturalized by passing a civil exam and taking an oath. We must do that by remembering the horrors of the Civil War, and the promise of the Statute of Liberty.

The second way to expand the meaning of constitutionally guaranteed rights was to write a new amendment, and that is what I am proposing to do in this book. The amendments to the Constitution *are* the Constitution, and their intent was to always have our country be united, which is why any state who disagreed with the 3/4 rule of approval would no longer be part of the Union. The dilemma we are in today is that the end-result of all those differences of opinion was that a variety of terms were used, such as "right of privacy," and "personal liberties," to refer to some of the rights that were implied in the Constitution by the Supreme Court cases that followed. This generality has caused much consternation between liberal and conservative Justices, and politicians alike, as to the reliability of those designations, and whether the specific right which was present was intended to include a wide range of similar, but not identical, rights.

In her book, *A Question of Choice*, Sarah Weddington, who argued the case of *Roe* to the Supreme Court, stressed that *Griswold* guaranteed "zones of privacy," and this was consistent with the wording of the Ninth Amendment. She relied on this argument before the Federal Court, and she was correct to do so, for the Federal Court in its decision said that the Texas abortion laws were unconstitutional because of the Ninth Amendment, which gave her the right to choose not to have children.[38] The Federal Court directed her to the Ninth, rather than the First Amendment, and during her argument, to the Supreme Court she noted that Thomas Campbell Clark (1899-1977), a former United States Supreme Court Justice from Texas who served on the Warren Court, said that "to say that life is present at conception is to give recognition to the potential rather than the actual," and her argument was well accepted.[39]

The legal team representing *Roe* responded well at both the Federal and Supreme Courts, and I believe that their victory at the Federal level gave them the confidence to succeed at the Supreme Court hearing. At the end of the presentation to the Federal court, John Tolle (1933-2024), of the Dallas DA's office, claimed that "the state's position will be, and is, that the right of the child to life is superior to that of a woman's right to privacy," and that claim not only ended the hearing, but, in my opinion, led to the victory of *Roe v. Wade* at the level of the Supreme Court, as Blackmun would accept Weddington's arguments, as I will explain in Chapter III.[40] In promoting his position that the fetus had a right to life, he, in essence, was admitting that a woman had a right to privacy, which supported Blackmun's position.

The very essence of our Constitution is that it allows for both the Federal and State governments to make laws to govern their citizens, but the Federal Constitution, along with its Amendments, governs whether state laws can be legal or not. If a state law is written that differs

---

38 Weddington, <u>A Question of Choice</u>, 62, 68.

39 Ibid., 64.

40 Ibid., 66.

from what is in the Constitution, as interpreted by the Supreme Court, the law is invalid. The problem is that the Supreme Court composition changes over time, and a decision they make can also change if a future Supreme Court interprets the Constitution differently than the one before. That is why Abraham Lincoln (1809-1865), the fifteenth President of the United States, sought an amendment to change the Constitution, rather than overturn *Dred Scott v. Sandford, 60 U.S. (19 How.) 393 (1877)*, the racist Supreme Court case that approved slavery.[41] That is also where I am at with the issue of abortion, as the Supreme Court in *Roe v. Wade 410 U.S. 113 (1973)* and *Dobbs v. Jackson Women's Health Organization 597 U.S. 215 (2022)* came to totally opposite conclusions on the same issue. The approval in *Roe v. Wade* was no small matter, for thirty states at that time had laws which forbid abortions under a number of differing conditions that were then negated by the Court decision. This initiated a massive anti-abortion movement in America, resulting in a promise made by Republican presidents that only conservative justices would be nominated for the Supreme Court until the *Roe v. Wade* decision could be overturned. It was very surprising that it took almost fifty years for changes to take place, but in 2022, the new Supreme Court that became staunchly conservative after Donald Trump vowed to get *Roe v. Wade* overturned during the third election debate with Hilary Clinton, finally achieved his goal in *Dobbs*.

If Supreme Courts are going to interpret the same Constitution, on the same issue, so radically different, it is clear to me that we cannot rely on judicial interpretation to set the standard for our country, and I will therefore use the amendment process to set the standard, which still can be modified if wrong. I can correct the error made by the Supreme Court in abortion, but it will still leave open interpretation on many other rights that have been protected by prior Supreme Court decisions that the present Supreme court can overturn. We cannot pass enough amendments for every right to be safe from the actions of this Court, and we must also demand that separation of Church and State become something that every Supreme Court Justice must agree to, or recuse themselves from dealing with issues like abortion.

As I see it, the dilemma has left us with only three options if we

---

41 Blackmun admired Abraham Lincoln and kept a photograph of him in his office. Koh, "The Justice Harry A. Blackmun Oral History Project," 8.

want to return to the status where abortion of nonviable fetuses is legal, as we were when *Roe v. Wade* was passed. First, we can wait and see if an appeal of the *Dobbs* verdict is filed, and then winds its way into the Supreme Court to see if the decision to overturn *Roe v. Wade* can be vacated. This will likely take years, however, and I do not think it is possible that a Supreme Court filled by Trump nominees will ever take that step, so I am not going to wait and see what happens before proceeding with my amendment proposal. Second, we can find a new case where a state passes an abortion law that allows abortions similar to my proposal, and after it is turned down by the Federal District Court, which now would have to follow the *Dobbs* decision, the case can be appealed to the Supreme Court. Donald Trump is now the sitting President, however, and I don't think we have a chance with any of his Supreme Court appointees to overturn *Dobbs*. The third, and final, option is to follow the same process that made slaves citizens of the country, and gave women the right to vote, and that is to pass an amendment making abortion of unwanted, nonviable fetuses the right of a woman to choose.

Since I believe the majority of our country now wants the law in the United States to be similar to that which developed after the *Roe v. Wade* opinion was given, I will present my suggested amendment in Chapter VII, and work to finish this book ASAP.

Am I concerned about the amount of time it may take for the amendment to pass? Of course I am, but I am also aware that the right for a woman to choose whether to have an abortion should be chiseled in stone, and not dependent on judicial interpretation alone. I personally find it egregious that the Supreme Court in *Minor v. Happersett 88 U.S. (21 Wall.) 162 (1875)* decided that the Constitution did not give women the right to vote by their being citizens of the United States, basing their opinion on the *Privileges or Immunities Clause* of the Fourteenth Amendment.[42] To make matters worse, the vote was 9-0, with Chief Justice Morrison Waite (1816-1888), who was appointed by Ulysses S. Grant (1822-1885) in 1874, giving the opinion of the Court. *Minor* interpreted the Constitution to "not confer the right of suffrage upon women," for the qualification to vote was a state issue, and was not written into the Constitution proper.[43] He

---

42 "Minor v. Happersett," 1.
43 Ibid.

was correct, of course, and the amendment would take 14 months to be passed, but the decision of the Supreme Court is reflective of what Alito wrote in *Dobbs,* and I will try to initiate an amendment as soon as possible. The need to assure that all American women could have the right to vote no matter where they live was seen to require the same constitutional process that allowed the nation, and not the individual states, to provide that legality by law, and that was the reason that an amendment had to be passed. That process began in Congress in 1878, when the amendment was first proposed, and it then began the process of ratification, which took until August 18, 1920, forty-two years later, so I will not wast that much time with this process.

It is clear to me that the majority of people in this country now favor abortion limited to nonviable fetuses as the proper way to legislate abortion in this country. Every citizen has learned to appreciate, and respect, that the intent of our Founding Fathers was to offer an equal opportunity to every citizen who lived in the United States by writing a Constitution that would become the fairest "law of the land" on earth. We have come to understand, however, that intentions are one thing, and results filled with that intent are another. It is vitally important for us all to understand this fact as we try to explain why one Supreme Court ruled abortion should be the law for all Americans in *Roe v. Wade*, basing their judgment on their interpretation of the Constitution, and another, fifty years later, ruled that it was unconstitutional, and required passage of an amendment to make it legal because the word "abortion" had to appear to be a personal right guaranteed by the original Constitution. The fact remains that it is possible that a case could arise in the future with different characteristics, and with different judges on the Court, and find that *Roe v. Wade* was actually correct. That ruling could reinstate the *Roe v. Wade* decision, but not prevent a future supreme Court from reinstating *Dobbs*, and so the wheel of judicial reinterpretation would keep turning.

While many countries are concerned about the need to control population growth, the ability to direct attention to unwanted pregnancies, whose children are likely to be subjected to child abuse, is particularly another important point to consider on a worldwide basis. Many countries across the globe now approve abortion of nonviable fetuses, and according to the *Center for Reproductive Rights* (CRR), a global legal advocacy organization headquartered in New York City, over the past 30 years, more than 60 countries have liberalized their abortion laws.[44] The American journalist, Talia Lavin, has described the influence creating "the rhythm of war music, the kind that shakes the ground under your feet," and I agree with her concern, for it reminds me of the animosity that developed between the north and south before the Civil War.[45] America began this acceptance with the passage of *Roe v. Wade*, and we now must add an amendment to our Constitution to highlight the rights of all citizens, black and white, male and female, to have full citizen protection of their God-given rights.

Not only should the abortion of a nonviable fetus be seen as feticide, rather than infanticide, the fact that it is the mother choosing the abortion should be emphasized, for in England and Wales, the realization that women who kill their babies are a special reason to be lenient since the Infanticide Act in 1922 defined infanticide in England as a unique offence, which applied only to "mothers who kill their biological children aged under 12 months."[46] This takes into account the recognition that women are susceptible to postpartum depression, and have a long history of known tendencies to harm, and even to kill their unwanted newborn infants, as I explained in my book *Hardness of Heart/Harness of Life: The Stain of Human Infanticide*. The specifics of this causation was added to the Infanticide Act of 1938, which said that it was because "the balance of her mind was disturbed by the reason of her not having fully recovered from the effect of giving birth to the child or by reason of the effect of lactation consequent upon the birth of her child."[47] Northern Ireland, where the Catholic Church is a dominant political force, enacted similar legislation in 1939, as did certain Australian states and territories. I should add, however, that in 1983, the Eighth Amendment was added to the Ireland Constitution which said that the unborn child had an equal right to the mother, effectively banning abortion, although it was repealed in 2018.[48]

---

44 "The World's Abortion Laws," 1.

45 Lavin, <u>Wild Faith: How the Christian Right is Taking Over America</u>, 2.

46 Brennan and Milne, "100 Years of Infanticide: The Law in Context," 1. Numerous scholars have argued that the legal roots to the Infanticide Act lie in the 1624 *Act to Prevent the Destroying and Murdering of Bastard Children*. Ibid., 9.

47 "Infanticide Act," 1.

48 Microsoft CoPilot (6/13/2025). Personal Communication.

While I applaud the foresight of the legislation to understand the dangers an expectant mother faces if she proceeds to give birth to any child, I must point out that the real dangers encountered here is that it is the pregnancies that are unwanted which led to this problem, and the reason the infanticide rate is so high throughout human history is that there has never been effective and safe means to abort the pregnancy before the fetus is viable. I am going to stress this fact throughout the book, and I ask for the help of anyone who agrees with me to please try and publicize this fact with all you know so that we can assure the passage of the abortion amendment. It is vital that part of this instruction is to explain why the position of the Catholic Church is within the control of their Papal hierarchy, and while it is within their right to decide this matter without scientific support, they still should realize the effect their teaching has on criminal codes across the world.

In conclusion to my Introduction, let me emphasize that at the root of why we need the legality of abortion in the United States is the enormous danger to allowing unwanted pregnancies to be carried to full-term births instead of being allowed to continue the benefits that followed the legalization of abortion by *Roe v. Wade*. No, let me change that terminology to *forcing* unwanted pregnancies to not be aborted, so they *have* to be carried to birth. The enormous danger we face if we do not pass the amendment to approve their abortions, are that the resultant deaths that will take place, along with a rise in the frequency of child abuse that will also result in premature deaths, is enormous.

The World Health Organization estimates that there are 73 million abortions performed globally every year, and no country can seriously think of totally eliminating abortions of unwanted children, and expect to maintain crime and economic control in their country.[49] In the United States, there were 3.6 million unintended pregnancies in 1988, and of those, 1.6 million resulted in abortion.[50] During that same era, in Russia there were more than three million abortions performed each year, more than double the number of births, while in France there were almost one million abortions each year, equal to the number of births.[51] In 1991, the Chinese government noted there were over

---

49 "Abortions Worldwide This Year," 1.

50 Chicago Tribune (June 6, 1993): section 4, 1.

51 Filshie, "Termination of Pregnancy," 234; American Medical News (November 20, 1995): 15. For a brief time, France even considered

fourteen million abortions, and in India, there are over five million abortions performed each year.[52]

The problem of unwanted pregnancy is not only worldwide, it has been present throughout recorded history, and now that the right to perform these abortions have been eliminated by *Roe v. Wade* being overturned, I am publishing this book to begin the process of calling for an amendment to the United States Constitution to legalize abortion of nonviable fetuses in all American women before the rate of infanticide rises to 10-15% per year once again. I do this because most discussions of unwanted pregnancy across the world are generally directed to the fate of the child's development, rather than the fact that I have shown that throughout the history of mankind that 10-15 percent of children have been killed by their parents. Let us face this dilemma together with understanding and knowledge, and not let misguided efforts to promote that life begins at conception interrupt what has become an effective device to relieve the burden of having to raise unwanted children across the world.

I will end my Introduction by noting that Professor Emeritus David Tennent Baird (1935-2022), the former eminent specialist in Obstetrics and Gynaecology at the University of Edinburgh, wrote the *Introduction* to a Ciba Foundation Symposium on Abortion in 1984 by noting that many countries have recently legalized abortion because: "The need to check the unlimited growth of the world's population has been accepted by most responsible authorities for about 20 years."[53] I accept that in many areas of the world, population-control is an important concern, but fortunately in America, at least for the present, things like "form a more perfect Union," and "establish Justice," are more important goals, and by approving the right of a woman to abort an unwanted, nonviable fetus, I believe we can achieve both ends.

---

abortion to be a crime punishable by death, but this was changed in the 1970s. Glennie, Milwit, and Zucker brod, "The World's Abortion Laws," 16-17.

52   Aird, "China's War on Children," 59; Hale, "The Brutality of Growth Control," 1 A.

53   Baird, "Introduction," 1.

Chapter II
History Of Abortion In America

In this Chapter, I have the difficult task of trying to explain how our country could be the place where Democracy began its evolution to become the most respected form of government in the world, and then, after a spectacular record of glorification as the bastion of freedom, became entrenched in a campaign to turn our country from a Democracy into a Theocracy, where the Catholic Church is seen as the most important religion in the world, and the arbiter of how our government should be run. This is because President Donald Trump has allied himself with Christian fundamentalists and openly declared that our government should not follow the rigid interpretation of the Separation of Church and State that the First Amendment forced our country to follow, and not allow public display of standard Christian worship in governmental buildings and schools. He has publicly stated on April 29, 2025, after the funeral of Pope Francis (1936-2025), when he was asked who he thought should be the next Pope, and responded: "I'd like to be the Pope. That would be my number one choice."[1] This answer seems more like a science fiction novel than a historical fact, but there is no question in my mind that what is happening in America right now is an attempt to change our Democracy into a Theocracy, and we must pass a Twenty-Eighth Amendment to put an end to the dangerous path he is trying to put us on.

Trump has many attributes that could have made him more popular than Franklin Delano Roosevelt (1882-1945), our 32nd President, who was seen as the one to get us through World War II, but his "my way or the highway" attitude has caused people to either passionately love him or hate him as much as Adolf Hitler. In my opinion, there is no middle ground with Trump, and I have seen close friendships among my neighbors vaporize away because of a refusal to associate with one who has an opposite opinion of Trump from their own. As I said in the Introduction, my primary interest in this book is the status of abortion in America, and the need to pass an amendment to obtain a written constitutional right for women to obtain an abortion for unwanted, nonviable fetuses, but to understand why this is so vital to all Americans in today's world, you must know why abortion became

---

1   "Trump reveals his top pick for the new Pope - himself," 2.

so crucial to women thousands of years ago, and why it is suddenly imperative today to have it be seen as a constitutional right of privacy. *Roe v. Wade* was overturned because that was what Trump wanted done, and Justice Alito decided that was the road he would also travel on. The love and hate for the man who caused this is so intense that I am forced to enter the fray to try and solve the problem by a popular vote, rather than a second Civil War.

From the time mankind first evolved from the apes, as described by Charles Darwin, if you believe in evolution, women, and men as well, have often resorted to disposing of unwanted births because they felt unable to care for every child that was born for a variety of reasons. The prevalence of this problem is directly related to both an inherited human trait of violence, coupled with an incredibly prolonged period of time that human infants require constant care before they mature enough to be able to live independently from their parents. On January 22, 1973, when *Roe v. Wade* was passed, the right to an abortion was finally legally provided in America, and for almost 50 years, we saw the benefits of having that right in the world-at-large. The case was finally overturned by the *Dobbs v. Jackson Women's Health Organization* Supreme Court on June 24, 2022. I will explain in this chapter why the history of abortion in the world, and in our own country, shows that the primary reason why we must pass an amendment which allows the abortion of unwanted pregnancies, as long as the fetus has not reached the state of viability outside the uterus, is that forcing the birth of unwanted children to reach the levels of 3.65 billion worldwide abortions that took place over the last 50 years will result in the death of over 350 million unwanted children, and that is a disaster that we cannot allow to happen.

I first alerted the world to this problem in 1998, when I published *Hardness of Heart/Hardness of Life: The Stain of Human Infanticide*, and showed how, throughout our recorded history, 10-15% of unwanted pregnancies resulted in either infanticide shortly after birth, or child abuse that led to an early death of the child.[2] The book was mostly ignored by the general public, probably because the births of unwanted children were already becoming a rarity due to the passage of *Roe v. Wade*, with the rate dropping from 10-15% to less than 1%

---

2   Milner, Hardness of Heart/Hardness of Life: The Stain of Human Infanticide, 27-28.

during the 50 years it was the law of the land. Now that we are back where we started from, or will be soon, we must prevent the horrible abuse and deaths of millions of unwanted children, whose births could have been prevented before their viability even began. Unwanted children are all now in danger of returning to the land of "what was," and I am determined not to let that happen just because our President decided that the Catholic Pope was correct to claim that abortion was murder.

In 2023, I republished the book after *Dobbs v. Jackson Women's Health Organization* overturned *Roe v. Wade*, and began to write this book to propose an amendment to approve abortions on the guidelines set by the *Roe v. Wade* Supreme Court, including the description of our common law that life of a "person," as described in the Constitution, begins at 20-weeks gestation of the fetus, and not at conception as decided by a Papal edict. I will not try to summarize my prior book in this chapter or pass judgment on why so many parents have acted this way for thousands of years. Still, it is a fact that has been present throughout human civilization, and the only time its frequency was reduced was when these pregnancies were able to be safely prevented because of the *Roe v. Wade* ruling. I will highlight my findings about the history of this unfortunate fact in this chapter, but I encourage you to read that book if you are interested in the extent of my research, as it is available on Amazon, and contains 3,150 footnotes to document my findings. Don't worry, I am used to inquiring minds about why my email is infanticide@ameritech.net, but if you have any questions about the subject after you read my book, that is where you can contact me.

The critical point to stress is that this amendment is not only necessary for the right of a woman to choose whether to give birth to an unwanted child or not, but it is vital to prevent the crimes that unwanted children have been victims of since *Homo sapiens* began to first populate the earth. The reasons unwanted births have resulted in this carnage are many, but basically, while other mammalian species become independent enough to walk and follow their mothers around either from birth, or soon thereafter, human beings take years for this to happen, and children are unable to survive on their own for many years, instead of just weeks to months, as takes place in other mammalian species. The longest gestational period for an animal is the elephant, which typically does not give birth for 18-22 months, but when the delivery does take place, the newborn can usually walk within minutes or hours. The need to spend so much time raising a human child is not always a problem, for when pregnancies are wanted, because larger families have a better chance of survival, given the high death rate of young children for thousands of years, families have been able to deal with the prolonged care by sharing in the burden. The human species has prospered despite our necessity for long-term care, as evidenced by our evolutionary success in the historical record. If the pregnancy was unwanted for a variety of reasons, however, this extended dependency put severe stress on the parents, as well as the extended family, to survive when problems arose that needed the assistance of all on board, including the mother. This is one reason why the English polymath Herbert Spencer (1820-1903) developed his theory of the "survival of the fittest" in his book *Principles of Biology* (1814), which was later used by Darwin in the fifth edition of *On the Origin of Species* in 1869 to show how the human species, *Homo sapiens*, prospered because only the most genetically strong individuals produced offspring, and this kept our genetic line strong, and adaptable to the changing world around us. However, when births took place that were not wanted, human beings also inherited a trait that kept those births from interfering with the necessity to survive by eliminating them 10-15% of the time.[3] This statistic is fact, not fiction, and is the reason I am writing this book.

It is important to stress that the only reason we don't see this many deaths today is because 50% of unwanted pregnancies in the Western World have been aborted since *Roe v. Wade* was passed. The reason for this is clear, as I have already discussed, and that is because in the 50 years after *Roe v. Wade* was passed, there have been 3.65 billion abortions performed worldwide, and that is why the infanticide rate fell to below 1%. The ease and safety afforded by modern abortion techniques have almost eliminated the birth of unwanted babies, and by reducing the sheer volume of such births, the stress on handling the ones that cannot be aborted is much easier for our social systems to handle. So the headlines of mothers killing their newborn children have greatly diminished. The problem with infanticide of unwanted infants is also still evident in many animal species as well, where young children of mothers who are found desirable by dominant

---

3   Ibid., 33.

males often find those children killed by their mother's new mate, so that the mother could become fertile, and give birth to new genetically stronger children, who will provide a way to keep the weaker offspring from bearing weaker children in the future. In my opinion, we are at a point in our evolution where we no longer need to rely on infanticide to improve our genetic structure, since it has done nothing to eliminate our inherited desire to kill others in holy wars.

If this trait of familicide sounds familiar, you may also remember that in the biblical story of the first human son ever born, Cain, that was soon followed by the birth of Abel, and then, when they were older, by Cain killing Abel, because of jealous rage over God's liking his sacrifice better, an act we now call fratricide. This crime, taking place at the start of the second generation of mankind, was clearly a story designed to deal with the laws of Nature, and it characterized much of our recorded history ever since. It is an inherited trait that will remain in our genetic inheritance forever, and the behavior of the first generation of mankind was so bad that God decided to eliminate all mankind, and start over with the family of Noah in a Great Flood, and select pairs of every animal species to repopulate the earth as well. Why is such a sordid history included in the Torah, whether the story was told by God to Moses on Mt. Sinai, as Orthodox Jews believe, or was written during the Babylonian Exile (598-538 BCE) from documents recorded by rabbis beginning in the 10th century BCE, as believed by the Documentary Hypothesis, according to the biblical scholar Julius Wellhausen (1844-1918)? I do not have a satisfactory answer to that question, but I have no doubt that it was a purposeful attempt by the originators of monotheism to remind everyone that even God can make a mistake, and no one should consider themselves to be "nearer, my God, to Thee," as said in the Christian hymn about Jacob's ladder reaching up to the sky.[4] I will point out many things in this book that you may not find appealing to accept, but when you deal with facts of human nature in a discussion of history, you often are faced with the dilemma of accepting "man's inhumanity to man," as the Scottish poet Robert Burns (1759-1796) said in his 1785 poem, *Man Was Made to Mourn: A Dirge*. The history of mankind is a violent story, and while there is no denying the fact that the life we live today could never have been imagined by those apes who

---

4   Gen 28:11-19; Microsoft CoPilot (9/8/2025). Personal Communication.

first transmuted into the human genus from appreciating their origin, our history proves that we have a violent nature, and so my goal is to instruct you about the facts of our heritage in order to show why we need an amendment to guarantee the right to terminate a pregnancy that is unwanted, and nonviable, because it is a benefit both to the mother, and to the suffering unwanted product. In the end, if you agree with my proposal, we can hopefully assure the survival of our world, as well.

This need, and desire, to end an unwanted pregnancy has been evident since mankind first discovered that sexual intercourse could cause a pregnancy, even when it was not desired. It is presumed that from the start of our evolutionary path to success, attempts were made to kill an unwanted child at birth, followed then by improper care or abuse, leading to an early death if the child was not eliminated shortly after birth. We don't have definite archaeological evidence of actual attempts at this happening until about 1550 BCE, in ancient Egypt in the early New Kingdom era, since record keeping was not often directed at providing that information until the proliferation of writing began to appear in ancient Egypt and Mesopotamia, c. 3200 BCE. That does not mean that our Stone Age ancestors did not practice ways to eliminate unwanted births before they were born, but to "know" that they did requires evidence in the historical record that is confirmatory, and this is first found in a document known as the Ebers Papyrus, which was dated to c. 1550 BCE. However, it is believed to have been copied from earlier texts that have not been located to date.[5] The Ebers treatise listed about 700 magical formulas and folk remedies already in use at the time to end a pregnancy, and even though the word "abortion" does not actually appear in the text, the methods described therein state that the result was that "the woman empties out the conceived in the first, second, or third time period," a clear description of an artificially induced abortion in terms that even described it as taking place during a trimester pregnancy.[6] It is interesting that this first notation already mentions a system that is still in use today, and was part of Blackmun's analysis in *Roe v. Wade*, but similar recordings can be found in early Chinese manuscripts, so

---

5   "Ebers Papyrus," 1.

6   "A Brief History of Abortion – From Ancient Egyptian Herbs to Fighting Stigma Today," 1.

the practice was not limited to Egypt alone, and exists in the historical record of every country.[7]

There are other indications of this practice in ancient Egypt, as a 4,000-year-old papyrus which bore the title "Recipe Not to Become Pregnant," describing how to mix crocodile dung with fermented dough, and placing it in the vagina, a notation that shows how desperate some of their methods were to obtain positive results.[8] These types of records clearly show that from the time writing first began, there were unwanted pregnancies, and efforts were made to try and end the pregnancy before an infant could be born. This activity had likely been going on from our earliest existence on earth, at least until methods to utilize tools to remove the fetus from the uterus were discovered, which first appeared in the writings of Tertullian (c. 155-240) and Celsus (2nd century CE), during the Roman Empire (27 BCE- 476 CE). Tertullian was a Christian theologian who described surgical implements that resembled those used in modern dilation and evacuation procedures, so their experience was likely not a rare occurrence.[9] We don't have extant details of how it was actually done, but if there were surgical instruments available, they likely were used in a manner that is similar to what we do today. Aulus Cornelius Celsus was a Roman encyclopedist who described a highly detailed account of a procedure to extract an already-dead fetus in his *De Medicina*, which indicates that abortions may have also been used to treat a complicated miscarriage, in addition to ending an unwanted pregnancy.[10] Soranus of Ephesus (1st century CE) was a Greek physician who did not appear to do abortions, and actually advised against the use of sharp instruments to induce miscarriage, recommending instead to engage in various activities, such as herbal baths, to induce a miscarriage.[11] This clearly resembled the information proscribed in the Ebers Papyrus, as well as many other references, all of which attests to the fact that the desire to end a pregnancy was not rare.

---

7 Klabusich, "Abortion Is as Old as Pregnancy: 4,000 Years of Reproductive Rights History," 2-3.

8 Peters and Kamitsuka, "Introduction," 2.

9 "History of Abortion," 3-4.

10 Ibid., 4.

11 Ibid., 3. Plants which were used back then were rue, Italian catnip, savory, sage, soapwort, cyperus, white and black hellebore, and pennyroyal. Ibid., 4.

Hippocrates of Kos (c. 460-370 BCE), who is known as the Father of Medicine, also was said to have forbidden the use of pessaries to induce abortion, but while all of these references indicate that abortive techniques were available in the ancient world, we cannot tell how often they were actually utilized, or how often they were successful.[12] The aphorism "where's there's a will, there's a way," however, is an appropriate description of how unwanted pregnancies were dealt with throughout our existence on earth. I contend that we should be seeking to assure the right of safe abortion technology to finally be able to stop the mistreatment of unwanted births today, since we finally have safe methods that are less dangerous than normal childbirth, and obviously widely desired, given the statistics of their use following the passage of *Roe v. Wade*.

What is clear is that throughout our history on earth, women have desired to end unwanted pregnancies by whatever means possible, for reasons that were often out of their control. Despite the prominence of this fact, the emotional dispute taking place today between the Republican Pro-Lifers, and Democratic Pro-Choice advocates, is becoming even more intensified because of the edicts against abortion, primarily from the religion of Christianity, which arose out of Judaism following the death of Jesus Christ, a Jewish heretic who was crucified sometime between April 7, 30 and April 3, 33, during the reign of Tiberius Caesar, who was the emperor of Rome from 14-37 CE. Before that period of time, little attention was paid to how infants and children were treated, as noted by Laila Williamson, an anthropologist and Senior Scientific Assistant with the American Museum of Natural History, who summarized the data she collected on the presence of infanticide throughout the history of mankind in 1978, and came to the following conclusion:

> Infanticide has been practiced on every continent and by people on every level of cultural complexity, from hunters and gatherers to high civilizations, including our own ancestors. Rather than being an exception, then, it has been the rule.[13]

Her conclusion did not mention that the practice was intended for unwanted births, but it is clear that the unfortunate history was

---

12 Ibid., 5.
13 Williamson, "Infanticide: An Anthropological Analysis," 61.

primarily directed at those pregnancies because there were not enough adults available to help protect the family from other dangers, and many times arose when an unwanted newborn had to be disposed of soon after the birth. Williamson's conclusion was agreed to by the American historian Lloyd DeMause (1931-2020), who believed that "all families once practiced infanticide," . . . and "all religions began with the mutilation and murder of children," which failed to clarify whether the religions in question were the cause of those murders, or whether they arose in response to them.[14]

I believe that DeMause may have made this statement in an attempt to claim that religion was a way to end that behavior, rather than begin it, but I'm aware that the facts are not so clear. What most historians who discuss this issue forget is that in Monotheism we find that the description of human activity from the time Adam and Eve were first created is consistent with the prevalence of violence and murder, eventually resulting in the tenth generation after Creation by God deciding to obliterate all mankind, and all animal life, and start over with a new human species from the family of Noah in a Great Flood, and select pairs of every animal species to repopulate the earth. This clearly indicates that God was not happy with His Creation, and apparently was unaware of the science of genetic procreation He utilized, since this method of starting a new population would not change the DNA structure of the human population. I note this discrepancy with tongue in cheek, however, for I believe the Torah we read is from human hands, and not reflective of the exact Words of God. I respect the fact that loyal monotheists believe that their holy books are sacred because they were written, or at least inspired, by God, but although I am a believer myself, I don't take every word of the Torah to be the literal truth.

Our Creator, according to the human story, also decided to pick one Patriarch named Abraham from Shem, the middle son of Noah, along with the elder Japheth, and the younger Ham, to found a group of ancestors that would be known as the Chosen People, because they would be the favored few who would worship this God as the One Almighty God, and be preferred above all other humans on earth. Abraham would give birth to two sons, the elder Ishmael from Sarah's maid Hagar, and Isaac, his legitimate son from Sarah. The

---

14 DeMause, "The History of Child Assault," 1.

initial Chosen People, according to the Torah, only came through the offspring from Isaac, and then from Jacob, who was the younger twin son along with Esau, from Isaac's wife Rebekkah (Rebecca). Jesus would be one of the heirs from King David, and so the three monotheistic faiths would all derive from Abraham's offspring, but I'm not going to discuss this family derivation in further detail in this book, and only point out that all three monotheistic religions accept this lineage to Abraham, and thereby see themselves as not only being related by a belief in the same God, but also by the same primal father, which makes their current differences more of a family fight, than just a Holy War, even though those battles killed more than 1-3 million people during the Crusades in the 11th-13th centuries.[15]

The importance of the rise of Christianity in the Roman Empire is related directly to the reason that I claim Trump is desirous of wanting America to resemble a Theocracy, rather than a Democracy, because he, personally, as well as politically, is a right-wing Christian who wants religion to be a greater part of the American governmental structure. This is why he is so anti-abortion, and desired to change the character of the Supreme Court to a super-majority of Catholic Justices, so that abortion could be characterized as a crime of murder. The Constitution of the United States did not define person in the same way as the Catholic Church does today, and the common law throughout the world, and two United States Supreme Courts, *Roe v. Wade* and *Casey*, accepted that a fetus became a person when "quickening," or the feeling of movement of the fetus by the mother, took place. The Catholic Church at the time the Constitution was written, also accepted quickening as when the fetus was a person, but later changed that designation when Pope Pius IX, who reigned as Pope the longest period of time from 1846-1878, made the stunning majority opinion in his apostolic constitution, *Apostolicae Sedis* in 1869 that there would no longer be a distinction between animated and unanimated fetuses, and that all abortions would be punished by immediate excommunication, because it was an act of murder. This is what was taught to our present Supreme Court Catholic Justices, and how they view what the common law must therefore be today. We face in the *Dobbs* decision to find *Roe v. Wade* unconstitutional this dilemma, and this is why I must outline why it is essential that I

---

15 "The Human Toll: How Many People Died in the Crusades?" 1-11.

educate the reader as to why I believe the present Supreme Court was designed to change our government from a Democracy to a Theocracy, so that the common law can be corrected to the Catholic view. In our country, however, that cannot be done by the Supreme Court, and that is why I am writing this book in response to his desire to become one of the next Popes. I therefore will now expand on how Christianity became a dominant force in the world, and then in America in this chapter.

Christianity arose to become the state religion in ancient Rome, and their law codes became the models for the Western World, given the fact that Christianity became the dominant religion in the Roman Empire at the same time that era became the model for Western Law. The birth of children in ancient Rome and Greece did not automatically change when Christianity first appeared on the scene, however, and both of these Empires continued to require that the father had to agree to keep the child after it was born, and undertake the responsibility of rearing it to adulthood, before it became a crime to kill it. This meant that under Roman law, if the infant was undesired because of physical disabilities, or even if it was unable to be sustained because of economic necessity, it could be exposed or killed at birth without committing a crime.

The worth of children was not given much attention until the time of the Renaissance, as the reality of survival was still the major concern during most of human history, and while children were "possible adults-to-be," they were not on a moral level of necessity equivalent to adults. This approach was also present in the earlier Greek Empire, which preceded the Romans, and Solon, who lived from 640-560 BCE, laid the constitutional foundations of Athenian democracy, and agreed that the Athenian father had the legal right to slay his own child,[16] likely based on the fact that in Greek mythology, even the gods could kill any of their children, as Cronos (Kronos), the father of Zeus, did to his son Uranus after he was warned that he would be defeated by one of his own sons by swallowing each of them at birth.[17] When Zeus was born, his mother Rhea tricked Cronos by giving him a stone to swallow, and then, true to form, when Zeus was grown, he forced Cronos to regurgitate his siblings, overthrew him, and became

---

16 Epicurus, Outlines of Pyrrhonism, III.211, 467.
17 Hesiod, Theogony, 464-465, 24.

the most powerful of the gods. It would take much time for the world to recognize the rights of children to equal that of adults, and until it did, infanticide and child abuse were a common occurrence. When the Roman Empire took over control of the region, they incorporated the Greek gods into their own polytheistic hierarchy, and so very little changed in the way both these pagan societies saw the way their gods acted.

Once the Emperors Constantine the Great (272-337) and Valentinian I (321-375) banned the killing of newborn children in the Roman Empire in the 4th century CE, however, they started the world on a change in the rights of children that would begin a long reassessment of human rights that would not reach fruition until the Renaissance took place from 1300-1600, finally preparing our passage into the Modern Age.[18] Christianity became the accepted religion in the Roman Empire under these two Emperors, but it would take much time for the values they applied to children to become accepted by the majority of civilized society. The killing of children by their parents would eventually be defined as a heinous crime, and since Christianity would eventually define a child as beginning at conception, we can see how we wound up with two Supreme Courts finding that abortion was a constitutional right, because both of the Courts had a minority of Catholic Justices, and then the *Dobbs* Court finally decided that abortion was not a constitutional right of murder because the supermajority of Catholic Justices applied the standard of a Theocracy.

Although Judaism never became a religion with as many followers as Christianity and Islam, it continued to support the rising belief in the value of children. However, it never changed its stance by accepting that life began at conception. Moses Maimonides (1135-1204), the renowned twelfth century CE Jewish philosopher and physician, put it best when he pointed out that the Torah was created "to teach us that if any man destroys a single life in the world, scripture imputes it to him as though he had destroyed the whole world," showing the importance of fetal life, but accepting that life began at quickening.[19] Maimonides' teaching was clearly influenced by the rising popularity of Christianity, reflecting not only what was happening in Monotheism

---

18 "Infanticide," 1.
19 Maimonides, "The Book of Judges," 35.

at the time, but in the world-at-large. I don't believe he foresaw the future development of Papal edicts in Catholicism, and the definition by later Popes that life began at conception; however, as children were not yet becoming recognized as having rights equal to adults when Maimonides was alive. There would still be centuries of development ahead before the expanded rights of children became the law of the land. It should be noted that child discipline was never strongly condemned in Colonial America, Massachusetts, where a law was enacted in 1646 that allowed the death penalty for a rebellious child, even though the law was never enforced.[20]

When our Constitution was written, the viable fetus would have protection for their safety, as evidenced by the fact that if a pregnant woman was found guilty of a capital crime, her execution would have to be delayed until after the child was born.[21] All of this showed a growing concern for the rights of children to be equal to adults, but neither Judaism nor Islam ever promoted the view that life began at conception.

Although the killing of a child would be considered as murder throughout the world as Christianity developed further, the followers primarily of Catholicism began to consider that even the killing of a fetus should be considered as murder because their interpretation of the New Testament would be under the sole discretion of the Pope, something which the German theologian Martin Luther (1483-1546) disagreed with when he initiated the schism that split Christianity into Protestantism and Catholicism.

When Pope Pius IX made his proclamation and changed the common law determination of life as quickening, to when conception took place, Catholic Justices found themselves in a real dilemma when it came to the issue of abortion, because over time, the Pope's stance became more concerned with the question of when life began than with the other two monotheistic faiths. Justice Alito would eventually take the position to the level of the Supreme Court interpretation of the Constitution when he declared that life began at conception in *Dobbs*, the first Supreme Court Justice to ever make that statement, and because he did, we find ourselves now at a dangerous crossroad, which

---

20 Hattery and Smith, <u>The Social Dynamics of Family Violence</u>," 21.
21 Freidenfelds, <u>The Myth of the Perfect Pregnancy: A History of Miscarriage in America</u>, 26

I believe threatens our entire structural integrity of the Constitution, which has guided us up until now to the position of being the poster-boy for the political rule by Democracy, but now allowing the Supreme Court to become the spokesman for the Catholic Pope.

Christianity rightly became outraged at the degree of killing of newborn children in ancient Greece and Rome, as did Judaism, but their actions to claim that abortion was murder did not alter the outcome of the killing of unwanted fetuses that were born at term. Judaism was their forerunner, but Jews never became integrated with the cultures in Greece and Rome. Although they made up about 10% of the population of Rome in the 1st century, numbering 2-7 million people, they mostly lived in their own neighborhoods, following rigid social and dietary restrictions that isolated them from the rest of the population, something that Christians did not do.[22] In addition, while the Jewish revolts led to the destruction of the Second Temple in Jerusalem by the Romans in 70 CE, and the destruction of the revolt of Bar Kokhba from 132-136 CE, the Christians were being fed to the lions in the Roman Coliseum in the 1st-3rd centuries, before Christianity became accepted by Constantine the Great.

All of the benefits that the United States Constitution brought to the world we live in was because our country was a beacon for Democracy. The monotheistic religions helped promote the concepts of Justice to all citizens, but the values came from the principles of Democracy, not that of any particular God. I will now try to explain why Christianity took this radical position of when life began, and why it was not followed by Judaism and Islam.

I explained that Monotheism began with the teaching of the Hebrew Bible, but more succinctly, it was the Torah that Christianity and Islam were interested in, and unlike Islam, Christianity was started by Jews who were made aware of the Hebrew Bible through their own translation in the *Septuagint*, which was the Greek translation of the Hebrew Bible that was written c. 280-250 BCE. This was necessitated by the fact that those Jews were living near where Jesus was born. The population in that location was primarily Greek-speaking, and so the Hebrew Bible written in Hebrew and Aramaic was of no use. According to the *Letter of Aristeas to Philocrates*, a Hellenistic work of that era, the Library of Alexandria collected all the published books

---

22   Microsoft CoPilot (7/29/2025). "History of Jews in Rome."

at that time in Greek translation so that the Greek-speaking residents of the city would be able to read them in their own language. Because it was written in Hebrew, the Library asked 72 Jewish interpreters, six from each of the twelve Hebrew tribes, to come and translate the Torah into Greek, hence the name *Septuagint*, which means seventy in Greek.

While many sections of the Hebrew Bible were translated into Greek with little change, there were modifications in some sections of the *Septuagint* which made a significant difference for those Jews who became Christians. For example, in the book of Isaiah, the Hebrew Bible says that the Lord will give you a "sign of His own accord" by the birth of a son to a "young woman" with child, and let her name him Immanuel.[23] In the Greek translation, however, the passage by Isaiah was translated in Greek by using the word for young woman as "virgin," which then allowed them to see the birth of Jesus as not being the adopted son of God, but the actual Son of God.[24] We often forget how much a translation can change the meaning of a text, especially in our modern era, where few people speak and read multiple languages, and translations are almost readily available on any subject. It is important to not forget, however, how this is the reason the three monotheistic religions have portrayed their God so differently that it is difficult to remember that we are speaking of the same Almighty Deity in each religion.

Another section which became important to the early Jewish Christians was such a great discrepancy in the evolution of Judaism and Christianity. Christians, as well as Philo, read the *Septuagint* Greek translation of the Hebrew Bible, rather than the standard rabbinic translation, which resulted in many of the variations which took place, both in their view on abortion, and in the nature of God, as I earlier discussed. The Hebrew Bible may not have used the word abortion, but in *Exodus 21:22-23*, which discussed injury to a pregnant woman resulting in a miscarriage, instead of following the Jewish translation, which did not consider life to begin at conception, the *Septuagint* differentiated whether the fetus was formed or unformed, and that the penalty, if formed, would be "life for life," which allowed

---

23 Isa 7:14. The Jewish Study Bible, 798.
24 "Does Isaiah 7:14 Refer to as Virgin?" 1-2.

later Christian Popes to consider the fetus at conception was formed.[25] The translation of this passage again shows how different the Jews who followed Jesus were taught what the Hebrew Bible said, and why their schism from traditional Jewish teaching was dramatic from the start. It should be noted that Josephus clarified the Jewish position of abortion as being "of what is begotten," but the Hebrew Bible itself did not consider the death of a fetus as murder, and the Qur'an did not mention the word abortion, as well. The earliest condemnation of abortion in Christianity is found in the *Didache*, as I will soon discuss, which was written around the same time Josephus wrote his own work, but it is hard to know which came first, and who may have influenced who. It is apparent to me, however, that both the Jews and the Christians were aware of what was going in the Greek and Roman Empires, and Monotheism would be taking a similar stance against the killing of children, although it is only Christianity that would extend the concept of life beginning at conception.

It is incredible how easy it was for Monotheism to develop into three radically different religions worshiping the same God in such different ways, but what it says to me is that our Constitution is correct to separate Church and State, and follow the principles of a Democracy, and not those of a Theocracy. All three monotheistic religions still had the same view of early mankind, for they all accepted that mankind was created with a violent nature from the fact that Cain, the first child born to Adam and Eve, killed his first brother Abel, and this violence continued for ten generations until God decided to kill all mankind except Noah and his family, in order to start Creation over again. They also knew that God told Abraham to sacrifice his son Isaac, and in my book, *Hardness of Heart/Harness of Life: The Stain of Infanticide*, I referred to this killing of children as a "stain," both because I believed that all mankind had inherited a violent nature, which left its presence as a "stain" on our nature, which is why our history has been riddled with constant warfare and strife, as well as causing the raising of unwanted children a difficult, and dangerous, undertaking. I believe completely in the existence of God, but I also believe that we must remain a Democracy.

Why did Trump decide to make Catholicism his focus for turning

---

25 Da Silva Carvalho, "The Bible and Abortion: Exodus 21:22-23 in the Septuagint and Other Opinions," 7-8.

our Democracy into a Theocracy? I believe this came about because of the effect the American Medical Association had on the judicial view of abortion. When the AMA was first formed on May 7, 1847 by 250 delegates representing 40 medical societies and 28 colleges, the common law description of personhood began at quickening, just as it was when the Constitution was written.[26] The American Medical Association became an anti-abortion activist organization because of the efforts of Dr. Horatio Robinson Storer (1830-1922), who steered the AMA into believing in anti-abortion legislation because he came to believe that life began at conception.[27] In 1860, he was able to convince the AMA to launch a campaign to convince state legislators to prohibit abortions, an action that was "legislatively successful," according to Simone Caron, Professor of History at Wake Forest University.[28] He apparently was able to do this because in 1859, he won the support of Dr. Henry Miller (1800-1874), the newly appointed AMA president and Professor of Obstetric Medicine at the University of Louisville.[29] Storer was raised in a Unitarian family, but later converted to Episcopalianism in 1869, and a decade later became a Roman Catholic, devoutly influenced by the Church's stance on abortion.[30] He became an anti-abortion activist when he graduated from medical school, and the leader of the Physicians' Crusade Against Abortion, and is widely seen as "largely responsible for the increase in laws criminalizing abortion in the late 1800s."[31] He took the stance that "By the Moral law, THE WILFUL KILLING OF A HUMAN BEING AT ANY STATE OF ITS EXISTENCE IS MURDER," and in so doing, he convinced the entire American Medical Association at its inception to follow his directives.[32] It is incredible to me that Storer was able to have this much control over the newly founded AMA, but we must remember that this was when the state legislatures began to enact anti-abortion legislation, so that by 1880, every state had some type of restriction after Connecticut began the process in

26 "American Medical Association," 1-3.
27 Ziegler, <u>Dollars for Life; The Anti-Abortion Movement and the Fall of the Republican Establishment</u>, 2.
28 Caron, <u>Who Chooses?: American Reproductive History Since 1930</u>, 14.
29 Ibid., 22.
30 Microsoft CoPilot (3/5/2025). Personal communication.
31 "Horatio Storer," 1.
32 Storer, <u>On Criminal Abortion in America</u>, 3.

1821. Storer was not only acknowledging the developing common law, but said that their reasoning was erroneous, and the accepted law had to become more restrictive, for it was unlawful.[33] His argument was compelling, as he explained that: "Lawyers and physicians should stand to each other, in medico-legal matters, as associates working together for the common good of society, rather than as adversaries liable to be thought endeavoring to make the worse appear the better reason," and while he had the right to make these claims as a physician believing in life beginning at conception, I contend that Justice Alito does not have that same right in a courtroom because of the oath he gave to follow the United States Constitution, and not the Catholic Pope.[34] It is one thing to proclaim that your religion is correct for you and your loved ones, but it is another thing altogether for a Supreme Court Justice to say that he can determine that the common law is wrong, and that he can make a new law by his judgment alone.

In 1865, Storer delivered a lecture to the American Medical Association at its session in Boston, and then had it published as *The Causation, Course, and Treatment of Reflex Insanity in Women*, where he claimed that the cause of the mental illness which caused women to desire abortion was "functional or organic diseases of the uterus and its appendages," and he was planning on looking into this problem to help explain why there were so many women seeking to have an abortion when it is consistent with murder.[35] It is clear to me that declarations such as these were influential in convincing not only the early AMA to undertake their anti-abortion legislative actions, but for others to continue to promote their belief that life begins at conception, which was directly influenced by the Papal decrees that life began at conception. I once again decry this position, but I cannot say it should be prohibited for doctors whose Hippocratic oath says nothing about the need to follow the common law. The problem with Storer is that he called abortion a criminal act, and convinced many who followed his teaching that his charge was correct, but he was following his faith that made him believe that abortion was murder, and there were no declarations about what the common law was so

33 Ibid., 6-7.
34 Storer and Heard, Criminal Abortion: Its Nature, Its Evidence, and Its Law, v.
35 Storer, The Causation, Course, and Treatment of Reflex Insanity in Women, 39.

he accepted what the Pope said as a legal declaration. In so doing, he ignored the fact that unwanted children had been treated by abuse, and killed 10-15% of the time by their parents, and that women who did not want to give birth to a nonviable fetus should be allowed to follow the common law, and have an abortion once it could safely be provided. The man who wrote his biography, Frederick N. Dyer, a research psychologist at the Army Medical Research Laboratory, was so enthralled by his talents that he titled his book *Champion of Women and the Unborn: Horatio Robinson Storer, M.D.*, a title I found to be most inappropriate, since his position was founded solely on his belief that life began at conception, but, like Storer, it was his right to follow Papal edicts if he so desired.[36]

Storer was able to be so adamant that abortion was a criminal act, that he convinced the Suffolk District Medical Society to form a Committee on Criminal Abortion to influence Massachusetts laws on the subject, and then extended this influence to the entire American Medical Association.[37] His efforts were directed at having the crime not be seen as a simple misdemeanor, but "to at least a felony," that both the physician and the mother should be charged with committing.[38] During his career, he wrote more than 200 published articles, seven books, and hundreds of extant letters, and all were vituperant, creating the atmosphere which erupted into the battle we see today between Republican and Democrat opponents.[39] His efforts were referred to by others as a "Physicians' Crusade Against Abortion," and while it may have not been as detrimental as Justice Alito's declaration that life begins at conception, it was instrumental in tilling the ground for the problem we are in today.[40]

Storer's most offensive publication, in my opinion, was a work he entitled as *Criminal Abortion: Its Nature, Its Evidence, and Its Law*, published in 1968. In that work, he charged that: "The Crime of unjustifiable abortion is now recognized by both the professions [of law and medicine] as of frequent occurrence, and as going too often

---

36 Dyer, Champion of Women and the Unborn: Horatio Robinson Storer, M.D.

37 Ibid., 104.

38 Ibid., 108-109.

39 Ibid., 2.

40 Mohr, Abortion in America: The Origins and Evolution of National Policy, 1800-1900, 147.

unwhipt of justice."[41] He claimed that the profession of medicine failed to prevent the practice because of a "moneyed interest," and that "the duty of the medical and legal professions" was necessary to be directed at "its general suppression."[42] His vehemence against abortion was broad, and he defined it as "the violent and premature expulsion of the product of conception, independently of its age, viability, and normal formation."[43] While he claims to throw aside, "as does the law, every case occurring from accident or from justifiable cause," he finds that those justifications are few and far between, and the effect of his campaign is one reason I believe that the Republican Party was able to convince their supporters to have anti-abortion become part of their National Platform in 1976, when Ronald Reagan ran for President.[44] I mention him in this book to show how the Republican party did not undertake their present stance without support from some medical men that were prominent at the time, but I contend that the promotion of this position primarily came from Catholics who developed their hatred from the belief that life did actually begin at conception, and they allowed their ignorance of the fate of unwanted pregnancies to totally blind them to the frequency of need that resulted in billions of abortions being done in the fifty years that abortion was legal worldwide. Two wrongs don't make a right, and while murder is wrong, abortion of a viable fetus is also wrong, but abortion of a nonviable fetus is right, and so my amendment should be passed, for it is the right thing to do.

I believe that the early political stance of the American Medical Association was inappropriate at the time they promoted the anti-abortion legislation, and it was one reason why the Republicans saw the advantage of aligning with Catholic Justices, who could aid their case in lawsuits across the country. Christianity was the religion that became outraged at the killing of children in the Holy Roman Empire, and over the centuries which followed, they helped combat the disastrous killing of unwanted children that littered the Middle Ages with the bodies of dead children. Their Popes moved closer and closer to considering the fetus in development as a living being with rights

---

41 Storer and Heard, <u>Criminal Abortion: Its Nature, Its Evidence, and Its Law</u>, v.

42 Ibid., 3-4.

43 Ibid., 5.

44 Ibid., 6.

equal to that of adults, however, and eventually resulted in their claim that life begins at conception. While I am not Christian in my belief in God, I do understand this attitude, which is why Luke claimed that Jesus Christ at the Crucifixion looked up and said: "Father, forgive them; for they know not what they do," because belief in God has not prevented individuals from committing horrible sins, both in real life, and in the holy books of all three monotheistic faiths.[45]

In the Hebrew Bible, however, God may have created mankind "in His image," but somehow that *imago dei* became tainted by a tendency to kill, perhaps reflective of God's Own decision to kill all life on earth and start over with Noah in the Great Flood.[46] I must admit that I asked myself at the time I wrote the book, that if what I found was truly factual, "why has there been so little overt reaction among either governmental, religious, or academic sources," except for the response of the Catholic Church?[47] I did not have an acceptable answer back then, but I now realize that the explanation is because there were never safe ways to abort unwanted pregnancies until *Roe v. Wade* was passed, and that is why I have reformed the Society for the Prevention of Infanticide, so I can do my part to assure that an amendment is passed, allowing for unwanted pregnancies to be aborted before the fetus reaches the state of viability. There is an old saying that if it ain't broke, don't fix it, but in my opinion, the *Dobbs* decision broke our long-standing trust in how the Supreme Court operates, and I'm damn-well going to fix it if I can.

Although early Judaism did not get as involved with the process of abortion as much as Christianity did, the two most famous ancient Jewish philosophers and historians, Josephus (c. 37-100) and Philo Judaeus (10-15 BCE – 45-50 CE), who lived around the same time as Jesus, did comment on abortion in a negative way, and their writings were read by the Jews who were becoming influenced by what Jesus said, and who would form a new religion after he died under the guidance of the Apostle Paul, originally Saul of Tarsus (c. 5-64). They provide important information about what Jews at the time likely thought about abortion, but they were not considered reliable

---

45 Luke 23:34. The Holy Bible, 733.

46 Gen 1:27. The Jewish Study Bible, 14.

47 Milner, Hardness of Heart/Hardness of Life: The Stain of Human Infanticide, 13.

spokesmen for Jews when they lived, and their works only survive today because their books were collected and passed on by Christians, because both men lived at the time Jesus was alive, and were felt as important sources for his memory. I, like many other Jews growing up hearing only about Josephus and Philo from that era, always thought they were revered by the ancient Jews as well, and I was very surprised to eventually learn that their books were only saved because of Christian libraries, so I have benefitted by their foresight.

Josephus was the son of Matthias, a Jewish priest, and became the most prominent, and thorough, Jewish historian writing about the war of the Jews against Rome. In his book *Against Apion*, Josephus actually mentioned the word "abortion," and told how: "The law, moreover, enjoins us to bring up all our offspring, and forbids women to cause abortion of what is begotten, or to destroy it afterward; and if any woman appears to have done so, she will be a murderer of her child, by destroying a living creature, and diminishing human kind."[48] Since he was not a trained rabbi, his opinion did not carry any religious weight, but he was accepted back then by both Jews and Christians alike as a reliable source for understanding Jewish practices. His writings were primarily historical, however, and like many other historians from that era, the reliability of what he said is often questioned.

The most dramatic change in the *Septuagint* translation, of course, was in the description of the birth of Jesus, which allowed him to not only be seen as a Messiah by Christians, but as the Son of God, which Jews and Muslims both found to be a violation of the entire concept of Monotheism, as I discussed earlier. The other ancient Jewish commentator who also was popular among Christian theologians like Clement of Alexandria (c. 150-215) and Origen of Alexandria (185-253), was Philo Judaeus, a Greek-speaking Jewish philosopher who was very representative of Jewish thought during the Hellenistic Age (323-30 BCE), and, as I said, likely learned much of his Hebrew Bible information from reading the Septuagint Greek translation because he lived in Alexandria, where it was used by most Christians, and Greek-speaking Romans. Unlike Josephus, Philo did not actually use the word "abortion" in any of his writings, but in his book *The Special Laws*, he relates that if a pregnant woman is injured, and "the child

---

48 Josephus, "Against Apion," II.25, 632.

which was conceived within her is still unfashioned and unformed, he shall be punished by a fine," which is consistent with the biblical text, and with the common Jewish law at the time that causing the death of an unviable fetus was not murder.[49] He obviously did not agree with life beginning at conception, but he likely lived before the *Didache* was written, for he does not comment on how some Christian leaders were beginning to take that status. Philo did not believe the fetus was considered to be a "person" is evident by his addition that "if the child which was conceived had assumed a distinct shape in all its parts," then it was treated as a man who was slain, which is similar to our present description of a fetus as nonviable or viable.[50]

Philo went on to add, however, that: "The exposure of infants is forbidden, which has become a very ordinary piece of wickedness among other nations by reason of their natural inhumanity," which clearly is a reference to the common practice in both the Greek and Roman empires.[51] Philo then went on to castigate the treatment of unwanted children by saying: "Let those parents who deprive their children of all these blessings, giving them no share of any one of them from the moment of their birth, know that they are violating the laws of nature, and accusing themselves of the very greatest enormities, of a devotion to pleasure, and a hatred of their species, and murder, and the very worst kind of murder, infanticide."[52] We cannot tell exactly who these remarks were directed to, or whether they included Jewish parents as well, although I believe it was likely primarily the Greeks and Romans living in Alexandria where he lived. Philo would have been aware of the writings that were available in other parts of the world for the Library of Alexandria was still open, and filled with books that were collected from all important authorities until it was destroyed in the 3rd century CE. Philo continued his specifying the nature of a viable fetus by explaining that when the child is "brought forth and separated" from the mother, "they then become real living creatures, deficient in nothing which can contribute to the perfection of human nature, so that then, beyond all question, he who slays an infant is a homicide," a clear indication that he did not think of life beginning at conception, which would become the hallmark of

---

49   Philo, "The Special Laws, III," XIX.108, 605.
50   Ibid.
51   XX.110. Ibid.
52   XX.112. Ibid.

Catholicism alone.[53] Exposure was also found in ancient Akkadian texts, derived from *ezbu*, which meant "to cast out," and was even used by the prophet Ezekiel as personifying the relationship Jerusalem had with YHWH as a girl abandoned at birth by her natal family.[54]

The belief in Catholicism that life begins at conception allowed the Christians to claim that there was an eternal existence of the soul, which began to exist when the sperm and ovum first united, and then continued to exist after the death of the body to find peace in Heaven, or punishment in Hell, after the body died. Modern Catholics still believe that the soul lives on after death, but in doing this, they also accept that the elimination of the body by abortion is murder, which is a belief completely dependent on faith, with no possibility of proof. The Hebrew Bible does not contain a reference to the soul until the book of *Ecclesiastes* was written, which, according to rabbinic tradition, was by King Solomon, but by most scholars was somewhere between 450-180 BCE, well before Christ was even born.[55] If life begins at conception with the formation of the soul, as Christians believe, and then goes to Heaven or Hell, then unwanted, nonviable fetuses who are aborted under this teaching will likely pass into eternity in Heaven, without undergoing the Hell of childbirth, or the painful existence of a life filled with child abuse.

The problem is that there is a question whether the soul can go to heaven without first being baptized, for according to the New Testament, Jesus said: "Verily, I say unto thee, except a man be born of water and *of* the Spirit, he cannot enter into the kingdom of God."[56] This problem was discussed by the *International Theological Commission,* which is a body of the Roman Curia of the Catholic Church that consists of no more than 30 Catholic theologians that are appointed to no more than 5-year terms. They studied the question of the fate of un-baptised infants, which would include those who are aborted, and they noted that in the *Catechism of the Catholic Church* in 1992, it taught that "infants who die without baptism are entrusted by the Church to the mercy of God," which is their way of accepting

---

53 XX.118. Ibid., 606.

54 Garroway, "Claiming the Unclaimed: The Role of Feet in Adoption and Levirate Marriage," 76; Ezek 16:1-7.

55 "Ecclesiastes," 1. https://en.wikipedia.org/wiki/Ecclesiastes, (8/3/2025), 1-12.

56 John 3:5. The Holy Bible, 736.

that they should go to Heaven, and I believe the same should be applied to the fate of aborted fetuses.[57] The Commission does not declare a position of the Church on this issue, however, and so for the present, it must be said that the determination of where the soul of those aborted resides cannot be determined with certainty. They added that infants, "who do not yet have the use of reason, conscience and freedom, cannot decide for themselves," which obviously would be the case in both viable and nonviable fetuses.[58] They noted that the Church had used for many centuries the idea of Limbo to designate the destiny of infants who die without Baptism, but the concept of Original sin excludes the possibility of the vision of God for those who die without Baptism.[59] Their conclusion was that there is "*hope, rather than grounds for sure knowledge,*" but however the Church makes an eventual decision, we will still be left with a concept that is based on faith, and not fact.[60]

The Talmud does suggest that there could be a soul that persists for a short time after death, but does not in most sections suggest a continuing life until the Resurrection takes place.[61] In any case, since the soul does not die, it cannot be murdered, but more importantly, not all modern Catholics or Protestant Christians believe that life begins at conception, even if they accept that the soul continues to survive after the death of the body, and that is why many Catholics accept the definition of *Roe v. Wade* for "personhood" as quickening, rather than conception. I have repeatedly said that this should represent the constitutional definition of personhood, and I hope that we can lessen some of the misunderstanding that exists about this history by educating the public in general, and Catholics in particular, about the need to understand that conception is only the potential for life and the soul, if it does truly exist, and it does not define the viability of the fetus to survive outside the womb that is the true definition of when life begins, and when a fetus becomes a "person." To protect unwanted children from suffering, I contend that it is necessary to pass the amendment I present in this book, and if the soul does exist at conception, it will then live forever in heaven, as many Catholics

57 "The Hope of Salvation for Infants Who Die Without Being Baptised," 1.
58 Ibid., 2.
59 Ibid., 3.
60 Ibid., 25.
61 Microsoft CoPilot (8/3/2025). "Berakhot 10 a, Sanhedrin 65 b, 91 ab."

today believe, allowing fetuses who have a soul to participate in the afterlife that exists for all eternity.

As I said, I am not going to try and present all my data from the history of infanticide in this treatise, but I will stress that the primary reasons for the killing of children throughout our history has included not only our inherited propensity for violence, but also other more reasonable explanations, like population control, which was often necessary because of times food resources were very limited; depression and insanity, which led to irrational behavior, including a belief that the devil had taken over their children's actions, and in legal cases this can be an excuse for insanity in committing a crime; revenge, which occurs when one parent seeks to severely harm their mate by killing their offspring, as vividly portrayed in the Greek legend of Medea; shame, which seeks to hide the fact that the child is illegitimate, and is a frequent cause of infanticide even today; and the propensity for child abuse because the birth was unwanted, and not able to be safely aborted. The word that is most informative in why all of this happens is "unwanted," for once a human being decides that their pregnancy was not only unexpected, but intensely unwanted, it became part of their nature to try and either abort the pregnancy, or kill the child shortly after birth, before others knew of their condition. If they realized that they were not capable of killing their newborn, they generally resorted to raising the child with abuse that truly represented a Hell on earth for the child, because the constant reminder to the parent that the attempt to abort was not successful, leading to a constant irritation that had to be suppressed. Physical abuse of the child for misbehavior became a worldwide problem, and in the United States, over 90% of parents have admitted to using physical punishment at some during their child's life, which is another "stain" that puts infants in particular at risk of a fatal injury, or life-long mental damage, both from physical damage to the brain, and emotional trauma.[62]

The sad part about child abuse is that the abuse is not always only for unwanted children, as some parents are simply prone to the process from being abused by their own parents, and so they continue with that behavior, even if they wanted to have more children. It is sometimes difficult to know when the abuse becomes intense enough to be defined as illegal "child abuse" as a crime, as opposed to just strict parental

---

62 Scott, "The Psychiatrist's Viewpoint," 191.

control, but the range of damage from the abuse includes "child maltreatment, cruelty, deliberate injury, abandonment, intimidation, sexual offenses, and avoidable death."[63] Many parents simply raise their children in the same way they were raised, not realizing that what they are doing is abusive, and we can only hope that public education about the problem will help reduce its prevalence in the future. The bottom line is that the end-result of an unwanted pregnancy is usually anger and sadness for the parent, and frequently death for the child, and so I believe that mothers who adamantly do not want to give birth once they find they are pregnant should be given the right to have an abortion as long as the fetus is nonviable, especially if they are of minor age.

Although Emperor Constantine is credited with being the man who made Christianity a legal religion in the Roman Empire, Christianity actually became the official state religion in the Roman Empire under Emperor Theodosius I (347-395), and it was then that abortion truly began to be seen as a morally wrong sin in the Western World. We are not sure that Theodosius I actually said that life began at conception, but when he convened the First Council of Constantinople in 381, he was considered a champion of Christian orthodoxy, and his teaching began the path toward greater acceptance of that concept, so that not only *some* abortions, but *all* abortions, were eventually seen as a mortal sin once Catholicism entered the modern era. Constantine the Great is said to have converted to Christianity in 312, but this is often ascribed to the fact that he decriminalized Christianity by the Edict of Milan in 313 in the entire Roman Empire. There is much controversy over whether he was actually a practicing Christian, and it is therefore generally accepted that it was Theodosius I who truly started Christian theology on its way to becoming the most prominent religion in the Western World. From the popularity Donald Trump has gained by allying with the Christian Fundamentalists, it is easy to see why he is promoting Theocracy, but I again point to politicians like John F. Kennedy who were as popular as Trump, but still as loyal to the Constitution, and to Democracy, while maintaining the principle of Separation of Church and State.

Even before Christianity became the official religion in Rome, the first Christian text to condemn abortion was the *Didache*, as I

---

63 Montgomery, Familiar Violence: A History of Child Abuse, 6.

previously mentioned, also known as *The Lord's Teaching Through the Twelve Apostles to the Nations*, a book thought to have been published in the 1st century CE, shortly before the New Testament was published in the 2nd century CE. Even though the *Didache* was not accepted into the New Testament canon, it was accepted by the Church Fathers as an important part of Christian ethics, and in its explanation of the meaning of the Second Commandment as stated in the Torah, "Thou shalt not murder," the *Didache* added: "You shall not murder a child by abortion, nor kill a child at birth."[64] This is why abortion was seen by many Christian theologians as part of their religious code, and it was fostered by many advocates for hundreds of years before becoming a papal edict that life began at conception, and abortion was murder.

The book states that it was written by the Twelve Apostles, and it has often been compared to the *Community Rule* book that was part of the Dead Sea Scrolls, originally called the *Manual of Discipline*, and this is one reason some scholars suggest that there is a similarity between the early Jewish Christians, and the Essene sect at Qumran. We don't actually know whether Jesus actually ever talked about infanticide, since it is not directly mentioned in the New Testament text or the Hebrew Bible, but the appearance of the reference in the *Didache* indicates that the author was aware of its presence, which means the Twelve Apostles who were noted in *Matthew 10:2-4* were, as well. These would have included Peter, Andrew, James, son of Zebedee, John, Philip, Bartholomew, Matthew, Thomas, James, son of Alpheus, Thaddeus (Jude), Simon the Zealot, and John Iscariot, later replaced by Mathias.[65] Note that Paul is not considered an Apostle in this classification, although he is called one in other sections of the New Testament.[66] Apostle means "one who is sent," and the term came to mean different things to different scholars, but since Jesus never left anything he taught in his own written format, like the Greek philosopher Socrates (c. 470-390 BCE), the New Testament is filled with material written by others who knew him, i.e., the Apostles.

As I said, the *Didache* was supported by many Church leaders

---

64 "Didache, The Teaching of the Twelve Apostles," 7.

65 Matt 10:2-3. The Holy Bible, 671; Microsoft CoPilot (8/3/2025), Personal Communication.

66 Gal 1:1; 1 Corinth 9:1-2; Acts 9.

throughout early Christianity, including Clement of Alexandria, who emphasized the sanctity of life from conception; Tertullian, who explicitly condemned abortion, equating it with murder; and Saint Basil the Great of Caesarea (c. 330-379), who included abortion in his list of serious sins, and called for penalties against those who performed it.[67] That these were independent views from their Jewish heritage is evident from the fact that the Hebrew Bible never actually mentioned abortion, although it did explain that if two men fought, and a pregnant woman was hurt and had a miscarriage, the one responsible should be fined.[68] This harm was a legal action that required expiation, even if it was not seen as equivalent to murder. The *Halachich*, which is the rabbinic interpretation of Jewish religious laws that began to be written down in the *Mishnah* in 200 CE, and then collected in the Babylonian and Jerusalem Talmuds, inferred that Judaism saw the death of the fetus as feticide, and not murder. In the Talmud, abortion was also then permitted to save the life of the mother.[69] This goes along with the Talmudic phrase, *uber yerekh imo*, a counterpart of the Latin *pars viscera matris*, which consider that the fetus is deemed a "part of its mother," rather than an independent entity.[70]

Although life beginning at conception was mentioned in some sources of the early Catholic Church, it did not become a serious consideration until the 16th century, when Pope Sixtus V (1521-1590) issued the bull *Effraent* in 1588 declaring that abortion was a grave sin requiring excommunication. Catholics who lived when the Constitution was written may have been aware of this opinion, but it was not a formal decree, until 1869, when Pope Pius IX (1792-1878), who reigned as Pope the longest period of time from 1846-1878, made the stunning majority opinion in his apostolic constitution, *Apostolicae Sedis*, that there would no longer be a distinction between animated and unanimated fetuses, and that all abortions would be punished by immediate excommunication, because it was an act of murder. This left many of the Church Fathers that had given differing views, such as St. Augustine of Hippo (354-430), who was a very influential

---

67 Microsoft CoPilot. (2/9/2025). Early Christian writings condemning abortion.

68 Exod 21:22. The Jewish Study Bible, 154.

69 Rashi and *yad Remah* to *b. Sanh* 72b. Ibid., fn. 22, 154.

70 Feldman, "Abortion: The Jewish View," 201. According to Rashi, the fetus is not a "person" until it comes into the world. Ibid., 202.

Christian theologian who affirmed the thought of Aristotle that ensoulment occurred after conception, without Papal support.[71] From that time forward, all abortions were to be consistent with murder, and the determination was permanent unless it was reversed by a future Pope. The recent death of Pope Francis, who was born Jorgo Mario Bergoglio, and named Francis in honor of Francis of Assissi (1181-1226), continued that trend, and we will have to await to see what Pope Leo XIV, born Robert Francis Prevost in Chicago, Illinois, will do after he was elected on May 8, 2025, becoming the first American-born Pope in history on May 8, 2025. As of this writing, there is no expectation of that happening.

When the U. S. Constitution was written, this view was not followed, and it was taught that the soul entered the body at 40 days of gestation for males and 80 days for females, so for that period of time, abortion was not the killing of an actual human being, even if it was a sin.[72] Common law took the easier route of identifying it with quickening, and the *Septuagint*, which was the Greek translation of the Hebrew Torah commissioned by Ptolemy I Philadelphus in the 3rd century, and was used by Christians as the standard text for the Old Testament, as I previously explained, had translations which differed from those by Jewish rabbis, but did make a distinction between the formed and unformed fetus, and did not consider conception as being the start of human life.[73] Many Protestant faiths like the Episcopal Church and the United Church of Christ similarly developed more tolerant views of abortion, and this view generally persists today among many Protestant faiths. Despite the fact that the Catholic Church remains firm in its position that life begins at conception, modern pollsters have generally found that only about 8-10% of the general population agrees with that conclusion, a figure well below the percentage needed to approve an amendment, indicating that there is a clear difference between what the Papal decree became, and how many Catholics wish to live their lives in real-time circumstances. Although Justice Alito Jr. used this reason to overturn *Roe v. Wade*, I contend that it is a minority Catholic view, and there is enough public support to

---

71 "History of Christian Thought on Abortion," 1.

72 McBride and Keys, <u>Abortion in the United States: A Reference Handbook</u>, 9.

73 "History of Christian Thought on Abortion," 2.

pass an amendment proposal that should have popular support. It is estimated that 20% of the population in America is Catholic, but we will see if they retain that devoutness when it comes to vote for my abortion amendment proposal. I am not here to argue against loyalty to one's religion, but I am here to say that the welfare of unwanted children are at risk of every Catholic in America who votes against my recommendation, and I believe that many of the victims of their loyalty will be Catholic casualties.

To look more closely at abortion in America, which is my primary concern in this book, I want to now concentrate on what the colonists who first came to America after the Renaissance began in Europe in the 14th Century, had been taught by the Christian Church they came from, and why I believe they followed the common law definition of quickening when the fetus became a "person," when the Constitution was written. They had grown up with a more tolerant view of the rights of all children that developed during that era, but there was still evidence of child abuse of unwanted children, and the legal system throughout Europe began to see that such behavior was a more serious offense. Our Founding Fathers therefore grew up in a culture that taught that children had to be cared for by their parents in a more tolerant way, but not with a view that life began at conception. While there are few statistics about actual attempts at abortion in America during the time before the Constitution was written, there is evidence that native Americans knew about the use of herb plants, known as abortifacients, and other substances, since their lifestyle made childbearing very difficult.[74] The population quickly learned of these substances, which included aloes or black hellebore, a blend of mercurous chloride and turpentine, Black Root and mistletoe, Key-tse-Sing, Indian hem, Uva Ursi, extract of belladonna, Quinine, and many others.[75] As I discussed above, these substances were also known by physicians since the Greek and Roman era, and native peoples in

---

74 Olasky and Savas, The Story of Abortion in America: A Street-Level History, 1652-2022, 19. Pennyroyal was known to the ancient Greeks, and in Aristophanes play *Peace*, Trigatius was told to not worry about making a girl pregnant if you give her a dose of pennyroyal. Riddle, "Women's Knowledge of Abortifacients from Antiquity to the Present," 214. Another plant Silphium (*Ferula antiqua*) was used so much it became extinct in the fifth century. Ibid., 216.

75 Caron, Who Chooses?: American Reproductive History Since 1930, 16.

America obtained the same instruction about these medications, and utilized them in the same way as before, even if they may not have been aware of their prior use. The colonists clearly became very aware of their methodology, and likely used many of the same substances that were indigenous to where they lived. Tribes such as the Lenape, Cree, Mohegan, Sioux, Ojibwwe, and Chippewa knew of plants such as sweet flag (*Acorus calamus*), tansy (*Tanacetum vulgare*), pennyroyal (*Mentha pulegium*), and blue cohosh (*Caulophyllum thalictroides*), all of which were believed to aid in aborting an unwanted pregnancy.[76]

Although abortion was mostly considered illegal in the regions of North America in the 17th century, a charge of murder required proof that there was a living fetus by the presence of quickening, as had been the common law in Europe as well, but I have not been able to determine if any of the native Indian tribes had tried to utilize instruments in aiding abortion.[77] The number of court cases in America for abortion was very small, but there is no question that the heritage of most of the new colonists was based in their being Christian Bible-believing citizens who saw human beings as being born from the womb in the image of God, and therefore deserving of life so that abortion after quickening was the only time it deserved a possible charge of murder. This fact must be remembered when I later discuss the concept of constitutional interpretation known as Originalism in more detail, for it is clear that the Catholic opinion at the time the Constitution was written also did not include the ruling that life began at conception.

When the Constitution was written, this was the common law in England, as is evident in the writings of the English jurist William Blackstone, whose *Commentaries on the Laws of England* became a standard treatise on the subject of English common law, and who championed the long-held view that life "begins in contemplation of the law as soon as an infant is able to stir in the mother's womb," which was a reference to "quickening."[78] Lord Ellenborough's Act of 1803 expanded British common law when it prohibited abortions after quickening appeared, and this was accepted in America, as well.[79] The colonists would have followed that same standard in this country

---

76 Olasky and Savas, The Story of Abortion in America: A Street-Level History, 1652-2022, 19.

77 Ibid., 21.

78 Ibid., 65.

79 Caron, Who Chooses?: American Reproductive History Since 1930, 16.

when they began to legislate laws in their cities and colonies, and since Justice Alito followed the principal of Originalism, he never should have determined that life began at conception, since that was not what the colonists believed. He may have been a good Catholic when he made that judgement, as were his fellow Catholic Justices, but he was a bad Supreme Court Justice for not following the oath he gave when he was formally appointed to the Court to follow the Constitution, and not the Catholic Pope. Quickening was such a reliable indicator of a viable fetus during Colonial times, that if a pregnant woman was sentenced to be executed for a capital crime, if she had quickening, the sentence had to be delayed until she gave birth, so that the child would not die, as well.[80] No matter what was evolving in the hierarchy of the Catholic Church, life began at quickening, and not conception, in America when the Constitution was written, and the Supreme Court should never have made a ruling that went against that standard.

Not much is known about the first landing of colonists from England, which was sent by the Virginia Company of London, arriving at Jamestown, Virginia in 1607 aboard three ships: the Susan Constant, Godspeed, and Discovery. The second settlement took place when Pilgrims, who were Separatists from London and lived in Leiden, Netherlands for about 10 years before they landed at Plymouth Rock in Massachusetts on the Mayflower in 1620.[81] Following these two endeavors, expansion then began to increase while the English Civil War (1642-1651) was taking place, so that by the mid-1600s more than 100 towns were forming along the East coast of America. The residents slowly began to function together, and found strength through unification and cooperation, although each colony still retained independence in their own governance. We don't have much information about what actually took place in these various settlements, but we do know that they made much contact with the indigenous Indian population who practiced using plants to induce abortion, and while their primary religious influence would have come from their Christian beliefs, both Catholicism, which was prevalent in Ireland and Italy, Anglicism in England, and Protestantism in Germany, they would have guided most of their behavior with respect to the issue of

---

80 Freidenfelds, The Myth of the Perfect Pregnancy: A History of Miscarriage in America, 26.
81 Microsoft CoPilot (5/11/2025). Personal communication.

abortion as was present in their homeland in Europe.

Since Christianity, and especially Catholicism, was the religion that most ardently considered abortion to be an immoral act, even if it was not criminal before quickening appeared, there would have been some opposition to its acceptance by the English inhabitants in America. Catholics, however, were a minority of the Christians who migrated here, with most settling initially in Maryland, although in 1649 the government there then switched their allegiance to Anglicanism.[82] Catholics remained a minority in the Christian population in North America until 1850, when their numbers increased by large numbers of immigrants from Italy, Poland, Ireland, Germany France, and Mexico, where Catholicism was more prominent, rising from 195,000 in 1820, to over three million by 1860.[83] This was an incredible population increase, but anti-Catholic bias was still widespread among the general population, and the first Catholic to run for President was Al Smith (1873-1944), the governor of New York who lost to the Quaker Herbert Hoover (1874-1964) in 1928.[84] Because Catholics were few in number, most of the colonists who came to America would have accepted that quickening was when abortion became illegal, and they in general would not have been averse to considering the use of medicinal plants to induce abortion in early pregnancy, and did so, as evidenced by the fact that Benjamin Franklin even published a recipe for an abortifacient in the book "The Instructor," which is clearly indicative of its being well-accepted at the time, as Franklin was one of the leading politicians during the writing of the Constitution.[85]

We should not forget, however, that North America was first discovered by Norse Vikings who were led by Leif Erikson around the year 1000, so there was an awareness of the land available across the ocean for a long period of time in many regions of Europe before colonists began to arrive from England. We first see International problems begin to arise throughout North America from this immigration from multiple countries when the French and Indian War (1754-1763) broke out as the French began to stake their claim to the Ohio River Valley by building forts which threatened the British rule

---

82 Gillis, <u>Roman Catholicism in America</u>, 53.
83 Ibid., 60-61.
84 Ibid., 69.
85 Ibid., 7.

in that region. The French had first entered North America in 1524 when Giovanni da Verrazzano (1485-1528), an Italian explorer sailing for France, explored the east coast from Florida to Newfoundland, followed by Jacques Cartier (1491-1557) in 1534 leading an expedition to the St. Lawrence River, and claiming land for France, laying the foundation for what became known as New France.[86] This, of course, was shortly after the Italian explorer Christopher Columbus (1451-1506) discovered America on October 12, 1492, when he landed on an island in the Bahamas, seeing America although never stepping on its mainland. The French were therefore in North America earlier than the British were, but they concentrated their early settlements on the region in Quebec, before beginning to extend into the areas where the English settlers were starting to prosper. Eventually George Washington led some forces under English control against the French, and this resulted in the Seven Years War (1756-1763), which ended with the first Treaty of Paris signed on February 10, 1763, when France ceded most of its territory in North America to Britain and Spain. This conflict eventually led to disputes of the American colonies with England, since the English tried to rule the colonists from across the Ocean, and the Revolutionary War would eventually begin with the Declaration of Independence signed on July 4, 1776, and ended with another Treaty of Paris on September 3, 1783 at the Hôtel d'York, which was on neutral ground.

I am not going to detail the Revolutionary War in this chapter, but the conflict began with the Boston Tea Party on December 16, 1773, when the so-called Sons of Liberty, who were a political organization that opposed British taxation, protested the tax that Britain imposed on merchants, causing England to then pass the Coercive Acts (Intolerable Acts), which were a series of five punitive laws in 1774, eventually resulting in the Revolutionary War in April 1775. The American motto during that conflict was "no taxation without representation," but during this entire period of time there was no legislation against abortion anywhere in North America, as in 1800, when there were 16 states in the country, but there were no abortion statutes in effect in any of the state governments. Instead, the legal status of the practice "was governed by traditional British common law as interpreted by the local courts," which meant that "abortions undertaken before quickening did not constitute homicide, and were not considered criminal" acts.[87]

---

86 "French Colonization of the Americas," 1.
87 McFarlane and Hansen, <u>Regulating Abortion: The Politics of US</u>

This means that the problem with abortion being seen as a crime did not take place until after the Constitution was written. There were no laws in the colonies against it, and there was very little discussion of the problem in any of the newspapers, but by 1900, however, there were 45 states on American soil, and "every state had an anti-abortion law," according to most scholars.[88] So what happened to bring this situation about? The answer, I believe is that the American Medical Association, which was first established in 1847, and was being encouraged by Dr. Horatio Storer to ban abortion, was very anti-abortionist from its inception, partly because of the dangers associated with the procedure during that era, but mostly because the governance of the Association was very Catholic at the time. I believe that part of this development may have been due to social pressure against what was considered sinful also increasing throughout America in the nineteenth century, as this was the era when the Eighteenth Amendment was passed on January 16, 1919, for Prohibition to prevent the sale of alcoholic beverages. The problem was exacerbated because herbal remedies were being used to cause abortion during Colonial times, mostly because repetitive pregnancies were very common, and because the remedies seldom worked, few pregnancies were actually prevented, and abortions began to rise by unqualified practitioners, leading many of the colonies to begin to legislate against abortion.[89] This included homeopaths, hydropaths, botanical physicians, and eclectics, in addition to MDs who had very little postgraduate training and saw a way to quickly make a living.[90] Berries and plants were plentiful in New England during this period of time, and often were cultivated by women for other women who would need them, but in the 18th century, but there were few prosecutions for abortion.[91]

After the Constitution was written, many non-physicians in America discovered methods to abort women who did not want to remain pregnant, and they did it in facilities that were not under state medical licensure control. Their presence became quickly known, and

---

Abortion Policy, 45.

88 Shannon, "Abortion: A Challenge for Ethics and Public Policy," 3.
89 Freidenfelds, The Myth of the Perfect Pregnancy: A History of Miscarriage in America, 27.
90 Caron, Who Chooses?: American Reproductive History Since 1930, 20.
91 Phillips, "Abortion in Colonial America: A Time of Herbal Remedies and Accepted Actions," 2.

many women who wanted abortions began to utilize their services, both because they were less expensive, and less likely to broadcast their treatment to the country-at-large. This greatly bothered the newly formed AMA, who saw the practice as not only dangerous to patients, but was something that was not under their own control, and not providing them recompense for their advice or treatment. They encouraged the state judiciaries to prosecute for deaths from these procedures, and the earliest trial of this type was in 1745, before the Revolutionary War took place, when Dr. John Hallowell was arrested and charged with murder for the death of Sarah Grosvenor and her baby in British Colonial America, as I will soon discuss.[92] At that time, savin, also known as juniper (*Juniperus communis*), and pennyroyal were the two most commonly used abortifacients, but since they were often not effective, a growing number of practitioners made themselves available to perform abortion when the other methods failed, and some of them were physicians who began to learn the same technique.[93] There are almost no accounts that described how abortions were done at that time, but there is some information on the case of Hallowell, because there are records from his trial in Connecticut, which was handled by Joseph Fowler, king's attorney for Windham County, on a charge of "highhanded Misdemeanor," for attempting to destroy the "fruit of her womb."[94] There were also times that miscarriages took place, and the fetus was not totally expelled, and the woman's uterus became infected, and had to be evacuated, so licensed physicians who practiced in approved hospitals became familiar with the procedure, because when an illegal abortion was performed, and the patient became ill with complications, the follow-up care had to be done in hospitals by registered doctors.[95] Miscarriages were very frequent during that era, affecting as many as

---

92 Ibid., 8-9.

93 Dayton, "Taking the Trade: Abortion and Gender Relations in an Eighteenth-Century New England Village," 19. Juniper was the most common folk abortifacient in America in the early nineteenth century, and was noted in the Egyptian Ebers Papyrus. Riddle, "Women's Knowledge of Abortifacients from Antiquity to the Present," 218.

94 Dayton, "Taking the Trade: Abortion and Gender Relations in an Eighteenth-Century New England Village," 20-21.

95 Freidenfelds, The Myth of the Perfect Pregnancy: A History of Miscarriage in America, 28.

30% of pregnancies, and so techniques had to be developed to try to eliminate the products that were not totally expelled, and those same methods were then used to try to abort a pregnancy as well. When the intent was clearly not abortion, the procedure was not a crime, but if a death took place, it still had to be explained in the courts. What is clear in the records we do have is that at the time the Revolutionary War took place, abortion was not seen as a common crime, and was not prosecuted unless it took place after quickening was detected, but the practice was becoming commonplace, and many states sought to have the procedures banned.

Because there were no laws in the colonies against abortion, there were no trials for abortion, but trials did take place for infanticide of newborns. One well-described event was of a bastard infant killed after birth, which is not actually abortion, but rather infanticide. It took place in Massachusetts in 1648, when Mary Martin, a twenty-one-year-old unmarried servant, killed her newborn child and then confessed to the crime.[96] She was hanged for the crime, which was a common sentence at that time in the thirteen colonies, as killing a newborn after birth was clearly murder. The first conviction for intention to abort, followed by death of the infant, took place in Maryland in 1652, when Captain William Mitchell was indicted for murder after he forced his bondservant, Susan Warren, to drink an abortifacient, and the baby was stillborn.[97] He was let off with a fine for conviction of murderous intention; however, it was likely because it could not be proven that the infant was alive before the drug worked. Other cases followed in the colonies, with Massachusetts having fifty-one infanticide convictions from 1670-1807, but details of the punishments were not available, and all we can say is that the tables were turning, and the opponents of abortion were gathering their forces to begin an intense anti-abortion effort in America that would be promoted by physicians who were founding the American Medical Association shortly thereafter, but all of that would take place in the nineteenth century.[98]

The first criminal trial, which included a charge of abortion, was in 1742 in New York City, when Sarah Grosvenor (1723-1742) died

---

96 "Did Colonial America have abortions? Yes, but . . .," 2.

97 Ibid.

98 Ibid., 3.

during an abortion performed by Dr. John Hallowell, who had taken an abortifacient which failed, and so she then had an abortion, and died ten days later.[99] Three indictments were brought against Dr. Hallowell that were dismissed, but he did eventually go to trial after a fourth indictment. He was only found guilty of a misdemeanor, as the abortion was not held to have caused her death.[100] It would take time before state laws against the legality of abortion became common enough to increase the legal actions against abortionists, but once the anti-abortion train was put into high gear by the formation of the American Medical Association (AMA), the battle lines would become drawn, and states began to enact anti-abortion laws in greater frequency.

James Mohr, the Distinguished Professor of History and Philip H. Knight Professor of Social Sciences at the University of Oregon, wrote *Abortion in America* in 1978, and believed that the abortion laws that were being written at that time did not focus on the fetus, but on the "health status of the mother and the safety of the procedure that was used."[101] He was referring here to the fact that in the mid-19th century, abortion had become a lucrative business throughout America, and at the time it was not utilized by well-trained physicians, but rather by many "abortionists," whose primary goal was felt by the medical profession to not be the health and welfare of the patient, but the means by which to obtain wealth.[102] While I agree that this may have been one reason the American Medical Association developed such a negative position on the practice of abortion, I do not accept that Mohr's intent to place a benevolent nature on the AMA when he made this assessment is accurate, and I do not agree that the mother's health was their major concern. What was taking place across America at that time was a reaction to the changing social structure that followed the liberalization that took place with the amendments that abolished slavery, and gave women the right to vote. Women did not want to deliver pregnancies that were not planned, and this is what prompted the increase in doctors willing to perform the procedures in non-hospital settings. As this practice increased, and the AMA

---

99   "Death of Sarah Grosvenor," 1-2.

100   Ibid., 1-3.

101   Shannon, "Abortion: A Challenge for Ethics and Public Policy," 3.

102   McBride and Keys, <u>Abortion in the United States: A Reference Handbook</u>, 5-6.

continued to support anti-abortion legislation, the Republican Party saw the opportunity in states where the legislatures were dominated by Republicans in the Southeast, as well as Ohio and Pennsylvania, although Democratic states, like Massachusetts and New York, also passed similar laws. The 19th century was an era when the Christian right-wing influence took on an active extremist political tone that continues to push its radical beliefs on the issue of abortion today, particularly in the last half-century.

Before I end my discussion of abortion in America, I want to show how our modern history after the Constitution was written continued to show other aspects of infanticide remaining a problem in America, as it was throughout Europe in the Middle Ages and the Renaissance. In my book on the history of infanticide, I discussed many of the methods that women had to use in the past to dispose of unwanted births, and this included how many Churches often made it easier for unwanted births to be left for adoption at their doorstep, without evidence of who the mother was who was responsible. They became aware of the problem because of a practice known as "overlaying," where a baby who was sleeping in bed with the mother would be found in the morning to have died because of being "accidentally" rolled over upon during the night while the mother slept. Churches throughout Europe during the Middle Ages were aware of these stories, and they developed a process in which parents planning to do this were encouraged to drop the infants off anonymously at the Church, so that no one would know who was involved in the transfer. In Medieval England, this was a very common means of infanticide, according to Catherine Damme, who was an Assistant Professor at the University of Texas, Dallas.[103] During the initial period of time this was done, the punishment for the crime was quite mild, although church legislation against the practice increased in the 1200s because it was found that the number of events was increasing greatly. It was considered a venial sin by the Church initially, and in almost every case it was directed at the mother, but for women who could not stand the burden of raising a child they did not want, they saw no other choice to make, and not be seen as guilty of murder.[104]

Infant mortality was very high in ancient days, and so the deaths

---

103   Damme, "Infanticide: The Worth of an Infant Under Law," 3.
104   Ibid., 4.

were initially not questioned. Fatal illnesses among infants was common, and there were no antibiotics to treat the problem until Sulfa medications became available in the 1930s, and Penicillin was discovered by Alexander Fleming (1881-1955) in 1928. Infanticide after birth was therefore usually not a discoverable event, but attempts to restrict the practice were made by many Catholic responses, such as the Penitentials of Columbanus (seventh century), the St. Hubert Penitential (ninth century), and the Penitential of Haltigar (ninth century), directed at both mothers and fathers.[105] Unfortunately, the production of unwanted children continued without interruption. In 1237, overlaying was elevated from a venial to a major sin in the Catholic Church, although the ease of the excuse led to its continued existence.[106] For the most part, from the Middle Ages until 1869, when Pope Pius IX extended excommunication for all stages of pregnancy, "it was commonly accepted in the West that the human person did not begin until several weeks after conception."[107]

This method of eliminating unwanted newborns had clearly begun to diminish in the Renaissance, however, but it did not totally disappear in the United States during this era, as there were also cases of overlaying in ante-bellum Virginia during the 1850s, when the mortality of children under the age of one year of age was 16-20%, even when they were well cared for, and overlaying was stated to be the cause in 4% of the cases, which is not likely an accurate figure for it is almost impossible to prove.[108] In addition, Todd L. Savitt, Associate Professor in the Department of Bioethics and Interdisciplinary Studies at the Brody School of Medicine believes that many of these were actually due to what is now known as Sudden Infant Death Syndrome (SIDS), which continues to be a significant cause of death in modern times, because many investigators do not believe that an unwanted child would actually be killed by a mother.[109] They have invented this

---

105   O'Connor, Child Murderess and Dead Child Traditions, A
        Comparative Study, 26-27.
106   Greenwald & Greenwald, "Medicolegal Progress in Inquests of
        Felonious Deaths: Westminster, 1761-1866," 238.
107   Ford, "The Human Embryo as Person in Catholic Teaching," 231.
108   Savitt, "Smothering & Overlaying of Virginal Slave Children: A
        Suggested
Explanation," 402
109   Ibid., 400.

"disease" as the only rational explanation, hoping that they will find a cause that will not suggest the parent actually killed their own child. I hope I am wrong, and there is such a diagnosis that can be treated, but the history of overlaying is factual, and the disease descriptions are incredibly similar.

All Bible-reading monotheists, however, are aware of this problem because of the decision of King Solomon, who lived during the 10th century BCE, and was said to have shown uncommonly wise justice. In that famous case, a woman had claimed that another woman rolled over on top of her three-day-old baby as they slept in bed, and caused the baby to smother to death, but she now claimed that the living baby was hers, and not the one that died. The problem for Solomon was that the other woman said the same thing, but charged that it was the first woman who killed her child, and laid her dead child in her arms, taking my child from me.[110] Neither would change their story, despite all attempts at resolution, and Solomon then decided that he would slice the living baby in two with a sword, and then give one-half to each woman to settle the dispute.[111] When he took a sword and raised it to divide the child in two, one woman suddenly gave up her claim to save the baby, and Solomon knew that she was the real mother. This was primarily the story that led to King Solomon's fame as being a wise king, but I bring this story up because in real life, it is often hard to know the real truth about the death of a young infant, but it is easy to understand how difficult it is for many women who give birth to an unwanted child to be able to accept the reality of their actions.

As I have already explained, many countries accept that the hormonal changes after birth create a mental disturbance in mothers that legally provides a medical excuse for infanticide up to a period of time when normality returns. I am not against such leniency, but I am concerned for trying to prevent many of these cases by allowing for the legalization of abortion in cases of mothers who have unwanted, nonviable fetuses that they do not want to carry to birth.

Overlaying was a simple way to eliminate an unwanted newborn and escape any claim of responsibility, but many cases throughout history were not so innocent. The problem became so widespread during the Middle Ages that various ecclesiastical decrees stipulated

---

110   1 Kgs 3:20.
111   1 Kgs 3:25.

that mothers were not to sleep in the same bed as their children under the age of one year. In 1217, the Synod of Salisbury issued warnings to nursing mothers not to take their children in bed with them because of the dangers of overlaying, and many of these instructions were directed to the wet nurses as well.[112] In the *Statutes of Winchester I* in 1224, which were secular laws enacted by King Henry III (1207-1272) of England, the Catholic Church warned of excommunication and instructed that: "Women should be restrained from keeping their children close by in bed lest they smother them while in sleep."[113] Catherine Damme, found at least fifteen other references in ecclesiastical statutes of councils during this era that pointed out the dangers of taking a child into bed, so the practice was common over a far region.[114] While the overlaying could easily occur during breastfeeding, when a lactating mother exhausted from her labors could easily fall asleep while feeding, there were a number of cases that developed during the night when either the husband or wife could suffocate the child, and explain it away as simply an accident. Whether the problem was truly one only of feminine causation, or whether this was another example of sexism in the Ecclesiastic courts, has not been clearly determined, but in most cases, it was the mother who was charged. The Danish synod had seen overlaying as a responsibility of the mother alone, but tribunals elsewhere would also bring various men before the court to be charged.[115] The prosecution in a case of overlaying did not need to allege an intent to kill the infant, as careless negligence was enough guilt and was punished with an equal intensity.[116] The twelfth-century Catholic theologian Peter Abelard (1079-1142), for example, considered overlaying an inadvertent act and not murder, but he nevertheless did not question the imposition of heavy penance on the mother, not because she had sinned, since she was innocent and had acted out of compassion for the infant, but as a caution to her and other women to act more carefully in the future.[117]

The problem of overlaying continued well beyond the Middle

---

112   Damme, "Infanticide: The Worth of an Infant Under Law," 3.

113   Ibid.

114   Ibid.

115   Shahar, Childhood in the Middle Ages, 130.

116   Helmholz, "Infanticide in the Province of Canterbury During the 15th Century," 381.

117   Shahar, Childhood in the Middle Ages, 129.

Ages, and so I believe it was likely to have been utilized in Colonial America, as well. The English playwright William Congreve (1670-1729), in *Love for Love*, depicted Valentine, the central character and eldest son of Sir Sampson Legend, as putting a pox on Twitnam who was the mother of one of his children: "A thoughtless, two-handed whore, she knows my condition well enough, and might have overlaid the child a fortnight ago, if she had any forecast in her."[118] It was a common cause of death in Norway in the sixteenth century, and the frequency was too high to be explained by accidents alone.[119] There was also evidence, as late as 1745 in Pomerania, on the southern coast of the Baltic Sea, of the punishment of overlaying by public penance. In The Gentleman's Magazine, from January 1746, a Florentine device called an "arcutio" was highlighted, which indicated active public interest in the problem.[120] Even up to the nineteenth century, overlaying remained a problem in England. In 1894, for example, the London coroner noted that a thousand infants were overlain each year in London alone.[121] It was particularly frequent on Saturday nights when the cause was believed to be gross carelessness brought on by excess alcohol intake, but finding excuses was never different throughout its long history of causing infant deaths. An article in the British Medical Journal noted that: "Perfectly healthy children are sacrificed to the bad habit of making them sleep with their parents," a snide way of explaining where the blame truly lay.[122] In 1909, England finally made overlaying a specific criminal offense, and there were twenty reported deaths from it in 1920 in Birmingham, England.[123]

Once the colonists moved to America, these same problems that afflicted people in Europe, affected their lives here as well, and the medical profession found itself discovering a new cause of infant death that many feared may have been a variant of the same way of disposing of unwanted children. In antebellum Virginia, during the 1850s, the mortality of children under the age of one year was 16-

---

118   Congreve, Love for Love, Liv. 190-193, 20.

119   Martinson, Growing Up in Norway, 800-1990, 29.

120   History of Auricular Confession and Indulgences in the Latin Church, Vol. II, 90; Fildes, Breasts, Bottles, and Babies, 196-197.

121   "A Thousand Infants Overlain," 36.

122   Ibid.

123   Radbill, "Children in a World of Violence: A History of Child Abuse," 9.

20%. Despite extensive investigations, the cause of this condition was often unknown, but it is said to primarily affect healthy babies between two and twelve months of age, a situation that sounds to me very much like overlaying.[124]

It is believed that 7-10,000 young infants die in this country every year from SIDS, but separating the homicidal death from the so-called "crib death" can be very difficult.[125] SIDS became a certifiable cause of death in 1963, and in 1968, Stuart S. Asch (1923-2002), former Professor Emeritus in Clinical Psychiatry at New York Presbyterian Hospital, presented the hypothesis that the majority of SIDS deaths actually represent maternal homicide secondary to postpartum depression, but his paper was not substantiated by any case reports.[126] When forensic evidence of suffocation is evident in a SIDS death, however, it is likely that the underlying causation was homicide, and some researchers have pointed out that up to ten percent of such "unexpected" deaths may not have been natural.[127] According to one pediatric pathologist, "It is not just difficult to tell the difference between a child who died from SIDS and one who is suffocated, it is impossible."[128]

It should be emphasized that although childbirth was an ordeal for women in America before the Constitution was signed, it was not as dangerous as undergoing an abortion, which at that time was like "playing Russian roulette," as the reporters Martin Olasky and Leah Savas described in their treatise on abortion in America.[129] The mortality rate for mothers giving birth in the 1800s was about 1%, given the unavailability of antibiotics to treat infections, so despite the pain and suffering, they would not be risking their life as greatly, as they would with an illegal abortion. They also knew that about 20% of children died before their fifth birthday, so if a child was unwanted you not only had to give them birth, you also had to deal with the

---

124   Raring, Crib Death, 19-20.

125   DeFrain, Taylor & Ernst, Coping With Sudden Infant Death, 3.

126   Asch, "Crib Deaths: Their Possible Relationship to Post-Partum Depression and Infanticide," 214.

127   Emery, "Child Abuse, Sudden Infant Death Syndrome, and Unexpected Infant Death," 1097.

128   Chicago Tribune (September 10, 1993): Section I, 16.

129   Olasky and Savas, The Story of Abortion in America: A Street-Level History, 1652-2022, 55.

likelihood that their survival was limited.[130] Women were limited by society, and were terrified by both giving birth and by dying from an abortion, and through it all, they couldn't even vote in an election for representatives that might be more tolerant of their needs. Despite this fact, "by the beginning of the twentieth century, some two million women each year resorted to illegal abortions," and this was the primary reason, in my opinion, that Blackmun's court voted seven-to-two to recognize a constitutional right of women to terminate an unwanted pregnancy.[131] One statistic I am sure he was aware of is that in the mid-1950s, there were between 200,000 and 1.2 million illegal abortions a year. Only 8,000 abortions took place inside a hospital annually.[132] How many people died from these unsafe abortions is not known, but most of the time their problems were hidden from view unless there were lawsuits filed for medical malpractice. What we do know is that in 1973, there were forty-seven deaths from abortions reported, and this number decreased to five in 2021.[133]

I believe that all Catholics who read my book will reconsider their public stance on abortion, while maintaining their view on a personal level only. When John F. Kennedy Jr. (1917-1963) addressed concerns about his Catholic faith during his 1960 presidential campaign in a speech to the Greater Houston Ministerial Association on September 12, 1960, he emphasized the necessity of separation of Church and State on a governmental level, while maintaining his religious views personally, stating:

> I believe in an America where the separation of church and state is absolute – where no Catholic prelate would tell the President (should he be Catholic) how to act, and no Protestant minister would tell his parishioners for whom to vote – where no church or church school is granted any public funds or political preference – and where no man is denied public office merely because his religion differs from the President

---

130   Microsoft CoPilot (1/12/2025), citing Miss Cellania, "The Historical Horror of Childbirth."

131   Bollinger and Stone, "Opening Dialogue," xvi-xvii.

132   Abortion Care as Moral Work: Ethical Considerations of Maternal and Fetal Bodies, 1.

133   "Number of abortion-related deaths reported in the U.S. from 1973 to 2021," 1-4

who might appoint him or the people who might elect him.[134]

Kennedy sought to reassure voters that his Catholicism would not influence his decisions as President, and that he would uphold religious liberty for all Americans. William D. Delahunt (1941-2024), a Catholic Democratic former Congressman from Massachusetts, remembers that Kennedy influenced many other Catholics who knew him to be able to follow his example by remembering how he would invoke the biblical maxim, "Render unto Caesar what is Caesar's, render unto God what is God's."[135] This is what I believe Justice Samuel Alito Jr. should do as well. Kennedy's speech was a pivotal moment in his campaign, helping to counter anti-Catholic sentiment, and with our present contention over the constitutionality of abortion, we need to have that same reassurance that it will be our Constitution, and not our religious beliefs, that determines the law of our land. If a Justice feels they cannot put their religious training aside, they can recuse themself from the case, as many have done in the past. No Justice has to deny their religious training, but they have to be true to the Constitution, rather than the Catholic Pope, when they enter the courtroom.

It is interesting that another well-known politician of Italian descent, Mario Cuomo (1932-2015), who was the 52nd Governor of New York, privately opposed abortion but supported public funding of abortions, defending his position by stating that: "The values derived from religious belief will not – and should not – be accepted as part of the public morality unless they are shared by the pluralistic community at large, by consensus."[136] He also said that he knew the Catholic Church didn't believe in abortion, but "I'm not here to legislate religion."[137] This is the attitude I believe Supreme Court Justices should use if they are asked to judge an abortion case, and if they cannot separate their Church and State views, they should recuse themselves and refuse from voting on this issue. This issue just came up this week on the Supreme Court in *Oklahoma Statewide Charter*

---

134   Microsoft CoPilot (5/12/2025). Personal communication.

135   Walbert, "Politics, Religion, and Abortion in the United States,"
        192-193.

136   Gillis, Roman Catholicism in America, 180.

137   Walbert, "Politics, Religion, and Abortion in the United States,"
        195.

School Board v. Drummond 605 U.S. (2025) where the Supreme Court was asked to judge whether an Oklahoma Catholic charter school was found by a District Court to not be able to have funding by the federal government, but the Supreme Court gave a 4-4 decision because only one of the Justices recused herself because she had ties to Notre Dame University. This case proves that my concerns are valid, and I am demanding that this issue of separation of Church and State be fully debated in the many discussions that will surround the passage of an amendment to approve abortion of unwanted, nonviable fetuses.

The legal system in America before *Roe v. Wade* was already preventing most women from seeking safe abortions for unwanted pregnancies because of the costs of traveling long distances to get the procedures in America out of the state where they lived. This resulted in two million women each year resorting to illegal abortions, despite the dangers associated with the procedure.[138] Once the Supreme Court ruled that they could get abortions close to home, our country settled into a safe haven for mothers who did not want to give birth to unwanted pregnancies. She did not have to risk abortions performed by unqualified individuals in non-sterile environments, which carried the risk of a much higher mortality; she did not have to hide the pregnancy for months by wearing loose clothing, disappear from public view until the baby was born, and then often kill and bury it, so the body would not be found. Throughout our history, this need to hide the shame of what had to be done had caused many women, often emotionally burdened by post-partum depression, to dispose of their infants after birth in this fashion in order to return to a normal life, and so infanticide became an uncommon event for the first time in American history once *Roe v. Wade* was passed. I believe that Blackmun knew this would happen, and also knew that the benefits of abortion would be able to be indelibly proven, so much so that the chance for passage of a future amendment would be much assured, something that was not possible at the time the trial was held. Blackmun truly changed the way unwanted pregnancies across the world could be prevented so that infanticide and child abuse could become a rarer social problem, which hopefully could be handled by programs designed to care for those children after birth.

---

138   Bollinger and Stone, "Opening Dialogue," xvi.

Chapter III
Roe v. Wade

So it is now time to finally carefully analyze each of the two Supreme Court cases that have greatly divided our country, and created a situation that threatens to escalate into the same disturbance that the issue of slavery caused after the Constitution was written -- a political Civil War that almost destroyed the efforts of our Founding Fathers to form a true Democracy in North America. So far, the dispute is not being threatened by soldiers on the frontlines, but rather by political parties in Congress, and the White House, who refuse to accept any facet of the other parties' platform, leading to disputes that are tearing our democratic process to shreds. The Constitutional Congress was similarly hotly divided, but their foresight in designing our governance in a timely fashion was superb, and even though their initial inability to provide a solid assurance of equal rights to all citizens of the country almost tore their structure apart because the issue of slavery could not be settled, the lesson we learned the hard way was to be sure we include the voice of the united populace of the United States in settling the social disputes that arise in our country. The voice of the people must decide important issues, and not the opinion of nine Supreme Court Justices alone. The issue of abortion is the dominant lynch-pin dividing our country at the present time, and unless we can pass an amendment that satisfies 3/4 of the population, and at least is accepted by the 1/4 that disagree without violent dissent, our ability to unify on other issues will be lost, and our legacy of Democracy will be destroyed. For that reason, I will analyze the two Supreme Court cases that led to this dispute, and show why an amendment should be passed to settle their differences peacefully, and we can maintain our position as the Beacon of Democracy.

It was after *Roe v. Wade* was decided that the dispute over abortion erupted into a battleground that now splits our two major political parties into the same type of Federalist and Anti-Federalist dispute that threatened the success of the Continental Congress. The legalization of abortion transformed the present Republican Party into an aggressive Pro-Life faction, backed by Religious Right Christian Evangelicals who claim that abortion is murder, and must be banished. Basing their model society on conservative Christian values, they found a leader in Donald Trump, who clothed their beliefs into his slogan of Making America Great Again (MAGA), which has made a mockery of First Amendment rights in its formula for success. The Democrats then transformed themselves into a similarly rabid Pro-Choice legion, led by a Progressive Social Justice Movement that demanded that women have the constitutional right to decide whether to keep an unwanted pregnancy if the fetus is nonviable, and coupled that feminist proclamation with the demand that people have the right to live lives that allow them to identify themselves in ways that have led to their designation as LBGTQ, which stands for: L-Lesbian, G-Gay, B-Bisexual, T-Transgender, Q-Queer or Questioning, and sometimes adding I-Intersex, and A-Asexual, to further make their point.

These political differences closely resemble how different the two sides of our Founding Fathers were when they wrote the United States Constitution. They savagely fought over what powers should be allowed to the federal government to decide what rights should apply to every citizen in the United States, and what control each individual state had in deciding the rights which applied to every citizen of their state. During the writing of the Constitution they were unable to agree on the issues of slavery, which allowed slaves to be considered as property rather than citizens, and the right of women to vote, both of which had to be settled by the passage of amendments to the Constitution many years later. According to the Pew Research Center, a nonpartisan American think tank based in Washington D.C.: "Today, 92% of Republicans are to the right of the median Democrat, and 94% of Democrats are to the left of the median Republican," a recipe that is not conducive to productive give-and-take legislation.[1] To make matters worse, the basis for their dispute is the position of the modern Catholic Popes that life begins at conception, rather than the common law definition that it begins at quickening, and this has resulted in a call to terminate the separation of Church and State in our Constitution.

When the Constitution was written, the Federalists wanted a strong central government, which is how the Democratic Party tries to legislate today; and the Anti-Federalists wanted the states to retain much independent authority, like Republicans argue for today, and the result back then was that 620,000-750,000 American lives were

---

1   Pew Research Center, "The United States Has Become More Politically Polarized," 12.

lost before the issue over slavery could be resolved in a bloody Civil War.[2] If we don't settle the issue we face in America today by passing an amendment to legalize abortion of unwanted unviable fetuses, I predict over the next few years an equivalent number of unwanted births will take place, resulting in the same carnage of children, but without an identifiable winner like ended the Civil War on the battlefield. The casualties today, if peace cannot be made, will not be soldiers, but rather innocent unwanted children whose lives will be lost because unwanted nonviable fetuses will not be able to be safely aborted without pain and suffering, and their souls allowed to continue to Heaven if they are Catholic, instead of a Hell on earth. The Bill of Rights which was voted on by the first Constitutional Congress included 12 Amendments that were accepted by the two sides, but only 10 of which were approved by the states, which was a good start, but not expansive enough to prevent a violent conflict. I am hopeful that we can avoid another violent confrontation by settling the matter by the passage of an amendment now, before the dispute over abortion really turns deadly. George Santayana (1863-1952), the Spanish-American philosopher, once said "those who cannot remember the past are condemned to repeat it," and this adage has long been agreed to by many others who fight for the liberty of all mankind, as I do in this book. Hopefully, my efforts will not be wasted.

The present rhetoric on abortion has reached proportions of violence that I personally did not encounter during the Civil Rights demonstrations that radically divided our country in the 1950s and 1960s, while I was in high school and college, and the disagreements over the Vietnam War in the 1960s and early 1970s, while I was beginning my career in Medicine. Violence has recently turned deadly at times, and all that I can think of is what President Abraham Lincoln had to say in his Gettysburg Address in 1863 that the battlefield before him had to be dedicated so: "that these dead shall not have died in vain."[3] I'm not concerned that the combatants in this present battle will be the ones who are arguing so vehemently, but rather the numbers of unwanted babies that will return to being mistreated and killed if their birth cannot be prevented before they reach the status of viability. I firmly believe that if we can pass an amendment similar

---

2   "Civil War Casualties," 2.
3   "Text of Lincoln's Speech," 1.

to the one I propose in this book, we can remove the confrontations before they become too violent to be contained, and we can put an end to the bloody history which the human race has demonstrated by the infanticide and child abuse that was inflicted on unwanted children that have been born since our civilization first began.

In the next two chapters, I will analyze both *Roe v. Wade 410 U.S. 113 (1973)*, and *Dobbs v. Jackson Women's Health Organization 597 U.S. 215 (2022)*, in detail in order to show where I believe the essence of their dispute lies, and why I contend that our country can pass an amendment that will satisfy at least 3/4 of the states to approve my proposal. I will show why both Supreme Courts made significant errors in their interpretation of the Constitution when they decided the issue of abortion, and that the dispute is still not being properly argued today, because there is a basic failure to understand that abortion of an nonviable fetus is not truly "abortion," as is the abortion of a viable fetus, which is infanticide or murder, but rather is a crime known as "feticide," which is not equivalent to murder, because a nonviable fetus cannot be considered to be a living "person." This issue has not been able to be accepted by Republicans because of their adherence to the Catholic position in modern times that life begins at conception, which I disagree is either a medical, or a legal, fact, and certainly is not the common law. Modern Popes have taken this stance, as I will soon discuss in detail, and if you are Catholic, I am not telling you that you are wrong to think life begins at conception, for that is a religious belief, and you can accept that as a matter of faith, which is your right when you believe in a particular God. What I am saying, however, is that if you decide to accept that holding, you should also not charge that others are committing murder when they decide to abort a nonviable fetus, for that decision is also based on their own religious faith that accepts the scientific belief that life begins at quickening, when the fetus is viable, and so the death of a nonviable fetus is therefore not murder, it is feticide, because the fetus has not yet reached the age when it can be considered to be a person under the Constitution.

This is what lies at the heart of why a basic principle of Democracy in America is that we must have freedom of religion that allows all individuals to choose to believe in a God, or not, because of their faith. If they to choose to believe in One God, or many gods, or even in no god at all, they can know that in our Democracy there cannot be one God that is better than all the others, for that would then be a

Theocracy, and not a Democracy. If you are Catholic, you can believe whatever your Pope tells you about when life begins, whether you are the President of the United States, or a peon with very little formal education. But you must also allow others to accept their religious teaching, as well, and you cannot tell them that your God is the One and Only Correct God, and if that God says life begins at conception, it is true. There are many things that cannot be proven, and must be taken on faith, which is the basis of all religious beliefs, and the present Catholic position that life begins at conception is not even accepted by all Christians, Jews or Muslims, who believe in the same God. I will explain in this Chapter, and others which follow, that the current United States Supreme Court was deliberately filled by Republican Presidents with a majority of Catholic Justices in order to overturn the *Roe v. Wade* decision by reasons which are based on religious faith, rather than the Constitution. In so doing, they did not follow the common law at the time the Constitution was written, which accepted that quickening was when life began, and instituted a new common law that they were taught as children, which the Catholic Pope said began at conception.

The Justices that made this their decision in the *Dobbs* case did not follow the oath they took to base their judicial judgments on the Constitution, and instead attempted to make a new common law about when life begins, even though they demanded in their opinion that those who believe in abortion must do that by an amendment, because the Constitution did not mention the word "abortion." *Roe v. Wade* had said they based their decision on the common law which declared quickening as when life began, and here *Dobbs* was changing the common law, which they are not authorized to do, by simply saying life begins at conception, and stating that now the prior two Supreme Courts that approved abortion must pass an amendment. There is an old proverb that says "what is good for the goose is good for the gander," and it is time that the Catholic Justices that voted for the *Dobbs* verdict realize that they cannot make new law unless they submit a new amendment, as well.[4] The *Dobbs* Supreme Court is attempting to change the principle of separation of Church and State,

---

4 The earliest known written version of this line appears in John Ray's 1670 collection of English proverbs as: "What's sauce for the goose is sauce for the gander." "U.S. Dictionary," 1.

and I contend that they do not have the authority to do that. If I am correct, the amendment I propose will pass; and if I am not, it will be defeated; but either way, it will be decided by a Democracy, and not nine Supreme Court Justices, seven of whom believe in the Catholic faith, and six of whom acted like a Theocracy, and not a Democracy, when they overruled *Roe v. Wade*. If that Supreme Court wants to change the common law and claim that life begins at conception, let them propose an amendment to that effect, and see what happens. If my amendment loses, I guarantee we will come closer to a 3/4 majority then they will. If both amendments fail, we can return to the *Roe v. Wade* verdict which followed the common law at the time the Constitution was written, and the Republicans and Democrats can argue about what to do next.

What is truly remarkable about both of these abortion cases is that each of the two Supreme Courts in question were composed of a majority of Justices appointed by Republican Presidents, and both selected the cases they wished to hear, but their decisions interpreted the Constitution in totally opposite extremes. This took place despite the fact that another Supreme Court in *Planned Parenthood of Southeastern Pennsylvania v. Casey,* later also approved the *Roe v. Wade* verdict as consistent with the Constitution, and when the *Dobbs* case was decided, both of the verdicts were overturned. One would not have expected that to be the case at the level of the Supreme Court, but after researching the issue exhaustively, I believe it is easy to see why we are now in such a dangerous state of contention that our political parties, and our citizens who voted them into office, are threatening to destroy the Union which has persisted for almost 250 years, and been the pride of Democracy, since the Declaration of Independence was adopted on July 4, 1776, and finally signed on August 2, 1776. I am confident we can find a peaceful resolution to this problem, and I will show you why, and how, in the pages which follow.

I will start my analysis with the case of *Roe v. Wade* in this chapter, which the United States Supreme Court agreed to hear on April 19, 1971, after it was submitted by the state of Texas District Court directly to the Supreme Court, rather than to the U.S. Court of Appeals. It did this because when it ruled the State law unconstitutional, it denied an injunction, which meant the law remained enforceable, and this qualified the appeal to be made directly to the Supreme Court, rather than delaying the matter to an intermediate court whose judgment would not matter. Everyone at the time knew it was going to become one of the most closely watched cases ever held, since the matter could only be decided on what the Supreme Court ruled the Constitution determined. Few expected the final outcome that was read 643 days later to decide that abortion was a constitutional right given to all citizens of the United States, because the Court was now altered by Richard Nixon to change from the liberal Warren Court, to a now conservative Burger Court, and finally, the issue could be brought to judgment in the manner the recent anti-abortion legislation throughout the country demanded.

By accepting the *Roe v. Wade* case to review in this manner, Chief Justice Warren E. Burger (1907-1995) was able to schedule it alongside another case, *Doe v. Bolton, 410 U.S. 179 (1973)*, from the state of Georgia, so that two cases with the constitutionality of abortion at issue, would finally be decided by the Supreme Court, and women would hear if abortion was a legal right in the United States based on a Supreme Court interpretation of the Constitution. I personally believe Burger, who was only recently appointed at the time as Chief Justice by Richard Nixon, did this because he believed the attorneys in *Roe v. Wade* were neophytes, with no prior appearances ever made in any courtroom, and while his logic was understandable, it would prove to be a decision he would regret for the rest of his life. Women the world over would finally be able to cheer for the next fifty years, but the political effect it had on our country would divide the Republican and Democratic parties into radically different sides that would find little to agree upon on a number of issues, and the dispute on the issue of abortion would bring us to the brink of a Civil War because of the emotions that rose to threats that suggested such an outbreak was a necessary solution.

But I proceed too quickly, because that outcome does not take place until the next chapter, so let me step back and explain how the issue in *Roe v. Wade* came to be handled by a newly appointed Chief Justice who found himself suddenly in over his head on an issue that had festered for too long, and would have been better handled by the experienced Warren Court. The Supreme Court had purposely evaded the issue of abortion for many years because it was a liberal Supreme Court headed by Earl Warren (1891-1974), and it was primarily interested in promoting liberal agendas, such as equal rights for people of color and women, and did not want to risk a Supreme

Court decision that could possibly take away the right of a woman to not carry an unwanted pregnancy to term delivery. Many states were passing anti-abortion laws during their term in office, and when the Republican candidate Richard Nixon was elected President on November 5, 1968, and inaugurated on January 20, 1969, he was openly opposed to abortion. Earl Warren, the Chief Justice who directed the infamous Court Nixon hated, had resigned on June 21, 1968, and President Lyndon Johnson tried to nominate Abe Fortas as Chief Justice, but his confirmation was filibustered, and the delay then allowed President Nixon to force Fortas to retire once he was sworn in as President, as I will soon explain. Nixon would then soon nominate four new Supreme Court Justices that he believed would assure that the anti-abortion laws would be found to be constitutional, and that is where my story begins.

The liberal Warren Supreme Court had primarily functioned during the Democratic Presidencies of John F. Kennedy Jr. and Lyndon B. Johnson (1908-1973), but many of the Justices on that Court were actually approved by Dwight David Eisenhower (1890-1969), a Republican President who did not demand conservative agendas from the Justices he nominated. The Warren Court, when Nixon was elected President, consisted of Earl Warren as Chief Justice, along with John M. Harlan II (1833-1911), William J. Brennan Jr. (1906-1997), and Potter Stewart (1915-1985), all four appointed by Eisenhower; Hugo Black (1886-1971), and William O. Douglas (1898-1980), who were both appointed by Franklin D. Roosevelt (1882-1945); Byron White, who was appointed by John F. Kennedy; and Abe Fortas (1910-1982), and Thurgood Marshall, who both were appointed by Lyndon B. Johnson. That Court may have had six Justices appointed by Republicans, but their actions represented Radical Left politics, more than the Radical Right, which developed from Republicans who followed after Nixon was elected President, and *Roe v. Wade* was passed. Nixon falsely believed he could change the behavior of the Court by first nominating a conservative Chief Justice who he thought would modify the behavior of the entire Court. He was obviously not very knowledgeable of matters such as this, which is why his choices would fail miserably to achieve his plans, but he did succeed in showing the Republican Party what had to eventually be done to finally develop a conservative Supreme Court that would fit their plans, as I will soon explain. It would take the Republican leadership almost 50 years to achieve their goal, but their task was well thought out, if totally undemocratic.

Richard Nixon was elected as President because the incumbent Democratic President, Lyndon B. Johnson had refused to run for reelection, and so Nixon ran against the Democratic candidate Hubert Humphrey (1911-1978), who had been the 38th Vice President of the United States under Lyndon Johnson, and George Corley Wallace (1919-1998), the governor of Alabama who ran as candidate of the American Independent Party, on November 5, 1968, in a close election, because all three candidates for President were not popular among the voting public.[5] Nixon won by 511,944 votes, but Kennedy beat Nixon by only 112,827 votes, in one of the closest elections in U.S. history[6] .Most people alive today did not live through the Nixon presidency, and so their awareness of the events comes from lessons in a history class, and not personal involvement, which more deeply affects your memory of important events. It is estimated that only about 1/4 of Americans alive today were 16 years old or older during Nixon's presidency, which makes the term "Tricky Dick," which became a derogatory common name tag applied to Nixon at the time, not a frequently remembered fact.[7] I am going to explain some of the history of this era for the rest of you to understand why this is so important, for Nixon's involvement in this abortion case requires some understanding of his strengths, as well as his faults, which explains why this case turned out the way it did. The nickname "Tricky Dick" was first used by the Democratic Representative who ran against Nixon in his 1950 campaign for the Senate in California, Helen Gahagan Douglas (1900-1980). She blamed her loss to him on his using "dirty tricks" against her in that effort, but the nickname did not become well-known until Nixon ran against John F. Kennedy Jr. for President in 1960, and the term became the name tag all of Kennedy's supporters used to identify their foe. This timing is important because Harry Blackmun's daughters were in college during this era, and like most youths of that age at the time, they were fans of Kennedy, and not Nixon. Kennedy's speech when he told the youth of the country at his inauguration on January 20, 1961: "Ask not what your country can do

---

5   Microsoft CoPilot (9/12/2025). Personal communication.
6   Ibid.
7   Microsoft CoPilot (8/10/2025). Personal communication.

for you, ask what you can do for your country," made him extremely attractive to the younger generation, and Nixon did everything he could to try and gain votes, but during the televised debate with Kennedy on September 26, 1960, he refused to wear makeup, and his appearance came across as sweaty and nervous.[8] The nickname stuck from that point forward, and throughout his presidency, after *Roe v. Wade* was decided, everything he did went downhill until he was forced to resign because of the Watergate Scandal, the only U.S. President who ever resigned from office.

It is important that you understand that what I am going to describe about the *Roe v. Wade* case all took place at the start of his election, when he was mostly an unknown entity, without the reputation of what would take place in the Watergate scandal that occurred at the end of his Presidency, causing his resignation. I will discuss this in further detail later in this chapter, but I want you to first see how disastrous the *Roe v. Wade* case turned out, and how I believe it was instrumental in his responding in ways that led to his eventual resignation. I realize this makes my book seem like a fictional soap opera, but the incredible part of everything I say is that I am only repeating the truth, and it's the "whole truth, and nothing but the truth," which originates from English common law and became a formal part of courtroom oaths by the 13th century.[9] I graduated from law school *cum laude* in 1987, and I can tell you that almost nothing you read in this book was ever part of my legal education, and I think that ignorance of the facts of both of these cases is why we are having a constitutional crisis today.

Nixon's term began on January 20, 1969, and shortly thereafter he was able to nominate Warren E. Burger as Chief Justice on June 23, 1969, replacing Earl Warren, who had presided over one of the most liberal Supreme Courts in United States history for 16 years from 10/5/1953 to 6/23/1969, and also one of the most popular among citizens who were not Republican voters. Warren had been the Governor of California from 1943 to 1953, and gave the job up to become the Chief Justice of the Supreme Court, replacing Fred M. Vinson (1890-1953), who died in office, as would later take place with Justice Rehnquist, as well. His influence on American law was as profound as any Chief Justice in history, but, as I said, he had hoped

---

8   Ibid., (8/13/2025).
9   Ibid., (8/19/2025).

to retire while Lyndon Johnson was President, so that his legacy could have been maintained. That plan failed when he did retire, and John's choice Abe Fortas did not pass a vote in the Senate, and now his greatest fears were to become a reality as Nixon would choose his successor, rather than Johnson. The Senate voted 74-3 to confirm Burger as Chief Justice, and the process took only 18 days, which was not a record, but showed that he was generally well-respected by both Democrats and Republicans alike.[10] There had always been competitive animosity between Republicans and Democrats in American politics, but the *Roe v. Wade* decision would turn the two sides into bitter enemies that has continued to worsen and present us with the dangerous state we are in today. Americans at this time knew little about conservative politics, which did not significantly develop until after *Roe v. Wade* was passed, and Barry Goldwater (1909-1988), the United States Senator from Arizona, and Ronald Reagan, the Governor from California, began to campaign for President on conservative ideologies.

Did that relatively easy acceptance by the Democratic Senators for Burger to be Chief Justice foreshadow problems for Republicans in the future because they knew something Nixon didn't? If it did, no one paid attention, for all that mattered was that Chief Justice Warren was gone, and his replacement was a Republican who most pundits believed would alter the way the Supreme Court viewed a variety of issues, but first and foremost, the legality of abortion. The mood of the country at that time was clearly anti-abortion, but liberalism was still evident in the civil liberties that were extended by both the Kennedy and Johnson regimes, primarily through the Warren Court decisions, and that influence would prove more difficult for Nixon and Burger to change. The Vietnam War initiated a wave of protest and a rise in Republican conservatism, but it would not become ingrained until the Presidency of Ronald Reagan. What was not remembered by most citizens, however, was the fact that Warren, the man they hated most, had also been appointed by a Republican President as well, Dwight D. Eisenhower, and Nixon's choices for Supreme Court Justices would eventually number four, but at the time *Roe v. Wade* was decided, only one voted as a true conservative. Warren Burger had much experience serving on the U.S. Court of Appeals in the

---

10 Woodward and Armstrong, <u>The Justices Behind Roe v. Wade: The Inside Story</u>, 22.

District of Columbia for 13 years, but he had no experience in the handling of the important issue of abortion, and he was inheriting Justices who had been on the Warren Court for many years, all of whom had developed ideas about the Constitution that were not any longer being accepted by conservative Republican Presidents. While Nixon was a new President, the Warren Supreme Court had developed a solid history of success with liberal decisions, and we will see that Nixon, as well as his choice for Chief Justice, Warren Burger, was not up to the challenge to decide *Roe v. Wade* in a conservative manner, and that would create an iron wall barrier between the Republicans and Democrats for the next 50 years.

Although the new Chief Justice was a known conservative Republican, it would be a year before Nixon could appoint Harry Blackmun as another Justice, because he had to do some back-door meddling in order to get Abe Fortas to agree to step down from the position he held since October 4, 1965, after he was appointed by Lyndon B. Johnson. Fortas had known Johnson for many years, and had been his adviser since his 1948 Senate race, so Johnson hoped he could make him Chief Justice to continue his liberal legacy on the Supreme Court. In early 1969, Nixon began to investigate Fortas for security violations from his financial ties to the millionaire industrialist Louis Wolfson (1912-2007) in 1966, and John Mitchell (1913-1988), the Attorney General under Nixon, had found that Fortas had accepted a $20,000 annual fee from a foundation funded by Wolfson, and was able to convince Fortas to resign, in order to open up his seat for another conservative Justice.[11] Fortas had taken a pay cut of 90% in salary when he joined the Supreme Court, and he apparently needed the extra funds, although the reasons were never detailed publicly. The important point to the Republicans was that another piece of the liberal Supreme Court was lost, and, as Bob Dylan sang in his 1964 album of the same name, "the-times-they-are-a-changing," they saw it as a declaration that Nixon believed he could take to the bank. Now that he had two appointees on the Court, Nixon began to make plans to find a way to ban abortions at the start of his presidency, and become the major force in the Republican Party, which had always been his desire since he lost the election as President to John

---

11 Woodward and Armstrong, <u>The Justices Behind Roe v. Wade: The Inside Story, 14-15.</u>

F. Kennedy, Jr. on November 8, 1960. Nixon and Burger were too confident in how only two new appointees to the Warren Supreme Court were going to immediately change the most liberal Supreme Court in history; however, they were destined to find out that there would be little change in the deliberations of the Court at all. In fact, the Burger Court would go down in history as more similar to the Warren Court than to conservative principles, as I will soon detail. It would be a lesson that conservative Republicans would remember in future elections, dividing the country into two radically different factions that would find no middle ground to agree upon for the next 50 years. It is difficult to believe that Nixon's ultimate demise, and the passage of *Roe v. Wade* lasting 50 years, was all due to the drama I am about to detail in this book, but my story is factual, so buckle up your seat belt as you find out the true story behind this incredible saga.

On April 14, 1970, Nixon then nominated Harry Blackmun to replace Abe Fortas, after two other nominees failed to be approved by the Senate. Nixon's first choice was Clement Haynsworth, Jr. (1912-1989), a Circuit Court Judge who was turned down by Democrats who were upset with how Fortas was treated.[12] Nixon's second choice, Judge G. Harrold Carswell (1919-1992), was also turned down one year later, supposedly because he was a white supremacist, so John Mitchell then decided to interview Blackmun for the job, likely because Burger made the recommendation.[13] Mitchell brought him to meet with Nixon, and the President was happy to see that he grew up with Burger, and was the best man at Burger's wedding in 1933.[14] Little did Nixon know that when he agreed to next nominate Blackmun for the position of Supreme Court Justice, that he would be the one who would read the opinion of the Court on *Roe v. Wade*, and I have not been able to determine if Burger asked Nixon for advice on who should determine the opinion of the Court in the case, but it is likely that both Nixon and Burger thought Blackmun would act as a conservative Justice, since that plan was widely circulated at the time. Blackmun later said after he was retired that Burger always intimated that he recommended Nixon appoint him, but he never knew for sure

---

12 Ibid., 44.
13 Woodward and Armstrong, <u>The Justices Behind Roe v. Wade: The Inside Story</u>, 60-61.
14 Ibid., 63.

if it was true.[15] I also have been unable to know the answer, but based upon Burger's multiple instances of ineptitude, I'm sure he probably did, given the fact that by then he felt he needed a friend to help him with his unexpected workload.

I believe that Burger recommended to Nixon that he appoint Blackmun as Justice because of the position Blackmun had as the attorney for the Mayo Clinic for ten years, and his own lack of experience with that issue in his career. The problem is that both Burger and Nixon ignored the fact that Blackmun's attachment to the Mayo Clinic may actually have been detrimental to their conservative agenda, because the Mayo Clinic was not a bastion of conservative or Christian thought at that time. In addition, when Blackmun was later asked about his experience there, he said that he never dealt with the issue of abortion, and it was not his prior training that led to his decision, but his research at the Mayo Clinic library once the trial began again, as I will soon explain.[16] Burger also did not pay attention to the fact that Blackmun had three daughters in college at the time, which should have alerted him to a possible liberal opinion on abortion, for as it turned out, all three of his daughters hated Nixon because of his political views according to many commentators, although Blackmun later said that they did not affect his judgment.[17] Nixon was not popular among college students at that time, and Burger only had one daughter, and Nixon had two, but both of Nixon's children were active in his administration, and were married at the time he became President, so their political positions were in lock-step with their father. Neither Burger nor Nixon left any commentaries on Blackmun's actions in their memoirs, but hidden doors cannot keep away their secrets forever, and I am sure the future will provide more information for inquiring minds to find out.

Let me take a moment and note another resource that I used in this book, and was lucky to find in my research, and that is the interviews that Professor Harold Hongju Koh, from Yale Law School had with Justice Blackmun after he had retired, which were recorded at the U.S. Supreme Court and the Federal Judicial Center from July 6, 1994-December 13, 1995 and available on the website of

---

15 Koh, "The Justice Harry A. Blackmun Oral History Project," 50.

16 Ibid., 192.

17 Ibid., 199.

the Manuscript Division of the Library of Congress, after Blackmun served his last term in October, 1993. Koh had clerked for Blackmun during his October 1981 term, and noted that Blackmun had heard 3,875 Supreme Court cases, and his nickname in law school was "Black Horse Harry," minutiae which are lost to most historians, but more importantly, the 514 pages of his interview provided an incredible insight into Blackmun's life, that I contend proves much of what I provided in this chapter.[18] On the first page of the interview, Blackmun confessed that he used to eat his lunch in his office and look outside to "see who's picketing us," because he was "often the target of good picketing."[19] He noted this on July 6, 1994, which was 21 years, 5 months, and 14 days since he read his verdict. When he was asked about what he thought about *Roe v. Wade* at that time, he said it was a correct decision and "had to be made if the country was to go down the road toward the complete emancipation of women. Period."[20] Everything I read made me understand Blackmun's motives in *Roe v. Wade* more and more, and I thank him for a book that reflects why I consider Blackmun one of the more important Justices to ever serve on the Supreme Court.

The idea that family discussions at home around the dinner table can affect a Justice's opinion was admitted to by Amy Coney Barrett in her recent book about *Roe v. Case*. She had seven children, and she admitted that they often had different opinions, "which don't always align with mine."[21] I can understand that, given her ultraconservative stance, and I am sure that Blackmun faced this same scrutiny. She admitted that dissent in deliberations was often helpful in coming to a correct decision, and she sometimes changed her vote by the arguments provided by colleagues, but I have pointed out that the supermajority of six Justices on the *Dobbs* Court was the reason the case was overturned, and I do not accept that it was based on views of Democracy, but rather those of Theocracy.[22] Her claim that Scalia, who was a Catholic conservative, and Ginsburg, who was a Jewish liberal, became close friends did not offer me any insight into

---

18   Koh, "The Justice Harry A. Blackmun Oral History Project," i-iii.

19   Ibid., 1.

20   Ibid., 25.

21   Barrett, Listening to the Law: Reflections on the Court and Constitution, 38.

22   Ibid., 39.

what is taking place on the current Supreme Court, and I continue to see a united force intent on ridding their focus of concern over the Separation of Church and State.[23] I will summarize my view of Amy Coney Barrett in the Conclusion to the book, but I found little of value in her supposed explanation of the *Roe v. Wade*, which was seldom even mentioned.

Blackmun was confirmed as a Supreme Court Justice on 5/12/1970, and this timing is very important in understanding why Nixon wanted to rush for a decision on abortion. In June 1970, one month later, the AMA's House of Delegates voted to permit licensed physicians in those states that allowed abortions to perform them as long as it was in a hospital, and two other doctors had been consulted. Nixon knew the AMA had a strong anti-abortion stance, and also that many states had begun to pass anti-abortion legislation with their support, so he wanted to try an abortion case as soon as possible to assure that the immoral procedures could be prevented from gaining in popularity, now that the procedures had gotten approvals to be performed.[24] If abortion was going to finally be adjudicated, Nixon wanted it to be done under his term as President, a desire I would have thought that Burger would have had as well, but we will see that this was not to be the case, as he elected Blackmun to write the opinion, rather than himself.

As happened in the personal lives of many of the participants in the *Roe v. Wade* case, Blackmun's middle daughter Sally, had become pregnant in 1966 while a sophomore at Skidmore College. She dropped out of college and got married, but had a miscarriage three weeks later, so the issue of abortion never came up.[25] Incredibly enough, we will see that the attorney for Roe also would actually have an abortion while in law school, so the case would wind up involving a number of the participants in a direct and personal way, which I find incredibly serendipitous.

Nixon would eventually be able to appoint four new Justices to become the new conservative Burger Supreme Court when the *Roe v. Wade* case was selected, although only two of his Justices, Burger and Blackmun, had been appointed when the case was eventually put on

---

23 Ibid., 40-41.
24 Greenhouse, <u>Becoming Justice Blackmun: Harry Blackmun's Supreme Court Journey</u>, 74.
25 Ibid., 74-75.

the docket. William O. Douglas was then the senior Supreme Court member helping Burger decide what cases to select, and he knew that Burger wanted to reduce the number of federal court cases brought by activist attorneys, and so he decided to take some of the cases, realizing that they would have to be presented to a seven-man Court because the new appointees, Lewis F. Powell and William Rehnquist, had not yet been sworn in.[26] Douglas was still known as a liberal Justice at that time, however, and Burger would not be able to rely on him to make selections that Nixon wanted, but we will see how Douglas nevertheless played an important role in the final outcome of the case.

How do I know what really caused this furor over abortion to happen? Is this just my best guess about what everyone thought, and why they did what they did? In a sense, the answer is yes, but my knowledge came about because of the enormous interest that both of these Supreme Court cases created across the country, and the resultant publication of more than 3,000 books investigating both trials, trying to understand how the outcomes could wind up the way they did. We have more insight into these two cases than any prior Supreme Court decisions in history, and you will be amazed in reading these next two chapters on how the story played out. In Blackmun, we have a man whose fame from how he decided *Roe v. Wade* became so widespread that many authors have peered into his past and provided me with an incredible array of material to allow me to rely on many facts that were unknown when the trial of *Roe v. Wade* took place. This interest only accelerated after the *Dobbs* trial was publicized, and the material uncovered provided an enormous amount of information that I could use to psychoanalyze both Blackmun and Alito. In the three-volume biography I wrote about Sigmund Freud, I realized how much insight I had gained from assisting my cancer patients through their difficult dealings with family and life during their prolonged treatments, and I was able to utilize the information that many investigative reporters uncovered about both of these cases to help understand how these Supreme Court Justices came to the conclusions they did.[27] In particular, the information that Blackmun

---

26 Ibid., 85-86.
27 Milner, The Three Lives of Sigmund Freud: Evidence of an Important Identity Crisis.

left in a diary that he began in his youth, beginning on December 30, 1919, just weeks past his eleventh birthday, and continuing throughout his twenty-four-year tenure on the Supreme Court, was very revealing, and, more importantly, told me how much he relied on his own instincts about what was right and wrong. This material was available to Linda Greenhouse, the American legal journalist who won a Pulitzer Prize for her coverage of the Supreme Court, and the information she provided from the diary was particularly helpful.[28] All of this material was essential for me to come to the conclusions I did, so let me save you the bother of doing your own research, and explain why I believe both Blackmun and Alito are responsible for the reason we are today in a constitutional crisis that must be resolved if our Democracy is going to continue the way it has in the foreseeable future.

Another fateful decision on the outcome of this case was that Nixon was soon able to have two new Justices on the Court, because around the same time *Roe v. Wade* came up, two other aging Justices who had been part of the Warren Court had become ill, and Nixon knew that he soon could appoint two more Justices to replace them, which meant that in just over his first two years as President, he was going to appoint *four* Justices to the United States Supreme Court. The only modern President who was able to accomplish that feat at a faster pace was Franklin D. Roosevelt, who nominated four Justices in under two years, and eight Justices altogether. He was famous for his liberal ideas during his time in office, and the "New Deal" directives which he was able to put through as President to take America out of the Great Depression, and lead the country through World War II. Nixon's choices would wind up not making a true "conservative" majority on the new Burger Court, however, but in his desire to be the President who found abortion illegal, Nixon pushed ahead and encouraged Burger to select a case to deal with abortion as soon as possible. Nixon was power hungry from the start of his presidency, and I believe his rush to press for a Supreme Court decision on abortion was a major reason he then degenerated into the actions that led to the Watergate scandal, as I will explain later in this chapter.

As I said, the push to prevent abortions nationwide had begun after

---

28 Greenhouse, Becoming Justice Blackmun: Harry Blackmun's Supreme Court Journey, 1-2.

the AMA made recommendations to ban abortions, and the first state to pass such legislation was Colorado in 1967, the year before Nixon's election. By 1970, 16 states had passed such legislation, and Nixon let Burger know that he wanted action on this issue sooner rather than later. Burger decided that he would first hear *United States v. Vuitch 402 U.S. 62 (1971)* on October 5, 1970, with oral arguments made on January 12, 1971, in order to help him decide which case to then hear about the constitutional right to have an abortion. This was only one year, eleven months, and twenty-three days from his inauguration as Chief Justice, and at the time, he and Blackmun were the only two appointees to the most liberal Supreme Court in United States history. The disaster to take place was clearly, in my opinion, due to Nixon's rush to become famous. If he had waited a little longer, I might not have needed to write this book because *Roe v. Wade* would not likely have been decided the way it was if it had come to the Court a few years later.

The *Vuitch* case did not involve the constitutionality of an abortion statute, but rather dealt with the requirement that a doctor had to determine whether the mother's life or health needed to be preserved by an abortion, and the United States District Court for the District of Columbia found that the statute in question was unconstitutionally vague because it was a criminal statute, and the word "health" in the statute was not properly defined. Blackmun was well aware that the case was a procedural issue, and not substantive about abortion, and he therefore did not do any research on the issue, for he would not be writing the decision.[29] This information is very important, for it shows how the discussion of the Justices in the case were never focused on the issue of abortion, but rather on legal procedural issues so there would be no way for discussions on the right for abortion to have been raised, and no substantive information provided that would help Burger plan for what to case to select to review. Dr. Milan M. Vuitch (1915-1993) was a Serbian-born gynecologist who performed thousands of abortions in his Washington, D.C. clinic, charging 100-200 dollars for what were determined to be illegal abortions, and he contested that the statute was vague and the abortions were legal because of his diagnosis.[30] This was not an actual issue of a mother's

---

29 Koh, "The Justice Harry A. Blackmun Oral History Project," 192.
30 Greenhouse, Becoming Justice Blackmun: Harry Blackmun's Supreme Court Journey, 75.

right to have an abortion, but Burger believed that the topic would allow him to posit a Republican-based view on abortion when the other Justices were eventually appointed, and so he decided to begin that task by reviewing the *Vuitch* appeal in order to better be able to choose which actual abortion case to put on the docket. As far as I know, Burger was never pressed by reporters to answer questions on why he may have asked for this particular case to be decided, but we will see that his neophyte status as a Supreme Court Justice was instrumental in his failing to properly prepare for the decision that Nixon desperately wanted. No benefit could possibly have been achieved from reviewing *Vuitch* before *Roe v. Wade*, but Burger's inexperience did not allow him to realize this fact at the time.

I obviously could not read every book written on the details of both of these trials, but I found little investigative reporting done on verifying how much Nixon pressed Burger to initiate this case, so it is obvious to me that the reason it took so long for the *Dobbs* Court to be put together was the care Republicans spent in forming a strong conservative majority before deciding that the time was right to overturn the verdict with *Dobbs*. Nixon's election was a disaster for the rising wave of Conservative Republicanism, and beginning with the election of Ronald Reagan twelve years later in 1980, a more careful and dedicated course was set up and followed with precision on the selection of District and Supreme Court Justices, and their foresight eventually showed the formation of a formidable and loyal *Dobbs* Supreme Court that is likely to allow modification of the way our Constitution is going to be interpreted for many years to come. At the time *Vuitch* was first heard, the Burger Supreme Court had five Republican-appointed Justices, with Potter Stewart, John Marshall Harlan II, and William J. Brennan Jr. appointed by Dwight D. Eisenhower, and Burger and Blackmun appointed by Richard Nixon, and although they would eventually have a 7-2 Republican appointed majority on the Burger Court, they would act more like the liberal Warren Court then what *Dobbs* would later become.

It should be remembered that Nixon had won the Presidency because his opponent would not be Lyndon Johnson, who had completed his one full-term presidency after finishing the shortened term of President John F. Kennedy after his assassination in 1963. Johnson had defeated Barry Goldwater for President in 1964, in a landslide victory that seemed to put an end to the conservative Republican hopefuls, and that left Nixon as the only notable Republican or Democrat to run for President. By the end of his term, however, Johnson had lost much public appeal because of his involvement with the unpopular Vietnam War, and also because he had health problems, which later caused him to die of a heart attack on January 22, 1973. His refusal to run for a second term allowed Nixon to defeat a make-shift Democratic slate, and when he was elected, he was anxious to make a name for himself as the top conservative Republican, ready to take over the liberal Democratic agenda. He had much state-wide support from legislatures across the country who were passing anti-abortion bills in expectation of his victory, and he had been Vice President under Eisenhower, and then lost the election to John F. Kennedy after a disastrous televised debate, and he was excited to now take center-stage as President, and resurrect his Republican leadership.

Attempts to deal with the issue of abortion by outlawing it on a national level in America had first begun when Dr. Mary Calderone (1904-1998), medical director of Planned Parenthood Federation of America, organized the first-ever national conference on abortion in the United States that ran from April 15-17, 1955 near Newburgh, New York.[31] This meeting eventually led to the anti-abortion reform laws I referred to beginning to be passed in Colorado on April 25, 1967 that allowed abortion only in cases of rape, incest, or when the mother's health was at risk,[32] followed by similar laws in California on June 15, 1967, and then New York on April 11, 1970.[33] Nixon saw that the time was ripe for his ascension, but his ability to read the tea leaves was as bad as his decision to make secret audio recordings of his conversations in the White House between 1971 and 1973, as I will discuss shortly, and in his haste, we will see how rapidly his rising star would vaporize into ignominy.

With successful anti-abortion laws showing up in many states, Nixon and Burger decided to bring the matter to the Supreme Court once they held a majority vote, and the fact that he acted this fast, before

---

31 Planned Parenthood was founded in 1916 by crusader Margaret Sanger (1879-1966), an American birth control activist. Barnes & Clinton, "Introduction," 13.

32 This became known as the PRIM justification for abortion, which included Prenatal diagnosis, Rape, Incest, and the Mother's life. Peters and Kamitsuka, "Introduction," 6.

33 "First Abortion Conference in the U.S.," 1.

the two new nominees were even selected, shows how important the issue of abortion was becoming in Nixon's mind. He was convinced that the Court would pay attention to the mood of the country, and the recommendations of his new Chief Justice, and he likely had few advisers in his new Cabinet who believed he was making a mistake. Both Burger and Blackmun were on the Supreme Court when the first case dealing with some aspect of abortion, *United States v. Vuitch, 402 U.S. 62 (1971)*, was argued before the U.S. Supreme Court on April 21, 1971, and decided on March 22, 1972, and I believe this case is important because even though the testimony during the trial did not deal with the issue in that manner, Burger was convinced that Blackmun would act like a conservative Justice. He was wrong to do this, since the case really had nothing to do with the constitutionality of abortion itself, but he had been friends with Blackmun since they were children, and Blackmun had even been his best-man at his wedding. The close friendship that Burger and Blackmun had before they were appointed to the Supreme Court one year apart would begin to dissolve shortly after *Roe v. Wade* was decided, as I will soon detail, and it is important that you understand how disorganized the Republican plan was under Nixon, so that you can realize how carefully those who followed once Reagan was elected President were to make sure they formed their conservative Supreme Court with Catholic Justices, in order to be sure they could pass a judgment that had life begin at conception.

The final decision in the *Vuitch* case held that the District of Columbia's abortion law banning the practice except when necessary was not unconstitutionally vague, and both Burger and Blackmun voted with the majority.[34] What this case did was to place the issue of abortion on a constitutional level, and allow the Supreme Court to see how the public would react to a decision on abortion, and then choose which case to resolve from all the lower court cases that were requesting an appeal from a District Court ruling to outlaw abortion altogether. The majority votes on *Vuitch* were from Hugo L. Black (1886-1971), who was appointed by Franklin Roosevelt in 1937, and who wrote the opinion, Warren E. Burger, William O. Douglas, Potter Stewart, and Byron White, while John Marshall Harlan II and Blackmun were in dissent on jurisdiction, but joined Black on the merits, and William Brennan and Thurgood Marshall were the only

---

34 United States v. Vuitch," 1.

ones to fully dissent, both liberal judges, although Brennan had been appointed by Eisenhower, as well.[35] Although Hugo Black and John Harlan II were nominated by Republican presidents, they were seen as moderate or independent in their philosophy, and they both would soon be replaced by Nixon with the appointments of Lewis F. Powell and William Rehnquist, so that the new Court under Burger would have a majority of so-called conservative Justices when *Roe v. Wade* was decided. I can see why Burger believed they could expect that the case would be able to judge abortion as unconstitutional, given the fact that only two dissents were rendered in *Vuitch*, but Nixon would be shocked to find that three of his appointees would vote with the majority in *Roe v. Wade*, as I will soon explain. The day after the *Vuitch* decision was published, the Justices met and voted to hear two more abortion cases, *Roe v. Wade* and *Doe v. Bolton,* which would be the rulings that created the dilemma we are in today.[36] The fact that Burger accepted the case before the two new Justices were actually appointed meant that he had already decided that Blackmun would write the opinion, and it would be an error that he would later regret for the rest of his life.

Unfortunately, I was not able to determine exactly whether Burger made this decision alone, or in consultation with Nixon, but the decision to hear a case for Supreme Court review generally followed a "Rule of Four," where four Justices must vote in favor of reviewing a case for it to be chosen to be put on the docket. The Chief Justice carried much weight in the process, but the choice of picking cases to be reviewed was a difficult, and time-consuming task, as about 5,000 new requests were received each year, and the Chief Justice had to pick 150 to decide with full argument and signed opinions.[37] In *Roe v. Wade*, the four Justices who voted to review the case were Chief Justice Burger, Justice William Douglas, who was the Senior Justice, Justice William Brenner, and Justice Potter Stewart. What is amazing to me is that despite the fact that all three of the other Justices were appointed by Eisenhower, a Republican President, they were not conservative on the Warren Court, and Burger should have known this,

---

35 Ibid., 1-2.

36 Greenhouse, <u>Becoming Justice Blackmun: Harry Blackmun's Supreme Court Journey</u>, 78.

37 Graetz and Greenhouse, <u>The Burger Court and the Rise of the Judicial Right</u>, 9.

and waited until his next two colleagues were appointed, whether he was pushed by Nixon or not. He had only been on the bench for two years when he picked *Roe v. Wade*, so he did have some experience with the process, but Blackmun had been there for only one term, and so he really did not have much experience with cases to assist Burger in the process. Douglas was known as a very liberal Justice, on the Warren Court, as was Breman, while Stewart was often a swing vote, so Burger should have known that he was not getting good advice for making this selection, but he did it anyway.

The fact that Burger actually voted for the case to be heard makes it possible that he secretly did want the opinion that was rendered by Blackmun, and did not want his own name on it as the author. I set this consideration aside quickly, however, because even though I'm not sure why Burger put the case in the docket this early, his reaction to the result of the case clearly showed he was upset with the verdict, and never maintained a liberal posture during the rest of his term. I'm afraid that I can only explain his choice by assuming that he believed Nixon wanted a case as soon as possible, and that he truly believed the inexperience of the attorneys bringing the case was in his favor. We are likely never to know the real answer to this query, but based on the fact that over the years that followed, the friendship between them began to dissipate, I accept that Burger felt betrayed by his friend for his eventual decision, and silently kept his thoughts to himself, and never let us know why he did not write the opinion himself. It is intriguing that Chief Justice John G. Roberts would do the same thing with letting Samuel Alito Jr. write the opinion in the *Dobbs* case, as I will discuss in the next chapter, but in that case, Roberts disagreed with overruling *Roe v. Wade*, but did not label it as a dissent. In both cases, the Chief Justice did not take the most critical case they chose to review, and write the verdict, and it appears that neither one was truly happy with the result.

The most critical question that remains unanswered in *Roe v. Wade* is why Burger decided not to write the opinion himself, and I believe the answer is because he knew Blackmun's medical knowledge was superior to his own, and he did not believe he had the time to research it properly. Unlike Blackmun, Burger seldom dealt with the medical profession directly throughout his career, and he was likely influenced by the actions of the American Medical Association, which I have described were anti-abortion. He knew this case was vitally important to Nixon, and while I believe he should have written the opinion himself, using Blackmun's knowledge as a back-up, I think he simply became overwhelmed by the amount of work he suddenly was burdened with as being the Chief Justice, and the responsibilities were more than he realized. He did not believe he could spend the time researching the issue, so he gave it to someone he trusted, and who he thought would vote the way he would, which was his close friend Blackmun. He never had any identity with the other Justices before the next two were nominated by Nixon, and so it is understandable why he made the mistakes he did. I am sure he believed he knew how Blackmun would vote, but he would prove to be wrong, and in a case this important, it would not be long before two more Justices would be appointed, so there was no need to rush picking which Justice should write the opinion, or which case to take. He could wait until the other two Justices were on the bench before putting any case on the docket, and discuss the issue with all three appointees about their views, and what case should be chosen. That was not what happened, however, and his action makes me believe that Nixon pushed him to do this, but I have no evidence in the record to know whether that was the actual reason. Burger needed to be sure a conservative Justice would write the opinion, because if he did not believe he would be in the majority, he would have to give the case to William O. Douglas, who was known as a strong liberal on matters of civil liberties, environmental protection, and individual freedoms, which was not acceptable to Nixon.[38] He gave the case to Blackmun because he believed he was a conservative Justice at heart, but he was wrong, and all he could do was swear *c'est la vie*, and move on, not a good option to be left with for a newly appointed Chief Justice.

To make his decision even more confusing to understand, the case decision on *Vuitch* was publicly read on April 21, 1971, which was two days *after* the *Roe v. Wade* case was put on the Supreme Court docket by Burger on April 19, 1971. That means Burger decided to hear the appeal in both abortion cases, already knowing that he was not going to write the opinion, and that by giving Blackmun that honor, he was going to have to agree with his decision. He did not know who the future Justices were to be, but he was aware that Nixon wanted to adjudicate the constitutionality of abortion rights from the time he was

---

38 Microsoft CoPilot (February 10, 2025). Supreme Court's process.

first interviewed for the job of Chief Justice. Both he and Blackmun voted in the majority decision of *Vuitch* that the legislation was *not* unconstitutionally vague, but he really had no idea what Blackmun's views on abortion were, since that issue was never discussed during the case.[39] I am sure that Burger's stance at this time was to not approve *Roe v. Wade*, and Blackmun was undecided about what to do, but Blackmun planned to extensively research the issue before making his decision, after he was told by Burger that he would write the opinion. As it turns out, Blackmun was surprised he would be writing the opinion as well, for when he was interviewed after he retired, he said that: "I didn't have any inkling that I would catch the case."[40] I cannot necessarily believe that recollection, but the entire sequence is hard to believe, and as I have already said, and few people in America understand how incredibly unique these two abortion decisions are, and why the American public needs to know the facts of why we are in a constitutional crisis today. I am under stress as well, for I believe we must pass this amendment I propose, and put ourselves back into the path of a true Democracy or the very foundation our country is built on is in danger of being sabotaged, so please do your best, if you agree with me, and help get the vote out.

Blackmun did not say much in his concurring opinion in *Vuitch*, simply stating that because the majority opinion was divided on the merits of the case, he agreed that the Court did have jurisdiction of the appeal.[41] I am not privy to what may have been said in the discussions of the Justices before the opinion was delivered, but the case didn't really deal with the legality of abortion, and I don't think Burger realized how much research Blackmun planned to do at the Mayo Clinic medical library before reaching his decision on *Roe v. Wade*. He knew that he would not have time himself for this task, but Blackmun was used to doing medical research at the library during the time he worked for the Mayo Clinic, and the staff at the library also was aware of his intense interest in medical issues. He probably had more knowledge about medicine than any other prior Supreme Court Justice, and when Blackmun asked the staff at the Mayo Clinic library for assistance, they set aside a place for him to work, and

---

39 "United States v. Vuitch," 1.
40 Koh, "The Justice Harry A. Blackmun Oral History Project," 12.
41 "United States v. Vuitch," 96.

compiled a stack of books and articles on the history and practice of abortion, which I believe was material generally favorable to the future acceptance of safe abortion. Although Blackmun later said that many commentators claimed he spent the whole summer there, he actually spent about ten days at the library, which I can attest is a lot of time to spend on the case, given the assistance he had with the library staff.[42] The fact that he did not have to search for the material like I did made the time he spent reading the material much more productive, and I admire his devoting this much time to be sure he understood the issues thoroughly before rendering his verdict.

That Blackmun paid attention to what he read is evident in his careful notes that he collected from his research, one of which was from an article in the *American Journal of Public Health* for March 1971, which said how important the Supreme Court case was going to be, and that: "Safe, legal abortion is now recognized as a fundamental right of women, a protection of maternal health and family welfare, and an assurance that every child is a loved and wanted child."[43] There is no question, in my opinion, that Blackmun's research in the Mayo Clinic library is what led to his remarkable opinion to find a constitutional for the right to abortion, and that Burger would not have done that amount of work, or come to that conclusion. In those same notes was an article of a Gallup poll in June 1972 finding that "two out of three Americans think abortion should be a matter for decision solely between a woman and her physician," including a majority of Roman Catholics.[44] It is clear to me that Blackmun decided the case directly from his research at the library, and I do not believe he discussed any of this with Burger before the final vote was taken when the Justices met at the end of the reargument.

Most commentators have agreed that Burger did not dissent in the case because there was still a majority without his vote, and it would anger Douglas if he didn't vote in the majority, because the standard practice in the Supreme Court was that if he didn't vote in the majority, he should have offered the opinion to Douglas to write, which he did

---

42 Koh, "The Justice Harry A. Blackmun Oral History Project," 197. He said the research fortified his views, particularly about the Hippocratic Oath. Ibid., 197-198.

43 Greenhouse, <u>Becoming Justice Blackmun: Harry Blackmun's Supreme Court Journey</u>, 90-91.

44 Ibid., 91.

not do. I agree with that view, and it is supported by the fact that Burger later dissented in *Thornburgh v. American College of Obstetricians and Gynecologists 476 U.S. 747 (1986)*, to show his conservative opinion, and Blackmun found his defection difficult to understand at that time.[45] This tells me that Blackmun likely did not initially realize how upset Burger was with his opinion, but it showed even more how distant the two became as the years passed. Blackmun wrote the opinion for the shrinking majority in *Thornburgh*, now down to a 5-4 majority, and noted in his decision that "few decisions are more personal and intimate, more properly private, or more basic to individual dignity and autonomy, than a woman's decision – with the guidance of her physician and with the limits specified in *Roe* – whether to end her pregnancy."[46] By now, it was clear that their friendship had begun to vanish, and over the next few years they seldom met except during actual deliberations of Supreme Court cases.

I believe this sequence clearly shows that Burger picked Blackmun to write the opinion on the case because he was not able to properly research the subject, and he did not think Blackmun was going to rule the way he did. They had been friends since childhood, even meeting over the summers when Burger went to the University of Minnesota and Blackmun went to Harvard, and they were both appointed by Nixon. In addition, before accepting the position on the Supreme Court they even considered working together as lawyers in a private practice.[47] I don't think Burger believed the verdict would have been to approve abortion, but the real question is then why did Burger vote to accept the case, when he did? He could have waited until the other two Justices were appointed, and then have a joint discussion on who should write the decision. This tells me that it is likely that Nixon either pressed Burger to act more quickly, or Burger at least thought that Nixon wanted him to act quickly. That is not the way I thought the Supreme Court always acted, but this entire case is unusual, or I at least hope it is, and I don't believe we are ever likely to know the true answer. What I do know is that all Pro-Choice supporters can thank their lucky stars that Burger acted the way he did, and that his decision

---

45 Ibid., 183.

46 Ibid., 185.

47 Ibid., 8. They often corresponded while in college as well. Ibid., 9. He was Burger's best man at his wedding, and remained friends after both were married. Ibid., 15, 17.

affected him greatly, for a few days after he rendered his decision on *Bowers v. Hardwick 478 U.S. 186 (1986)* on June 17, 1986, he resigned his position as Chief Justice to lead a commission on the Bicentennial of the Constitution, which was to be celebrated on his birthday.[48] I believe this decision shows that he felt responsible for his actions in *Roe v. Wade*, and that he needed a cleansing of his inner turmoil over how his tenure on the Supreme Court did not end as he hoped it would have when he first began. He will go down in history as being the Chief Justice in the *Roe v. Wade* case, and will either be hated or revered for that position, but few will realize how devastated he was by being remembered for that fact. Being the Chief Justice of the United States Supreme Court is more gratifying to a graduate of law school than being the President of the United States, and I feel sorry for how he must have felt as a lifelong conservative Republican for being forever known as the man who's Supreme Court approved the constitutional right of a woman to have an abortion.

I now want to discuss how the case started out because to fully appreciate how this issue became so divisive to the country as it did, you must understand how both sides in this dispute fostered the battle over abortion without fully appreciating the reason for their dispute. *Roe v. Wade* did not start out looking like a landmark case that would stun the world by its outcome, for it had begun as a class action lawsuit at the District Court level, "on behalf of herself and all other women similarly situated," in March 1970, when Norma Leah Nelson McCorvey (1947-2017), who took on the pseudonym of Jane Roe, in a case that was initially listed as *Roe et al. v. Wade, District Attorney of Dallas County 410 U.S. 113 (1973)*, but the citation shifted to *Roe v. Wade* after the arguments began at the Supreme Court.[49] McCorvey had been working for a carnival that was traveling through the southern region of America in August 1969, while living in Dallas, Texas, when she was raped outside Augusta, Georgia, and became pregnant.[50] This was her third pregnancy, and she knew that she did

---

48 Toobin, The Nine: Inside the Secret World of the Supreme Court, 21, 27. The eventual celebration took place on September 17, 1987, which happened to be his eightieth birthday. Graetz and Greenhouse, The Burger Court and the Rise of the Judicial Right, 1.

49 Microsoft CoPilot (2/18/2025). Personal communication.

50 Faux, Roe v. Wade: The Untold Story of the Landmark Supreme Court Decision That Made Abortion Legal, 7-8.

not want the child, as she did not even know the name of the father, and had no means of support, but had been denied an abortion under Texas state law. In addition, she had given up her two prior children by adoption, and she was anxious to get an abortion, because she was already 10-weeks pregnant.

Her lawyers filed the lawsuit against Henry Wade (1914-2001), the district attorney who defended the constitutional legality of the law, although the lawyer in the courtroom at the District Court was actually Jay Floyd, the Assistant Attorney General, who would also be the lawyer in the first argument at the Supreme Court, and then was replaced by Robert C. Flowers, Floyd's supervisor, in the reargument, because his initial performance was criticized.[51] It is interesting that Weddington handled her case well at the District Court level, but when the Justices there asked her why she sued Wade, when if she won, other Texas District Court attorneys could still sue her, she admitted that "we goofed," and the case went on.[52] Weddington was probably just being honest because that was the first time she had ever appeared in a courtroom, but she was a quick learner, and I will soon show how good she especially was in her second courtroom appearance at the Supreme Court level.

This is the most incredible fact in the case, and I asked Microsoft CoPilot if any other attorney had ever argued their first courtroom case at the Supreme Court level, and their answer was no.[53] I could not find any such case in my own research as well, so it is likely true, but I find it incredible that such a situation could arise, given the number of cases that over the years tried to reach the Supreme Court for a decision on this matter. Abortion was a hotly debated national issue for years, and there were many famous lawyers trying to reach the Supreme Court to make a name for themselves, whether they won or lost. How could the case chosen be one that was handled by representatives who had never even appeared in a courtroom as an attorney before? The District Attorney of Texas, Henry Wade, was well-known, and had a fierce reputation, in time seeking thirty death sentences, and securing all but one, and Texas had the most abusive

---

51 Microsoft CoPilot (3/23/2025). Personal communication.

52 Bridge, Pushback: The Political Fallout of Unpopular Supreme Court Decisions, 146.

53 Microsoft CoPilot (6/28/2025). Personal Communication.

laws in the entire country, so I could understand why the plaintiff lawyers thought their case would be the most appropriate for the Supreme Court to want to approve abortion, but this was a Republican president who clearly was anti-abortion, so what gives?

Jay Floyd did not start out arguing the case well, opening with: "It's an old joke, but when a man argues against two beautiful ladies like this, they are going to have the last word."[54] This case was unusual because he was the only male lawyer in the courtroom, with the plaintiff attorneys in both cases female, as well as the Georgia State Attorney. Wade did not suffer any job insecurity after being named the defendant in this case, eventually prosecuting Jack Ruby (1911-1967) for the murder of Lee Harvey Oswald (1939-1963), President John F. Kennedy's assassin, and retiring peacefully in 1987.[55] He never appeared in either the District or Supreme Court trials, and he remained loyal to the Republican position on abortion for the rest of his life. Floyd, on the other hand was replaced in the reargument because of his poor performance, but it was too little, too late, as I will soon explain. His replacement was male, so the same sex differential took place in the reargument, as did the result of the verdict, so the entire drama was a win for Women's Lib.

I believe that this entire case turned out to be an anomaly because of the inept way Burger chose this unusual way to pick the cases the way he did. The inexperience of the *Roe v. Wade* attorneys made him believe that the case would be easier for Blackmun to handle, and the Georgia case was not handled by a well-known attorney, even though she was associated with the American Civil Liberties Union (ACLU), a nonprofit civil rights organization founded in 1920. He couldn't get on the job advice from Justice Warren because of the animosity that was set up by Nixon's maneuvering against Warren, and he had no prior experience on the Supreme Court, either as a lawyer or a Justice. He also didn't really know any of the other Justices from the Warren Court, and it was common knowledge that Nixon picked him to get rid of Warren, so he was pretty much on his own. Even once Blackmun arrived, they had been friends for a

---

54 "Transcript of First Oral Argument in Roe v. Wade, 410 U.S. 113 (1973)," 15.

55 Faux, Roe v. Wade: The Untold Story of the Landmark Supreme Court Decision That Made Abortion Legal, 86.

long time, but Blackmun had relied on him for knowledge about the Supreme Court, and he was overwhelmed with a a work load he had totally unexpected, so Blackmun could not do much else than write the opinion. His frustration is evident in the fact that in the 1980s he warned Congress that something had to be done to reduce the Court's caseload, which was beyond all expectations, and they responded by making the Court's jurisdiction "almost entirely discretionary."[56]

As for the case itself, McCorvey had first tried to find a local Dallas attorney, Henry McCluskey (1943-1973), but he was not taking any abortion cases, and referred her to two women attorneys who he knew were looking for a case to contest the state abortion laws, Linda Coffee and Sarah Ragle Weddington.[57] The two newly-graduated lawyers had gone to the University of Texas Law School together, with Weddington graduating in June, 1967, and Coffee in February, 1968. Even in law school, Weddington became interested in abortion cases, and studied the law in Texas, deciding early on that she wanted to file a lawsuit challenging the Texas abortion law. But she had no experience except for her training in law school, and she eventually thought of asking her former classmate who had returned to her hometown in Dallas, and clerked for Federal District Judge Sara T. Hughes, to join her, as she realized that at first she would have to maintain her present job.[58] After they both graduated, they both had trouble getting jobs at prestigious law firms, and eventually they decided to open a practice together, specializing in feminist concerns.[59] At the time they did, Weddington was still working with other law school students who were interested in abortion at *The Rag*, an Austin underground newspaper which was a job she would have to forego

---

56 Barrett, Listening to the Law: Reflections on the Court and Constitution, 94.

57 When Norma McCorvey gave birth, she used McCluskey to handle the adoption of her daughter. Weddington, A Question of Choice, 68.

58 Ibid., 46, 48-49.

59 They were two of only five women in the class, and Sarah Ragle was not yet married to Rod Weddington, another law student. Prager, The Family Roe: An American Story, 79. Ragle had gotten pregnant before the marriage and had an abortion in a clinic at the border town of Piedras Negras, which was one reason she wanted to specialize in the field of abortion. Ibid., 80.

when McCorvey's case was filed.[60] They particularly were looking for a case on abortion in Texas, because the Texas abortion statute was enacted in 1854, and was written in an "old-style" law format, compared to the "new-style" reform laws that were written in the 1960s. The old-style laws only allowed abortion when the mother's life was in danger, and did not allow cases which resulted from incest or rape, as took place with McCorvey.[61] Texas seemed to be the perfect state to test the anti-abortion laws, and her interests would prove true in time.

When McCorvey finally agreed to let them handle her case, they apparently did not tell her they had never tried any case in a courtroom before, but they were undaunted, and determined to proceed by themselves, and McCorvey was happy with the arrangement because she found someone who would take her case *pro bono*, since she couldn't afford to pay for their services. Think of it – the most famous case in the history of abortion in the United States, and the lawyers in charge had to work for free because that was the only way their client would let them represent her. They changed McCorvey's name to Jane Roe, because they were told this was common in abortion cases so that the plaintiff's name was anonymous, and on March 3, 1970, filed their pleadings in the federal courthouse, and their case was accepted. When it later was reviewed by the Supreme Court, it was combined with a separate suit from Georgia, *Doe v. Bolton,* referring to Arthur K. Bolton (1922-1997), the Attorney General of Georgia, a case that had been filed by Margie Pitts Hames (1933-1994), an Atlanta based ACLU attorney.[62] The original name of the plaintiff in *Doe v. Bolton* was changed to Mary Doe from Sandra Cano (1948-2014), whose maiden name was Sandra Benning before she married Carlos Cano, a convicted child molester. Cano would later say she was Pro-Life, and her attorney lied to her in order to have a plaintiff case.[63] Some articles about the *Roe v. Wade* case have mistaken *Doe v. Bolton* as being filed by Coffee and Weddington along with their *Roe* case, but that was because they had filed an additional case with *Roe v. Wade* at the District Court that involved John and Mary Doe as

---

60 Ibid., 74.

61 Faux, <u>Roe v. Wade: The Untold Story of the Landmark Supreme Court Decision That Made Abortion Legal</u>, Ibid., 67.

62 "Doe v. Bolton," 1.

63 Ibid., 1-2.

plaintiffs, but that case was dismissed at the federal court level, and was named *Does v. Wade*, and involved a childless married couple, but the case lacked standing to sue.[64]

The irony of the outcome of this case is that it made abortion a legal right for every woman in America, but it took so long before it was decided, that McCorvey had already given birth to a daughter, which she put up for adoption after her birth on June 2, 1970. Because she had no further need for an abortion when the case finally came up for trial, the state tried to argue to the District Court that her case was moot, but the District Court allowed the case to proceed, stating that pregnancy is a condition that is "capable of repetition, yet evading review.[65] As I said, McCorvey would wind up having three pregnancies during her life, with all three births of girls given up for adoption. The last child born from the *Roe v. Wade* pregnancy would be adopted by Ruth Schmidt, and named Shelley Lynn.[66] To complete the theatrical nature of how history will remember this case, McCorvey eventually became an avowed anti-abortionist, and shared these sentiments in a documentary called "AKA Jane Roe," where she revealed that she felt used by both sides of the abortion debate, and was convinced by the religious right that abortion was wrong.[67] This entire sequence, including the case being overturned by *Dobbs*, will likely one day wind up in movie theaters across the world, but I only hope that the last scene will be a triumphant passage of the amendment I propose, so that we can have a true Hollywood ending, and I can ride off into the sunset, or like Mel Brooks' *Blazing Saddles*, be driven in a limousine off the set. It would be a fitting ending to a case that had incredibly unique features, but was a truly landmark Supreme Court case that can hopefully end up providing the impetus for the passage of an amendment that is vitally important to the future of our country.

It was at this early stage of my research that I realized that destiny had to have played a role in this trial, for I found it absolutely incredible that these two lawyers could file a case attacking the anti-abortion laws from Texas, and then reach the Supreme Court where they tried the case by themselves, having never even been in a courtroom before this

---

64 Weddington, <u>A Question of Choice</u>, 62, 70.
65 Microsoft CoPilot (4/18/2025). Personal communication.
66 Prager, <u>The Family Roe: An American Story</u>, 125.
67 Stewart, "Fx's Jane Roe Deathbed Confession Reveals the Abortion Lie at the Heart of the Religious Right," 1.

case was begun. Not only were they totally inexperienced in the field of abortion, but, as I said, this was an era when abortion had become a key issue in the United States, backed by well-funded organizations like the National Organization of Women (NOW), and Planned Parenthood, allied with an army of experienced attorneys. Why then did Burger pick this case to review when there were cases pending in Colorado, Illinois, Indiana, Kentucky, Michigan, Minnesota, New Jersey, North Carolina, Oregon, and Vermont, all wanting to be appealed to the Supreme Court?[68] Also, why did Burger decide to take this case from Texas as the first test case on the constitutionality of abortion, when Texas had the most egregious law in the entire United States, and the Supreme Court would likely not want that law to be found to be legitimate? My only answer is that Burger must have decided that Blackmun would know that their new Supreme Court had to act conservative, and he was well-versed in medical issues, so likely was against abortion like most of the AMA, even though he had no reason to make such a foolish judgment. Burger must have believed that the inexperienced lawyers would be overwhelmed by having to present their case in such a lofty setting, with all of the media attention and publicity, despite the fact that it was an important case for both him and Nixon, and he decided that he would let Blackmun write the opinion, and, in his mind, this would make it easier for him to not be misled by an experienced lawyer who had often handled Supreme Court cases before. I'm sorry, I know this sounds ridiculous, but it is exactly what happened, and I had nothing to do with it, don't shoot the messenger.

As it turned our, however, having an inexperienced attorney was an advantage, and not a handicap, for instead of a protracted trial in a courtroom with a jury that could last for weeks, the presentation to the Supreme Court was for only 30-60 minutes on one day, with submission of a brief that was 50-100 pages in length. The brief from the party who lost in the federal court was known as "the petitioner," and was bound in blue colors, and the party who won, which was Roe, was "the respondent," and was bound in red colors, while the solicitor general, if one was present, represented the United States, and added a brief called "the tenth justice," in gray colors.[69] *Roe v. Wade* had a

---

68 Weddington, <u>A Question of Choice</u>, 72.
69 Barrett, <u>Listening to the Law: Reflections on the Court and Constitution</u>, 54.

solicitor general Erwin Griswold (1904-1994) file a brief without an opinion attached, and in *Dobbs,* Elizabeth Prelogar filed an amicus curiae brief forcefully recommending that *Roe v. Wade* be upheld.[70] There was no appearance before a jury, and their inexperience was actually a benefit at the Supreme Court level, with Blackmun writing the opinion on the case, instead of Burger handling it by himself. Burger may have also picked the Texas case because the powers-to-be there were also confident they would be victorious with the Warren Court gone, not realizing that the Court only had one Catholic who would not be partial to their argument that life began at conception.

I listened intently to the entire oral transcript of the first argument to the Supreme Court on my computer, and it was clear to me that Weddington was nervous at the start of her presentation, just as Burger thought she would be. But as the case went on, her performance was superb, and as she gained confidence from the ineptitude of the Texas assistant Attorney General's presentation, she began to believe she really could win the case. Because she was a neophyte lawyer, Weddington discussed in the book she later wrote about the case, she had problems in filing the brief in time, and if she had not been working at the Institute in New York with Roy Lucas (1941-2003), I do not believe that she ever could have completed the brief in the time allotted.[71] Yes, she was fortunate enough to have an experienced attorney helping her prepare for her appearance at the Supreme Court for free, although when the case finally came up, he tried to be the one to actually present the argument. Yes, there would not be a jury to appear before, and the publicity they would get would make them famous, as the ending indeed revealed, but the courtroom was not a public spectacle, and the proceedings were short, and quickly concluded. But still, this was the first major trial on abortion in America, and their performance shows how sometimes a "Miracle on Ice," event can happen on land, like when the American amateur hockey team defeated the Russians in the hockey medial round of the Olympics on ice on February 22, 1980, and then went on to beat Finland in the

---

70 Microsoft CoPilot (9/10/2025). Personal Communication. Any person may submit an amicus brief, including the federal and state governments, and Amy Barrett said that her law clerks read all the briefs, but she read only select amicus briefs. Barrett, Listening to the Law: Reflections on the Court and Constitution, 54-55.

71 Weddington, A Question of Choice, 89-91.

finals two days later. I don't know about you, but I found this trial to be a "Miracle of Justice," forcing me to carefully analyze the cases to see why it turned out as it did.

Weddington surmised in her book that the Court accepted the two cases because each involved a different type of statute with Texas having a "restrictive" law, and Georgia a "liberalized" law, and I appreciate her view of what happened. I truly believe, however, that Burger saw the *Roe* lawyers as an "easy catch," with the Georgia case seen as a throw-in addition, and his inexperience as a Supreme Court Justice turned out to be the problem, and not her inexperience in ever being in a courtroom before.[72] I thought I was an educated man about the law when I began to write this book, but the details of all the cases I researched astounded me about how unprofessional the entire sequence truly was. I still believe in the value of our Constitution, but I am terrified about our future from the way I found our past has been handled on this issue, and in the next chapter, I will amplify this to show why we are in a true constitutional crisis today, and our future stature as the Beacon of Democracy is under assault.

When the Supreme Court agreed to hear their case, Weddington and Coffee were stunned, for the Court had chosen not to review decisions involving anti-abortion laws eight times before finally deciding to hear *United States v. Vuitch* on January 12, 1971, which I discussed above. Not only that, but the Supreme Court agreed to hear this particular case as a direct appeal from the District Court, rather than have it first be directed to the Fifth Circuit Court, a possibility that Linda Coffee had already prepared for, despite her neophyte status.[73] When it came time to decide who should present the case to the Supreme Court, for only one attorney could present the argument at that level, Coffee knew that despite the fact that she was the one who started the case in the District Court, her outward appearance was not very professional, and Weddington "was blond, [and] blue-eyed," and "enjoyed the limelight as much as Coffee disliked it," so Coffee agreed to let Weddington argue the case.[74] Even when the wire service later reported that Weddington was the one who submitted the class action suit that led

---

72 Ibid., 81.

73 Ibid., 69. This was only possible if the state authorities were going to continue their prosecution of the case, which Henry Wade announced he would. Ibid. 69-70.

74 Prager, The Family Roe: An American Story, 89-90.

to the *Roe v. Wade* ruling, neither she nor Coffee ever corrected the record, with Coffee going unrecognized throughout much of the trial, and claiming that "I don't particularly care."[75] I'm not sure how true that statement is, but from my research I can say that both of their names were associated with the case in a majority of the publications from that time forward, and Weddington later wrote a book about her experience, even though Coffee did not. I don't care how much money either of these women eventually made from this trial, their efforts were truly one of the greatest courtroom miracles of all time, and I think you will find the details of their argument to be convincing enough for the majority of Americans to vote "yes" for the amendment, even if many of them are Pro-Life advocates. Weddington told how her mother asked if she could bring a camera into the courtroom to film her first argument, as everyone was unexpectedly thrilled that these two young women were going to appear in the first abortion case the Supreme Court would hear, but that was not allowed, and the only tape I could find was an audio recording on the internet.[76]

What is especially incredible about the book Weddington wrote about herself, *A Question of Choice*, is that she tells how in her third year of law school, and dating her future husband-to-be, she became pregnant and had to go and get an abortion in Piedras Negras, Mexico, across from Eagle Pass, Texas, so that she could finish her schooling, and get her degree.[77] The book was published when she was famous from the trial, in 1992, twenty-one years after the *Roe v. Wade* decision was made, and it tells why she had decided to make law her career, and probably why she was so good at this, her first case in a courtroom. As I already mentioned, she was smart enough to mention "unwanted" pregnancies that were at issue in the trial, and that was something I believe impressed the entire Court, as I hope it will 3/4 of the American legislatures, for it stresses the main reason why so many women want, and need, an abortion before the fetus is viable.[78] The abortion rights

75 Ibid., 115.
76 Weddington, <u>A Question of Choice</u>, 106. Sarah and her husband stayed in Washington with friends that once lived in Texas, which also "blew my mind," but then moved to the Capitol Hill Hotel to be close to the Courthouse. Ibid., 106-107.
77 Ibid., 13-14.
78 Her answer in the book, however, was because women in Texas were an independent breed, for it is where "men are men, and women are elected officials." Ibid., 17.

activist and lawyer Roy Lucas provided legal direction during the trial, so Weddington and Coffee were not totally alone in preparing their appearance. After he heard of their success at the federal court level, he contacted Weddington and offered his help on the appeal, and Weddington accepted his offer as "a godsend."[79] A feminist heiress named Ruth McClean Bowman Bowers (1920-2013), a longtime supporter of Planned Parenthood in San Antonio, and the industrialist Thomas Cabot, of the chemical company Cabot Corporation, also footed many of the bills, so the two new lawyers were not at a loss for funds, or advice, and so one of the most famous trials in the history of America at the Supreme Court level began with a well-funded, but totally inexperienced duet of trial lawyers, and a Supreme Court that all thought was going to be a conservative tribunal, but instead became a final gavel in the rulings of the Warren Court.[80]

At the time *Roe v. Wade* was accepted for review by the Supreme Court, Weddington was still working at *The Rag*, and had moved with her husband to Fort Worth where he had found a new job. She realized she could no longer continue on that path if she was to appear before the Supreme Court, and so they moved back to Austin, and she began to work full time on the *Roe v. Wade* appeal with Coffee.[81] In order to prepare for the trial properly, Weddington then moved to New York, in Greenwich village, to utilize Lucas' office where he was president of the James Madison Constitutional Law Institute, and as they prepared for the trial, her commitment was intense.[82] She communicated with Linda Coffee by telephone every day because Linda had to remain at her paying job in Dallas, and while I know this sounds crazy, and even made-up, the facts I am presenting are all true, and why I believe that they may have had some divine assistance to reach the end it did.[83] This entire episode almost ended in disaster, for as it came time for the Supreme Court hearing to begin, Lucas had said he should present the case because he was more experienced, but Weddington was not

---

79 Lucas was the one to write most of the appeal work for the Supreme Court because Coffee was busy with her bankruptcy work at her firm, and Weddington and her husband were moving to Fort Worth. Ibid., 72.

80 Prager, The Family Roe: An American Story, 90.

81 Weddington, A Question of Choice, 83-84.

82 Ibid., 72, 86.

83 Ibid., 89.

accepting of his offer.[84] She had become admitted to the Supreme Court Bar, and all of her associates agreed that it would be better for a woman to present the case than a man.[85] When the Court asked who was to present the case, Lucas had responded that it would be him, but the client has the final answer on the choice of attorney, and Linda wrote back that it would be Sarah, despite Lucas' request that he be the one to appear, and although he was upset by her demands, the outcome showed that her decision was correct.[86]

As the first argument to the Supreme Court began, Weddington was twenty-six years old, standing in front of the Supreme Court of the United States, in the first real abortion case of consequence to appear in that tribunal. I'm not sure how she was able to perform as well as she did, although she said that she relied on the faith that the plaintiff Norma had in her, and the grit it took to get through law school in Texas as a woman, but that was all written by the woman she eventually became, and not the one who was appearing at the trial. She talked about her excitement on that day in her book, noting that there was "a sense of the historic proportions of the moment," and that Betty Friedan (1921-2006), the first President of the National Organization of Women (NOW) movement, even showed up saying that her "'historical Geiger counter' was clicking madly," as I believe her own was as well.[87] It is interesting that she noticed that in the lawyers lounge the only restroom facilities were marked "Men," and this hadn't changed when she returned to visit the Court again on April 22, 1992, an indication that her awareness of discrimination of women was acute, which may be one reason she performed so well.[88] She presented her case on *Roe v. Wade* first, and *Doe v. Bolton* was second, both in the morning session, so she was able to witness how both cases were argued, which may have helped her prepare when both of her cases had to be reargued.[89] The two cases took all morning to complete, and was unique for there were four oralists, with three women as the Georgia statue was argued by Dorothy Beasley (1937-2024, an assistant attorney general who became the first woman on the

84 Ibid., 100.
85 Ibid., 101.
86 Ibid., 102.
87 Ibid., 109.
88 Ibid., 111.
89 Ibid., 112-113.

Georgia Court of Appeals.[90]

Blackmun remembered her as having "large blond hair, rather pretty, plump," with Coffee at her side, and he graded her performance as a C+, which was modest in my opinion, making him a definitely tough grader.[91] In an interview after he retired, he claimed all three female attorneys in the reargument "did an acceptable job, not a triple-A type, but acceptable."[92] The first hearing of the trial of *Roe v. Wade* was on December 13, 1971, when the Court only had seven active members because there had been two deaths of Justices, and their replacements that were appointed by Nixon had not yet been confirmed. This was unusual, but there had been a few times when less than nine Supreme Court Justices have decided a case, such as when seven Justices decided *The Justices v. Murray 76 U.S. 274 (1869)*, which dealt with issues elated to the authority of Federal and State Superior Courts, and when eight Justices ruled in *United States v. Nixon 418 U.S. 684 (1974)*, when Justice Rehnquist recused himself in the trial that ruled Nixon had to deliver tape recordings in the Watergate Scandal. All four of the Justices that Nixon appointed to the Supreme Court were still on the Court when Nixon was ordered to produce the tapes in that trial, and Nixon was furious, feeling completely betrayed by three men he had put on the Court himself who had found him guilty, but satisfied that Rehnquist did not participate.[93] Burger allowed the case to proceed in this manner, planning to have a reargument in order to have all nine Justices present when a decision was made, and I believe that this was an even greater mistake on his part than deciding which case to choose to begin with, as I will detail later.

Three days after the arguments were made, the Justices met to discuss the case, and although there are a number of published accounts on what took place, Blackmun's cryptic notes of the discussion made no record of his own remarks. What is known, is that all seven Justices, for one reason or another, agreed that the Texas law was

---

90 Koh, "The Justice Harry A. Blackmun Oral History Project," 194.

91 Prager, The Family Roe: An American Story, 90-91. The lawyer for Texas who argued the case was Jay Floyd, the Texas Assistant Attorney General, who Blackmun gave a grade of B, even though he eventually lost the case. Ibid., 91. In addition to being a tough grader, I would say Blackmun was also sometimes inept.

92 Koh, "The Justice Harry A. Blackmun Oral History Project," 198.

93 Graff, Watergate: A New History, 633.

unconstitutional, while the Georgia case was less clear.[94] As I already pointed out, Burger should have realized that this was a likely first impression, so I don't believe he should have been surprised. Their views were not strong, however, and all felt that more clarification was needed, and a reargument with all nine Justices present would be a good idea. Their reasoning was because they thought they would vote to find a constitutional bases for abortion, but they wanted more proof to be sure. Burger wanted it not to be approved, and he foolishly agreed to reargue the case, not realizing what a good job Blackmun would do after researching the Mayo Clinic library. Burger formally assigned the case to Blackmun to write the opinion when he decided to have the case reargued, and because there was division in the Justices after the first argument was made, Burger could have changed his mind, but Blackmun later said that this was the first time he knew he was writing the opinion.[95] Internal memos indicate that he did consider that move with Rehnquist and Powell now on board, but in the end he stayed with Blackmun to write the opinion.[96]

Linda Greenhouse thought that Burger's decision to have Blackmun write the opinion was because of Blackmun's medical background, and Burger believing Blackmun "would discharge the Court's duty without doing or saying anything more than necessary."[97] Ouch!! I don't know if she actually had reason to believe that latter part, but if Burger truly wasn't sure of what to do, I would say that the trauma he suffered after the decision was made would be the reason their friendship would soon begin to break apart. What Burger didn't realize is that the very next day, Blackmun wrote to Thomas E. Keys, who was the medical librarian at the Mayo Clinic and asked for anything they had on the history of abortion.[98] He was not well-versed on the subject, and I believe it was smart to ask Keys to prepare the material for him to review, but it also indicates that he was going to rely on somebody else's research, which skewed his final opinion. I do not doubt that the material he was given was mostly pro-abortion, but I

---

94 Greenhouse, <u>Becoming Justice Blackmun: Harry Blackmun's Supreme Court Journey</u>, 80-81.

95 Koh, "The Justice Harry A. Blackmun Oral History Project," 192.

96 "The Burger Court Opinion Writing Database," 1-38.

97 Greenhouse, <u>Becoming Justice Blackmun: Harry Blackmun's Supreme Court Journey</u>, 82.

98 Ibid.

have not been able to review the material myself, and since I agree with his holding in the case, I will say no more.

It was then that I believe the "dye was cast," however, as Julius Caesar supposedly said when he crossed the Rubicon River to war against Rome. Blackmun's dedication to thoroughly prepare a strong medical argument for his decision would win the support of his fellow Justices, and begin the division of the Republican and Democratic parties into forces ready for a Civil War. Interestingly enough, that night at dinner, Blackmun also asked his wife and three daughters about their views on abortion, and I believe he decided to take both sources to heart in deciding the *Roe* verdict, for his daughters hated Richard Nixon, and would have been Pro-Choice all the way.[99] Fathers of daughters, like me, understand Blackmun's reaction; Nixon had two daughters as well, but they supported him through all his trials as they were married, and agreed with his beliefs. The outcome of *Roe v. Wade* may have been a surprise to the American public, but the facts I have been able to uncover reveal to me that the result should never have been unexpected. I was surprised about the case when I began my research, but by the time I wrote this book, I understood how both cases wound up being decided the way they did. Both of these trials were not worthy of how a Supreme Court should be run, but this is a history lesson, and not a legal instruction manual, so let me proceed.

Burger, despite their friendship, in my opinion, never understood how deeply Blackmun was researching the issue in the Mayo Clinic medical library, and how this was affecting his past conservative training. In a case as important as *Roe v. Wade*, Burger did not want the verdict to be suspect because of a less than full complement of Justices, so he allowed the first argument to be given before seven Justices, and then ordered a reargument to be given on October 11, 1972, when Justices Lewis F. Powell and William Rehnquist replaced Hugo Black and John Marshall Harlan II, so that the full nine-member panel could be present, and vote on the outcome. Harlan II was nearly blind, and resigned on September 23, 1971, and Black died two days later, so the process of beginning to name their replacements was able

---

99   At the time he was appointed he had been asked if his daughters could be typifies as hippies, and although I don't know what he answered, his youngest daughter, Susan, "was at the time a self-described hippie and political radical who regarded Nixon as the ultimate enemy." Ibid., 47.

to begin, and Nixon chose candidates who would not have problems being passed by the Senate.[100] This decision to reargue the case, while definitely a smart judicial tactic, and based on logical legal foundations, would make it less likely to be overturned because of only seven Justices deciding the case, but this tactic would prove to be disastrous for Burger, who I sincerely believe wanted, and expected, a vote to ban abortion. He wanted to be sure there was a strong conservative majority, so that he could be assured they would vote to ban abortion, but he could not choose the candidates, for that was up to Nixon.[101] His reasoning was logical, but because he did not expect the case to be approved, he wanted to solidify the verdict to find it unconstitutional, and wound up assuring that its passage would remain in force for another 50 years. We will see that as they waited for a reargument to take place, Blackmun corrected the mistakes he made in the first argument, and that allowed him to convince a majority of the Justices to agree with his view, so that the eventual verdict would find the Texas law unconstitutional, and abortion became an authorized constitutional personal right, and the law of the land.

When Rehnquist later wrote his dissent in the case, he told Blackmun that: "I have to take my hat off to you for marshaling as well as I think could be done the arguments on your side," a compliment that I agree was well-deserved, but Rehnquist would remain a strong opponent of Blackmun for his entire life, upset with the verdict as much as I believe Burger was.[102] When Blackmun was interviewed after he retired, he said that when he was being considered for the appointment of Supreme Court Justice, Rehnquist was the assistant Attorney General in charge of the Office of Legal Counsel, and when he would joke with Rehnquist later and say that he made a mistake in approving him, Rehnquist always allowed that he did.[103] Blackmun also said that after he was sworn in as a Justice, he never spoke directly to Nixon again, so that Rehnquist, Burger, and Nixon would represent a trio of men who regretted the approval of *Roe v. Wade* for the rest of their lives.[104] As I now discuss the second argument that would take place, I want

---

100   Ibid., 76.

101   Ibid., 89.

102   Ibid., 95. Blackmun returned the favor by sending Rehnquist a copy of the ruling and asking him to autograph it. Ibid.

103   Koh, "The Justice Harry A. Blackmun Oral History Project," 27.

104   Ibid., 28.

you to realize that there have been very few such cases of this type in the history of the Supreme Court, and although I have not been able to determine the precise number, Microsoft CoPilot noted that there were four cases that were reargued and turned out to be important, including *Roe v. Wade*, *Brown v. Board of Education* in 1952 and 1953, *Citizens United v. FEC* in March and September 2009, and *Kiobel v. Royal Duct Petroleum* in 2012.[105] I feel secure in stating that no reargument in the history of the Supreme Court ever shocked the world as much as *Roe v. Wade* did, and none which caused a Political Party to work so hard to have the case eventually overturned.

Blackmun did not go by his instincts alone after the discussions were held before the rearguments took place, but he took advice from the other Justices on the Court, as is evident in the fact that he originally wanted to allow for abortions only in the first trimester, but Justices William Brennan and Thurgood Marshall objected that the first trimester didn't give women enough time to obtain an abortion.[106] In addition, Marshall was particularly concerned about poor and minority women, and since the eventual vote needed both of these justices to make a majority, Blackmun settled on accepting not only the trimester system, but also the onset of quickening as the evidence of viability, which was usually within the second trimester.[107] His eventual position would eventually convince most of the nine Justices to vote his way, with Rehnquist the only Nixon appointee to dissent, along with Justice Byron White, who despite being appointed by John F. Kennedy, was widely regarded as a strong conservative in constitutional law, having also dissented in *Miranda v. Arizona, 384 U.S. 436 (1966),* which was a landmark liberal decision of the Warren Court to rule that law enforcement must warn a person of their constitutional rights before interrogating them. The fact that only two Justices dissented was a severe blow to both Burger and Nixon, but the verdict shows to me that Blackmun was not only persuasive, but his ruling was a perfect model for what an abortion amendment should look like, and I followed him very closely except for changing the gestation period to 20 weeks, instead of 24-28 weeks.

When the first oral arguments were made in December 1971, Mary

---

105   Microsoft CoPilot (8/13/2025). Personal communication.
106   Balkin, "Roe v. Wade, *An Engine of Controversy*," 10.
107   Ibid.

Ziegler, the Martin Luther King Jr. Professor of Law at the University of California, Davis, School of Law, claimed that Burger did not want the decision to be made with only seven Justices because the opinion would then have been "unconstitutionally vague," because it would not have necessarily included a 5-2 verdict, but a 4-3 vote, which would not have been a majority on a 9-Justice panel, and his more liberal colleagues also pressed for a more sweeping ruling, so the case was ordered to be reargued in the Fall of 1972, when a full contingency of Justices would be present.[108] I'm not sure this was the reason or not, but I do believe that part of his uncertainty was from not yet having two more votes which he was "sure" to be conservative in nature. Burger's reasoning to reargue the case, in my opinion was brilliant from a legal standpoint, but I do not believe it would have taken almost fifty years to be overturned if the case had been decided and approved by only seven Justices, given the outrage which followed the final decision, so his instincts to have two more Nixon appointees voting was a good idea. I think Burger later rued the fact that he made it be reargued to not risk an appeal once he found out that Blackmun decided that abortion was constitutional, but that's water under the bridge, as the aphorism goes, and its effect was not a small trickle, but a tidal wave.

During the rehearing, both the liberal and conservative Justices became more assured by Blackmun's further study in the Mayo Clinic medical library, and they showed their approval in the final vote. In the reargument, Dennis Horan (1932-1888), who was Chairman of the Board of Americans United for Life, and who had wanted the Court to take his own abortion case, submitted a brief supporting fetal personhood, which may be one reason Blackmun faced that issue in his final opinion.[109] The eventual 7-2 majority vote included Blackmun, Burger, Douglas, Brennan, Stewart, Marshall, and Powell, Jr., and showed that Burger's vote was not necessary to make a majority. He voted with the majority for appearance's sake, and not because he agreed with the decision, and this was all necessary because he did not want the decision to be made with seven Justices voting.

I want to provide more details about the reargument, because it

---

108   Ziegler, <u>Dollars for Life; The Anti-Abortion Movement and the Fall of the Republican Establishment</u>, 15.

109   Ibid., 16.

shows how well I believe Weddington performed, and why I think the verdict survived the follow up *Thornbourg* case, which I will discuss in the next chapter. Weddington started her argument with the claim that Roe's rights to an abortion were protected by the First, Fourth, Fifth, Ninth, Fourteenth Amendments, which should override any state law, as she had before.[110] She also was able to cite an article showing that when the Constitution was adopted, there was no common law prohibition against abortion, which was very important, and I believe was particularly noteworthy to the members of the Court that were part of the prior Warren panel.[111] They were well aware of this type of argument, and were in general agreement with it, but now there were four Nixon appointees on the panel, and it was smart to set the table with all the utensils you may need. As I previously discussed, many prior courts during the Warren era had found a right of privacy, primarily in the Ninth and Fourteenth Amendments, which they argued included the right to choose whether to abort an unwanted nonviable fetus, even though the word "abortion" wasn't mentioned in the Constitution itself. As the Republican push to favor a conservative interpretation of the Constitution increased over the ensuing years, the question of whether there was truly a right of privacy came up more and more, so that in *Webster v. Reproductive Health Services, 492 U.S. 490 (1989)*, a friend of the court brief was filed by 885 American law professors who claimed that the right of privacy "is an essential component of constitutional liberty and privacy commanding reaffirmation by [the Supreme] Court."[112] We will see in the next chapter that by the time *Dobbs* finally came to the Court, Alito was looking to modify this right more completely, but in *Roe v. Wade*, Weddington's argument was directed at the nature of the Warren Court Justices, and her tactic worked. The lawyers from the Northern District of Texas had rebutted that the fetus had constitutional rights as well, but the federal U.S. District Court ruled in her favor, declaring that the abortion statutes were vague, and overbroadly infringing the plaintiffs' Ninth and Fourteenth Amendment rights, and so the case was then appealed to the Supreme Court.

It is important to point out that the ruling of the District Court

---

110   "Roe v. Wade, 410 U.S. 113 (1973)," 5.

111   Weddington, A Question of Choice, 116.

112   Tribe, "Finding Abortion Rights in the Constitution," 476-477.

based the constitutional rights of Roe on amendments, and since the Justices were all appointed during the Warren Court era, it meant that Weddington's argument was designed to follow their same mode of interpretation as what Blackmun did as well.[113] That argument would not work with the conservative Supreme Court in the *Dobbs* case, however, because the majority were Catholic conservatives utilizing the argument of Originalism, which deemed that approach erroneous, even though I have argued that they were only pretending to use that tactic, and were instead following the teaching of the Catholic Pope that life began at conception. Although this was the Burger Court, it was acting more like the liberal Warren Court, and there was no way that Weddington's approach would lose. As Geoffrey R. Stone, the Edward H. Levi Distinguished Service Professor at the University of Chicago Law School, explained, the Ninth Amendment had recognized that there were other freedoms beyond those expressly spelled out when it provided that "the enumeration in the Constitution, of certain rights, shall not be construed to deny or disparage others retained by the people," and that was why he found the "right of privacy" to be present.[114] Warren was no longer the Chief Justice, but his effect on Blackmun persisted, even if Burger was upset by the ruling.

There was one major event that took place in Weddington's life during the period before the reargument took place that I want to relate because I believe it altered her for the rest of her life, and helps explain why I knew so little about her when I began to research this book. While I do believe that her first argument in *Roe v. Wade* was very good, and deserves a better grade than she was given by Blackmun, her local fame from the first appearance spread like wildfire, even though no decision was yet made in the case. The fact that she actually appeared before the Supreme Court was enough for the local papers to acclaim her feat, and as a result, she was convinced to run for Travis

113   Judge Sarah T. Hughes (1895-1985) was appointed by John F. Kennedy in 1961. Judge William M. Taylor Jr. (1909-1985) was appointed by Lyndon B. Johnson in 1966. Judge Irving Goldberg (1906-1995) was appointed was appointed in 1966, shortly after Warren retired. Microsoft CoPilot (4/18/2025). Personal communication.

114   Bollinger and Stone, "Opening Dialogue,"xix. He did not choose to claim discrimination against women because the Supreme Court did not hold unconstitutional a law for that reason until Reed v. Reed, 404 U.S. 71 (1971). Bollinger and Stone, "Opening Dialogue,"xx.

County state Representative after the incumbent decided to run for state Treasurer. The county she lived in had never been represented by a woman, and in her book she related how she was proud of this fact, and felt capable because she went to a law school in Texas, where women were looked on as second-class citizens and she still wound up getting to the Supreme Court with a case. In the end she won a runoff against a man who had spent more money than she did to become a State Representative, and once she knew she was able to beat a man who was more well-known, and experienced in political matters, her confidence grew exponentially.[115] As is often the case in Politics, however, how able you are to do a good job is less important than how good your public appeal is, and in the district she lived, there was no one better than she because of her Supreme Court appearance. While I understand her positive reaction to the opportunity of running for political office, I think it was more reflective of an underlying character fault, which helps explain why she is relatively unknown today, despite the fact that her eventual victory provided as much success for the Women's Lib organizations as did the right of women to vote, as I will explain in short order.

Weddington's appearance in *Roe v. Wade* showed an incredible legal talent that could have made her legal career a formidable legacy in my opinion, and yet we never hear of her ever appearing in a courtroom again. A one trial career, with her only appearance before the Supreme Court? Sounds too incredible to be true, but that is exactly what happened. She then served in the Texas legislature from 1973-1977, and later became a law professor at the University of Texas, Austin, and at Texas Women's University, and a public speaker, of course, about the *Roe v. Wade* verdict. Rather than continue a career as a practicing attorney, she wound up being the General Counsel for the U.S. Department of Agriculture, and White House Director of Politic Affairs under President Jimmy Carter, but I believe it was all too much for Weddington to handle, and after the trial was over, her fame in the courts flickered like a candle in the wind. She was happy with her career in Politics, but I believe she could have done much better, both for herself, and the Women's Liberation cause, if she would have dedicated herself to her legal talents. When she wrote her book, *A Question of Choice*, you can see why this change took place in how

---

115 Weddington, <u>A Question of Choice</u>, 123-129.

she described the manner in which she handled the success in a manner that often ruins people who win the lottery. Not only was she elected the first woman representative from the district she lived in, but she described herself as suddenly feeling "an opportunity to broaden my focus to other areas – rape-law reform, parental custody matters, the needs of children and the poor, health care, working conditions, the environment, and a long list of other concerns I could move on. After all, [she continued] I had never meant for the abortion issue to be my focus forever."[116] At least she was honest about her feelings at the time, and so I am sure she also was happy with her life, at least for a while, but I truly believe she could have been the female version of Clarence Darrow, and helped promote a more successful campaign to prevent Republican inroads on their anti-abortion promotions. She died on December 26, 2021, at the age of 76 years old, shortly after the oral arguments were made in the *Dobbs* case, and about seven months before the opinion was delivered, a fitting end so that neither she, nor Blackmun, had to read about it in the newspaper.

I show my age when I say all this, for while this attitude is not an uncommon response to sudden success, I remember it more from when I was growing up, and became intrigued by a book called *The Peter Principle*, written by Dr. Laurence J. Peter (1919-1990), a Canadian educator who claimed that people are promoted in their life for success they have in each role they undertake, and eventually they reach a point where their skills no longer match the job requirements, and their promotions end. I was immediately struck by how much throughout history this end result was true, and how with Weddington it was absolutely true. Her only time in a courtroom was *Roe v. Wade*, and she never took on another case again. Weddington was truly a remarkable lawyer in her appearance before the Supreme Court in *Roe v. Wade*, but she let her honors "go to her head," as the saying goes, and her list of things she wanted to do in her life was simply a "pipe dream," which was a 19th century idiom that was prompted by the effect smoking opium had on smokers of opium pipes. Few people are truly important enough and talented enough to make a difference in the world they live in, in multiple aspects of life. When those aspirations hit, you often search for a public spectacle like Politics to pursue, and seldom perform in the special manner you did to get that

---

116   Weddington, <u>A Question of Choice</u>, 151-152.

job. Weddington did play a significant role in getting *Roe v. Wade* approved, and I hope my amendment proposal doesn't fail, for we vitally need that assistance, and I owe my potential success to her reargument in *Roe v. Wade*.

After the first argument was completed, she soon was informed that the reargument with all nine Judges present would take place shortly, and that Justice Burger had appointed Blackmun, "the justice with the best background in medical-legal issues," to write the opinion, and so her preparation for that important event was made as she relished being an elected public official, and not just a lawyer making her appearance at the Supreme Court level in her first case she ever filed.[117] Her new position would have to be put on hold until the case was completed, but once you taste the nectar of public appeal, your fate is sealed. I will now explain what happened in the reargument, and let you contemplate what you would have done if you were in her shoes.

In the transcript of the reargument of *Roe v. Wade* that took place on October 11, 1972, we can see how much the work Blackmun put in at the Mayo Clinic Medical library prepared him to convince the majority of Justices to agree that there was a true constitutional protected right of privacy that permitted women to choose abortion in the Constitution. His success, however, was also aided by Weddington's performance, as she began her presentation to the Court by smartly asking the Justices "that you affirm the ruling of the three judge court below which held our statute unconstitutional for two reasons," an action that she said "interfered with the Ninth Amendment rights of a woman to determine whether or not she would continue or terminate a pregnancy."[118] She focused the argument on both the decision of the District Court, and the fact that since the original action, there had been an intervener accepted, Dr. James Hallford, who was a physician who performed abortions in Texas, but had not seen the Roe defendant, in order to buttress her argument that physicians in Texas were still being negatively affected. The Supreme Court did not let Dr. Hallford intervene, but her argument was made in writing, and she hoped the realization remained in the Justices' mindset, as we will see it did.[119]

---

117   Ibid., 131-132.
118   "Transcript of Reargument in *Roe v. Wade, 410 U.S. 113 (1973)*
       U.S. Supreme Court October 11, 1972, October 11, 1972," 1.
119   Ibid., 2.

Hallford's position had pointed out to the entire panel the importance of this case to all physicians in the state of Texas, for he had joined the case at the Federal District Court level, where he was under indictment for performing an illegal abortion, and Weddington accepted him as a third plaintiff because he "added weight to our arguments that the statute was vague.[120] This tells me that Weddington was coached well by Roy Lucas on her performance in the first set of arguments, and she was going to add to her success by working on her C+ grade and raising it to an A+ at the time she was done, but I don't have access to Blackmun's diary to see what comments he made, although he did later decide that all the female attorneys "did well," retaining his reputation as being a tough grader. In their decision supporting Roe's case against the state of Texas, the District Court did not refuse to allow the District Attorney of Texas to sue doctor's for abortion, and did accept that both Roe and Hallford were appropriate plaintiffs, so Weddington was able to add that information to her written argument.[121]

The text of the trial testimony indicated that Burger was still acting as Chief Justice during both the argument and the reargument, beginning the interrogation in each section. Weddington answered his questions about the prosecutions of doctors for abortion by noting that 1,600 Texas women still had to go to New York in the first nine months of 1971 to get an abortion, and so the case was not moot because it was almost three years since they instituted their original action, and the problem was still continuing.[122] I believe she sensed Burger's reputation of being a conservative Justice wanting to get rid of this case, and faced the issue directly at the start of her testimony

---

120   Weddington, A Question of Choice, 59. The Texas Attorney
        general, Crawford Martin was the attorney at the Federal Court level.
        Ibid. They had amended the case at the Federal Court to include it
        being class-action in order to paint a larger picture than just the facts
        of their one plaintiff. Ibid., 61. Both Weddington and Coffee spoke at
        the Federal Court level. Ibid., 63. The addition of class-action would
        prove to be important at the Supreme Court because the Texas attorney
        Floyd argued that Roe did not have standing because she was no longer
        pregnant, and when reminded by one of the Judges that it was a class-
        action suit, that argument was voided. Ibid., 119,

121   Ibid., 68.

122   "Transcript of Reargument in *Roe v. Wade, 410 U.S. 113 (1973)*
        U.S. Supreme Court October 11, 1972, October 11, 1972," 2.

to him about the need to change the law. She added that the legal abortions in New York were very safe, with the maternal death rate dropping to 3.7 per 100,000 abortions in 1971, which was half the death rate of normal deliveries for women.[123] I must emphasize this aspect of her argument because the statistic was extremely important to Blackmun, and she knew he was going to write the opinion of the case, so she brought this up at the very start of her testimony, primarily for his attention. By adding that the holding of the right to determine the use of birth control was a constitutionally protected right, she was answering Burger's questions, but she was also focusing on Blackmun's concerns, although she likely kept her eyes directed at Burger during her testimony.

I truly believe that Weddington was an important reason Blackmun wrote the decision the way he did, and I don't know if it was advice she was given by her team of lawyers, or her instincts that took control during her argument to be sure she focused her attention on everything he was interested in. Her law school training obviously was important, but in a courtroom you either exude confidence, or you don't. You either breath in confidence, and exhale what the Judges want to hear, or you don't, and I contend that Weddington did this, and deserves praise for her bold approach. Juries take sides much of the time, and here, it is obvious to me that Justices on the Supreme Court do it as well. Early in her testimony she began emphasizing how the state's argument that the fetus at conception is a person, and that this meant abortion was therefore a crime in Texas was vital, but yet, she explained, that Texas law did not subject criminal prosecution if a woman performed self-abortion, which was something that you would have expected if Texas law truly saw the fetus as a legal person.[124] This information effectively attacked the inconsistent position of the Texas statute, and she was simply backing up the decision of the District Court to find the law unconstitutional. Her argument, in my opinion, could also be used to invalidate the *Dobbs* decision, if that case is ever appealed, but I will hope that my amendment proposal will pass,

---

123   Ibid., 3. In a recent paper she changed those statistics to a death rate of twenty deaths per 100,000 childbirths in the United States, and three per 100,000 pregnancies in Eastern Europe. Weddington, "The Woman's Right of Privacy," 27-28.

124   "Transcript of Reargument in *Roe v. Wade, 410 U.S. 113 (1973) U.S. Supreme Court October 11, 1972,* October 11, 1972," 4.

and like the *Dred Scott v. Sandford* decision on slavery, the *Dobbs* decision will lay dormant for all time, bathed in the same slime as *Dred Scott v. Sandford* Justice White broke in during her testimony to ask her if the right of the fetus is a factor in the case, and Weddington smartly brought up the *Vuitch* case that allowed abortions to continue in the District of Columbia, and yet wouldn't have done it if the fetus had any rights in the Constitution, and then clarified that if there was any right at all, it had to be "compelling" rights, and in this case it was not.[125] She was carefully highlighting the difference between how she, and the medical profession in general, saw the difference between the rights of the mother, and that of an unviable fetus, and this was something that Blackmun was doing, as well. In addition, she was letting the Court know she carefully had studied their position, which is good for a neophyte to do. I don't know if she was aware of the extent of Blackmun's research in the Mayo Clinic library, but Microsoft Pilot declared that during the trial itself, that information was not generally known.[126] What the library research did show was that common law when the Constitution was written declared life to begin at quickening, and that was the stance that Blackmun would take as well.

Justice Burger at this point in her testimony then asked whether she made any distinction between the first month and the ninth month of gestation, which, of course, clearly dealt with the issue of viability, which was the issue in both Supreme Court cases because the state continuously declared that life began at conception. I believe that Blackmun found her argument compelling and correct, and due to his medical knowledge, it was something he agreed with from the very start.[127] I am sure that at this point, all nine Justices sat up to hear her response as well, which was that the Texas statute did not define a point of viability, but that some states did have time limits, but "they have not yet been challenged."[128] This, of course, was to point out that Texas's stance that life began at conception was not supported by the evidence, and was not supported by any other state statute. She added that she thought the Texas Supreme Court should look into it

---

125   Ibid., 5-6.

126   Microsoft Pilot (8/1/2025). Personal communication.

127   Ibid., 6.

128   Ibid., 6-7.

because they were not likely to agree with the stance taken by the District Attorney, and her answers, to me, could not have been put better by Alan Dershowitz, who is considered one of the best living constitutional lawyers.

After the research Blackmun put in at the Mayo Clinic Medical Library, I am sure he found her information to be consistent with his own general medical knowledge, and the information he uncovered in his research, as well, and by now his mind was close to made up, but if it was not, I will show where the door was soon to be shut. Rather than state a strict viewpoint, she was comfortable leaving Texas stating that life began at conception without specifically commenting on it at her level of expertise, and this is something that I contend Blackmun appreciated.

I am amazed at how well her reargument went, and I am certain that Blackmun took much of his final opinion in the case from this sequence of events. I will argue in the next Chapter that Justice Samuel Alito Jr., who wrote the opinion in the *Dobbs* case that overturned *Roe v. Wade*, went beyond his own authority when he did not follow the Mississippi statute, which put the limit at 15-weeks gestation, and instead acceded to the Catholic Church position that life began at conception. His opinion has not been yet challenged, and if my amendment passes, it won't have to be, like with *Dred Scott v. Sandford*, but I contend that there is no way the *Dobbs* decision can be valid unless you accept that the Catholic Pope, and not the Constitution, is the authority being followed. I will discuss in the next chapter how the Republicans shortly after *Roe v. Wade* was decided thought of presenting an amendment to deny the right of abortion, but decided they could not get it passed, which I guarantee is true. I also contend that if my amendment fails, they should be required to pass an amendment themselves, for they changed the common law with their passage of *Dobbs* and, in their own words, that is an unacceptable action. If my amendment fails, their's will fail by a much larger margin, and their *Dobbs* decision can then be overturned by someone else. I will be saddened by the failure of my amendment, but as long as *Roe v. Wade* is once again an accepted Supreme Court ruling, I will be satisfied. Because Weddington was arguing a position that Blackmun knew was consistent with his own experience at the Mayo Clinic, her deference in the courtroom was very effective, and

I believe the Republicans saw that they would need to have a solid majority of Justices who would agree with the Texas stance, which is why they decided there and then that the Justices would have to be Catholic, so that their religious training would convince them that life began at conception.

When Blackmun directly questioned her in the reargument, I carefully followed his questioning, for I knew this was the pivotal moment of the case. He asked her about her attacking the statute on two grounds, vagueness and the Ninth Amendment, and wanted to know if one was more important than the other, which was an issue he was still dealing with, and was interested in knowing her position, for by now he was assured that her preparation for the case was as intense as his own.[129] Her answer was that the Texas Court of Appeals held that the statute was not vague, but when he asked her about the Hippocratic oath, which he would later say was very critical to him, she held firm to the fact that the medical profession has adopted a position "that says the doctor and the patient should be able to make the decision for themselves in this kind of situation," and there is no question in my mind that this was identical to his own position.[130] This was something emphasized in the material that the Mayo Clinic library staff collected for him to review, and he was impressed by what she said, and how she said it. She then added that "there has never been established that the fetus is a person, or that it's entitled to the Fourteenth Amendment rights, or the protection of the Constitution," like the mother is, and, and this was where he knew what his final decision on the case would be.[131] The fact that the Texas attorney Robert Flowers answer to her statement was that he did not have in the time allowed the ability to explain the development of the fetus from conception to birth, but declared that the State of Texas believes that "upon conception, we have a human being; a person, within the concept of the Constitution of the United States," a position that was taken almost verbatim by Alito.[132] This was when Blackmun's decision was made in my opinion, for there is nothing in medical or legal literature to support such a proposition, and it would take fifty

---

129   Ibid., 7.
130   Ibid., 8.
131   Ibid., 9.
132   Ibid., 11.

years, and a collection of six reverent Catholic Justices, before another Supreme Court would find that *Roe v. Wade* was unconstitutional because life began at conception. I know that this will never pass in an amendment, for it is a minority opinion made even by religious believers who are Catholic according to most polls.

In her own book, Sarah Weddington noted that Justice White commented to Flowers: "You've lost your case, then, if the fetus or embryo is not a person, is that it?" and Flowers admitted it was true.[133] In response, she ended her own presentation with a statement that I believe assured her victory:

We are not here to advocate abortion. We do not ask this Court to rule that abortion is good or desirable in any particular situation. We are here to advocate that the decision as to whether or not a particular woman will continue to carry or will terminate a pregnancy is a decision that should be made by that individual, that in fact she has a constitutional right to make that decision for herself, and that the State has shown no interest in [or sufficient legal status to allow] interfering with that decision.[134]

I'm not sure if she had help in writing that closing argument, but I believe she was speaking directly to Justice Blackmun, and to all the Justices who had been on the Warren Court, had read their minds with the astuteness of Clarence Darrow, a remarkable feat by a lawyer in her first legal case, and arguing to the Supreme Court of the United States. As if to reward her for her efforts, on November 7, she won the election from Travis County to the Texas House of Representatives, becoming the first woman to do so, defeating the Republican candidate, Dwight Wheeler, a win she cherished, and deserved, but she was giving into the notoriety that was coming to her from political fame in her town, rather than national attention, and that is why we read little of her name today.[135] Her legal acumen could have made her career in the arena of women's rights equal to many others I have named in this book, but while her political career did eventually land her position in the White House, her political value never rose to an important role, but her performance in *Roe v. Wade* is worthy of all the plaudits I have bestowed upon her.

---

133   Weddington, <u>A Question of Choice</u>, 141.

134   Ibid., 142.

135   Ibid., 142-143.

The eventual decision of the Supreme Court agreeing with Weddington's argument came as a shock across the country at the time it was made, because three Republican appointees of Nixon joined in the majority opinion, including Blackmun, Warren Burger, and Lewis F. Powell, and they all were aware that the Constitution, or the amendments, did not specifically list the word "abortion" as a right.[136] When they were appointed by Richard Nixon, all four Justices were thought to be conservatives who would not approve of abortion because it was not specifically listed as a right, and it was only Rehnquist, the fourth justice appointed by Nixon, who dissented in the case. Because the Court at the time the decision was made it was a full panel of Justices, and not just the seven who were at the first argument, Burger had made sure it would not easily be overturned, which was the reason I believe it lasted almost fifty years, despite the raging argument that would be unleashed by the Pro-Life Republican Party. Rehnquist would later become Chief Justice on September 26, 1986, after Burger resigned, appointed by President Ronald Reagan, in my opinion as a reward for his dissent in *Roe v. Wade*. Rehnquist was replaced as a Justice by the appointment of Antonin Scalia, a rigid conservative Justice who avidly agreed with the concept of Originalism espoused by Robert Bork.

Kathryn Kolbert, the ACLU attorney who I discuss at length in the next chapter since she was the lead attorney in both the successful *Thornburgh* and *Casey* cases which followed, approved the *Roe v. Wade* verdict, claimed that the Republican anti-abortion movement launched its efforts to appoint ultra-conservative anti-abortion judges into the lower courts nationwide following this case, and prepared a short-list for Supreme Court nomination, after Reagan was elected President, in order to change the composition of the Court that appeared to reflect Warren, more than it did Burger. It is clear that Reagan's efforts were successful eventually to modify the mistakes made by Nixon with his appointees, but the time it took for the changes to take place, and the proven evidence of the effectiveness and safety of the abortions that were done worldwide, now gives me a good chance to pass an amendment that I believe will be accepted by 3/4 of the American public, something that never would have happened if *Roe v. Wade* had not ended the way it did.[137] The reason I am so confident is

---

136   Chemerinsky, "Justice Blackmun Got It Right in *Roe v. Wade*," 67.

137   Kolbert & Kay, <u>Controlling Women: What We Must do Now to</u>

that despite their care to appoint six Catholic Justices to the Supreme Court, and not have anyone question their reasoning, I am going to be the first to charge that this was a deliberate action intended to fulfill a Republican plan to eliminate the principle of Separation of Church and State in America, and promote favoritism to Christianity as the national religion of America, just as Constantinople did in the Roman Empire. I will fight against this attempt because it destroys the very essence of what our Founding Fathers did when they wrote the Constitution of the United States, and I believe that my amendment will be passed by a greater that 3/4 majority of the states in our great Union because it is consistent with our claim to be a Democracy, and not a Theocracy.

Weddington's success in Politics came in 1978 when she was appointed as General Council for Agriculture by Jimmy Carter, but it took some time for her career to advance, and the fame and appeal which the *Roe v. Wade* case brought to her name finally caused such a sensation that in 1989 a made-for-TV movie, *Roe v. Wade*, appeared with Amy Madigan playing Sarah Weddington, and Holly Hunter playing Ellen Russell, which was the fictionalized name of Norma McCorvey. It was written by Allison Cross, and directed by Gregory Hoblit, and emphasized the struggles of McCorvey, and the effectiveness of Weddington.[138] In 2020, another movie with the same title reappeared, this time produced, written, and directed by Nick Loeb and Cathy Allyn, showing that Weddington's choice for a career in Politics, more than Law, was more suited to her personal goals, and she would begin to become a more well-known commodity, but not because of her legal talent. Sadly, to me, this glorification on the Silver Screen helped her political career, but wasted her attributes that were evident in her Supreme Court appearance. Greer Grammar played Weddington, and Summer Joy Campell played Norma McCorvey, and according to Loeb, the movie was about "the women's rights movement versus the pro-life movement," rather than the personal lives of the main characters. He described it as a "social war movie," which I find to be a perfect analysis of what I am writing

---

Save Reproductive Freedom, 66. She added that the redrawing of state legislative district lines following the 2010 census swept abortion opponents into power in state capitals nationwide. Ibid.

138   Microsoft CoPilot (5/9/25). Personal Communication.

about in this book.[139] It should not have been a surprise that *Roe v. Wade* would find its way into Hollywood, as the topic of abortion had become popular the decade before with movies like *Cabaret* in 1972, followed by 44 productions between 1983-1992, and 58 from 1993-2002.[140] I remember nothing about Weddington during the many years I worked and studied in the field of law and medicine, but when I began to write this book, I wondered why I had known so little of her fame, and now I knew.

As I said, Blackmun's decision to find a constitutional justification in the case came about during his intense research at the Mayo Clinic medical library when he became convinced that the Constitutional Amendments supported the right to abortion, in particular the Ninth and Fourteenth Amendments that were used by the Warren Court to expand personal liberties. He obviously had known of the liberal interpretations of the Warren Court, and agreed with many of their concepts, so I'm not sure how he was believed to be a conservative when he interviewed with Nixon. My only explanation is that it came from his friendship with Burger, who also is guilty of not properly knowing the legal views of his friend before letting him write the opinion in *Roe v. Wade*. Blackmun apparently never gave any hint of being liberal before given this case to write the opinion. His behavior after *Roe v. Wade* shows that he definitely was Pro-Abortion for the rest of his life, however, and from that point forward, he never his that fact. I truly believe that his life-long appointment as a Supreme Court Justice, and the level of pride that any Jurist has by having that honor, is clearly the reason he decided to take pride in what he had done, and promote it for the rest of his life. When Blackmun took on the task of writing the opinion in *Roe v. Wade*, he believed that Texas was the first state to enact a criminal abortion statute in 1854, even though that honor actually belonged to Connecticut, which passed a law against Ammi Rogers (1770-1852), a Puritan preacher who was arrested and charged with murder for procuring an abortion for Asenath Smith (1797-1848) in 1820.[141] This shows that he was not

---

139   Ibid.; "*Roe v. Wade* (film)," 1.

140   Barnes & Clinton, "Introduction," 20-21.

141   Olasky and Savas, <u>The Story of Abortion in America: A Street-Level History, 1652-2022</u>, 71-73. The first criminal abortion case in the newly constituted United States came in Massachusetts in 1810. Ibid., 79. New York was the first state to criminalize abortion making

very knowledgeable about the history of abortion, and I contend that he became so emotionally involved with this case during his research that he put aside his prior legal training to rigidly read the Constitution as a conservative Judge, in order to approve a constitutional right that the Warren Court supported, even though he knew it would likely one day be overturned if the Court became composed by a majority of conservative Judges.

Why did Blackmun do this? In my opinion, he did it because he had three daughters, he was not Catholic, and I sincerely believe that he became offended by the severity of the Texas statute against abortion, and convinced that the right of privacy was contained in the amendments. I don't think he thought much about abortion before Burger told him to write the opinion, and I really don't think he would have put as much research into the project if he was not given the responsibility of writing the opinion. He understood that the decision of Burger to let him write the opinion before the reargument was made as a declaration of trust because of their friendship, but once he began the project, he no longer worried about what Burger, or Nixon, or anyone else, thought about abortion, and found a reason to become a devoted Supreme Court Justice in the opportunity he was given to write the opinion in the case that would determine the legality of abortion in the entire country. He spent almost a year devoting himself to this project after only being on the Supreme Court for two years, and he wound up being associated with decisions that rivaled those of any made by the famous Warren Court Justices, who he was appointed to help discard.

Burger never really had much of a chance to know about Blackmun's legal opinions or training on the Supreme Court before *Roe v. Wade* was tried. The first case Blackmun took part in as the named Justice on the Court was to write the opinion was in *Wyman v. James 400 U.S. 309 (1971)*, and in that case he simply reversed a District Court ruling that found a violation of the Fourth Amendment.[142] Surprisingly

post-quickening abortions a felony and pre-quickening abortions a misdemeanor. "Timeline of Reproductive Rights Legislation," 1. James Mohr claims the Connecticut law was part of a "Crimes and Punishment" law passed in 1821. Mohr, Abortion in America: The Origins and Evolution of National Policy, 1800-1900, 20.

142   Greenhouse, Becoming Justice Blackmun: Harry Blackmun's Supreme Court Journey, 62. Burger told him it was clear and to the

enough, his hometown newspaper carried an AP story with the headline BLACKMUN RATED MORE CONSERVATIVE THAN BURGER.[143] I'm not sure why they came up with that rating, and it was local news only, but his reputation in that regard would not last for very long. He also had participated in *Vuitch* which was decided on 4/21/71, and two other opinions during his tenure on the Court up to the time *Roe v. Wade* began, including *Flood v. Kuhn 407 U.S. 258 (1972)*, which dealt with antitrust issues, and *Parisi v. Davidson 404 U.S.34 (1972)*, which dealt with a conscientious objector's right to avoid military service, but nothing which would suggest how he might vote on an abortion issue. In addition, he was working on another case *United States v. Kras 409 U.S. 434 (1972)*, which was decided on December 18, 1972, and did not deal with abortion. *Roe v. Wade* was decided on January 22, 1973, and talk about a "bolt from the blue," we don't know who first said that idiom, but it well-describes what happened when Blackmun announced his decision to the world-at-large. By the time he retired, he would participate in 3,875 cases during his career on the Supreme Court, but none were more important than *Roe v. Wade*, and none created the furor which followed for the next 50 years, before *Dobbs* would overrule its validity after he died 23 years, 3 months, and 23 days later.[144] I have not been able to find how many cases William O. Douglas, who had become famous for his tenure on the Warren Court, voted on, but I added up what I found in *The Supreme Court Compendium*, and found that he voted in 4,827 cases.[145] Douglas was on the Warren Court when Warren was first appointed as Chief Justice, and he remained on the Court until 1975, ending up with the longest tenure in Supreme Court history. His presence on the *Roe v. Wade* Court, in my opinion, helped Blackmun do what he did, and while Blackmun may not have equaled the stature of Douglas in the history of Supreme Court Justices, but he sure came

---

point, and was an important case. Ibid. The opinion in the case was not unanimous, however, and Blackmun later remembered Justice Brennan coming in and apologizing for that. Koh, "The Justice Harry A. Blackmun Oral History Project," 175.

143   Greenhouse, <u>Becoming Justice Blackmun: Harry Blackmun's Supreme Court Journey</u>, 63.

144   Koh, "The Justice Harry A. Blackmun Oral History Project," i-iii.

145   Epstein, Segal, Spaeth, and Walker, <u>The Supreme Court Compendium: Data, Decisions and Developments, Second Edition</u>, 452.

damn close.

In his early years on the Supreme Court, Blackmun had trouble making up his mind when he was a swing vote on certain cases, according to both Hugo Black and John Marshall Harlan II, but now he was imbued with the life-long appointment as a Supreme Court Justice, and determined to do the right thing.[146] He had previously struggled to get out his views forcefully, and his influence on most cases was slight up to this point, but in this case he developed an emotional attachment to the right of a woman to choose an abortion, and it gave him the strength to power through an opinion that would create a literal war of words between Pro-Choice and Pro-Life advocates that often would lead to violence over the next fifty years. He would not only stun Burger and Nixon, he would shock the entire world by his opinion, and change the American political system into opposing sides that had only existed in this way during the writing of the Constitution, and during the Civil War. I believe his influence on the other Justices on the bench not only led to the verdict in *Roe v. Wade*, but also helped win victory in the case of *Casey,* which surprisingly upheld *Roe v. Wade* when the conservatives on the Court were increasing their numbers. As I will discuss in the next chapter. Rehnquist was now the Chief Justice in that case, but the other Justices refused to throw *stare decisis* aside, while Blackmun was still sitting on the Court, and Rehnquist could not change their minds. To me, the *Casey* case showed the respect other Justices had for what he had done, and if he had not still been on the bench, I don't think the decision would have been the same. I will discuss *Casey* at length in the next chapter because the passage of that case was almost as unexpected as *Roe v. Wade*, and Alioto was a Justice on the Circuit Court and wrote a dissent that forecast his view in *Dobbs*. It is an important adjunct to understanding the effect *Roe v. Wade* had on the world, and, oh yes, it was also how I believe Alito got selected to be a Supreme Court Justice, and author of the decision I will detail in the next chapter.

I have no doubt that the reason the *Roe v. Wade* Supreme Court decided as they did was because they had only one Catholic Justice,

---

146   Woodward and Armstrong, The Justices Behind Roe v. Wade: The Inside Story, 68. Black had graduated from the University of Alabama Law School without a high school diploma or college degree. Woodward and Armstrong, The Brethren: Inside the Supreme Court, 70.

William Brennan, while the *Dobbs* Court had seven Catholic Justices, six appointed by Republican Presidents who all voted to approve the case. I believe that this difference in the religious training of the Justices was the reason one tribunal defined life as beginning at quickening, and the other demanded it began at conception. The problem with claiming that life begins at conception, is, of course, the fact that any abortion suddenly becomes the crime of murder, and that is a legal principle that is unsupported and absurd, and will never become the common law in the United States. True life undeniably begins when a fetus is viable, and can survive outside the fetus with support until it is mature enough to breath on its own. That is why abortion of a nonviable fetus is feticide, and abortion of a viable fetus is infanticide, or murder, and medical science backs up both of those definitions.

As I previously noted, when Justice Samuel Anthony Alito Jr. overturned the *Roe v. Wade* case in 2022, he based his argument on the fact that the fetus was a person because he was taught all his life that "life" began at conception in the Catholic Church, and therefore the fetus was a person with equal protection under the Constitution. He did not come to this conclusion from medical training, or citations of any ability to grow a human being in the laboratory, and nurture it to become a fully grown child. He did not do it because any fetus has been able to be kept alive and then live independently before reaching a 20-week gestational age. He did it because he went to a Catholic school, and was taught at home by Catholic parents, both of whom told him that life began at conception. This allowed him to say in his decision that Blackmun's rational was wrong, and so the case had to be vacated. In doing this he based his entire argument on something that cannot be proven in a court of law, and while there are many physicians who accept that same principle, they do it because they *feel* it is so, and their religion tells them that is so, and that is where their proof ends. Alito followed his Catholic upbringing, and decided that life began at conception, so there was no such thing as a nonviable fetus, because the essence of humanhood was present in the zygote.

I will discuss this issue of viability from a scientific sense in Chapter V, but for now I want to continue with the details of the case, and show why abortion of unwanted pregnancies that are nonviable because there is no scientific evidence that any fetus ever delivered before a gestation period, and supported by mechanical assistance, has ever survived for very long. The first issue we must discuss is that despite the widespread use of a right to privacy in the Constitution in many Supreme Court cases decided by the Warren Court, the word "privacy," like the word "abortion," does not appear anywhere in the Constitution.[147] The right of privacy first appeared in the case of *Griswold v. Connecticut, 381 U.S. 479 (1965)*, when Justice William O. Douglas (1898-1980) wrote that the Connecticut statute which prohibited the use of birth control was unconstitutional because it violated "the zone of privacy created by several fundamental constitutional guarantees," including the First, Third, Fourth, Fifth, Ninth, and Fourteenth amendments."[148] I have already pointed out that Douglas was an Associate Justice who prospered on the Warren Court, serving from 1939-1975, becoming the longest-serving Justice in history. His tenure lasted for 36 years, 7 months, beating that of Stephen J Field who served for 34 years, 8 months, and John Marshall (1755-1835), who is known as the "Great Chief Justice," served 34 years, 5 months.[149] Nominated by Franklin Delano Roosevelt in 1930, he was also one of the youngest Supreme Court Justices to ever serve, and wrote more opinions than any other in our history. He was raised Presbyterian, not Catholic, but I don't know if he had an opinion on when life began. Douglas knew that the word "privacy" did not actually appear in the amendments, but he used his judicial reading of them to decide that the wording of the amendments implied the right to decide not to have children, even though it was not stated as such. In his majority opinion in *Griswold*, Douglas wrote that the case involved "a right of privacy older than the Bill of Rights – older than our political parties, older than our school

---

147   Huq and Wexler, "*Dobbs* and Our Privacies," 299.

148   Faux, <u>Roe v. Wade: The Untold Story of the Landmark Supreme Court Decision That Made Abortion Legal</u>, 71. Supreme Court decisions dating back to *Meyer v. Nebraska* and *Pierce v. Society of Sisters* dating back to 1925, however, had recognized that there were "unenumerated" but fundamental constitutional right to privacy. Bollinger and Stone, "Opening Dialogue,"xix.

149   Epstein, Segal, Spaeth, and Walker, <u>The Supreme Court Compendium: Data, Decisions and Developments, Second Edition</u>, 336. Marshall was the Chief Justice who initiated the requirement that the Justices of the Supreme Court should only wear simple black robes to symbolize humility. Barrett, <u>Listening to the Law: Reflections on the Court and Constitution</u>, 25, 42.

system."[150] The case became particularly important in the issue of abortion because both *Roe v. Wade* and *Doe v. Bolton* would rely on the "personal liberty" and "right of privacy" which *Griswold* afforded to pregnant women.[151] His judgment would be followed by many of the other Justices on the Supreme Court, and was the primary reason that the Republican nominees for the Supreme Court were conservatives who did not follow the same interpretation of the Constitution. The Warren Court was known from the leadership of Earl Warren, but William O. Douglas deserves to be considered an equal founder of Civil Rights, and the "one man, one vote" principal of United States Justice. As I said, I believe his presence on the Court helped *Roe v. Wade* be approved, and the presence of Blackmun on the *Casey* Court helped that case be approved, so Douglas and Blackmun can both take credit, while Nixon and Burger can be minor characters, in the story of abortion in America.

The problem with the *Dobbs* decision is not only because the definition of life changed to the point of conception, it was because the only reason that conclusion was made was because it was what a Catholic Pope decided when life began. What does this do to all other personal rights of women who are pregnant, and what does it do to the long accepted standard of Separation of Church and State in constitutional interpretation, is a question that must now be discussed and debated on a national level, and I am opening that debate with my proposal of a 28th Amendment to approve the abortion of unwanted nonviable fetuses before the age of 20 weeks gestation. Other Supreme Court cases did hold that there was a right to privacy, such as *Eisenstadt v. Baird, 405 U.S.479 (1972)* which invalidated a state law the kept unmarried individuals from having access to contraceptives stating: "If the right of privacy means anything, it is the right of the individual, married or single, to be free from unwarranted governmental intrusion," further extending the acceptance of a "right of privacy."[152] It is easy to see that liberal Justices like Douglas and

---

150   Weddington, <u>A Question of Choice</u>, 41. In his concurring opinion, Justice Arthur Goldberg (1908-1990) cited former Justice Louis Brandeis' (1856-1941) analysis of the principles underlying the Constitution's guarantees of privacy. Ibid., 42.

151   Greenhouse, <u>Becoming Justice Blackmun: Harry Blackmun's Supreme Court Journey</u>, 78-79.

152   Chemerinsky, "Justice Blackmun Got It Right in *Roe v. Wade*," 69.

Brennan saw the opportunity to expand the constitutional protection, while the conservative Justices appointed by Donald Trump wanted to negate that expansion. Erwin Chemerinsky, Dean and Jesse H. Choper Distinguished Professor of Law at the University of California, Berkeley School of Law, agreed that there is a right to privacy in the Constitution, even though abortion was not mentioned, but that was not going to be the way that the Justices on the *Dobbs* Supreme Court were going to view the Constitution.[153] Although the *Griswold* case itself was very narrow in focus, Douglas' description of the right to privacy opened up all aspects of a woman's pregnancy to a potential constitutional support, and created the two diverse cases on abortion that I am discussing in this book.[154] I maintain that we cannot allow this decision to last, and I am writing this amendment to prove that it is wrong, but if my amendment fails, I hope others will take up the gauntlet and try their best to overturn *Dobbs* on that basis.

Many critics of the *Dobbs* case have worried that the entire issue of a "right to privacy" might not be followed in other future cases, but we will have to see if that holding will ever be tested and denied, as took place in *Dobbs* with abortion. The one thing that is apparent so far is that the right to "informational privacy" has continued to be followed in both the federal and state courts, and the issue of whether the acceptance of this interpretation will expand in the future, as many of the ultra-conservative Justices want it to, will have to await future Supreme Court decisions.[155] I am not suggesting in this book that this same right to privacy should have unlimited expansion to a large number of personal liberties, because the burden of carrying for an unwanted child, and the clear danger that history shows is associated with this necessity in the incidence of infanticide and child abuse is not present in many other cases. But while I concentrate on the primary issue of abortion, I am concerned that many of the recent Supreme Court decisions continue to suggest that they want to change the leniency the Warren Court showed to many other Catholic religious moral determinations that are often not followed by many parts of our population. While I don't have a problem with the Supreme Court deciding appropriate social standards, I continue to demand that the

---

153   Ibid., 68-69.
154   Ziegler, <u>Dollars for Life; The Anti-Abortion Movement and the Fall of the Republican Establishment</u>, 9.
155   Shachar and Zubrzycki, "Informational Privacy After Dobbs," 1-3.

Justices separate their religious beliefs from their interpretation of the Constitution, and rely on fundamental principles that are not religious in nature.

Before concluding this chapter, I want to discuss the opinions of Lewis Powell Jr., one of Nixon's appointees who was, in my opinion, the key vote in the majority opinion that made Burger's vote moot. As I previously noted, there were two dissenters to the *Roe* decision, Justices Byron White, who was selected for the Court by John F. Kennedy, a staunch conservative Justice, and William Rehnquist, who had just been appointed by Nixon, both of whom did not agree that there was constitutional authority for the right of abortion. Lewis F. Powell, Jr., who was approved along with Rehnquist after the first argument in *Roe v. Wade* took place, and was by reputation also a conservative Justice, had voted with the majority, making it three of Nixon's appointees voting to approve the privacy right of abortion. The decision was a true surprise, but the real deciding vote in this case was that of Powell, Jr., who seldom is mentioned in most of the books I have read about the *Roe v. Wade* decision. I'm not sure exactly why he voted the way he did in *Roe v. Wade*, except for the fact that I believe he was swayed by Blackmun's arguments in the meetings the Justices had when they discussed the case, both before and after the reargument. He was appointed by Nixon after he had written "Attack on the American Free Enterprise System," however, which was considered to be a blueprint for conservative business interests to retake America, and became known as the *1971 Powell Memorandum.*[156] This publication is clearly consistent with conservative beliefs, and it indicates to me that Nixon definitely considered Powell Jr. to be a true conservative Justice. He had also been a corporate lawyer and director on the board of Phillip Morris, the tobacco company, from 1964 until he was appointed by Nixon in 1971 to replace Hugo Black, and I have not found much other information on why he voted the way he did, but Microsoft CoPilot reports it may have been because he was a proponent of *stare decisis*, which is an unusual explanation, since there was not a true prior decision to rely on.[157] In my opinion, *stare decisis* had nothing to do with his vote, and Blackmun likely convinced Powell that it was the right decision, even though I am not sure how, or why, he was successful. His vote remains a strange

---

156   "Lewis F. Powell, Jr.," 4.
157   Microsoft CoPilot (4/23/2025). Personal Communication.

footnote never fully explained, but a blessing to all who believe that the abortion of unwanted, nonviable fetuses should be regarded as a benediction, not a crime.

Another future liberal Justice, Ruth Bader Ginsburg (1933-2020), wrote critical comments on the decision, agreeing that the Constitution protected abortion rights, but objecting that "*Roe* went too far, too fast, and that it did so unnecessarily because the normal political processes were working as they should."[158] I'm also not sure why Ginsburg did not realize that the normal political process would never have allowed the decision to stand, but it is possible that she simply wanted to lessen the brunt of the decision by having a liberal dissent, knowing how much of society would react against approval at this time. It is interesting that when President Clinton was thinking of nominating Ginsburg to the Court, he was concerned about her position on abortion because of this incident, but concluded she was for abortion, but on different reasoning than in *Roe*, and it was a form of sex discrimination.[159] If she were on the Court, and passage did not occur because of her opinion, I believe America would not have been able to pass an amendment for abortion at that time because the infanticide rate I am showing in this my second book on the subject, would not have been known and an amendment would have been defeated. For Ginsburg to make this comment when three of Nixon's appointees approved the decision is an embarrassment to her legacy and status as one of only a few Supreme Court female Justices. However, it did not affect her appointment to the Supreme Court by President Bill Clinton in 1993.

The final statistic I want to emphasize in this chapter is the effect that *Roe v. Wade* had on the availability of abortion in the United States, which is evident in the statistics kept by the Centers for Disease Control (CDC) based in Atlanta, Georgia. In 1972, the year before the opinion of the Supreme court was rendered, there were 587,000 legal abortions performed in the United States, while each year thereafter, the number increased every year with 616,000 in 1973, 763,000 in 1974, 855,000 in 1975, 988,000 in 1976, 1,079,000 in 1977, 1,158,000 in 1978, 1,252,000 in 1979, 1,298,000 in 1980, and 1,301,000 in 1981.[160] This dramatic increase clearly showed, in my opinion, that

---

158   Strauss, "Liberal Critics of *Roe*," 4-5.

159   Toobin, <u>The Nine: Inside the Secret World of the Supreme Court</u>, 83.

160   Grimes, "Provision of Abortion Services in the United States," 27.

the ability to finally now have a safe procedure to erase an unwanted pregnancy was the primary reason for the significant increase, and this showed up in the reduction of infanticidal deaths to below 1%, when throughout the history of mankind, levels approaching 10-15% were universally present. The statistical analysis of who obtained abortions showed that 78% of the women were unmarried, and 28% in 1981 were teenagers.[161] Because *Roe v. Wade* allowed them to now get abortions throughout the country, less than 8% of women obtaining an abortion crossed state lines to obtain services in 1981, while in 1972, this occurred in 44%.[162] It is obvious that the ability to get safe abortions when a pregnancy was unwanted for whatever reason showed clear evidence of preventing the rate of infanticide against those children who were otherwise likely in the past to be killed or mistreated. We cannot afford to lose the benefit of legal abortions in our country, and I will now move on to an analysis of *Dobbs v. Jackson Women's Health Organization* in order to determine how that decision wrongly overturned *Roe v. Wade*.

---

161   Ibid., 30.
162   Ibid.

Chapter IV

Dobbs v. Jackson Women's Health Organization

So now we know that Justice Harry Blackmun in *Roe v. Wade*, which was decided on January 22, 1973, concluded that the Constitution guaranteed personal liberties to women, including the right to an abortion, even though the word "abortion" never appeared in the text of the Constitution, and he did this because other Courts had expanded the meaning of the Ninth and Fourteenth Amendments to indicate that this right was intended, and he was convinced that the Founding Fathers knew that life began with the onset of "quickening," which was movement felt by the mother, and that this was why state legislatures made abortion illegal only once quickening occurred, so abortion was therefore acceptable before that took place. Blackmun was also aware that many other countries had recently found abortion to be legal before quickening took place, in particular the British Abortion Act that was passed four years earlier, and he utilized the same time frame for his definition of when viability of the fetus was present. Since our Constitution followed many of the same precepts as English law, the fact that England passed this Act was very supportive of the principle that our Constitution would see the right as one of the intended personal liberties that would extend to all American citizens, and it was an attestment to the fact that common law in both countries accepted quickening as a definition of what it meant to be a person. Being a lawyer, he would have learned that fact about British law, and the eminence of the English jurist William Blackstone, in law school, so although he was not knowledgeable about abortion when he became a Supreme Court Justice, we know he took a crash course at the Mayo Clinic library when *Roe v. Wade* was adjudicated, and I contend that we can accept that the conclusions he came to after the reargument was completed were well-researched, and worthy of being put into a proposal for a Twenty-Eighth Amendment.

Blackmun not only decided that abortion before the fetus was alive and moving was protected under our constitutional law, he then convinced a majority of his colleagues on the Supreme Court after the second reargument took place that these two Amendments were intended to include this right, despite the fact that he also knew, in my opinion, that this interpretation would likely one day be overturned by a future Supreme Court.

The passage of many anti-abortion statutes in America before *Roe v. Wade* was decided made it clear that public opinion at the time was not in favor of passing an amendment to judicially approve abortion, so he decided to approve the *Roe v. Wade* case so that enough procedures could legally be done in order to show the safety and effectiveness of abortion at some point in the future. He believed the benefits would become part of an international acceptance that could provide a permanent benefit to women who did not feel capable of taking care of a child at that point in their life, and his considering it a "right of privacy" followed many of the decisions by the Warren Court, which five members of his present Burger Court at the reargument were part of. I am sure that the final decision came from the discussions he had with all of his fellow Justices who agreed with his decision, and he was then satisfied that he had made the right choice. He was not alive to witness all of the future events which followed, but I am sure that when he did pass away, he considered that his life was a success because of the value he served many women, for many years, by providing them with a choice he truly believed they deserved.

The one flaw with his plan, however, was that Chief Justice Burger had been his close friend all of his life, and did not approve of his decision to find constitutional support for abortion, and this resulted in their friendship rapidly evaporating away. When Blackmun initially spoke to various audiences after Burger was appointed Chief Justice, he showed his ignorance of Burger's conservatism by telling them that: "The Burger Court under its 'active, energetic new chief' might not prove so different from the Court under Earl Warren," adding later, that "Mr. Burger's entire background, believe it or not, is in the liberal tradition and not in the conservative tradition."[1] This assessment turned out not to be true, however, and in all of my research I never heard him talk about how much that change in their relationship affected him, but I am sure that he was bothered greatly by how difficult that made their remaining years together on the same Supreme Court. The American lawyer and legal analyst for CNN, Jeffrey Toobin, told how the Burger Court, in many ways, was even more liberal than the Warren Court, for it "approved the use of school busing, expanded free speech well beyond *Sullivan*, forced Nixon himself to turn over

---

1   Greenhouse, Becoming Justice Blackmun: Harry Blackmun's Supreme Court Journey, 43-44.

the Watergate tapes, and even, for a time, ended all executions in the United States."[2] The Burger Court may have done all this, but I do not believe it was because Burger himself was not a conservative Justice, and did not try his best to guide the Court in that direction. The problem was that he was overwhelmed and inept in his position of Chief Justice, and was wrong to pick the *Roe v. Wade* to be tried before the other two Justices were appointed, so that he never had the opportunity to discuss with them the decision to have Blackmun write the opinion for the Court. He was not being a liberal Justice when he made these decisions, he just never expected to be remembered as the Chief Justice whose Court approved the constitutional right for abortion, but that was to be his fate, and he had to live with it as best he could.

I say this about the Burger Court because even after Burger retired, and William Rehnquist, the only Nixon appointee to dissent in *Roe v. Wade*, became the new Chief Justice of that same Court, it still did not overturn the verdict when it had a chance in the *Casey* decision, as I will discuss shortly. It would take the appointment of six Catholic Justices by Republican Presidents for the *Dobbs* Court to finally overturn the case almost fifty years later. Burger's Court had only one Catholic Justice, William J. Brennan Jr., who was appointed by Dwight D. Eisenhower, and he wasn't even a conservative Justice; and the *Casey* Court had four Catholic Justices, Antonin Scalia, Anthony Kennedy, Clarence Thomas, and Byron White, and still did not overturn *Roe v. Wade*, but four does not make a majority on a nine-Justice Supreme Court, but six does, and the legality of *Roe v. Wade* remained the law of the land for almost 50 more years. Richard Nixon had made no dent in the continuation of the liberal Warren Court with his appointees, and it was not until Ronald Reagan was elected the fortieth President in 1981, that the transition of the Republican Party into the American conservative political movement truly began. The change was put on hold during the Bush presidencies, but then shifted into high gear with the inauguration of Donald Trump as the forty-fifth President on January 20, 2017, so that a true conservative Supreme Court could be formed, as I will detail shortly.

When *Dobbs v. Jackson Women's Health Organization* was initially granted *certioari* to be heard by the Supreme Court on May 17, 2021,

---

2   Toobin, The Nine: Inside the Secret World of the Supreme Court, 14.

forty-six years and one-hundred-fifteen days after the *Roe v. Wade* decision was given, the Court was now finally staunchly conservative, and on June 24, 2022, four-hundred-three days later, Associate Justice Samuel Anthony Alito Jr. finally overturned *Roe v. Wade*, claiming that abortion was never intended to be seen as a personal right in the Constitution, and therefore would need an amendment to provide that interpretation, just like women needed an amendment to get the right to vote. In this chapter, I am going to carefully analyze the *Dobbs* case, and point out the errors which I have found in Alito's decision, so that if anyone wants to appeal the judgement, and try to overturn it, they are free to do so. Because Donald Trump is in office for the next four years, however, I do not think that the composition of the Supreme Court will act in that manner, and so I am publishing this book with an amendment proposal that I believe will be approved by at least 3/4 of the states, so that we need not worry about what the *Dobbs* decision determined, and why it was wrong. My job now is to assure that Blackmun's legacy will continue to be a success by offering an amendment that I believe will pass because of his efforts to show that his legalization of abortion has proved that abortion is safe, and should be done if a pregnancy is unwanted, and the fetus is nonviable. I believe voters across the country can now understand why the requirement to pass an amendment approving abortion of nonviable, unwanted fetuses is as important as eliminating slavery, and giving women the right to vote, and passage of the amendment will also end judicial interference in the issue of the legality of abortion forever, and maintain our government as a Democracy, and not a Theocracy, as President Trump, and the present U.S. Supreme Court, want it to be.

Time is moving quickly, however, and since it is now more than fifty-two-years since *Roe v. Wade* was passed, and more than three-years since the Supreme Court finally decided to take the case that was originally titled as *Dobbs, State Health Officer of the Mississippi Department of Health, et al. v. Jackson Women's Health Organization et al.*, and used it as the vehicle to declare *Roe v. Wade* unconstitutional, I need to move quickly. The explosion of negative sentiment over the decision to overturn *Roe v. Wade* was intense, but "when the shit hit the fans," as I used to say when I was growing up in Skokie, Illinois, after *Dobbs* was announced and people across the country were shocked by abortion clinics being closed down, the country was basically told that abortion was no longer legal, and women in the United States were now in a major crisis. Women who found they had an unwanted pregnancy suddenly saw their one escape hatch closed, and panic began to spread throughout the country, as this was not a state-by-state issue, but a national ban that left no states immune. Before *Roe v. Wade*, many states refused abortions, but women could still travel to find a state to obtain an abortion. It may be far, and more expensive, but women still had an option to find a safe abortion. Now, there was no where to go. The response mimicked that seen among Republicans after the *Roe v. Wade* news hit the same fans, but the calls for Civil War were less prominent by the Democrats, who frantically searched for what to do in the immediate future. Many states issued immediate bans against abortion, with 13 states already having "trigger bans" in place that would kick in if *Roe* was overturned. Five states had abortion bans on hold while the *Roe* ruling was valid; twelve states had six-week bans in place; and four states already had constitutions stating there is no right to an abortion, all of which went into law once *Roe v. Wade* was overturned.[3]

To make matters worse, the sudden change left Americans totally unprepared for how to deal with the changes that had been thrust upon a country that had depended on easy access to abortion for now over 50 years. For those of you who don't like statistics, deal with this reality: in the past 50 years, about 65.5 million abortions were formed in the United States, and in the rest of the world there were 73 million abortions every years, giving a total of 3.65 *billion* abortions worldwide. Let me repeat that figure slowly: 3.65 B-I-L-L-I-O-N. Yes, I understand that is an appalling number, but whether you like it or not, or you think it is murder or not, what do you think is going to happen if we suddenly make abortions illegal, and force women to give birth to every one of those babies they do not want? I recently republished by book, *Hardness of Life/Hardness of Heart: The Stain of Human Infanticide*, which showed how 10-15% of unwanted pregnancies have resulted in infanticide or child abuse worldwide since mankind first evolved, and if my amendment is not approved, these figures will once again dominate our crime statistics. If that doesn't scare you, don't bother to finish reading this book, because

---

3   Ibid., 23.

you must be a robot without human emotions. The fact is that we need to figure out what we are going to do about this right now, for if my amendment doesn't pass, these numbers will begin to rise quickly, like it or not, and that is a condition that we cannot allow to take place.

The shock of abortion once again being considered a crime has been an intense trauma that has angered and frightened many Americans, and as I write as fast as I can to get this book published, there are unwanted children being born into a life that I fear will be filled with child abuse, and early death, making it critical that I finish this book STAT. For those of you who do not understand medical lingo, that means NOW! Once again, family gatherings across the country are divided because of harsh debates such as those that took place during the 2024 Presidential Election, but despite the rhetoric which has filled the airways and newspaper pages from both Republican Pro-Lifers, who proclaim abortion to be infanticidal murder, and Democratic Pro-Choice advocates, who charge that Republicans are against the civil rights of women, and people of color, nothing beneficial will take place unless my amendment proposal is passed, so I press on with that goal in mind. Demonstrations across the country have once again begun to grow violent, and I am also concerned that the damage being done to our reputation across the world from this enmity is dangerous to the Democracy which our nation has stood for from its inception when the Constitution was first written. Democrats have been so angered and shocked by the *Dobbs* verdict, that Merrick Garland, the then U.S. Attorney General under President Joe Biden, issued a statement strongly disagreeing with the Supreme Court's decision once it was published by stating that: "This decision deals a devastating blow to reproductive freedom in the United States. . . [and] The Justice Department will use every tool at our disposal to protect reproductive freedom."[4]

Of course, there was nothing Garland could do to achieve that goal, and the outrage over what is now the loss of the ability to obtain abortion in many states across the country is once again rising among Democratic supporters. The intensity of the debate has been very great, and the desire to get more information so enormous, that when I began to research the number of books that have been written about these two cases on my public library's website, I was astounded to

---

4   Mooney, Overturned: The Constitutional Right to Abortion, 5.

find more than 3,000 titles to review. This demand for an explanation of why the two Supreme Court decisions was so disparate is evidence to me that the lack of knowledge about the issue at hand is the real cause of the problem, and not whether abortion is immoral or not. The real problem is that we are allowing religious claims to overshadow whether there is a Constitutional right for a woman to have an abortion of a child she does not want before it is viable, or not. The debate taking place, and discussed in all of the books I have read, does not ever deal with the vital issue of viability, however, and whether the claim that abortion is murder or not is truly valid. More importantly, we must clarify whether our focus should be only on the question of whether it is a constitutional issue alone, with a focus on what the common law says, or whether it matters what the Catholic Pope says about when life begins. We are in the courtroom of the Supreme Court here, not a synod or a philosophy congress, and yet we are allowing our Supreme Court to change our common law without any complaint that their action is unconstitutional. How? Why? I'll tell you why at the conclusion to this book, but let me first describe how we got here, and how we can correct the problem permanently by passing an amendment that will carry the full authority of the Constitution – an amendment.

I have written this book to explain why we must pass an amendment to allow abortion to take place because the *Dobbs* decision is purely an attempt to put religion above the Constitution because of the claim made by a Pope that life begins at conception, and not at quickening, which has been the essence of common law not only in America, but across the world since civilization first began. Our debate in this country is out of control, and I will show in this book that both prior Supreme Court decisions that approved unwanted, nonviable abortions showed why the issue cannot be left to a judicial decision, but rather to the people of America, who must decide whether we will continue to follow Constitutional Law, or allow the view of one religion to determine what our law should be. I will argue that women should have the right to choose when they believe they are capable of properly raising a child, as long as the abortion is done before the fetus is viable, and unable to survive outside her womb, and that abortion of a nonviable fetus is feticide, and not murder, and that is a right that is protected by our Constitution. I accept that the Catholic Pope has the right to decide what the Catholic position is on that subject, and every Catholic has the right to either follow that decision or not, but that has nothing to do about how America decides what is the law in our country, and how the Supreme Court is supposed to function according to our Constitution. In America, our Constitution says that we must consider what all religions have to say on the laws in our country, and that means that we must decide the justness of our laws by the Separation of Church and State, which means that we do not favor the views of any one religion, no matter how popular that religion may be. Our Founding Fathers declared that all citizens had inalienable rights under the law, and the common law when that document was written said that every person under the Constitution became that way when the fetus the pregnant mother was carrying showed signs of "quickening," or that she could feel in her abdomen.

Mary Ziegler, who I have already referenced, has written many books on the effect of *Roe v. Wade* on the abortion debate in America, and has pointed to the fact that James Bopp Jr., a passionate conservative lawyer who was the deputy attorney general in Indiana from 1973-1975, switched his interests after *Roe v. Wade* was passed, and became the general counsel for the National Right to Life Committee (NRLC), which was the largest national anti-abortion group in America. He was instrumental in mobilizing networks that became adept at influencing judicial nominees, and who pledged their support to pass a constitutional amendment to ban the procedure.[5] They soon realized, however, that they could never pass such an amendment, so they switched their focus to changing the composition of the Supreme Court, which finally came to fruition with the election of Donald Trump. Bopp's efforts led to reform legislation that allowed great sums of money to be donated to politicians who backed anti-abortion legislation, and this tactic was particularly prosperous, helping to elect Donald Trump to both of his successful campaigns to become President of the United States. The amount of money being donated, and spent, to try and stop abortion from being legalized, is truly, in my opinion, a tragedy in itself because instead of that money going to help prevent child abuse, and stop the purposeful infanticide of unwanted children, we have coffers supporting anti-abortion access in our country, and I will do my best to end this injustice. "Power to the People" was a political

---

5   Ziegler, Dollars for Life; The Anti-Abortion Movement and the Fall of the Republican Establishment, xii.

slogan in the United States in the 1960s, and was used by a vast array of voices, including Civil Rights activists, the Black Panther Party, Anti-Vietnam War protesters, and various counterculture and youth movements, and while I was a passive participant back then, I am today an avid proponent to demanding that we remain a Democracy, and not let a President and a Supreme Court with a supermajority of orthodox Catholic Justices turn our country into a Theocracy. The Constitution under common law allowed a woman to choose to end a nonviable pregnancy before quickening appears, because that is not murder, as prohibited by the Ten Commandments, but is feticide, which is a normal process of pregnancy, and naturally ends about 30% of all pregnancies which take place by a process known as a miscarriage.

What nobody has pointed out in this entire debate over abortion is how the make-up of the present Supreme Court has been masqueraded as becoming a more conservative majority of Justices under the guidance of a policy of Originalism, which I contend is intended to hide the fact that devout Catholics were chosen purely because they accepted the teaching of the Pope that life begins at conception. They decided to make a common law to that effect by a Supreme Court decision, and if that isn't fraud, then I don't know what is. Robert Bork, who first proposed the concept of Originalism, was born into a German Lutheran heritage, and wrote his book on the subject in 1990, suggesting that the Constitution should be read as it was intended when it was written, but not fully accepting the amendments at the time they were written. He later converted to Catholicism in 2003, and that move is what showed me the true reason *Roe v. Wade* was overturned. When he was nominated to be a Supreme Court Judge in 1987 by President Ronald Reagan, he claimed he was an atheist, but after he met Father C. John McCloskey III (1953-2023), a Catholic priest of the Prelature of Opus Dei, and a former director of Catholic Information Center (CIC) in the Catholic Archdiocese of Washington, D.C., he converted to Catholicism, and he then became popular with Republican conservative politicians who were all engrossed in the Right-wing Christian belief that life began at conception, and so all abortions were equivalent to murder. A decision was made that the best way to ban abortion was to promote this claim that life began at conception, and so every pregnancy was a "person" with rights equal to that of the mother, and abortion would be considered to be murder, and not accepted by the U.S. Constitution. How do you set about to do that? You appoint Justices to the Supreme Court that are practicing Catholics who accept the modern Papal ruling that life begins at conception, and assure that abortion under the ruling of *Roe v. Wade* will be overturned because they will in their hearts have accepted that the Pope's decision is equal to the common law, and agree that every abortion can now be seen as murder.

The problem here is that common law, as defined by William Blackstone, the English jurist who was recognized as an expert in the development of English Law, is "quickening," and that is what has been the law in America as well for our entire history. Attempting to claim that life begins at conception is changing the common law in our country, and making a new law, which cannot be done by a judicial ruling, but must take place by either an amendment, or a legislative action by the Congress and Senate of the Legislative branch of the government. Justice Alito knew this, for in his opinion to overturn *Roe v. Wade* he stated that such an action would require that an amendment be passed to approve abortion, because the word "abortion" was not mentioned in the Constitution. He added to his legal opinion, however, that life began at conception, and not quickening, relying on a prior Papal edict, which our Constitution does not allow. Perhaps because our Constitution does allow free speech, he thinks he can say anything he wants, but that does not include his speech as a Justice, and it is therefore null and void, in legalese.

State legislatures are allowed to make anti-abortion laws as long as they are not against federal laws, as interpreted by the Supreme Court. This allowed many of the states to pass what became known as Targeted Regulation of Abortion Providers, or TRAP laws, which imposed legal requirements such as higher licensing fees and annoying minutia which made it more difficult, and expensive, for health care professionals and the facilities they worked in. They were able to do this because the U.S. Constitution gave them that right, and as a result, between 2011 and 2017, half of the abortion clinics in Arizona, Kentucky, Ohio and Texas were forced to close down.[6] But they cannot make laws that go against the accepted common law of the United States, and the two Supreme Courts that *Dobbs* overturned

---

6   Becker, You Must Stand Up: The Fight for Abortion Rights in Post-*Dobbs* America,9.

both said that the common law was that life began at "quickening," and Alito could not, on his own, claim that the common law was wrong without requiring that either the federal legislature make a new law or an amendment be passed. The decision that Justice Alito made to require an amendment was appropriate, but he could not by himself make a new law.

As I have said repetitively in this book, the animosity between the two political sides of our government has reached dangerous levels for after *Roe v. Wade* was decided, Republicans set about on a course to declare abortions unconstitutional. Although the response to *Dobbs* has not been as intense, it is because people do not yet realize what the implication of the ruling was, and those that do, do not generally have the funds to put their view across. This issue was not about abortion alone, but rather about the authority of the Supreme Court to ignore the First Amendment requirement that there be separation of Church and State. The *Dobbs* Court, with seven Catholic Justices, six of whom appointed by Republicans, and four of whom recently voted against separation of Church and State requirements in other Supreme Court cases, decided to accept a case where a Mississippi Law which allowed abortions at 15-weeks gestation was found to be constitutional, and in their decision changed the rule of *Roe v. Wade* that life began at quickening to life begins at conception. They did this without providing any justification for that ruling, and no one, from my research, has brought that up as a major fault. It is vital that I try to get back to reality on what the real issue entails in this book, and stop the progressive rise to levels of a holy religious war. We are a Democracy, not a Theocracy, and if you want to change the definition of a "person," then you must do it by an amendment as well, because our common law has already defined it as "quickening," and two prior Supreme Courts have accepted that definition.

Donald Trump had proclaimed in his first presidential campaign in 2016, in a debate with Hillary Clinton in October, that he would put Pro-Life justices on the Supreme Court if elected, and send the issue back to the states.[7] The gauntlet was thrown down because

---

7   Biskupic, Nine Black Robes: Inside the Supreme Court's Drive to the Right and Its Historic Consequences, 76-77. He had said in a debate with Hillary Clinton that if he became president, the overturning of *Roe* "would happen automatically." Waldman, The Supermajority: How the Supreme Court Divided America, 131.

Clinton had openly proclaimed that she was for the *Roe v. Wade* decision, and she essentially lost the election in large part because of her Pro-Choice stance, which failed to get Republican women voters to back her in large numbers. After Trump won the election, he eventually appointed three conservative Justices to the Supreme Court, including Neil Gorsuch in 2017 to replace Antonin Scalia; Brett Kavanaugh in 2018 to replace Anthony Kennedy, who retired; and Amy Coney Barrett in 2020 to replace Ruth Bader Ginsburg (1933-2020), turning the Supreme Court into a true ultra-conservative Court that had six Catholic Justices, as he had promised he would do during the presidential campaign. All three of the Justices he appointed were raised Catholic, although Gorsuch later became Episcopalian, but remained deeply rooted in Originalism. Barrett at the time was a Federal Court of Appeals Judge appointed by Trump in 2017, and she had clerked for Justice Scalia after graduating Notre Dame Law School, and worked there as a law professor, so she was a popular candidate for the Supreme Court.[8] She is a deeply committed Catholic, and part of a very conservative group called the *People of Praise,* as well as self-proclaimed Originalist.[9] It was she who recused herself from the Supreme Court vote on the First Amendment in the recent case of *St. Isidorfe of Seville Catholic Virtual School v. Drummond, 605 U.S. . . . (2025)* because of her continuing association with Notre Dame Law School, and I applaud her for that action, but from what I read in the *Dobbs* verdict, she failed to recuse herself from the verdict, despite knowing that life does not begin at conception anywhere in any legal or medical text, but only in the holding of the Catholic Pope. This is clearly not Separation of Church and State, and she, as well as the other Popes, should have recused themselves by voting in this manner, and I contend that they will continue their campaign to alter our valid method of interpreting the Constitution until they can be forced to modify their views based upon the oath they took when they accepted their Supreme Court appointments. I will shortly explain why I believe this is supported by our Constitution.

This rearrangement of the Supreme Court included having seven of the nine Justices being devout Catholics, but one, Sonia Sotomayor,

---

8   Chemerinsky, <u>Worse Than Nothing: The Dangerous Fallacy of Originalism</u>, 7.

9   Ibid., 8.

who did not let her religious beliefs override her pledge to follow the Constitution as the basis for Justice. The other Catholic Justices are disregarding the principle of separation of Church and State, which has been followed by all who hold the Constitution to be the Law of the land, and this is the sole reason for the *Dobbs* decision, because of 6-3 conservative supermajority to approve the Mississippi law, with all six conservative Justices appointed by Republicans voting to approve, and three liberal justices appointed by Democrats, including, Sonia Sotomayor appointed by Obama in 2009, Elena Kagan appointed by Obama in 2012, and Ketanji Brown Jackson appointed by Joe Biden in 2022. The Court then decided by what is said to be a 6-3 decision to overturn *Roe v. Wade,* with Chief Justice John Roberts not voting yes on the question of overturning *Roe v. Wade*, so there was evidence that some chance for an overturn of that issue could still take place in the future, but that possibility was lessened when Trump won the reelection in 2024.[10] I am still not sure why the decision was listed as a 6-3 majority, since Roberts was against overturning *Roe v. Wade*, which would make me believe the vote should be 5-4, but I don't write the rules, so I will leave the explanation up to others. What is clear, however, is that the decision was based on what the Catholic Pope wrote, and not what our Founding Fathers believed, and certainly not in what two prior Supreme Courts said was the common law in our country.

When the *Dobbs* case was initially accepted for review, everyone knew what the eventual outcome would be, because it had become evident that the Republican conservative Justices were following the legal theory of Originalism, which, as I said, was first proposed by Justice Robert Bork in 1971 to always interpret the Constitution in a way that reflects the times when it was written, and it was obvious that the word "abortion" never appeared.[11] Bork served as a judge on the U.S. Court of Appeals for the District of Columbia from 1982-1988, and was nominated for the Supreme Court by Ronald Reagan in 1987, but was rejected by the Senate 58-42, and Anthony Kennedy was then approved.[12] Bork's influence on the Republican Party changed the

---

10 Mooney, <u>Overturned: The Constitutional Right to Abortion</u>, 21; "Dobbs v. Jackson
Women's Health Organization (2022)," 1.

11 "Originalism," 1.

12 Prager, <u>The Family Roe: An American Story</u>, 157.

entire future status of the Supreme Court, because his conservative extremism caused hundreds of left-leaning organizations to form a Block Bork Coalition, and the National Abortion Rights Action league vowed to spend $1 million to defeat him. This was primarily because of his assailing the Civil Rights Act which promoted the civil rights of Black Americans, and was supported by Democrats from the South that were elected with black support.[13] That attempt was a success, but their ultimate goal was a failure, for money poured into Republican coffers to elect conservative Justices who would put anti-abortion projects relentlessly on both the Federal District Courts and the Supreme Court. Both sides had vowed to continue their battle with renewed aggression, but because it was clear that Trump was going to support the overturning of *Roe v. Wade*, their focus shifted to being sure the Court was comprised of Justices who supported Originalism, or, in my opinion, Catholicism. Very few people who are not Catholic actually belief that life begins at conception, and even the country of Italy approved abortion of nonviable fetuses, although the Vatican, which is a sovereign-state within Italy, does not.

According to the *Encyclopedia Britannica*, the case of *Dobbs v. Jackson Women's Health Organization* overturned "two historic Supreme Court rulings, *Roe v. Wade* (1973) and *Planned Parenthood of Southeastern Pennsylvania v. Casey, 505 U.S. 833* (1992), which had respectively established, and then affirmed, a constitutional right to obtain an abortion."[14] I concur with their description, and believe that the *Casey* case has not gotten enough attention because its importance is often overlooked as it was also a true landmark decision and came at a time when the fury directed at the *Roe v. Wade* decision was so great that no one believed the opinion in *Casey* would agree that there was constitutional support for the approval of abortion. Everyone at the time assumed that *Roe v. Wade* would be overturned, and it was a shock when it wasn't, leaving abortion to remain legal for another thirty years, which was vital for it proved how safe abortion was, and

---

13 Toobin, The Nine: Inside the Secret World of the Supreme Court, 23.

14 "Dobbs v. Jackson Women's Health Organization," 1. Melissa Murray, Frederick I. And Grace Stokes Professor of Law at NYU School of Law, and Katherine Shaw, Professor of Law at Cardozo School of Law, refer to the *Roe v. Wade* and *Casey* cases as "the twin pillars of the Court's abortion jurisprudence," which is an appropriate accolade, in my opinion. Murray and Shaw, *"Dobb's* Democratic Deficits," 158.

confirmed that the 10-15% level of infanticide of unwanted children fell to levels below 1% because of the abortions that were able to be safely done. I am going to discuss that case in detail now because it confirms the value of legal abortion, and why my amendment proposal should be passed to assure that it can become a legal option for unwanted pregnancies. One important finding in *Casey* that is often overlooked is that it also held that a woman's right to terminate a pregnancy follows from her "'dignity and autonomy,' which are 'central to the liberty protected by the Fourteenth Amendment,'" a guaranteed right that supports the importance of maintaining all of the rights that are contained in the Ninth and Fourteenth Amendments, and a reason why *Dobbs* overturned *Casey*, as well as *Roe v. Wade*.[15]

The Republican reaction against *Roe v. Wade* had raged for almost fifty years trying to show the American public that abortion was wrong, and that *Roe v. Wade* needed to be overturned. The *Casey* Court, when it met, was composed of five Justices appointed by Republican Presidents, and the Chief Justice was now William Rehnquist, who had voted to dissent in the *Roe v. Wade* case, which is why I think it was vital that Blackmun was still on the bench when the panel made its decision. During the arguments in *Casey*, I believe it was his presence on the bench at the trial that made all the difference for how the other Judges voted, because the new Republican Justices on the *Dobbs* Court were Antonin Scalia, Anthony Kennedy, and Clarence Thomas, all known to be conservative, Originalists, and Catholics, and it was widely assumed that *Roe v. Wade* would be overturned because of their presence. It is truly remarkable that *Roe v. Wade* was not overturned with those new appointees joining with Rehnquist, and I will show how Antony Kennedy's decision to not dissent was the reason for the final opinion, and how his retirement in 2018, and replacement by Justice Brett Kavanaugh, was the reason for the different verdicts.

I do not think that the arguments for maintaining *stare decisis* in *Casey* would have been effective if Blackmun had not been sitting at the table next to them at the time the arguments, and discussions took place. Six days after Thomas was confirmed as a Justice, the United States Court of Appeals for the Third Circuit upheld the strict Pennsylvania law, rejecting only the part that said married women must get permission from their husbands, and the one Justice on the

---

15 "Amicus Curiae *Brief in* Whole Woman's Health," 174-175.

Court of Appeals who which did not reject that part was Samuel A. Alito Jr., who had just been appointed to the bench a year earlier, and this was his first major opinion, written to show that he was against abortion if his name came up for Supreme Court Justice consideration in the future.[16] As it turned out, incredibly enough, not only would his name come up, but he would wind up being the Justice who wrote the opinion in *Dobbs*. His voice was heard loud and clear at the trial, and I contend that it was the primary reason he was appointed by President George W. Bush (1924-2018) on 10/31/2005 to replace Sandra Day O'Connor on the Supreme Court. It was O'Connor, Kennedy, and Sauter who wrote the majority opinion, and who decided to vote for *stare decisis*, and their fellow Justices, Blackmun and Stevens, that kept *Roe v. Wade* as the law of the land, and provided the extra time needed to prove the value of abortion in America Law. We are seeing now, in the intricate modulations of the *Dobbs* case, the same unusual occurrences we saw in *Roe v. Wade*, and I once again must bring up the incredible circumstances which added to this incredible saga of judicial mystique.

When the *Casey* Court surprisingly did uphold the verdict, it invigorated the entire Pro-Choice community, but the political division was already so intense that the Pro-Lifers didn't flinch, and continued their vigorous campaign to eventually overturn the verdict of *Roe v. Wade* in the *Dobbs* case. The Supreme Court agreed to hear the *Casey* case after the appointment of Clarence Thomas was confirmed, making the conservative majority secure, and Republican think-tanks then met to strategize about how to argue the case, focusing on ways to overturn *Roe v. Wade*, an idea that had frightened the George H. W. Bush administration, who was then President, and who had publicly supported Pro-Life policies, but was supported by a large number of woman voters, and this worried him because he felt he needed their backing when he ran against Bill Clinton for a second term, a concern which proved to be true.[17] Bush tried to finesse the demands of the far right-wing of the Party, and swore fealty to conservative orthodoxies, but he chose a man for the Supreme Court, David H. Souter (1939-2025), who resembled his own temperament. As it turns out, this was

---

16 Toobin, <u>The Nine: Inside the Secret World of the Supreme Court</u>, 44-45.
17 Ziegler, <u>Dollars for Life; The Anti-Abortion Movement and the Fall of the Republican Establishment</u>, 81.

the primary reason *Casey* failed to overturn *Roe v. Wade*, because after Souter was nominated in 1990, he would participate in voting with the majority in *Casey*, and so Bush's decision was vital in not nominating a Catholic Justice who could have voted with the others to overturn *Roe v. Wade* at this earlier date. His Attorney General back then was Richard Thornburgh (1932-2020), who as Governor of Pennsylvania was the defendant in the 1986 abortion case.[18] Once again, we have incredible instances of serendipity that allowed this verdict to happen, and although the answer is now apparent, the case at the time was so crucial in allowing abortion statistics to continue in order to prove the future value of the procedure for another 36-years, that I want to discuss it in more detail before moving on to the *Dobbs* decision.

The primary reason that the *Casey* Court decided the way they did, in my opinion, was because only four of the Justices were Catholic, unlike the six that were on the *Dobbs* Court, and only three of the four voted to dissent, while on the *Dobbs* Court, six of the Catholic Justices who were indoctrinated by President Trump all voted to overturn *Roe v. Wade* except the Chief Justice, John G. Roberts Jr., who nevertheless still agreed with the majority opinion. Trump had indoctrinated the Justices he appointed, as well as the others on the Court, on the importance of repealing *Roe v. Wade*, and this was why when Pope Francis died on April 21, 2025, and a picture of Trump dressed as a Pope appeared on Truth Social, the social media post Trump launched in February 2022, scoffed at those saying it was in poor taste. I state with full conviction, that Donald Trump planned for the Supreme Court to become a religious tribunal that follows the law of the Pope, rather than the Constitution of the United States, and something must be done to require Justices to follow the oath they swore to when they accepted their Supreme Court appointment. How can this be done? Very simple, and I will detail it later in this chapter. All Supreme Court Justices take an oath to uphold the Constitution when they are sworn into office, and if they feel they cannot in a particular case, they can recuse themselves, as Rehnquist did when he had to sit on the Court that ruled against Richard Nixon in the Watergate trial, and he felt he was unable to disregard their friendship. You have to rely on the honesty of Supreme Court Justices, even though I may disagree with their loyalty to the Constitution alone. I still respect and admire

---

18 Toobin, The Nine: Inside the Secret World of the Supreme Court, 24.

them for their training, and the job they are appointed to do, and so while I will point out where I believe they have failed, I trust that their integrity will allow them to respond in a truthful manner once they are made aware of the mistakes they made.

The solution should be simple in future abortion cases – if they cannot follow the common law definition of when life begins, and believe they must follow what the Pope declares, they cannot vote in a case involving abortion. Pure and simple, and all based on trust that Supreme Court Justices will follow the principle of Separation of Church and State in all legal matters. I will carefully watch future cases to see if my trust is warranted, and I hope I am not disappointed, but I am sure if I am not there to voice my disapproval, others will take up the complaint. I understand that there will be variance on how the modern interpretation of Separation of Church and State may be seen, but how the Pope interprets when life begins is not a legal dictum that is accepted as truth.

William Rehnquist, Antonin Scalia, Anthony Kennedy, and Clarence Thomas were the four Catholic Justices on the *Casey* case, and the dissenters in the case were Rehnquist, White, Scalia and Thomas, with Kennedy helping to write the decision of the majority instead of adding his name to the dissent. The Majority who wrote the opinion therefore included Rehnquist along with Sandra Day O'Connor (1930-2023), who was raised in the Episcopal Church, and was a centrist voice on church-state issues, and who also was Rehnquist's law school classmate at Stanford, and the majority leader of the Arizona State Senate, as well as David Souter, along with Harry Blackmun and John Paul Stevens (1920-2019, and their primary reason was the claim that *stare decisis* supported the reaffirmation.[19] The word "conception" appears in the *Casey* opinion eight times, but never as the point of time when life begins as it does in the *Dobbs* case. I do not know if it ever came up in their private discussions, but my best guess is that did not once Kennedy was chose to take part in the majority opinion. The majority opinion noted the importance of our Constitution by declaring that: "Our Constitution is a covenant running from the first generation of Americans to us and then to future generations," and I find that this is something that the *Dobbs* Court

---

19 "Planned Parenthood of Southeastern Pa. v. Casey, 505 U.S. 833 (1992)," 835.

failed to do, because they chose to follow the teaching of the Pope, rather than the founding Fathers of our Constitution.[20] The lesson learned in this important opinion is that if you follow the Constitution, you will be a Democracy; if you follow the Pope, you are a Theocracy, as occurs in Islamic countries, but not in the United States of America, where all religions are equal under the law.

The decision in *Casey* was one of the most widely anticipated ruling in decades, but their reason for upholding the *Roe v. Wade* opinion was primarily that women had a Constitutional right to choose an abortion based on the Due Process Clause of the Fourteenth Amendment, rather than *Roe's* strict scrutiny standard of review, which was overruled.[21] This action enabled abortion to remain legal for many more years to come, and became known as an "undue burden" standard in its approval of the case. *Dobbs* found that the entire opinion was erroneous, however, because they negated the common law of quickening, which is why they overturned *Casey* as well, and confirmed the state's power to restrict abortions because of a legitimate interest in protecting the life of the fetus from conception.[22] The extra time it took was essential for being able to prove the effectiveness of abortion, so we can now have a good chance of passing the Amendment I propose because of the valuable data collected over the years.

Justice Antonin Scalia, who was a strong advocate of Originalism, in his dissent to the majority approval in *Casey* argued that: (1) the Constitution says absolutely nothing about abortion, and (2) the longstanding traditions of American society have permitted it to be legally proscribed, failing to mention that it was not just a tradition, but was common law, as well, accepted by both prior Supreme Courts.[23] The decision showed that there was still a deep division in the Justices appointed by a Republican President on the principle of Originalism, but by the time the *Dobbs* case came up, the Court was strengthened by Trump appointees, and they would wind up overturning *Casey,* as well as *Roe v. Wade,* a sign that no matter who was going to be President for quite a while, the Supreme Court was going to be a staunchly conservative Republican ally, even though Trump had lost

20 Ibid., 902.
21 "Planned Parenthood v. Casey," 1.
22 "Planned Parenthood of Southeastern Pa. v. Casey, 505 U.S. 833 (1992)," 902.
23 Mitchell, "Why was *Roe v. Wade Wrong?*" 52.

his reelection bid to Biden, and was not President when the *Dobbs* opinion was made. An interesting sidelight to the *Casey* case is that Alito had been appointed to the U.S. Court of Appeals for the Third Circuit by President George H. W. Bush, and was on that District Court when it heard the *Casey* before it was appealed to the Supreme Court. He had disagreed with his colleagues in that case, making it clear that he believed a woman should have to inform her husband before seeking an abortion, and this was clearly the reason he would have been anxious to overturn both *Roe* and *Casey* in his decision on *Dobbs*.[24] Like Alito, Scalia was Italian, Catholic, and educated at a Catholic High School, and so it is not surprising that he was able to accomplish his goal, but it is incredible how entwined the judicial system, and the Presidents who appointed the Judges, became in this entire sequence of cases, and it will be interesting to see if Hollywood ever decides to place the matter before the public in a movie, although I'm not sure it will be as good without Charlton Heston (1923-2008) playing either Blackmun or Alito.

Jeffrey Toobin has suggested that the decision in *Casey* came about because the lead attorney Kathryn Kolbert presented the case in her opening argument as simply being an issue of *stare decisis*, and spent her entire opening statement on that one issue alone, even when she was asked by Sandra O'Connor, who is an Episcopalian, whether there was any other issue she would challenge.[25] I think his opinion is on target here, and took advantage of the fact that Blackmun was still in the room as a Justice when the trial took place. It was this bold move by Kolbert that led to the eventual decision. She correctly saw that Blackmun being on the panel was a strong impetus to argue for *stare decisis*, and it appears that this worked on both O'Connor and Anthony Kennedy, as well as Souter, who has been suggested as the prime mover for using that argument. The successful 5-4 decision to not overturn *Roe v. Wade* meant that the "end justifies the means," as so appropriately said by the Florentine philosopher Niccolò Machiavelli (1469-1527), and the reason I believe it was successful is that Chief Justice Rehnquist left most Mondays and Wednesdays open as argument days when they were in session, and the Justices

---

24 Becker, <u>You Must Stand Up: The Fight for Abortion Rights in Post-*Dobbs* America</u>,31.

25 Toobin, <u>The Nine: Inside the Secret World of the Supreme Court</u>, 56.

had lunch together on those days, with conferences every Friday, so that Blackmun's presence was evident for all to see.[26] The Friday conference was always a very important part of deciding a Supreme Court case, and the Justices spoke and voted in order of seniority, with the Chief Justice beginning the process.[27] This allowed the more junior members of the panel to clearly know how their superiors were voting. In *Casey*, Souter, in particular, had contact with O'Connor, and it is believed that he may have influenced her to vote for *stare decisis* in the same way I believe Blackmun influenced him in *Roe v. Wade*, but it also influenced Kennedy, and all of the votes were necessary to prevent *Roe v. Wade* from being overturned.[28] The *Dobbs* Court filled with six orthodox Catholic Justices, however, left no room for *stare decisis* to be considered, but 50 years would be enough time, in my opinion, for my amendment to be approved.[29]

I know that judicial decisions are always potentially reversible, and I do believe that the *Dobbs* verdict is susceptible to being overturned, but I do not expect the Republican Party to give up on their control of the Supreme Court, so I will proceed with my amendment proposal, and hope for the best. I previously noted that three Nixon appointees voted in the 7-2 majority for *Roe v. Wade*, but *Casey* was passed with only a 5-4 majority, and all five justices approving were appointed by Republican presidents, including Justice Blackmun by President Nixon, Justice John Paul Stevens by President Gerald Ford, Justices Sandra Day O'Connor and Anthony Kennedy by President Ronald Reagan (1911-2004), and Justice David Souter by President George H. W. Bush, so the primary problem was the dependence on Originalism, and that was going to make the difference with the Court appointed by Trump.[30] Blackmun saw the writing on the wall, but fortunately for those who believe in the benefits of abortion of nonviable unwanted fetuses, this would not occur for another thirty years. I am amazed, but extremely heartened, by the outcome in *Casey*, because I truly believe the Justices felt an obligation to the obligation of following the spirit of the Constitution, and the importance of *stare decisis*, which

---

26 Ibid., 57.

27 Barrett, <u>Listening to the Law: Reflections on the Court and Constitution</u>, 62.

28 Toobin, <u>The Nine: Inside the Secret World of the Supreme Court</u>, 57-59.

29 Ibid., 65.

30 Chemerinsky, "Justice Blackmun Got It Right in *Roe v. Wade*," 67.

is a critical component of how a Democracy is run. Kathryn Kolbert, who argued the case to the Supreme Court, and was a co-founder of the Center for Reproductive Rights, has written a book about her experience in the trial, and provides much insight into how that case, and others, were important elements in fighting for abortion rights in our country. She had attended the confirmation hearings of Clarence Thomas, and was appalled by the then senator Joe Biden, who chaired the Judiciary Committee, refusing to allow a second EEOC employee to corroborate the testimony of Anita Hill that Thomas had sexually harassed her.[31] This all occurred one year before *Casey* reached the Supreme Court, and because she had also argued the *Thornburgh* case to the Supreme Court in 1985, she participated in the *Casey* case to the Federal District Court in Philadelphia, along with Tom Zemaitis, and her recollections provide much insight into how these cases were adjudicated.[32] I knew little about her until she published her book, but luckily I came across it during my research, and it shows how many important books get little recognition for the volume of books available on the subject is so great, that many gems are hidden from view. There was little chance, however, that the conservative majority in the *Dobbs* case would not stick to their guns, and to the promise made by Donald Trump to return the vote back to the states after the *Casey* opinion was given, and this showed up in the 30-year delay until *Dobbs* was decided, and overturned both cases. Republican majorities had approved the prior two abortion cases, but *Dobbs* was going to be sure and follow the demands of Donald Trump that abortion be banned, and their decision was loud and clear.

I argued in the prior chapter that the *Thornburgh* case, which was decided in 1986, had Blackmun write the majority opinion in the case, but Burger took the opportunity to dissent, in order to show his true conservative feelings about abortion, which he was not able to show in *Roe v. Wade*. When the Pennsylvania legislature passed another *Abortion Control Act* three years later, which was even harsher than the prior one, and it was signed with approval by Governor Casey, Kolbert and Zemaitis, along with Linda Wharton, who was a dedicated women's rights advocate, brought suit again and won the case in what

---

31 Kolbert & Kay, <u>Controlling Women: What We Must do Now to Save Reproductive Freedom</u>, 40.

32 Ibid., 41-42.

became known as the *Casey* case.[33] I find it incredibly ironic that this would now be the third time the *Roe v. Wade* Supreme Court, with significant changes in the Justices, but the same lawyers in the follow-up cases, were going to basically be arguing the legality of the *Roe v. Wade* decision in face of a growing number of conservative Justices, and, by chance, with perhaps divine assistance, in order to survive the onslaught. In *Roe v. Wade*, Burger was Chief Justice, and Blackmun read the opinion with Douglas, Brennan, Jr., Stewart, Marshall, and Burger voting with the majority, and White and Rehnquist dissenting. In *Thornburgh*, Burger was still Chief Justice, although he would soon retire, and Blackmun again read the verdict, with the majority including Brennan, Jr., Marshall, Powell, Jr. and Stevens, with Burger, White, Rehnquist, and O'Connor dissenting. In *Casey*, Rehnquist was now Chief Justice, and the verdict was read by O'Connor, Kennedy and Souter, along with Stevens and Blackmun, with dissents by Rehnquist, White, Scalia, and Thomas. I personally believe that these three cases show how brilliantly the lawyers in favor of abortion, Sarah Weddington and Kathryn Kolbert in particular, were able to have the case survive this onslaught before the changes made by Donald Trump caused the entire structure to collapse. I have not lost faith in the American Justice system after reviewing this entire sequence, but I am concerned that the present Supreme Court of *Dobbs* is ignoring the Separation of Church and State mandate, and I am strongly suggesting that this issue be discussed nationwide on a public level, because it is a change that I contend should not be accepted by the Supreme Court Justices. The Justices take an oath to follow the Constitution, and they clearly are not doing that, and this poses a serious threat to the separation of Church and State in America, and must end now, or our entire system of Democracy will be in serious danger. At the end of this chapter, I will show how this danger is being promulgated further by an attack on the First Amendment as part of the attempt to turn our country into a Theocracy, instead of a Democracy.

One fact which Kolbert admitted to in her book was that Justice O'Connor was the only woman on the Supreme Court at the time the *Casey* case was tried, "and was considered one of the swing Justices," an assessment which also proved vital to her case.[34] This correct

---

33 Ibid., 42.
34 Ibid., 44.

insight into how the Justices viewed *stare decisis* showed that she did her homework on the Justices quite well, as Weddington did in the *Roe* case, and I believe that those of us who believe in abortion rights for women owe a debt of gratitude to both of these legal teams who fought for *Roe* and *Casey* against all of the odds that were stacked against them. They gave us the opportunity to hopefully pass an amendment to eliminate the need for future lawsuits. In addition, Kolbert knew that if the case went to the Supreme Court, the final decision would be close, so she decided to ask the Supreme Court only one question on her opening statement: "Has the Supreme Court overruled *Roe v. Wade* holding that a woman's right to choose abortion is a fundamental right protected by the United States Constitution?"[35] By emphasizing the issue of *stare decisis*, she was directing herself directly to Justice O'Connor's vote, hoping to have her be the deciding vote that would allow abortion to continue. She was amazingly correct in her assessment, and *Roe v. Wade* would remain the law of the land for another 5 days shy of 30 years. This period of time was vital to show how effective and safe abortion would be, and how the ability to abort unwanted and nonviable fetuses safely were able to reduce the infanticide rate from 10-15% down to less than 1%.

I will now move on and analyze the case of *Dobbs* carefully, and show where I believe the decision was fatally flawed, and why my amendment is a vital necessity to vote for. It is clear that Justice Alito had two options in nullifying the decisions of both *Roe v. Wade* and *Casey*: he could overrule them entirely, as he did, and declare that life began at conception, which he also did, and which I believe Donald Trump told him to do; or he could declare that the decision that life began at 24-28-weeks was erroneous, and the new standard should be 15-weeks, as the Mississippi case declared, and which Chief Justice Roberts wanted him to do, as he said in his dissent along with his vote with the majority. The latter choice would be consistent with both the Constitution and the separation of Church and State, and the former choice was dependent solely on the position of the Catholic Pope and President Trump, and would be determining a new common law definition of viability. This is why I have declared that Alito, and other Catholic Justices, erred in their decision to not recuse themselves, given the fact that they did not have the authority to make a new common

---

35 Ibid., 48.

law determination, and disregarded the intention of the Founding Fathers. The first Chief Justice of the United States Supreme Court, John Marshall, who was the one to claim that the Supreme Court had the power to expound constitutional law in *Marbury v. Madison, 5 U.S. 137 (1803),* was also the one who acknowledged that the decision in *Chisolm v. Georgia, 2 U.S. 419 (1793)* was wrongly decided because it was overturned by the Eleventh Amendment.[36] *Marbury v. Madison* is the case which concluded that the Supreme Court had the power of judicial review to declare laws or judicial decisions unconstitutional, and the case is considered so important that pictures of Marbury and Madison both are displayed in the Supreme Court's Marshall Dining Room.[37] If my amendment fails, I believe this same decision could be applied to *Dobbs* in order to overturn their holding, and return to the standards that will at least allow earlier nonviable fetuses to be aborted, and the pictures of Marbury and Madison to remain where they are now.

What *Dobbs* could not change by their decision, however, was the fact that after *Roe v. Wade* was passed, the number of legal abortions in the United States began to rise every year thereafter, so that by 1981, eight years later, the number reached a high of 1.6 million in America, although in the 1990s the abortion rate started to fall steeply. The factors that led to the later decline were a reduction in the number of unwanted pregnancies due to an increased use of contraceptives promoted by public health campaigns; improved economic gains, which encouraged births to be wanted; and increased passage of abortion laws as the growing Republican anti-abortion campaign gained force, causing demonstrations at abortion clinics interfering with easy entry. The *Dobbs* decision declared all abortions illegal, except those where the mother's life was in danger, for the fetus was always viable, given the fact that life began at conception, and all abortions were therefore murder. Martha Bailey, Professor of Economics at the University of California, Los Angeles, accentuated the role of improved contraception methods and education in beginning to lower the abortion rate, estimating that at least 40% of the reduction in the birth rate in the 1960s was due to the introduction of the birth

---

36 Microsoft CoPilot (8/24/2025). Personal Communication.
37 Barrett, <u>Listening to the Law: Reflections on the Court and Constitution</u>, 101.

control pill in 1960, but this did not affect unwanted pregnancies, except to assure that a greater percentage of the abortions performed were truly unwanted.[38]

To give some background to the case before I analyze it in detail, it is necessary to understand that Mississippi had enacted a new anti-abortion law in 2018, referred to as the *Gestational Age Act*, and the statute was flatly unconstitutional, because *Roe v. Wade had* declared that abortions could be done until 24-28 weeks gestation, and Mississippi lowered that age to 15-weeks gestation because the legislature in Mississippi believed that fetuses at that age could survive with intensive care treatments, and therefore were viable at that gestational age. State legislatures have this right, but if the law is at variance with a Supreme Court decision, it is void, which did not happen in *Dobbs* because *Roe v. Wade* was overturned, and a new law was introduced which stated life began at conception, and so the 15-week gestation approval was also voided. I do not know the details that the Mississippi legislators used in making the determination of viability, but in my own research I have found evidence that the appropriate present-day limit should be 20-weeks gestation, since there are no recorded instances of younger gestational births eventually surviving with independent lives. I have no problem with the passage in the Mississippi legislature because when they lowered the definition of quickening to 15-weeks gestation, they still were refusing to deny abortion of nonviable fetuses, and they apparently were empowered to make that determination under state law without the criteria I require for my amendment, so the change was relatively minor. As I will shortly discuss, Alito in his opinion demanded that *Roe v. Wade* would require an amendment to do that under his interpretation of the Constitution, and by doing that he should have submitted himself to that same requirement, which he did not, and I believe that is a reversible error in his decision.

Because the Federal Appeals Court system in Mississippi was still accepting *Roe v. Wade* as constitutional law, the Federal District Court blocked the statute, and the state of Mississippi then appealed, all of this happening at the time Ruth Bader Ginsburg died in 2020, and was replaced by Amy Coney Barrett, who was appointed by Trump as a

---

38 Freidenfelds, <u>The Myth of the Perfect Pregnancy: A History of Miscarriage in America</u>, 50.

staunch conservative who would likely vote with the four who already wanted to strike down *Roe*. This was therefore seen as the perfect test-case for the Supreme Court to accept, and although it usually takes only 6-weeks for the Supreme Court to act once a petition has been filed, the State of Mississippi had asked the Supreme Court to take the case on June 15, 2020, but the Court waited 11 months before agreeing in order to be able to replace Ginsberg with Barrett. The new presidential election was taking place between Donald Trump and Joe Biden, and Trump was claiming that the Democrats stole the election, leading up to the famous attack on the Capital building on 1/6/2021 to stop the certification of the Electoral College results.

I believe Trump knew the *Dobbs* case was put on the docket, and desperately wanted to be the President when the results were read, having appointed the Justices to perform that function, and he was willing to do anything possible to prevent the Congress from performing the required transfer of power.

Was this his only reason for contesting the election? Probably not, but, in my opinion, Trump is clearly an all-or-none personality, and his actions during the "Capital Attack," and "January 6 Insurrection," is something that supports my contention. Only time will tell if the truth will ever be known about that horrible event, but while many Democrats believed his actions would never be accepted by the majority of American voters, their ignorance about how loyal Republicans are to Trump is legendary now, and I am sure that Judicial action is not going to change any time soon. I have no problem with Trump trying his best to Make America Great Again, but I do have a problem with his attempting to load the Supreme Court with Justices who refuse to follow the separation of Church and State, which is the issue I assert is an essential part of Constitutional interpretation.

As I said, when the Supreme Court received the appeal of *Dobbs*, it did not give an answer until Amy Coney Barrett was appointed, so that they could be assured of the end-result with another secure Trump appointee on board. Then, in May 2021, the Supreme Court announced it would hear the case in order to answer one simple question: "Whether all pre-viability prohibitions on elective abortions are unconstitutional." This brazen announcement that they were going to decide if life began at conception may have simply been Alito's goal at the outset, but I don't think he would have written that if he didn't already know that his support from the President was secure. I am sure he would have preferred that Trump was President when he made that announcement, but I do not know if Alito actually discussed the issue with Trump, but if he did, I am convinced that Trump told him to go ahead as planned. Any abortion would be murder under this principle, and could not be seen as consistent with the Constitution, since it would be a capital crime. This decision by Alito to follow his Catholic teaching may have been bold, but, in my opinion, it was demanded by Donald Trump, and while the effect was electric on all who read it, I do not think it will hold up to proper constitutional analysis.

Unless Catholic Justices swear to recuse themselves if they believe they must follow the belief of the Pope in abortion cases, there is no way that personal liberties that have been accepted by multiple Supreme Court decisions cannot be thrown aside by utilizing Originalism this cavalierly, and this is why I will proceed with my proposal to pass an Amendment to approve the right of abortion, and a declaration that life begins at 20-weeks gestation. Erwin Chemerinsky, Dean and Jesse H. Choper Distinguished Professor of Law at the University of California, Berkeley School of Law, noted that in the majority opinion of *Dobbs* there was referral to "potential life" twelve times, and despite his repetitive use of the term to try an apply the term viability to conception, there is no rational reason whatsoever to make that connection.[39] I have said it many times already in this book, and will continue to stress in the pages which follow, that separation of Church and State does not disavow the existence of God, but it must be a vital component of the analysis of our Constitution, and the Catholic Justices must search their conscience to be sure that they are able to follow that principle they swore to, or, like Rehnquist in the Watergate trial of Richard Nixon, they must recuse themselves from participating in the decision, as they swore to do at their appointment.

The news of *Roe v. Wade* being reexamined so distressed the then Democratic majority House of Representatives, that the House Committee on Oversight and Reform, with Carolyn Maloney from New York presiding, met to decide what to do in what they labeled: "A State of Crisis: Examining the Urgent Need to Protect and Expand Abortion Rights and Access." To show how flustered they must have

---

39 Chemerinsky, "Justice Blackmun Got It Right in *Roe v. Wade*," 73.

been from realizing that their right to abortion was likely soon to end, Maloney claimed that the anti-abortion bill was written by the state of Missouri, rather than Mississippi.[40] She claimed it was a crisis because "nearly 1 in 4 women in the United States will have an abortion in their lifetime," a figure that Microsoft CoPilot said the Guttmacher Institute gave, adding it meant that "if the trend continues" to allow abortion to be legal.[41] The Republican members of the Committee were upset as well, but only because so much time was being wasted on trying to "normalize the destruction of unborn babies, which is called abortion," an attitude that totally disregarded the numbers of abortions that have been performed worldwide, showing how difficult dealing with the decision of *Dobbs* is going to be for millions of women every year because of the bitter debate over whether abortion is murder or feticide.[42] This case has truly split our country into a dangerous controversy, and I am hoping that the amendment debate can bring our divergent views into a more reasonable understanding of how the lives of future unwanted children will be affected if we don't pass this amendment.

The division of Republican and Democrat understanding of the morality of abortion is so great that I have no other explanation but to write this book and try to bring some sense into what the claim that life begins at conception really means, and why I believe it has reached the dangerous level of being a constitutional crisis, as it has been described by many concerned legislators today. In January 2021, four months before the Supreme Court agreed to hear the *Dobbs* case, the United States had its highest number of deaths in the COVID-19 pandemic that began in January 2020, when the first case of COVID was diagnosed in the state of Washington. It also was when Donald Trump began to mount his ongoing campaign to overturn the 2020 presidential election, and Republicans and Democrats were taking sides on that political battlefield, as Americans were preparing for what turned out to be a horrible epidemic that resembled the polio epidemic that hit America in 1948-1952, and the Spanish Flu epidemic that killed 500 million people worldwide from 1918-1920. Although

---

40 Committee on Oversight and Reform, "A State of Crisis: Examining the Urgent Need to Protect and Expand Abortion Rights and Access," 1
41 Ibid., 2; Microsoft CoPilot (7/15/2025), Personal Communication.
42 Ibid., 6.

COVID only killed about seven million people, the function of the entire government was affected, and we are still dealing with the problem today.[43] The Press and media airways were filled with arguments and fear for years following the onset of that epidemic, but the chaos that would develop between the two sides was going to erupt into a battle that threatened to turn our country towards the brink of Civil War once Trump threatened to not let the House of Representatives certify that he lost the election.

On January 6, 2021, two weeks before Biden was sworn in as President, supporters of Trump stormed the U.S. Capitol building in what many have labeled as an insurrection, a demonstration that frequently takes place in undeveloped nations, but never in America before that day had such an event ever taken place. Trump claimed that it all stemmed from the election having been stolen by the Democrats, and he was simply trying to prevent the Congress from certifying the fraud until his investigations were completed. He remains convinced that his accusations were true today, and after being reelected President on November 5, 2024, he pardoned all the people that were arrested and sentenced to prison, calling them patriots. This action has further solidified the difference between Republicans and Democrats, and the only reason I believe my proposal will pass is because I truly believe that women will vote for the amendment, even though they voted for Trump for President. At the heart of the confrontation on January 6, 2021, was the deadly battle between those who were loyal to Trump's claim that the election was stolen, many of whom who were Republicans who also believed that abortion was equivalent to murder, and those Democrats who saw that Joe Biden was fairly elected President, and saw abortion as a woman's right to choose, were outraged by their actions. When it comes to giving up the right to have an abortion, however, I truly believe that many of those women who were present at the demonstration will be just as adamant to be sure that their vote for my amendment will not be ignored.

The *Dobbs* decision was made about 1.5 years after the incident took place, and the entire event was seen by Republicans as a vindication of their support for Trump, and clearly helped him to win the Presidency once again. Justice Alito has become the most dominant conservative

---

43 Ziegler, Dollars for Life; The Anti-Abortion Movement and the Fall of the Republican Establishment, ix.

voice on the Supreme Court, and has continued to loudly complain that many of the Supreme Court decisions are not following Trumpian mandates, taking on the role of being Trump's spokesman on the Supreme Court. It will be interesting to see what Trump does in the months and years to come during his Presidency if the current Chief Justice Roberts does not follow the path Alito has taken as second-in-command. Trump may very well try to oust Roberts, as he has with others who do not follow his Executive control orders to run the country as he sees fit. I believe this is a true Constitutional Crisis, and I hope the readers of my book press their legislators to obey the Constitution, rather than the Catholic Pope, because that is the path that truly made America great, and is the path we must continue to follow. If this amendment can be passed, then I believe that our Democracy will remain strong, and if Trump maintains his power and authority to run for President a third time, it will have to be approved by a Supreme Court that has learned that they have to rule in a manner consistent with a Democracy, and not a Theocracy, no matter how they rule on First Amendment rights.

To now return to the details of case of *Dobbs v. Jackson Women's Health Organization,* it was first argued to the Supreme Court on December 1, 2021, and was decided on June 24, 2022, about 8 months later, with Associate Justice Samuel Anthony Alito Jr. delivering the opinion of the Court. Like happened with Blackmun, Alito was relatively unknown to the general public when he was given the opportunity to write the opinion, but unlike Blackmun, he had written many opinions by that time, and was second in conservative seniority on the Court to Chief Justice John Roberts, so he was not as unknown to the powers-to-be in government as Blackmun was. As I previously described in the *Thornburgh* case, Alito was known to politicians while he was on the Appellate Court, as well as the judiciary community, for being the only Justice on the District Court to dissent with the verdict to approve the case, and this is what enabled him to get appointed to the Supreme Court. Both Roberts and Alito had been appointed by George B. Bush, with Roberts appointed on September 29, 2005, and Alito on January 31, 2006, similar to the way in which Burger and Blackmun were both appointed by Nixon. Because of the COVID pandemic, arguments to the Court at the time were heard by conference call only, and the Court would not reopen to the public until 9/28/2022, when medical deaths from the epidemic began to abate.

Alito was appointed to the Supreme Court following the resignation of Justice Sandra Day O'Connor in 2005, the first woman to be appointed to the Supreme Court. O'Connor was Protestant, and not Catholic, and had a moderate stance in religious freedom cases, and Alito's selection was delayed because Bush first proposed John Roberts for the position, but when Chief Justice William Rehnquist died, Bush appointed Roberts as Chief Justice instead, and then nominated Harriet Miers to be the Justice to replace him. Rehnquist died while still sitting as the Chief Justice, and he was given a rare tribute by his casket being displayed in the Supreme Court building.[44] Once again, similar to the *Roe v. Wade* process, Miers withdrew her name, and Alito was Bush's next choice.[45] This is the same pathway that was taken by Blackmun, although in this case I don't think John Roberts was surprised, or angered, by the outcome. Alito was an Italian-American Catholic who was born to immigrants in Trenton, New Jersey. His father, Samuel A. Alito, Sr. (1914-1987) was born in Roccella Ionica, Calabria, and immigrated to the United States as a child. He became a U.S. citizen, so his son would therefore be a natural citizen when he was born, but he would have been raised in the same manner as other Catholic Italian children, and I contend that he let his Catholic upbringing affect his judicial opinions, refusing to separate his Church and State allegiance, as has been customary since our Constitution was first written. He has maintained that stance to the present day, and is a prime reason I am campaigning for Congress to take notice, and legislate actions for Justices who refuse to separate loyalties to Church and State. Failing to follow an oath taken to become a governmental employee must be mandated by laws that can only be passed by Congress, and no one, even Supreme Court Justices, are above the law.

---

44 Toobin, The Nine: Inside the Secret World of the Supreme Court, 4-5. I was impressed by this honor in face of his playing in the same poker game for thirty-three years, and being the man who ran the Court's betting pools on NCAA basketball, NFL football, and the Kentucky Derby. Ibid. 135-136.

45 Miers became the only nominee to withdraw her name from consideration by the Senate even though she probably would have been confirmed. Ibid. 330. Robert Bork refused to withdraw his name, even though it was clear he would not be confirmed. Ibid., 344.

I have no doubt that Alito's decision to overturn *Roe v. Wade*, and claim that viability took place at conception, was strongly influenced by his Italian Catholic heritage. It is interesting that Jack M. Balkin, Knight Professor of Constitutional Law at Yale School of Law, agreed with my view, but put it more eloquently when he claimed in 2024 that the decision to overturn the case created opposition that "helped energize the conservative religious and social movements of the 1970s and 1980s, which argued that an unelected judiciary was imposing its personal (and immoral) views and casting aside those of democratically elected state governments."[46] I'm not exactly sure what immorality he was referring to here, but I totally agree that the *Roe v. Wade* judgment energized the religious movement in the Republican Party, and the primary reason Alito was picked to give the opinion in the *Dobbs* case, rather than have it written by the Chief Justice, because Roberts knew that the decision was made because Donald Trump wanted the Catholic Pope, and not the Constitution of the United States, to be highlighted, and Roberts did not want that opinion to be ascribed to him. He still voted with the majority, however, and did not label his disagreement as a dissent, so I cannot accept that his actions were appropriate. The Republican Party has been greatly energized by the Christian evangelical movement, and by including it in their political platform in 1980, which called for "a constitutional amendment to restore protection of the right to life for unborn children," they became labeled as a Pro-Life political party.[47] That amendment never had any chance of passing, and so it was never actually submitted, but the American philosopher Michael Tooley, now emeritus at the University of Colorado, Boulder, nevertheless claimed that the basic issue in both abortion and infanticide is whether "human fetuses and infants have a right to life."[48]

In addition to the profile that our Democracy is in danger of being destroyed, we are going to once again be forced to deal with rising infanticide rates of many of the unwanted births that will take place if the *Dobbs* decision is not overturned. There also will be a similar increase in childhood abuse, that is going to reach levels that our social service system simply cannot handle. The numbers of

---

46 Balkin, "Roe v. Wade, *An Engine of Controversy*," 11.
47 Ibid., 12-13.
48 Tooley, "Abortion and Infanticide," 15.

abortions performed worldwide, as I said were 3.65 billion in the last 50 years, makes it impossible for us to deal with the births of so many unwanted children, and it is this type of issue that keeps me up at night. The only way we can avert our unwanted infanticidal rate from rising to 10-15% once again is by passing the amendment I propose. Judith Jarvis Thomson (1929-2020), former Laurence S. Rockefeller Professor of Philosophy at the Massachusetts Institute of Technology, said that she had a problem with drawing fine lines like a point in time where viability suddenly begins, but facts are facts, and being able to have organ development that can survive with assistance outside the uterus can be estimated with reasonable accuracy by today's testing, in conjunction with the experience gained by careful study of premature births treatment in intensive care units, so it clearly supports defining a fine line.[49] Thomson agrees that an acorn is not an oak tree, but nevertheless wants to accept that life begins at conception, which is taking philosophy to the ultimate end of rationality, since it basically is saying an acorn is always an oak tree, despite the fact it is estimated to grow into an oak tree less than 1% of the time.[50] No matter how difficult it may be to draw a fine line that is absolutely the same in all human beings, there is a scientific point at which maturation can take over after birth, and a point when it cannot, and we must be able to define it within statistical significance if we are going to utilize it in a court of law.

Common law across the world has always accepted quickening as the fine-line to determine viability, as well as two Supreme Court cases. That point is very apparent today, and it can be determined more precisely by studying factual cases of premature births treated with intensive care unit life support. It may be difficult to decide which life is more important if we are forced to choose between the mother's life in danger, and the abortion of the fetus, but that is a different question than when the fetus actually becomes defined as a person. When the fetus is nonviable, I submit that there is no question that the fetus is not a "person" under the law. The moral issue of what to do about accepting abortion if the mother's life is in danger is an entirely different question, and all well-trained specialists have to deal with this problem on a daily basis when they are deciding whose life

---

49 Thomson, "A Defense of Abortion," 31.
50 Ibid., 32. Microsoft CoPilot (4/26/2025). Personal Communication.

in that situation must be saved. The Supreme Court does not have to enter that fray, except to decide whether the decision made is legal or not. In that situation I contend that the fetus is only an equal partner once it is considered viable. I agree that there are many levels of defining that danger on a theoretical basis, but I also accept that such decisions need accurate medical assessments to clarify how dangerous to life the continuation of pregnancy would be, and the likelihood of whether the fetus is viable is an important part of deciding what to do if both lives are endangered.

The problem with leaving this issue up to either philosophers, or religious devotees, is that they think like Patrick Lee, Professor of Philosophy at Franciscan University of Steubenville, and Robert P. George, Professor of Jurisprudence at Princeton University, who consider the embryo to be "a *complete* or *whole* organism, though immature," as if the path ahead was only a matter of time, and most of the time successful.[51] It may be true that an embryo, or a nonviable fetus, already has the "elements" of what will become a person, but stating that the fetus is "albeit in radical, i.e. root form," implies that scientifically it is acceptable to assume that it will naturally continue to develop normally, and that statement does not follow statistic likelihood.[52] The issue of viability must now be handled in that fashion, and we must also realize that maturation inside the uterus is a necessity of life after birth, even though we are making progress to improve our means to sustain life with artificial means so that some maturation with continue to take place after a certain gestation period in the uterus. I cannot know exactly at which point that will eventually be possible, but at the moment it appears to be 20-weeks gestation, and if it changes in the future, the abortion amendment can be modified to follow that progress as it develops. Don Marquis (1935-2022), former Emeritus Professor of Philosophy at the University of Kansas, considered abortion to be immoral, and "in the same moral category as killing an innocent adult human being," putting him, in my opinion, in the same category as Justice Alito, and I personally do not accept that their views are based on scientific data, which is the only criteria that provides the necessary data to know the likelihood of survival, and the

---

51 Lee and George, "The Wrong of Abortion," 43.
52 Ibid., 44.

only criteria that should be allowed in a court of law.[53]

Alito's upbringing, and his contention that life begins at conception is a spiritual, rather than judicial, opinion, and he should have recused himself in the case, knowing that he was disobeying the oath he took when he became a Supreme Court Justice. His opinion is based on faith alone, which is the foundation of all religious beliefs. He is entitled to that belief in his religious faith, but this is the Supreme Court, and when you don the judicial robe, in my opinion, you must leave your faith outside the chambers, and put on the gowns of the Constitution, which you swore to follow. You made an oath that you must put aside your religious beliefs when you adjudicate according to the Constitution, and if you cannot, you must recuse yourself from participating in the chambers. All Supreme Court Justices take two oaths when they are sworn in: the Constitutional Oath and the Judicial Oath. The Constitutional Oath is mandated by Article VI of the Constitution, and states:

"I, [name], do solemnly swear (or affirm) that I will support and defend the Constitution of the United States against all enemies, foreign and domestic; that I will bear true faith and allegiance to the same; that I take this obligation freely, without any mental reservation or purpose of evasion; and that I will well and faithfully discharge the duties of the office on which I am about to enter. *So help me God.*"[54]

I have added italics here, because when he swears to God, he lets his position as a Catholic be known, and I realize that is a problem for some devout Catholics that feel incapable of disobeying a Pope's edict. The problem is that he also swore to God to follow the Constitution, and if he cannot distinguish between the two obvious different views, he has no recourse but to recuse himself from the case.

He also took the Judicial Oath, which reads:

"I, _____, do solemnly swear or affirm that I will administer justice without respect to persons, and do equal right to the poor and to the rich, and that I will faithfully and impartially discharge and perform all the duties incumbent upon me as _____, according to the best of my abilities and understanding, agreeably to the constitution and laws of the United States. *So help me God.*"[55]

---

53 Marquis, "Why Abortion is Immoral," 54.
54 "Oaths of Office," 1-3.
55 Ibid.

The italics are again my addition, but in December 1990, the Judicial Improvements Act of 1990 replaced the phrase "according to the best of my abilities and understanding, agreeably to the Constitution" with "under the Constitution." The revised Judicial Oath, found at 28 U.S. C. § 453, reads:

> "I, _____, do solemnly swear (or affirm) that I will administer justice without respect to persons, and do equal right to the poor and to the rich, and that I will faithfully and impartially discharge and perform all the duties incumbent upon me as _____ under the Constitution and laws of the United States. *So help me God.*"[56]

The added italics again emphasize what the Justices are swearing to, and they are doing it voluntarily, so they must be held accountable to the oath they take.

There is no question that these oaths forbid Alito from ruling that life begins at conception. He cannot say he is following his oath to either one if they are not in agreement, and therefore he has to knowingly agree to pick the Constitution, or not rule in the case. One can be a good Catholic, however, and not accept every word of every Papal decree which changes over time. I personally never expected *Roe v. Wade* to be overturned, but that was because I was ignorant of the details of the verdict at the time it was made. I understand better today why it angered many anti-abortionists, but I don't believe that the majority of people who are against abortions, are against all abortion, but only those who want to abort a viable fetus. That is why the Mississippi statute allowed abortion up to 15-weeks gestation, but not beyond. It was Alito that made the change to conception, not the Mississippi legislature, and I am willing to find a compromise with people who understand that there are multiple issues at work here, and we have to rationally evaluate them, so that all concerned can see why each view has been thoroughly and thoughtfully, discussed, and a rational conclusion made, at least at the state level, if not the Supreme Court.

Just as I was surprised that Blackmun was allowed to write the opinion for *Roe v. Wade*, I also was surprised that John Roberts picked Alito to write the opinion of *Dobbs*, but knowing that he personally did not want to overturn *Roe v. Wade* tells me that he let his conscience be

---

56 Ibid.

appeased, but kept it hidden from view. When Roberts was appointed to his role of Chief Justice of the Supreme Court on 9/29/2005, he was only 50-years-old, and was younger than any other justice in that position, except for John Jay, who was appointed at age 44-years-old in 1789.[57] Alito had also excelled at all levels of his education, but he first went to an all-male Roman Catholic boarding school, La Lumiere, finishing first in his class, and then went to Princeton, graduating in 3 years, and then Yale Law School, where he graduated in 1975. Roberts attended law school at Harvard, where he received his J.D. in 1979, and served a clerkship with Justice Rehnquist, who had dissented in the *Roe v. Wade* case, which may be one reason he was picked for the more senior position on the Court.[58] Roberts kept a sofa in his house that John Quincy Adams (1767-1848), the sixth president of the United States, had died on, and so his devotion to American history was clearly ingrained in his way-of-life.[59] Alito went to Yale Law School, where I earlier mentioned that Robert Bork taught, and helped start what would be called the Federalist Society to promote conservative legal concepts. He joined the Justice Department shortly after Reagan was elected, six years later, and by then he was an avowed follower of Originalism.[60] This is why I am not surprised that Roberts gave the case to overturn *Roe v. Wade* to Alito, since he was known as a conservative judge when he was appointed by George W. Bush in 2005. It would seem, however, that Roberts would want his name remembered throughout American history as the one who approved the concept of *Dobbs*, but not to overturn *Roe v. Wade*, since he was so much a part of the Republican Party, and of America, that long supported the Constitution of the United States, and now he was giving into far-right opinions that do not abide by Constitutional mandates. Shame on him, and shame on the Catholic Justices who refuse to leave their religious beliefs aside when they enter the chambers of the Supreme Court. I can understand why President Trump did what he did, because he clearly is in favor of a Catholic theocracy running the country, but if he truly wants America to be Great Again, it has to be as a Democracy, and not a Theocracy.

57 Biskupic, <u>Nine Black Robes: Inside the Supreme Court's Drive to the Right and Its Historic Consequences</u>, 46.

58 Ibid., 45.

59 Ibid., 47.

60 Toobin, <u>The Nine: Inside the Secret World of the Supreme Court</u>, 19.

I contend that Roberts did not write the opinion in *Dobbs* because he knew he could not agree with Alito that life begins at conception, and he instead in his concurring opinion recommended "a more measured course" than overturning *Roe v. Wade*, because "it would hold that 15-weeks, the period allowed under Mississippi's law, is enough," rather than now claiming that life begins at conception.[61] To me, this is clearly a dissent, and I do not know why it was instead called a concurrence response, which adds his name to the whole opinion, but does not clarify that with the dissent it was 5-4, rather than 6-3. He added that the case was "'an ideal vehicle' to 'reconsider the bright-line viability rule' and that a judgment in its favor would 'not require the Court to overturn' *Roe v. Wade*."[62] Chief Justice Roberts then said that Mississippi allows three months to get an abortion, "well beyond the point at which it is considered 'late,'" and sees no reason to change that to conception without putting that in writing.[63] I truly believe that if Roberts had taken it upon himself to write the majority opinion, the case would have not overturned *Roe v. Wade* and *Casey,* but would have modified the gestation period for viability, and been more consistent with what was going on worldwide with most countries basically following their own common law acceptances for fetal viability. It is this reason that I believe Roberts allowed Alito to write the opinion, and why Alito has become the most ardent Justice calling for all Supreme Court decisions to follow the intentions of President Trump to expand the presidential authority to take over some of the authority the Constitution gives to the Legislative branch of the government. This includes modifying the First Amendment restrictions, as I will discuss at the end of this chapter.

I strongly maintain that Roberts wanted to write the opinion in *Dobbs*, but because he knew that President Trump wanted the case to be overturned, he let Alito write the opinion, and then had to find a way of dissenting without writing a dissent. He allowed Alito to write the majority opinion, and then concurred by dissenting on the issue of overturning the case. This is why the majority vote to overturn was listed as 6-3 instead of 5-4, but as I said earlier, I'm not sure why that

---

61 "Dobbs, State Health Officer of the Mississippi Department of Health, et. al. v. Jackson Women's Health Organization et al.," 72.

62 Ibid., 136.

63 Ibid., 137.

was allowed. Alito at the time, was second in seniority to Roberts on the right wing, and since Roberts change of vote to dissent did not alter the fact that overturning still had a majority vote. This action by the Supreme Court to collude with the President, and try and make Catholic teaching the law of the land is a very serious matter, and must be dealt with in many ways, but first by beginning to let both the President, and the Supreme Court, know that we do not want our Constitution disregarded because of a belief that we do not have to follow Church and State separation. To do this is simple, pass my amendment, and stand up for what is good for America, both in how we abide by our Constitution, and how we refuse to allow millions of births that are unwanted and nonviable to be safely aborted as approved by two Supreme Court decisions.

The dominance of conservative Justices on the Supreme Court at this time is the result of Republican billionaires increasing their support of influencing federal judicial selections from providing around $31 million in federal races in 2010, to $1.2 billion, a forty-fold increase, in 2020, an expenditure that, in my opinion, should alert more Americans to the danger that is now reaching us at a Constitutional Crisis level.[64] President Donald Trump after his election in 2024 nominated 13 billionaires to cabinet posts, an unprecedented change from past policy, and the *Dobbs* decision to overturn *Roe v. Wade* gave Republicans an enormous boost in political power, and clearly helped Trump to win the presidency in 2024.[65] Since entering office for his second term, Trump' personal wealth has been said to have increased two-fold. In November 2024, his estimated personal wealth was $2.3 billion, and by July, 2025, it was $5.1-5.8 billion.[66] This is not what America stands for, and it is time we put an end to greed that never was what our Revolutionary War was fought for.

The amount of money being funneled into political and judicial positions is not healthy, in my opinion, especially when it is accompanied by attitudes that threaten the very basis for how, and why, our Constitution was written. Politicians and Justices are not

---

64 Waldman, The Supermajority: How the Supreme Court Divided America, 85.

65 Charalambous, Romero and Kim, "Trump has tapped an unprecedented 13 billionaires for his administration. Here's who they are," 1.

66 Microsoft CoPilot (18 July 2025). "Conversation about Donald Trump's Wealth and Financial Ventures."

supposed to be bribed for their judgments, but I am witnessing a change in recent Supreme Court decisions that I contend is dangerous, and must be seriously investigated to assure that the Constitution remains the single most important source for Justice in our country. I truly believe Roberts was aware that Alito was going to declare that life begins at conception in his opinion, and knew that it seemed more like a Papal decree than a judicial opinion that he could not agree with. I am not able to do anything about that on the political level, but I can voice my opposition for this on the issue of abortion, and I leave it to the American public to determine whether we can allow women the choice to have the right to not give birth to an unwanted pregnancy by passing an amendment to show that is their constitutional right to make that choice. The Gallup polls show that more than 80% of Americans agree with me on abortion of nonviable fetuses, and it is time that you show that those polls are true, and feel free to vote for President if you believe in him, but to not allow him to convince you to vote no on this issue of allowing thee abortion of unwanted, nonviable fetuses. In the latest Gallup poll in May 2024, 35% of voters favored abortion "under any circumstances," 50% said "only under certain circumstances," usually meaning the first or early second trimester, and only 12% said it should be illegal "in all circumstances" meaning that they believed life begins at conception.[67]

Mississippi may be a state that was in the top 10 most voting for Trump in the last election, with 60.9% of the population voting for him, a figure that showed Wyoming in first place with 69%.[68] The legislature, however, had decided not to pay attention to the Supreme Court decisions approving abortion, and passed an abortion ban that took effect on midnight, September 1, 2021, and when the Supreme Court was asked to reject the new law, they said they needed to first assess its validity, knowing that the U.S. Department of Justice filed a suit claiming the "for half a century this Court has held that a state may not prohibit any woman from making the ultimate decision to terminate her pregnancy before viability," a clear sign that the court wanted the appeal to be directly from the judgment of the District Court.[69] The Syllabus to the 213-page decision of *Dobbs* indicates that Blackmun's attempt to find constitutional support for abortion was

---

67 "Where do Americans Stand on Abortion?" 1.
68 Microsoft CoPilot (7/2/2025). Personal Communication.
69 "Dobbs, State Health Officer of the Mississippi Department of Health, et. al. v. Jackson Women's Health Organization et al.," 1-2.

simply wrong: "The Constitution does not confer a right to abortion; *Roe* and *Casey* are overruled; and the authority to regulate abortion is returned to the people and their elected representatives."[70] There you have it, a simple answer to the problem, from a conservative Supreme Court that was ready to show how things in America were going to change. Like the right for women to vote, an amendment would have to be passed to approve abortion, but with as many states wanting to have more anti-abortion laws, the conservative majority knew that passing such an amendment was very unlikely. Because Trump won reelection to the Presidency, they also knew it was unlikely that *Dobbs* would soon be overturned, so in the near future they did not believe that an amendment would likely be passed. I find it necessary, however, to assure that women can choose abortion of an unwanted, nonviable pregnancy, and we can return our attention to following the tenets of the U.S. Constitution, rather than the opinion of a Catholic Pope, so I am going to take that route. As I said, I believe the polls show that more than 3/4 of the population agrees with the abortion of nonviable fetuses, but the question is whether they will put their effort into assuring that everyone goes to the poll and vote for the amendment on the day it opens. You can't complain about the outcome unless you add your name to those that vote on that day.

What I found truly remarkable in analyzing these two cases was how each Justice made their determinations not on constitutional law, which is what they were supposed to be the most capable of doing, but on emotions that were based on their personal views of morality. Alito's opinion began with a statement that shows that his stance on abortion, while totally different from Blackmun, was just as emotionally based, for he declared that "abortion presents a profound moral issue on which Americans hold sharply conflicting views."[71] By defining abortion as "a profound moral issue," Alito clearly showed that his focus was not on scientific and legal arguments, but instead was on his Catholic religious views, which defined abortion as a moral sin because it was seen as a case of murder since life began at the time of conception. Once again, we have a Justice, like Blackmun, not talking strictly about legal complexities, but rather on the morality of the issue, and because he was taught morality by a different Church

---

70 Ibid., 1.
71 Ibid., 9.

than Alito, he found no unusual behavior in the abortion of nonviable fetuses. The minds of both of these Supreme Court Associate Justices who delivered the opinions of the most important abortion cases in American history were not founded on legal precepts, but on religious morality, and each Justice then searched for legal citations to support their stance on a moral issue. They were both not relying on the Constitutional law for their initial decision, they were relying on what they personally believed, and then found Constitutional laws to refer to as the basis for their judgment. Alito, like Blackburn, knew nothing about the fact that 10-15% of all children ever born were killed by their parents, primarily because the pregnancy, and therefore the birth, was unwanted. I am sure Alito did not know that for most of its history the Catholic Church also did not find abortion of a nonviable fetus as morally wrong, but he knew what he was taught as a child, and cared little about what the past history of the Catholic Church was. Both Justices couldn't, and therefore didn't, want to change their opinions on the moral issues they faced, and they therefore relied on what their gut-reactions told them was the right thing to do. It is true that they both relied on the same United States Constitution, and they both were assured that their opinions were correct, but I believe that Alito, in particular, listened to the argument made by the Mississippi solicitor general Scott Stewart, who told the Justices in his argument that: "Nowhere else does this Court recognize a right to end a human life," and he agreed with it because he believed that life began at conception as the present Pope taught.[72] What he totally overlooked, however, was that he was approving a statute that, in essence, approved the commission of murder, since he believed life began at conception, and that opinion was totally unfounded by any other source than the Pope.

The other problem we face in both of these cases is that the question of whether a mother should be forced to have an unwanted child or not was being judged by very well-educated Supreme Court Justices in both cases, yet neither Justice had any idea about how unwanted children had been treated in the history of mankind's evolution, and how 10-15% of them were killed because safe abortion techniques were not available, as I detail in my book *Hardness of Heart/Hardness of Life: The Stain of Human Infanticide*. The issue of morality in

---

72 Biskupic, <u>Nine Black Robes: Inside the Supreme Court's Drive to the Right and Its Historic Consequences</u>, 8.

Dobbs was made simply because a death of a fetus that could possibly continue to grow and reach a stage of viability to live was to be considered the same as a fetus that had already reached that advanced stage of gestation because of a Catholic Papal bull. Alito did not accept that unwanted pregnancies who were nonviable are different from those that are wanted, and he did not realize that 10-15% of those fetuses would be eventually killed because they were unwanted in the first place. This is not something that the majority of people on earth want to think is true, but as I show in *Hardness of Heart/Hardness of Life: The Stain of Human Infanticide*, the facts are not only true, they have been true since Adam and Eve were Created. Religious leaders have always had opinions on this subject, but not educated opinions that dealt with the reality of how unwanted children were raised, and then mistreated for much of their life. They may have read about history, but not about how unwanted children had fared from the Stone Age to the time the United States Constitution was first ratified by the necessary nine states on June 21, 1788, and then went into effect on March 4, 1789.

There have been multiple accounts of the prevalence of infanticide in cases of unwanted children, but very few people have read the many books which have detailed this problem. Half the population in the world today is from a monotheistic religion that claims Abraham as their Patriarch, even though Abraham was willing to obey God's order to sacrifice his son. They do not remember that the Christian Father God sacrificed His Only Son to save the souls of all mankind, yet they look on all abortions as a moral wrong. I'm not saying that these biblical events factually took place, but they were written to teach all monotheistic believers a lesson, and the fact remains that today, the rate of such occurrences is only rare because more than 50% of unwanted pregnancies are able to be prevented by safe abortion. The moral issue of abortion is not whether abortion is murder, as claimed by many opponents to the procedure, because abortion of a nonviable fetus is not murder, it is feticide, which is elimination of a fetus that cannot live outside the womb, and cannot feel pain because it not viable. Infanticide *is* murder, however, and it becomes the true moral issue in this case only because if abortion is once again made illegal, and it will cause many parents to wind up committing infanticide, which is a crime that could have been prevented. It will cause millions of children to be abused, and billions of dollars to be spent on the medical and physical damage that will result. If conception alone defines viability, then making a scrambled egg is murder of a chicken, and that prospect is ridiculous. The general public must be educated on this issue, and then vote to approve of abortion on nonviable fetuses, before they become viable and truly inflicted with pain and suffering.

To expand upon this statistic, let me state that because 50% of unwanted pregnancies in the Western World have been safely aborted, the percentage of unwanted children who have been born has dropped to below 1%.[73] In 1966, before *Roe v. Wade* was decided, and the majority of states had passed anti-abortion laws, the United States had 10,920 murders, and one out of every twenty-two was a child killed by a parent."[74] That number does not indicate the many cases of hidden births, and uncharged deaths. From 1968 to 1975, infanticide of all ages accounted for 3.2% of all reported homicides in the United States, and from 1976-1979, out of every 100,000 live births, only 1.3 resulted in neonaticide, 4.3 in infanticide, and 3.5 in child homicide.[75] These statistics reflect how effective, and safe, abortion was in lowering the number of unwanted children born, and it also shows how vital Blackmun's decision to approve the right to choose safe abortion in unwanted pregnancies really was. There are many other statistics that show how the large number of abortions performed have lowered the rate of unwanted births, as well as their higher level of infanticide, and if we don't allow the abortions to take place again, we will see a change in the statistics.

Alito supported his decision by stating that he was giving authority back to the elected representatives of the country, since 30 States still desired prohibition of abortion.[76] He did not give a citation to this statistic, but in my research, I have found that why many states have some limitation to abortion, it is not total prohibition, but primarily restricted to viable fetuses, as it was in Mississippi. Yes, the law has changed, and today many states are defining life as beginning at

---

73 "Homicides Among Infants in the United States, 2917-2020," 1-2.

74 Hoover, Uniform Crime Reports - 1966, 5.

75 Saunders, "Neonaticides Following 'Secret' Pregnancies: Seven Case Reports," 370; Jason, Gilliland, & Tyler, "Homicide as a Cause of Pediatric Mortality in the United States," 191.

76 "Dobbs, State Health Officer of the Mississippi Department of Health, et. al. v. Jackson Women's Health Organization et al.," 10.

conception, but that is only because of the erroneous *Dobbs* verdict, which most states do not yet know is unconstitutional. The verdict has been accepted as making common law, despite the fact that Alito said that to be constitutional, abortion had to be approved by an amendment. His opinion does not create either common law or legislative action, as the Supreme Court cannot make common law, and changing the definition of a person from quickening under common law, to conception under a Papal bull, is not legal legislation. This is all happening in America, folks, a country which we say is the land of the free, and the home of the brave, and I am doing my damnest to warn you about what is happening before permanent damage takes place, and our Democracy is torn to shreds by a President who has already admitted that he would like to be the Pope.

The fact remains that there is an exception to the rule in almost every one of those states that are anti-abortion because that has basically been the common law since the time the Constitution was written, and has been the practice primarily all over the world. An amendment that is properly written should be able to pass in at least 3/4 of the total number of states in America because those states today, like Mississippi, accept that abortion is murder only when the fetus is viable. Alito may have been correct to say that the *Roe* decision struck down the abortion laws of every single State at the time, but I point out that all Constitutional Amendments do this, although that cannot be said to be true until the amendment is written, and passed. Women won the right to vote through an amendment in every state; slavery was abolished through an amendment in every state; and now we must give women the right to choose whether to have an unwanted child, or not, but do it before that fetus becomes viable in every state. My proposal is rational; my proposal is moral; and, more importantly, my proposal is the only one which will prevent 10-15% of unwanted pregnancies to eventually result in infanticide or child abuse.

What Alito further added to his discussion of the abortion issue gives us important insight into his reasoning throughout the case, and that was when he stated: "26 States have expressly asked this Court to overrule *Roe* and *Casey* and allow the States to regulate or prohibit pre-viability abortions."[77] The importance of this statement is that he is admitting that he was asked to declare that life began at conception

---

77 Ibid., 12.

by 26 states, even though the state of Mississippi, whose act was the only evidence presented, never hinted that his statement was true, and I have no evidence in any of the books I have read that such a declaration was ever made in any of the ancillary filings. Where did this information come from? Side-bar conferences? Irresponsible gossip? No legislators appeared at the trial; no other Justices talked in this manner. In my opinion, this information likely came from the District Attorney and the Governor, who wanted abortion banned, but since when does a judicial decision to claim life began at conception come from sources like that when it goes against the common law of almost every state in the Union. I know of no prior push for life beginning at conception at any time in my interest in this subject over the past thirty years. Yes, Dr. Horatio Robinson Storer, made this claim when the AMA was first formed, but his campaign has clearly been showed to be no more than an attempt to follow Catholic law, and not the faith of all religions, which is exactly was Justice Alito did in his *Dobbs* decision. Today, there still are no proponents of this Theocracy except those promoting Catholic theology. This is legal malpractice, pure and simple, in my opinion, and the 14 states that have declared that life begins at conception, have done so basing their legislation on what Alito said and did without any constitutional support for his action. I am hoping that this book will encourage those states to reconsider those laws, and accept that there is a clear distinction between viable and nonviable fetuses that should allow for abortion of nonviable pregnancies at whatever level the state in question accepts, and no amendment on the subject has yet been passed.[78]

Justice Alito had no accurate sense of what research on fetal viability showed when he defined it as beginning at conception, and he relied only what his religion taught him, and not on what medical research had shown. His legal training should have made him aware of what the common law was in America, and across the world, but he paid no attention to that information, and was acting more like a political Representative, or an altar-boy in a Church, than a Justice of the Supreme Court. The Supreme Court also once ruled that slavery was constitutionally correct, so we know that Justices can make mistakes, but this declaration affects millions of women, and many millions of future unwanted children, and we need more observance

---

78 Microsoft CoPilot (7/2/2025). Personal Communication.

of constitutional law than we do altar-boy obedience. Alito also knew that the Mississippi legislature did not follow that supposition, and yet he decided to make it as his own, never declaring that the statute would then mean that the abortion would be murder. The pressure to overrule *Roe v. Wade* had reached such intense proportions at the time *Dobbs* was decided from President Donald Trump, in my opinion, that was not present when the Supreme Court revisited the *Roe* case in *Planned Parenthood of Southeastern Pa. v. Casey* in 1992. That Alito decided to overturn both cases, and claim that life began at conception because he had no other basis to act as he did without such a declaration, is self-evident to me.[79] Very seldom has a Supreme Court case overturned two other Supreme Court cases at the same time, with the last taking place in 1937, when *West Coast Hotel Co. v. Parrish, 300 U.S. 379 (1937)* overturned two earlier decision in *Adkins v. Children's Hospital, 261 U.S. 525 (1923)* and *Lochner v. New York 198 U.S. 45 (1905),* allowing for minimum wage laws and greater government regulation. The actions in *Dobbs* are extremely unusual, and I believe shows how the Republican Party is trying to change our government from a true Democracy, and turn it into a Theocracy, which I find reprehensible, and frankly unconstitutional.

I believe that Alito's declaration shows not only how divided our country had become over the right to an abortion, but how uneducated our entire country is on the issue of unwanted pregnancies, and unwanted children throughout the entire history of mankind.

More importantly, I can say that the fact that 50% of unwanted pregnancies are now aborted is a statistic that should scare the Hell out of people who want to prevent safe abortion on everyone, for it shows that people are not paying attention to what is a fact-of-life concern for millions of unwanted children because their not-wannabe-parents are abusive, dangerous, and many will one day cause harm or death to the child they didn't want.

If 50% of unwanted pregnancies are aborted, what do you think will happen if all of those people suddenly are forced to give birth. Blackmun accomplished his goal of allowing abortion to be legal for more than 50 years, and in that era, we truly found out how pervasive is the desire to have a safe abortion. We must not allow every unwanted

---

79 "Dobbs, State Health Officer of the Mississippi Department of Health, et. al. v. Jackson Women's Health Organization et al.," 3.

fetus to become viable before it is aborted, or we will find ourselves dealing with the incredible statistic that 10-15% of them will be killed by infanticide or child abuse, and that will be a disaster that is truly immoral.

This is America, the land with a Constitution that affords all residents to have equal protection under the law, and it is time to accept that some parents are not ready to take care of a child when an unexpected pregnancy arises, and we must let them abort that pregnancy before it is a viable fetus that is not sufficiently developed to feel pain and suffering.

You ask how I know that what I say is true? We are talking here of millions of cases each year, as 930,160 abortions were done in America in 2020, and 1,037,000 in 2023.[80] If we assume a 10% infanticide rate that I presented in my book was the average infanticide rate throughout our history, that is 103,700 murders per year. If abortion is approved, and if the rate stays at 0.1%, then the number drops to 1037 murders. I rest my case.

Alito found that the case now before him meant that he had to provide the means to satisfy the request from the 26 States that wanted to ban abortion in some capacity. Mississippi had passed a law that prohibited an abortion after the 15th week of pregnancy, which was several weeks before a fetus was regarded as "viable" outside the womb in *Roe v. Wade*.[81] Many other countries in the world have passed similar laws, however, and so there is no clear figure the everyone agrees upon for when viability is possible, and my choice to use proven cases of survival after intensive care was able to be stopped after aiding their ability to mature is what I will be proposing in my amendment. Khiara M. Bridges, who has both a J.D, and a Ph.D. degree in Anthropology, and is Professor of Law at Berkeley School of Law, noted that Alito continued to use the word "womb" instead of "uterus," in her opinion, and also often referred to the fetus as an "unborn human being," which reflects a dispassionate opinion of medicine, an opinion I agree with.[82] Alito has no authority to make this judgment as a Justice without providing medical and legal

---

80 Microsoft CoPilot, 11/15/2024. Personal Communication.

81 Ibid. This was Mississippi's Gestational Age Act, Miss. Code Ann§41-41-191 (2018). Ibid., 15.

82 Bridges, "The *Dobbs* Gambit, Gaslighting at the Highest Level," 121-122.

support for his opinion. She also believes that the term "abortionist" is offensive, and is used four times in the *Dobbs* case to claim that those who provide abortion are not highly trained, credential medical providers.[83] It is possible that the fifteen-week gestation date was chosen because reform in Mexico City in 2007 had made voluntary abortion legal at 12-weeks gestation, along with Cuba and Guyana, and this would seem to be a reasonable response to not following *Roe v. Wade*.[84] It is immaterial, however, because, as I have already said, the Mississippi statute under Alito could not be valid because it would mean the abortion would be murder. Because the law involved the decision in both *Roe v. Wade* and *Casey*, however, the Federal Court found the law unconstitutional and both sides appealed to the Supreme Court. The question was whether that case could be used as a basis for *stare decisis*, which is a legal term that means "to stand by things decided."

In his opinion, Alito clarified that what was called "fetal life" in the prior cases, the Mississippi law calls an "unborn human being," indicating, in his opinion, that they are defining human life as beginning at conception, although that is not what they said in their legislation.[85] If he is correct, Mississippi approved a law calling for murder of fetuses, and that was not true because you can't "murder" a nonviable fetus, you can only commit feticide. He was aware that the state's concern was to protect the life of a fetus, so he added his own belief that life begins at conception, rather than accept their 15-week limitation. This put an entirely different element into all future legal discussions of abortion, however, because if conception is legally accepted as a definition of when life begins, then feticide disappears from the American lexicon, and any pregnancy termination is indeed infanticide, or murder. This statement does not belong in a Supreme Court decision. It is not up to a Supreme Court to decide when life

---

83 Ibid., 121.

84 Singer, <u>Lawful Sins: Abortion Rights and Reproductive Governance in Mexico</u>, 3. Most of these were done by giving two doses of mifepristone to produce contractions. Ibid., 1. Abortion is still illegal elsewhere in Mexico because the country is such a strong Catholic country that the only legal exception in every other state is rape. Ibid., 8.

85 "Dobbs, State Health Officer of the Mississippi Department of Health, et. al. v. Jackson Women's Health Organization et al.," 14.

begins if all they can cite is their religious upbringing as scientific proof. We are a country that is supposed to have separation of Church and State, and that means that our judicial system must not allow the Justices to rely on their childhood training to determine what our Constitutional rights are.

I realize I am making life on our planet more complicated with my present book, but it is time we all begin to think of what our underlying nature of being a *Homo sapien* truly is, and realize that our propensity to hate, and kill, and constantly try to eliminate those we don't like, will end life on earth unless we try to legislate in a more protective manner, and do our best to become tolerant of those who may have different beliefs, both religious and social in nature. These two Supreme Court cases, one finding a constitutional right for abortion, and one denying that right, demonstrates how one Justice was able to legalize abortion throughout our nation because he believed it was the right thing to do, even though he could not find true constitutional support for his decision, while another Supreme Court Justice was able to deny abortion by following his Catholic training on when life begins. While both believed they were doing the right thing, one based his judgment on the Catholic Pope, and one was relying on the common law which defined life as beginning at "quickening," Both Justices on this issue made mistakes on what they did, and even though I am glad Blackmun did it because he relied on what he believed the medical community supported, the result was that we were able to prove the value of allowing abortion of unwanted nonviable pregnancies.

I understand that I am not an accepted scholar on the subject of how Supreme Court Justices should act on interpreting Constitutional law, but I can say that my basis of making my decision is that religious principles are relied on by faith, and not proof, and that is not how judicial opinions should be made. The entire sequence of these two cases shows us that our legal system cannot protect us from our own biologic behavior unless we begin to understand that human life is not sacred with God-given rights, and the United States Constitution must carefully construct amendments which protect not only our personal liberties, but the safety of all our inhabitants from criminal behavior that endangers the lives of other human beings. This includes the lives of unwanted nonviable fetuses, whose life as a human being has not yet begun, and whose parental right to abort before viability exists should be allowed for whatever reason they desire. I will return to this issue in the Conclusion to this book, but I must continually remind the reader that when they enter a polling place to vote on whether the amendment should pass or fail, they must supplement their opinion with the arguments I make in this book. I am not here to change your religious beliefs on when the soul, or the chance for life begins, but rather when that fetus truly can feel pain, or survive outside the womb, for that is the legal issue which must be the factor that causes you to vote yes or no.

What is especially egregious about Alito's decision is that he was aware of the fact that abortion under common law was felt to be a crime after the first movement of the fetus was felt in the womb, usually taking place between the 16th and 18th week of pregnancy, an issue I previously discussed in *Roe v. Wade* as the reason Blackmun accepted that definition.[86] Alito discarded the importance of the quickening rule, however, saying that "the rule was abandoned in the 19th century," which is an outright lie.[87] He knew it was not abandoned in the 19th century because England had made it part of their Abortion Act in the 20th century, as did many other countries in the world, as well. It is clear that Alito was intent on following the Catholic view of when life begins, totally ignoring the view of the scientific medical community, and the judicial holdings throughout the rest of the world. The only place that it began to be abandoned in the 19th century was the Catholic Church, and it is clear to me that all of Alito's conclusions on when life began came from his Catholic education, ignoring the medical community, and the judicial holdings throughout the rest of the world. He said that the Mississippi legislature found at 5-6-weeks gestation a fetus heart begins to beat, at 8-weeks, the fetus begins to move, at 10-weeks the organs function, and after 15-weeks, surgical instruments are needed to abort, which is a dangerous practice.[88] He knew that other legislatures picked 15-weeks as when life began, but totally ignored that reality, and ruled that life began at conception. In making his decision, I believe he used the public support of others who follow that opinion by adding that: "In this country during the 19th century, the vast majority of the States

---

86 "Dobbs, State Health Officer of the Mississippi Department of Health, et. al. v. Jackson Women's Health Organization et al.," 24.

87 Ibid., 30.

88 Ibid., 16.

enacted statutes criminalizing abortion at all stages of pregnancy," in support of this stance, making the argument that an amendment to the Constitution would be required.[89] I don't doubt that an amendment is necessary, but I will show that his decision to pick conception as the beginning of viability is not generally accepted, not scientifically feasible, not legally possible, and to put it bluntly, is ridiculous. I will begin the process of starting a campaign for an amendment along with the Society for the Prevention of Infanticide, but hope that some legal scholars consider arguing that this position makes his own case faulty, and return to the *Roe v. Wade* decision.

I feel impelled to make a personal note here that expresses my concern for the legitimacy of this majority opinion of the Court. I am amazed at how far America has come since John F. Kennedy was elected President in 1961, when I was 20-years-old. I remember that during his campaign, it was widely stated that a Catholic had never been President, and shouldn't be because of the allegiance he owed to the Pope. When he was elected, I was proud, as I was when Barack Obama was elected as the first Black President in 2009, for the fairness shown by the American public, who showed through the amendment process that the United States Constitution would be able to combat the type of prejudice that was worldwide at the time it was written. By electing these two men as President for the first time, one a Catholic, and one a Black man, it showed me that our country was becoming less biased, and more open to change. This vote in *Dobbs*, however, with six Catholic Justices voting for a Catholic, rather than a scientific or legal, definition of what entails a "person," causes me to worry that our country is reverting to a narrowness of mind that could very well portend a possible future Civil War, which a number of Republican politicians have already called for.

Alito went on to state in his opinion that Mississippi initially only wanted clarification of *Roe v. Wade*, and it went out of its way to make clear that it was *not* asking the Court to repudiate entirely the right to choose whether to terminate a pregnancy, but in his concurrence, Roberts stated that after *certiorari* was granted, it "bluntly announced that the court should overrule *Roe* and *Casey*."[90] This information is also very disturbing, for I believe that Roberts was admitting that

89 Ibid., 31.
90 Ibid., 141.

there was much use of undocumented personal communications in the deliberations, and I cannot tell if it was intentionally put in or not because it is factual, or if there was pressure applied to truly overturn *Roe v. Wade*. It is clear to me that the entire Republican Party, and all the Republican states, wanted *Roe v. Wade* overturned, since that was what Trump said he would do in his debate with Hillary Clinton in 2016. I would not expect that two assenting Justices on a Supreme Court decision would write comments that are so disparate, however, and frankly contradictory on the issue of when life starts, defining personhood. Since when do the parties in a case, especially a Supreme Court case, get this much power in the decision making of the court? Roberts said that Mississippi went on to demand that the court reaffirm or overrule the cases, and "given those two options, the majority picks the latter."[91] My law degree does not authorize me to demand an explanation for these remarks, but I would like someone to explain what the Hell is happening here. The Chief Justice is adding a written concurring opinion, and it is voiced in language that sounds more like a dissent than a concurrence, and Justices Clarence Thomas, Neil M. Gorsuch, Brett M. Kavanaugh, and Amy Coney Barrett all concurred in the decision, making our Supreme court look more like a Catholic tribunal, than the highest Court in the land.[92]

Before I end this chapter, I want to add that the dissent in this case also failed, in my opinion, to focus on any of the truly faulty reasonings of Alito, and acted more like they were overwhelmed by the loss of support that they had relied on for almost fifty years while *Roe v. Wade* was the law of the land. Justices Stephen Gerald Breyer, who retired in 2022, shortly after the case was determined, Sonia Sotomayor, and Elena Kagan, all were appointed by Democratic Presidents, and

---

91 Ibid.

92 At his hearings to become a justice, Gorsuch testified that *Roe* "Is a precedent of the U.S. Supreme Court," and lauded the idea of respecting them. Waldman, The Supermajority: How the Supreme Court Divided America, 131. At his hearings, Kavanaugh also called an "Important precedent of the Supreme Court that has been reaffirmed many times." Ibid. Clarence Thomas, on the other hand, has said precedent is for suckers, and if the Court disagrees with it, "it can feel free to erase it." Ibid., 209. In his concurring agreement opinion, Justice Thomas disparaged the Due Process Clause, but none of the other Judges agreed. Strauss, "Liberal Critics of *Roe*," 16.

all dissented in this case, with some of their comments adding even more fuel to my gradually increasing flame of disappointment in the handling of this case. As expected, they opened their discussion with the statement that: "Respecting a woman as an autonomous being, and granting her full equality, meant giving her substantial choice over this most personal and most consequential of all life decisions," which was clearly reflective of the arguments raised during the fight to give women the right to vote, but I think it was not helpful to their case, since that right came from an amendment, and not a judicial opinion of the Constitution.[93] Women did attempt to get the right to vote by applying public pressure under what became known as the Women's Suffrage Movement led by Susan B. Anthony (1820-1906), Elizabeth Cady Stanton (1815-1902), and Lucretia Mott (1793-1880), but that was over one-hundred years ago, and the women's-lib movement is truly old news. In addition, while women were able to eventually get the Nineteenth Amendment passed on August 18, 1920, the fight to get 3/4 of the states to approve it took almost 72 years, and the prospect they now faced apparently made it difficult for them to respond.[94]

What Alito based his opinion on was the right of the fetus to have an equal right to live as a "person" under the protection of the Constitution, and the dissent did not really deal with that issue at all. Supporters of abortion rights all emphasized the right of a mother to choose whether to carry a pregnancy to term or not, but they were in an era when the right of a fetus to live was being considered as an alternate option, and Alito's verdict that the State had legitimate interests from the outset of the pregnancy in protecting" the "life of the fetus that may become a child," went uncontested.[95] The dissent argued that the mother had a right to choose, but they had no answer for the State arguing that the right of the fetus was just as great. The dissent argued that the Court was saying "that from the very moment of fertilization, a woman has no rights to speak of," but that was not what Alito actually said.[96] I am sure if the decision is challenged in the future, we will hear more powerful arguments than what was raised in this case, but I am not going to await for that event, and will

---

93   "Dobbs, State Health Officer of the Mississippi Department of Health, et. al. v. Jackson Women's Health Organization et al.," 148.

94   Ibid.

95   Ibid., 148-149.

96   Ibid.

press forward with vigorous effort. This is the reason I am writing this book to propose an amendment that allows abortions up to the 20th week of gestation, which is not that much above the Mississippi statute that was approved, and yet the dissent never pointed this out. If the Justices could vote to approve that level of life, the people of Mississippi should vote to approve my amendment, and every other American, as well.

I agree completely with the view of *Roe v. Wade* on both the right of a woman to choose whether to abort an nonviable fetus or not, and also that life begins when quickening appears. The dissent correctly noted that states are already lowering the bar for when abortion can take place, and they should have argued that Alito should have followed their 15-week gestational period, and not made his own determination that life begins at conception. These even included fears that a fetus with severe physical anomalies will not be allowed to be aborted in their forecast, and indicated that this could also include a failure to allow an abortion if there is a risk of death or physical harm to the mother.[97] These are all possible projections, in my opinion, and they are correct to emphasize that these possible outcomes will take place in many states unless my book can help to educate the public to the dangers of not allowing unwanted pregnancies to be aborted before the fetus reaches the age of viability, but their failure to bring it up in the dissent meant that the majority was not required to provide an answer. My analysis of history has shown that there is a 10-15% chance an unwanted child will be killed at some point after the birth, because "history will repeat itself," as first said by Karl Marx (1818-1883), and then embellished by, but that argument was also not raised.

The dissent also rightly claimed that "women lacking financial resources will suffer from today's decision," and showed that this causation was one major reason women in the past often committed infanticide because they could not stop working to provide sustenance to the family they already had.[98] This problem also was a major cause of female infanticide in countries when the birth-rate was limited to allowing the birth of only one child, and many families wanted that child to be a boy. According to the American journalist Nicholas D. Kristof:

---

97 Ibid., 149-150.
98 Ibid., 151.

At least 60 million females in Asia are missing and feared dead, victims of nothing more than their sex. Worldwide, research suggests, the number of missing females may top 100 million.[99]

Female infanticides in India and China have been particularly prevalent because of this preference for male offspring, but there are many reasons which parents killed children in the past, and I recommend you read my book before you come to any decision of your own whether abortion should be a right for all women to choose. I will discuss this issue in greater detail throughout this book, but none of these issues were raised, and so *Roe v. Wade* got overturned.

The dissenters also were against the cavalier way the Court tossed aside the important doctrine of *stare decisis*, which they feared would cause an upheaval in law and society, but even *Casey* used this tactic.[100] They pointed out that "women have relied on the availability of abortion both in structuring their relationships and in planning their lives," but such arguments did not attack the major conclusion that Alito made about life beginning at conception.[101] At the same time, we have to realize that *Dred Scott v. Sandford*, which was decided in 1857, and upheld the right of slavery in the Constitution, is generally considered one of the worst decisions ever made by the United States Supreme Court, and makes *stare decisis* a tactic to always be considered, but not infallibly. It clearly is not a barrier to overturn a case if it was not decided in a just manner, so I am not going to argue that the court should not have made their decision because of the principle of *stare decisis*.

The primary problem with the dissents' argument was that they were too devoted to the *Roe's* accepting that "a long line of precedents, 'founded in the Fourteenth Amendment's concept of personal liberty,' protected individual decision making related to 'marriage, procreation, contraception, family relationships, and child rearing and education,'" and while many of those personal liberties may have indeed included the attribute of personal liberty, the primary purpose of that amendment was for equal protection under the law.[102] Everyone knew that the

99   Kristof, "Stark Data on Women: 100 Million Are Missing," C1.
100   "Dobbs, State Health Officer of the Mississippi Department of Health, et. al. v. Jackson Women's Health Organization et al.," 153.
101   Ibid., 153-154.
102   Ibid., 155.

conservative Supreme Court was going to attack the interpretation of the Constitution in the manner which I said was begun by Robert Bork, and yet the dissent failed to argue against that topic effectively. When women needed to have the right to vote, it took an amendment of the Constitution for them to get it, and not a Supreme Court case. If state laws against abortion are so pervasive that an amendment cannot be passed, then I agree that using the Fourteenth Amendment as a reason for making abortion a personal right is not good constitutional law, and it is not the Supreme Court's proper role to make that decision for the entire country. We must remember that it took the Bill of Rights, and many other amendments, to include vital liberties under our Constitution, and the proper method to do it today should be to start a campaign now to inform the population of every state to realize that getting pregnant is too easy to try and prevent unwanted pregnancies from ever happening, and it is obvious that in the history of mankind from the time of Adam and Eve, when unwanted pregnancies take place, 10-15% of those births will eventually be killed. It will be very difficult to determine when a fertilized ovum becomes viable to live outside its mother's womb, but it is vital that we try and make a reasonable, scientific definition of that moment, and allow abortion to take place before that date as a personal right all women should have. After that date, States should have the right to limit the procedure as they see fit.

I earlier stated that I believe that the Supreme Court in *Dobbs* has been attempting to turn our political system into a Theocracy rather than a Democracy, and they are doing this by also attempting to modify the Separation of Church and State principle which has been applied to the First Amendment since the Founding Fathers first described the meaning of that amendment. In the opinion itself, I have stated that I believe the *Dobbs* verdict was an attempt by Donald Trump, in conjunction with the Supreme Court he designed, to change our political system to a Theocracy, instead of a Democracy, and this began with his desire to declare abortion unconstitutional by claiming that life began at conception, as declared by the Catholic Popes, instead of at quickening, as declared by American and English common law. The *Roe v. Wade* verdict had relied on the Ninth and Fourteenth Amendments, but the *Dobbs* verdict was going to rely on a modification of the First Amendment, which had been interpreted since its inception when it was ratified on December 15, 1791, to mean Separation of Church and State.

The text of the *Dobbs* case only mentioned the First Amendment eight times, but their intention was made clear when Alito claimed that *Roe v. Wade* "distorted First Amendment doctrines," "as well as the rule that statutes should be read where possible to avoid unconstitutionality."[103] This was the only mention that was put into this case discussion, but following this ruling, the Court has gone on to try and expand this theory to relaxing the relaxing of the rigid Separation of State and Court doctrine, that I want to discuss further at this time. In 2022, the Court ruled on four cases that expanded their allowance of not applying strict criteria to the separation concept, including *Carson v. Makin, 596 U.S. 767 (2022),* which dealt with public funding for religious schools; *Kennedy v. Bremerton School District 597 U.S. 507 (2022),* which dealt with religious expression in schools and the boundaries of the First Amendment; *Ramirez v. Collier 595 U.S. 411 (2022),* which dealt with religious liberty in the Execution Chamber; and *Shurtleff v. Boston 596 U.S. 243 (2022),* which dealt with free express and government speech. Each case sought to modify the criteria for separation of Church and State, and I contend that this is a dangerous precedent being put forward by the conservative Catholic

Before *Dobbs was passed,* other Supreme Courts had followed the First Amendment, including *Santa Fe Independent School District v. Doe, 530 U.S. 290 (2000),* which held student-led prayers in schools unconstitutional; *McCreary County v. ACLU of Kentucky, 545 U.S. 844 (2005),* which disallowed displays of the Ten Commandments; and *Van Orden v. Perry, 545 U.S. 677 (2005),* which also did not allow Ten Commandment displays. The trend began to change in 2014, however, as the *Town of Greece v. Galloway, 572 U.S. 565, (2014),* allowed a town's prayer service to not be nonsectarian, and *Trinity Lutheran Church v. Comer, 582 U.S. 449, (2017),* where grants were allowed to improve religious schools utilizing the interpretation of the Establishment Clause, so I believe that the *Dobbs Court* after overturning *Roe v. Wade* saw the opportunity to begin to eat away at what Trump was really interested in, and that was transforming our

---

103   "Dobbs, State Health Officer of the Mississippi Department of Health, et. al. v. Jackson Women's Health Organization et al.," 63.

country into a Theocracy governed by the Catholic Church.[104] In 2025, the Court held in *Mahmoud et al. v. Taylor et al., 606 U.S. — (2025)* that parents could opt out of school teaching that differs from their religious beliefs, further ignoring their responsibility to separate issues involving Church and State.

In my opinion, the attempt by Justices on the present Supreme Court to modify the principle of Separation of Church and State must be shown to be erroneous by passing an amendment to overturn their decision in *Dobbs*. Morgan Marietta agreed that the Supreme Court was redefining religious neutrality into "'coequal' neutrality, which abandons the view that secularism is the assumption and religion the exception, in favor of a new standard which assumes that both religion and secularism are co-equals present in the public realm."[105] He claimed that the Court's intention was that "mere existence is not endorsement and does not necessarily constitute coercion," but there is no question that in the issue of abortion, the Justices changed the definition of personhood from true life, to mere conception, and that is more than coercion, it is following the opinion of a Catholic Pope.[106] It is also attempting to redefine the common law definition of life beginning at conception, and that can only be done by an amendment, and not a Supreme Court decision, since two prior Supreme Court decisions accepted that quickening was the common law.

There have been many references in Supreme Court decisions to the need to follow the Separation of Church and State principles, as manifested by Justice John Paul Stevens, who is Presbyterian and was nominated by President Gerald Ford (1913-2006) in 1975, and in his concurrence in the case of *Wallace v. Jaffrey, 478 U.S. 38 (1985),* he emphasized that "the State's interest must be secular; consistent with the First Amendment the State may not promote theological or sectarian interest," which is exactly what I am claiming the *Dobbs* Court did.[107] It is one thing to allow some display of one's religion in the schools or workplace, it is another to modify the common law based on the opinion of the Catholic Pope. I believe Blackmun was worried about this trend developing, for in his concurrence he

---

104   Microsoft CoPilot (8/23/2025). Personal Communication.

105   Ibid.

106   Ibid., 10.

107   "Dobbs, State Health Officer of the Mississippi Department of Health, et. al. v. Jackson Women's Health Organization et al.," 915.

voiced my concerns when he added to his note that: "I fear for the darkness as four justices anxiously await the single vote necessary to extinguish the light," to me a clear indication why, in 1992, he delayed his retirement as long as he could until 1994.[108] He was correct in his concern, for the *Dobbs* Court has continued to attack the validity of the Separation of Church and State, as I will show throughout this book. The *Dobbs* Court would show its desire to become a Theocracy, but not actually mention the First Amendment, while a later case, *United States v. Hansen, 599 U.S. 762 (2023)* shows how they will be pushing the Theocracy envelope further in the future.

I will return to this issue in the Conclusion to this book, but I now want to move on and elaborate the issue of fetus viability, which, as I said in the Introduction, is the primary problem with the *Dobbs* opinion.

---

108   "Planned Parenthood of Southeastern Pa. v. Casey, 505 U.S. 833 (1992)," 924.

Chapter V
Fetus Viability And When Life Begins

I have made it clear so far in this book that the violent debate that has been going on in America since *Roe v. Wade* was decided over whether abortion is an act of murder or not is primarily due to a misunderstanding about the issue of fetal viability, and the determination of when "life" begins. This moment in time is critical because the long period of time a human fetus takes to grow from conception to birth in a woman's uterus is very unusual, and clearly, according to common law and medical science is not murder when the process begins, but becomes murder when the fetus is able to survive on its own outside the uterus.

Abortion is a term that is used to describe the artificial removal of the fetus. When it takes place when the fetus is nonviable, the result is feticide, which is not murder because the fetus at that point cannot survive outside of the uterus. When the removal occurs once the fetus is viable, it is equivalent to murder, and the term usually applied is infanticide, which is only approved by a court of law that must determine if the mother's life is in danger if abortion is not done. It is a difficult decision to make because it means that some living entity must actually be killed, so that the other can hopefully survive. No one wants to be the party making that decision, but in most societies, it has been a court of law making the decision. Abortion under common law across the world has generally only been done when the woman can feel movement of the fetus, a condition known as "quickening," for that is when it was accepted that a miscarriage, or purposeful removal of the fetus, can still result in the survival of the fetus. *Roe v. Wade* was the Supreme Court's case that decided that a citizen of the United States had a personal right guaranteed by the Constitution for feticide, but not for abortion of a viable fetus because that was equivalent to the right to kill during declared wars, or punishment for a capital crime. The common law restricted legal abortion to only nonviable fetuses.

It is for this reason that the issue of when fetal viability begins is of the utmost importance in deciding if, and when, abortion can be seen as the right of a woman to choose whether to give birth or not. Medical treatises have often attempted to define precisely when the viability of a fetus actually took place. For centuries, the only method available was determining when the mother could actually feel movement, indicating that the fetus was mature enough to have muscular function. Obviously, other means of determining the capacity to more accurately make this decision became available when newborn intensive care units (NICUs) first began to be developed in the late 1900s, appearing in America in 1922.[1] These units developed assisted-living devices like intravenous feeding and mechanical respiration, which allowed premature deliveries to be kept alive so that extended opportunities for maturation could take place outside the uterus, and hopefully, a child would then mature enough to eventually be able to live with assistance by the mother alone. *Roe v. Wade* was the first Supreme Court to decide in 1973 that the gestational age when this was possible was the common law definition of "quickening," which generally took place at 24-28-weeks gestation. The Supreme Court in *Colautti v. Franklin, 439 U.S. 379 (1979)* agreed with this judgment, holding that: "Viability is reached when, in the judgment of the attending physician on the particular facts before him, there is a reasonable likelihood of the fetus's sustained survival outside the womb, with or without artificial support."[2] Governments across the world accepted the standard, although since that time, the gestational age that defines the viability of the fetus has been lessened by variable amounts, as I will soon explain.

Pro-Lifers claim that all abortion is murder. They base their view on the definition of life beginning at conception, which is the banner that has been taken up by the Republican Party, based upon the modern position of the Catholic Church, which considered abortion to be murder when Pope Pius IX made the stunning majority opinion in his apostolic constitution, *Apostolicae Sedis*, in 1869 that there would no longer be a distinction between animated and unanimated fetuses, and that all abortions would be punished by immediate excommunication, because it was an act of murder.

Most countries of the world do not accept that life begins at conception, when the union known as a zygote then forms a round ball of cells known as a morula, and then a two-layered blastocyst, which consists of about 70-100 cells and a fluid-filled cavity, with an inner layer of cells that will grow into the fetus, and an outer layer

---

1   Microsoft CoPilot (9/15/2025). Personal Communication.

2   Selia, "The Meaning of Viability in Abortion Care," 106.

that will form the placenta, which will provide sustenance to the fetus. Once the zygote is formed, the lining of the uterus begins to thicken so that the zygote will have a place to nestle in and be nourished. The zygote is 70 microns across, while the blastocyst cells only measures around 10 microns, but because there is growth taking place, Pro-Lifers accept that this is true "life," even though there is no way that continued maturation can take place outside the uterus, which is when the blastocyst can develop into a fetus and begin the process of organ maturation that can support life after expulsion from the uterus once "quickening" develops.[3]

In this chapter, I am going to try and explain the life cycle of the human fetus in some detail so that those of you who are going to vote on may amendment proposal will have some scientific understanding of this process because there has been much research performed on animals that have been cloned in the laboratory from somatic cells, and then maintained at first artificially, and then in the uteri of living females, which has added to our understanding of how the maturation actually works. This took place with the birth of a famous sheep named "Dolly," which was born after scientists at the Roslin Institute in Scotland took a mammary gland cell from an adult sheep, and fused it with an enucleated egg cell, which had its nucleus removed, and then incubated in a laboratory dish for six days. They then implanted it into a surrogate Scottish Blackface ewe's uterus, and on 7/5/1998, 145-150 days later, a living sheep was delivered.[4] So far, no birth has taken place with an artificial uterus. However, researchers in Japan have come close to sustaining a goat embryo in a biology lab for several weeks, which does not yet assure it will be possible.[5] In addition, Jacob Hanna's team grew mouse embryos at the Weizmann Institute of Science in Israel by adding blood serum from human umbilical cords, agitating them in glass jars, and pumping in a pressurized oxygen mixture in an artificial womb, but not yet to completion, which is also promising.[6] . Hanna likens the process to putting a COVID-19 patient on a ventilation machine. Getting closer, however, is not yet

---

3   Zernicka-Goetz and Highfield, The Dance of Life: The New Science of How a Single Cell Becomes a Human Being," 51.

4   "Dolly, Cloned Sheep," 1-4.

5   Gargiulo, "Japan Has Created the First Artificial Womb," 1-8.

6   "A Mouse Embryo Has Been Grown in an Artificial Womb - Humans Could be Next," 2.

getting there, and while the future may hold an artificial uterus dream, our ability to grow human beings in the laboratory is not likely to be in the lifetime of anyone present today.

Our present-day research, however, assures me that my stand against the concept that life begins at conception is valid. I contend that we must accept the common law that is accepted in most countries of the world, which considers that life begins at quickening, when the mother can feel movement of the fetus as a sign it is alive. Pro-Choice advocates obviously prefer this definition of when life begins, and base their belief on science rather than faith because they are aware that when a fetus is expulsed by a miscarriage, it is easy to see why the majority are not capable of survival outside the uterine cavity for very long. Physicians, as well, are generally aware of these facts, but that does not prevent them, if they are devout Catholics from accepting the Papal pronouncements, and claiming that all abortion is murder. When it came to United States Supreme Court decisions, two agreed that life began at quickening, and one, the most recent *Dobbs* decision, held that life began at conception, but I have argued in this book that the decision was purposely made by being sure that conservative Catholic conservative Justices were appointed by Republican Presidents to the Court in order to have that determination take place. I will show in this chapter that the earliest premature delivery that has survived with life-sustaining intensive care unit (ICU) treatment and lived to become independently capable of life is at 20-weeks gestation, and for that reason it should be the definition of when life begins.

In the last Presidential campaign in 2024, the rhetoric between the Democrats and Republicans over the status of abortion rose to such levels that some prominent Republicans, such as Georgia State Senator Colton Moore, Ohio State Senator George Lang, and former Alaska Governor Sarah Palin, were calling for a Civil War to settle the issue once and for all.[7] Really, I'm not kidding, the conflict got so heated that threats of a Civil War were flung across the gauntlet, and I actually believe that the combatants were telling it like they believed it was, or how their muddled brains thought it was. The intensity of the dispute has reached the level of dispute that our Founding Fathers had over the liberty to have slaves when our Constitution was written, and the Federalists and Anti-Federalists fought over the issue of state-rights

---

7   "Republicans Just Can't Stop Calling For Civil War," 1.

– i.e., Patrick Henry's "give me liberty or give me death" demand. This means that our country has been through this type of political disputation before, and it shows how emotional an enraged populace can be, as we also saw in the French Revolution that followed shortly after our own uprising against English rule. America is just going to have to come to grips with the realization that before we can decide if abortion can be approved by an amendment to the Constitution or not, and we are going to have to decide when an individual can fulfill the definition of becoming a "person," as defined for individuals with guaranteed rights in our Constitution. In general, this boils down to the Catholic view that life begins at conception, or the common law view that it develops at "quickening," when a fetus can be seen as truly having "personhood" rights, which generally implies a living, human being in either a conscious or unconscious state. Because it also comes down to a decision whether it is the state that determines who has the rights, or the Catholic Pope, it is also the difference between a Democracy and a Theocracy.

When you vote on my amendment proposal, you will have to decide which of these positions is correct, because, as I said, you cannot claim that there is a constitutional right for an abortion if the act is actually a crime of murder. I have already mentioned earlier in this book how Catholic theology has come to its determination because they see the concept of life as having both a "soul," which is believed to be an inner mental nature of life that does not die according to Catholic theology, and a "body," which does undergo a physical death.

The existence of the soul, which then remains in either Heaven or Hell until the resurrection takes place, is a philosophical principle and cannot be proven or tested to determine if it is true. At the same time, a body can easily be defined as being alive or dead by medical testing, although today that decision is more complicated than it has been in the past.

Today, we have had to bifurcate the definition of death into two separate categories: that of the brain and that of the heart and lungs, which shows how complicated our understanding of "life" can sometimes become. The reason we have had to do this is because of legal complications necessitated by our previously defining death as a stoppage of heart function, and our ability today to keep a person alive by artificial support of heart and lung function that has created a condition where the brain has been so severely damaged that there is no brain function on electroencephalogram (EEG) tracings, which are permanent, but the life support treatment has continued to keep the patient "alive," by providing artificial support to heart and lung function, along with intravenous feedings. This state has become known as "brain death," which is permanent, and in order to stop the artificial support of the heart and lungs so the patient can actually "die," there has to be judicial intervention to allow the support to be discontinued, for the act is, in essence, murder. By allowing a court to declare that a patient is "brain-dead," we can allow artificial life-support to then be discontinued, so that death can finally take place.

In a way, this convoluted issue is very similar to the dilemma we are in when trying to differentiate between a viable and nonviable fetus, for murder is a severe crime that must be determined in a judicial setting, and we must have definitions that are as clear and concise as possible, in order to be sure that we continue the time-honored Sixth commandment to "thou shalt not commit murder," which is the basis of most ancient and modern Law Codes Because we are talking here of Constitutional law, however, and not a religious edict, we must also understand that the meaning of the term "person," which is how the Constitution describes those who are entitled to all the rights and liberties which are guaranteed to United States citizens, is not specifically defined in the wording of the Constitution, and because of that deficiency, we have had Supreme Courts differ in whether a "person" begins at conception or quickening. With respect to the right of an abortion, the word "fetus," like the word abortion," never appears in the Constitution, and therefore, whether an unborn fetus has rights separate from the mother who is pregnant is an issue that all Supreme Courts dealing with abortion have had to determine, and which *Roe v. Wade* and *Casey* decided that life began at "quickening," and *Dobbs* claimed it took place at conception. I have argued that Justice Alito was errant in declaiming that life began at conception because he was making a new common law by that decision, whereby both *Roe v. Wade* and *Casey* were simply following the long-held common law definition of a "person."

The conundrum we are in has left many commentators equally divided as to what is the proper approach to take. H. Tristram Engelhardt, Jr. (1941-2018), former Professor of Philosophy and Medicine at Rice University, tried to explain this dilemma by declaring that: "Zygotes, embryos, and fetuses, like brain-death but otherwise alive human beings, give no evidence of being persons," which helped him to explain our dilemma, but not satisfactorily in my opinion,[8] because all nonviable fetuses are not actually "brain-dead," but rather "brain not yet developed." A "brain-dead" person cannot recover, and will remain brain-dead forever, but a nonviable fetus, will eventually become brain functional unless some other process intervenes, which by the age of viability is not likely. We are therefore still left with a definition that does not differentiate between viable and nonviable fetuses, and also does not discuss how today some people want to include in the definition of "person" beings such as robots and pets.

In this chapter, I am interested in only the fetus, and I will not discuss robots and pets, but we cannot understand the true issue of abortion until we understand whether there is a difference between a viable and nonviable fetus, for that gets to the issue of "life" itself. I will try to settle this issue in this chapter firmly enough so that my amendment proposal will make sense to both sides of the abortion debate, and perhaps we can come to a sensible approach to what the status of a fetus truly is. If you only listen to the vociferous opponents of the abortion debate, it would appear that an amendment could never pass, but I believe that more than 3/4 of Americans believe that there is a distinction between viable and nonviable fetuses, and my proposed amendment should be able to pass, although the vote will be close, and hopefully not contentious.

I contend that there is only one Constitutional answer to this question of viability because of the accepted principle that there must be separation of Church and State if our Constitution is to be properly interpreted. As I said, I believe that America is Great because we follow the precepts of our Constitution that guarantee rights to all citizens, with the only caveat being that we understand who those citizens are. Our original Constitution did not answer that question properly, which is why our Founding Fathers left that issue to Amendments, and it took two of those amendments to eliminate slavery, and give women the right to vote.

Many more amendments have been added for a variety of other rights, but when it came to the issue of abortion, our Supreme Courts were divided on how the Constitution needed to be interpreted, so I am now proposing an amendment that will provide that understanding,

---

8   Engelhardt, Jr., "Introduction," xv.

and provide a unification that ends the debate. The belief that life begins at conception requires a faith in God to accept that it is true because there is no way that you can ever prove the existence of a soul that initiates life at conception, and this means you must also believe in God, which requires faith and not proof. That is what Alito did in the case of *Dobbs*, but in so doing he violated the principles of separation of Church and State, because he had relied on what his religion taught him, rather than what the Constitution supported.

You can prove when a fetus is able to survive outside the confines of a uterus by studying the results of premature deliveries that are supported by life-support measures after birth, and then eventually live independently without that support. That survival is proof, not faith, of viability, and even though the exact gestational age may vary over time as supportive measures improve, we do know that at the moment that age is about 20-weeks gestation. That is fact not fiction, and that is what I am putting in my amendment as the age at which abortion switches from feticide, which is abortion of a nonviable fetus, to infanticide, which is murder because the fetus changes from being nonviable to viable. It is necessary to point out that while the Catholic Pope states that life began at conception, not all Catholics follow that belief, and most other Christians, Jews and Muslims believe that life begins at quickening, so we cannot even be sure what the same One God Almighty, Who all monotheists believe in, actually said.

To turn to a more scientific method of making the determination of when life begins on the table, the earliest premature birth we know of today that actually survived long-term took place when a premature birth named Curtis Zy-Keith Means was born at age 21-weeks and 1 day gestation on July 5, 2020, at the University of Alabama, Birmingham Hospital, weighing 14.8 ounces (420 grams).[9] Since the normal gestation period in humans is generally estimated to be 266 days, or about 40-weeks, and the normal onset of quickening according to *Roe v. Wade* occurs at 24-28-weeks, the ability to survive birth at this early gestational age was considered a modern-day miracle. For convenience, I have chosen 20-weeks as the limit in my proposed amendment, realizing that some countries, like Germany, allow abortions without any danger to the mother's life only up to 12-weeks, or the first trimester, but these earlier determinations are

---

9   Echols, "UAB Hospital delivers record-breaking premature baby," 1.

not yet probable enough for me to utilize them, and I will demand that we only take into account actual cases which have undergone premature birth, and then survived, to utilize as valid gestational maturations to define a "person."[10] Because this may change in the future, my amendment proposal will be reevaluated every two years, and the age of gestation may eventually be lowered if proven instances of survival can be shown. There clearly is a limit to how low this can go, as sufficient organ maturation must take place, but our progress continues to rapidly improve, and I will not say more than "wait and see."

Claiming that life begins at conception not only affects how we view abortion, but it also creates an entirely different problem in trying to deal with the research in fertility issues that have been affecting the problems with fertility in America. In 1957, the United States' fertility rate for women peaked at 122.9 births per 1,000 women aged 15-44 years old, but by 2023, that rate dropped to 54.5, and there are many reasons that this is taking place, but I am not going to detail them in this book.[11]

It seems that the problem is likely to continue in the near future. The situation we now face is that many women today are dealing with this problem by using artificial insemination of their ovum, which immediately allows conception, so the ova become zygotes, and are immediately frozen for use when they are ready to begin their pregnancy. Multiple zygotes are created, but only a few are used to implant, and the rest can remain fertile in a frozen state and then be implanted up to 10-20 years later. A term has been invented to describe the state these embryos are in, because they are not "alive," and they are not "dead," and the term which has been accepted is Cryptobiosis, which creates a significant problem known as the "Paradox of Cryptobiosis," because if the future mother dies, or no longer wants more children, the disposal of the zygote, in one sense of the word, could be considered to be murder by abortion from the freezer.[12] Since the conceived ovum are not alive now, we also can't call them a person yet, as Justice Alito did, but since it can become

---

10 Ginsburg, "American Exceptionalism and the Comparative Constitutional Law of Abortion," 262.

11 "How Have US Fertility and Birth Rates Changed Over Time?" 1-2.

12 Gilmore, "What It Is to Die," 28.

a person in the future, similar to what has taken place at conception, what can we legally do to it if the mother dies, or no longer wants to use it to give birth. No matter what uterus the zygote is placed in, it will grow and mature, so in one sense of the word, it is a "person." Remember that the common law held that a mother convicted of a capital crime had to have her execution delayed until the fetus was born so as not to kill the fetus, so what do we now do with the product we have in the freezer? I bring this up not to answer it, because I am a doctor and a lawyer, but not an ethicist, so I'm not going to answer that question in this book, as my brain is already spinning out of control. You need to understand, however, how complicated life can get if you truly decide you are going to accept conception as the diagnosis of a "person." I contend that this issue is best left with the Catholic Pope.

The basis for the Catholic Church relying on the concept of the soul to decide that life begins at conception has expanded the need for us to make a clear legal decision on when life begins, and whether that is at conception, or a date determined to be when the fetus can survive outside the mother's uterus for a finite period of time. It is important to point out that advancements made in our knowledge of the Universe as a whole includes a better understanding of how our human condition is changed by that new information, which must be made part of our entire legal system, so that we can "keep up with the times," as the saying goes. Human life is no longer an issue of just being dead or alive, but has become increasingly difficult to define in modern times, both in the courtroom and in the hospital setting.

Today, there are medical and philosophical arguments on what actually defines what we mean by a person being "alive" or "dead." According to James L. Bernat, Emeritus Professor of Neurology at Cornell University Medical College, we must now define death as the permanent cessation of "the organism-as-a-whole."[13] Without brain function, there is no ability for the "whole" to function, so it is appropriate to consider a "brain-dead" person to be dead.[14] From a legal standpoint, this has necessitated defining criteria for when this condition can be accurately diagnosed so that a respirator can be allowed to be turned off, and the patient can be allowed to "die" in

---

13 Bernat, "Arguments Supporting Neurologic Criteria to Determine Death," 14.
14 Ibid., 17.

the permanent sense of the word, without considering the act to be murder. Many books have recently been written about this issue, and we must realize that we need to do the same thing with the issue of abortion. In order to bring abortion into the modern era, we have to realize that the nonviable fetus, which does not have a functional brain yet, is temporarily "brain-dead," with the only difference being that if it is allowed to mature with artificial support, it may be able to survive, and develop brain function, but that will not occur until we can call the fetus viable. The true definition of *personhood* is not applicable to a nonviable fetus because there is no evidence that, before viability, a nonviable fetus can be supported with artificial life support. This resembles what has been called the "Decapitation Gambit," which is raised in the issue of brain-dead patients, and asks if it is reasonable to consider that a person whose head has been removed to be allowed to die by turning off the machines that mechanically assist their heart and lungs to function.[15] By realizing that such a condition as the Decapitation Gambit is too absurd to accept, it allows us to proceed beyond the pure biological explanations of how to define death.

The issue of brain death was first raised in the Supreme Court case of *Cruzan v. Director, Missouri Department of Health, 497 U.S. 261 (1990)*, where a patient was diagnosed as being in a persistent vegetative state after an auto accident, and the family requested that a feeding tube not be inserted to artificially keep her alive. The Missouri Supreme Court said that it could not be done without a signed living will, which made it the first "right to die" case heard by the Supreme Court. Incredibly enough, this was the same Supreme Court that then was directed by Chief Justice William Rehnquist, who then ruled in a 5-4 decision that competent patients could refuse care that keeps them alive, but incompetent patients required a living will. The opinion, in essence, meant that the right to die was not a protection guaranteed by the Fourteenth Amendment without the addition of a living will, but that such a document would extend their desires after they were declared brain-dead.[16] Blackmun actually dissented in that opinion, along with Brennan and Stevens, but it shows that despite the similarity of the issues in this case, there are going to be variable results in how Justices react, because, in my opinion, it is better to rely

---

15 Lizza, "Defining Death in a Technological World," 13-14.
16 "Cruzan v. Director, Missouri Department of Health," 2-4.

on amendments to guide how the legal community should think. We cannot leave these issues up to nine Supreme Court Justices, and it should be an issue best handled by an amendment, if it is possible to get one passed without changing the criteria in our Constitution.

The fundamental importance of the *Cruzan* case was the question whether the Supreme Court in ruling that the patient has the "right to die" by writing a living will, and when the text, rather than use the term "brain death," refers to the condition as a "persistent vegetative state," does that mean that there is such a condition, and therefore a fertilized egg at conception cannot be a "person" because the zygote does not have a brain? In the *Cruzan* case, the word "persistent vegetative state" appeared 43 times, and Rehnquist said that the issue before the Court was whether the Due Process Clause allowed "Missouri to require a now-incompetent patient in an irreversible persistent vegetative state to remain on life support absent rigorously clear and convincing evidence that avoiding the treatment represents the patient's prior, express choice."[17] He added that the issue is important because "as many as 10,000 patients are now being maintained in a persistent vegetative state in the United States, and the number is expected to increase significantly in the United States."[18] The text indicated that Dr. Fred Plum, "the creator of the term 'persistent vegetative state' is a renowned expert on the subject," and best described as a loss of consciousness.[19] To me, the importance of this case is that it helps us to better understand how the growing fetus must be seen as a similar process, and not a single entity, and the best way to handle the issue on a cultural level is to try and determine when a fetus becomes viable, so that we can differentiate the issue of defining a "person" as when the essentials of life finally appear in a relatively permanent state. A zygote at conception cannot have a brain, and therefore must be "brain-dead," but it can eventually awaken and be alive when the brain is finally mature enough to function, and so when we come to these difficult decisions, we must be careful to rely on factual, provable analysis, and not on faith in a particular God..

As advancements in science continually expand our knowledge of

---

17 "Cruzan, By Her Parents And Co-Guardians, Cruzan Et Ux. v. Director, Missouri Department Of Health, Et Al" 18.

18 Ibid., 28.

19 Ibid., 41.

the world we live in, we have to be prepared to deal with difficult questions such as these, and the legality of abortion brings us in conflict with that dilemma because of the length of time it takes for a human fetus to grow to maturity, and undergo the birth process, which continues to require a long process of growth and maturation before independent life can exist. It is imperative that we set criteria to determine when abortion is feticide or murder, because it is an impossible problem to manage the problem that human society has had to deal with unwanted pregnancies that caused so many of our ancestors having to commit horrible crimes because they simply could not deal with every pregnancy that took place. Specifically, we can do this now by determining when a fetus becomes a "person" with the rights afforded to all other "persons" in the country. We can, and we must, develop answers to this problem, and so I will now argue for when the life of a fetus begins to afford the title of being a "person."

I believe we can find a happy medium in describing when a person's life legally begins, without resorting to our faith in God, or, in this instance, in a particular God. In monotheism, Courts cannot determine what God intended to say in the Torah, the New Testament, or the Qur'an, for only the Church tribunal has that authority. In America, however, the one place we can turn to in order to for advice on how to deal with this issue is the *Presidents Commission for the Study of Ethical Problems in Medicine and Biomedical and Behavioral Research*, which was established by Congress in 1978 to answer when death takes place so that the statutory law could be uniform among the several states.[20] This led to the Uniform Determination of Death Act (UDDA), which was a model state law that was approved for the United States in 1981 by the National Conference of Commissioners on Uniform State Laws, in cooperation with the American Medical Association, the American Bar Association, and the President's Commission for the Study of Ethical Problems in Medicine and Biomedical and Behavioral Research, to deal with this problem of brain-death. This Act has since been adopted by every state in America and the District of Columbia, and was intended "to provide a comprehensive and medically sound basis for determining death in all situations," and distinguish between a persistent vegetative state,

---

20 "Defining Death, A Report on the Medical, Legal and Ethical Issues in the Determination of Death (excerpt)," 3.

where there is still normal brain activity on an EEG, and true death when the heart and lungs stop functioning.[21] This procedure is clearly better than depending on nine Justices to make that determination, and it can allow either Congress to enact a law defining the issue, or the people to pass an amendment. I believe the people will be more important in this issue.

Death by neurologic criteria, rather than cessation of breathing and heart function, was first described by French neurologists in 1959, and called *le coma dépassé* (beyond coma or irretrievable coma).[22] In 1968, the World Medical Assembly recommended a reevaluation of the meaning of death, and an Ad Hoc Committee of the Harvard Medical School was formed to initially study this problem. In 1970, Kansas was the first state to legally adopt the recommendations.[23] The report they published was titled "A Definition of Irreversible Coma," a term they claimed should be considered death, and the term then became "brain death," and was used to allow the legal system to be able to turn off life support when there was still cardiac activity, because there has always been universal acceptance that killing another "person" is considered murder, and that can only be authorized as a punishment by a court for committing the crime of murder, or by being drafted into the army after a declared war so that you can commit murder to protect the safety of your country.[24] For courts to make the decision to allow "murder" in cases where the heart continued to beat normally, there had to be a legal definition of what "life" meant, and we were able to cross that barrier by the creation of the term "brain death," when the heart continued to beat normally and keep the body alive, but brain activity was absent. Although this concept has become widely accepted, it has only been utilized to define death in a small number of cases.

This term clarified that there were now two ways to call a patient dead, but we are still left with a need to define when "life" begins. This is what has left us in our present quandary with the two abortion cases differing on either conception, or quickening, on that term. We

---

21 "Uniform Determination of Death Act," 1. New Jersey has a "conscience clause" to allow rejection. Lizza, "Defining Death in a Technological World," 11.
22 Bernat and Lewis, "Historical Introduction," 1.
23 Ibid., 10.
24 Veatch and Ross, Defining Death: The Case for Choice, 2.

cannot have such disparity, however, and I maintain that we can only determine when "life" begins by showing that a fetus can survive initially with assistance after either birth or miscarriage in the hospital, and then be able to be discharged home with the care of the mother, and that is the youngest age when "life" begins. At the present time, that is a gestation period of 20 weeks, but it is possible that it will be earlier in the future.

I maintain that just as brain wave activity of an EEG is proof of a living brain, even if that brain may be disabled, life begins when it is proven that life exists outside of life-support methods being used to keep a fetus alive in the laboratory.

In *Roe v. Wade*, Justice Blackmun used the common law, and the information the medical profession gathered for him about working with minimal life-support modalities, to estimate that the common law gestational age of 24-28 weeks for life to begin was the correct criterion for defining a "person." In English law, however, William Blackstone held that any fetus *in utero* was considered a person for the purposes of inheritance, irrespective of the concept of viability, and in so doing, he created a legal "right" that was seen as "*nasciturus fiction*," which protected the right of the fetus, even in an nonviable state, as long as the child was eventually born alive.[25] Quickening alone would not satisfy that requirement, because the fetus had to eventually be born alive for his family to share in the inheritance.[26] That concept is not the issue I am dealing with in this book, however, so I will not discuss it further, but it points out how important it is to differentiate between a nonviable and viable fetus, and to take into account the long gestational period which clearly is provable evidence of survivability, which is necessary to label a fetus as a person.

After *Roe v. Wade* was first found constitutional, and 24-48 weeks of gestation was accepted as the definition of viability, various states attempted to pass laws to define a different standard when a fetus became a "person," such as the "Pain-Capable Unborn Child Protection Act" (LB1 1103), which was passed in Nebraska on April 13, 2010, banning abortion after 20-weeks gestational age on the grounds that

---

25 Shaw and Damme, "Legal Status of the Fetus," 4. Microsoft CoPilot (4/27/2025). Personal Communication.
26 Mo, "At What Point Can a Fetus Survive Outside the Womb?" 1; Microsoft CoPilot (4/27/2025). Personal Communication.

a fetus at that time "is capable of feeling pain and would, therefore, suffer immensely if aborted."[27] While this may have been what the Anti-Federalists wanted when writing the Constitution, the Civil War made that possibility unacceptable, and we cannot let individual states have that authority as the United States is simply too expansive to not make the definition a federal issue. For that reason, I am including in my amendment a proposal that the definition of a "person" is at present 20-weeks, and if that figure changes in the future, it can be modified. Other states passed laws after Nebraska and tried to reach the Supreme Court to test the *Roe v. Wade* verdict, such as Alabama, California, Colorado, Florida, Michigan, Missouri, Montana, Nevada, and Virginia, but it was only the *Dobbs* case from Mississippi that was accepted, and it had defined 15-weeks as the period when the fetus became viable, even though the earliest age proven for a fetus to actually survive was 20 weeks, as I will soon discuss.[28] *Dobbs* threw this entire issue aside, and bluntly stated that the fetus at conception was viable because the soul was created at that time, and that not only overturned *Roe v. Wade*, but overturned the *Casey* case, as well. In my opinion, the *Dobbs* decision was foolish and unscientific, but it threw the entire debate over abortion into a chaotic argument that left the arena of reason, given the fact that even in Italy, where the Vatican is located, and where Alito gained his heritage, under Law 194, abortion is legal within the first 90 days of pregnancy for health, economic, or social reasons.[29] If Italy was an American state, that edict would have been overturned as well.

While I find it ridiculous that Justice Alito, who is Catholic, allowed his religious beliefs to define when life begins in a court of law, and did it in a case where the legislature of Mississippi decided that life began at 15-weeks gestation, I realize that I cannot determine if this is a legal barrier to his acting in the manner, since he did it under our present judicial standard. There is a legal principle that does prevent his action, however, and that is the principle of separation of Church and State, and I contend that if he demanded that *Roe v. Wade* could only be approved by an amendment, then he had to know that his

---

27 Manninen, Pro-Life, Pro-Choice: Shared Values in the Abortion Debate, 12.

28 Ibid., 13.

29 Microsoft CoPilot (5/17/2025). Personal Communication.

proposal was changing the common law and needed an amendment as well. I may not have the requirement to be seen as a legal "scholar," but you don't need credentials to know that what I am claiming is true. In addition, Alito is contesting this concept as being unconstitutional under the theory of Originalism, which I have previously discussed is not accurate because all of the writings of the Founding Fathers, and all of the law during the Colonial America times, show that quickening was the age at which a "person" began. Alito is lying in his opinion, and that is legal malpractice and cause for overturning the verdict, but like Lincoln and the issue of slavery, I am more interested in having an amendment passed so we don't have to worry about Theocracy rearing its undemocratic head again.

Most of the social efforts directed at the care of children after birth have focused on the problems of child abuse, and not infanticide, and it is not surprising to me that there was a Society for the Prevention of Cruelty to Animals (SPCA) founded in London in 1824, fifty years before there was a Society for the Prevention of Cruelty to Children founded in New York in 1874. New York then became the first state in America to pass laws protecting children from child abuse in 1875, but it would take one-hundred years for federal legislation to mandate appropriate care to children, when on January 31, 1974, the Child Abuse Prevention and Treatment Act (CAPTA) was enacted, which included the so-called Baby Doe Regulations that were intended to develop procedures to report medical neglect, including the withholding of treatment for a disabled newborn's survival that was judged "virtually futile."[30] It was rewritten in the Child Abuse Prevention, Adoption and Family Services Act in 1988, and further changed many times thereafter. The fetus was not really addressed in any of these actions, and the first Act which dealt with the status of the fetus was the Born Alive Infant Protection Act (BAIPA), which was passed by Congress in 2002. This legislation extended legal protection to all infants born alive, regardless of gestational age, and was primarily intended for how to deal with cases after a failed abortion.[31] When the law was passed, 89% of California neonatologists who were polled believed that only palliative care options should be applied, but following the passage

---

30 Partridge, "Definitions of Viability and Their Meaning for Neonatal Care," 173.

31 Ibid.

of the law, a small percentage of infants born at 17-week gestation survived for a short period of time with continued care, but none to independent life.[32] This has led one of those specialists to conclude that there is a "grey zone at twenty-three to twenty-four weeks and at 500 to 650 grams where disagreement about appropriateness of intensive care is both ethical and legitimate."[33]

---

32 Ibid., 174.
33 Ibid., 175.

Chapter VI

Is Adoption An Acceptable Answer?

I have already discussed how important it is to understand that the solution to the treatment of unwanted births, being either killed after birth, or treated with child abuse leading to an early death, is to allow for unwanted pregnancies to be aborted before the fetus is viable. It has been suggested by many Pro-Lifers, however, that giving up the child for adoption is an equally successful answer to preventing the results I have described. Theoretically, according to many of these proponents, if every unwanted birth was put up for adoption, with payment provided to attenuate the cost and discomfort of carrying the fetus to term, the problem would be solved, and the "murder" of the fetus would be prevented, satisfying both parties without the need to cause a loss of life. This view was made after *Roe v. Wade* was found unconstitutional by the *Dobbs* decision, by Gretchen Sisson, a sociologist at the University of California, San Francisco, who said that since "abortion is unavailable and parenting is untenable, adoption becomes the only path forward."[1] The statement referenced an ancient practice fact that included the adoption of Moses by the Egyptian princess after the order to drown all the newborn Hebrew males was issued by the Egyptian Pharaoh,[2] as well as something that was present in ancient Ugaritic texts, as well, attesting to its acceptance throughout human civilization.[3]

Of course, this tactic ignores the psychological stress that is often associated with adoption, both in the birth mother and the children adopted, but the benefit of this solution has been accepted by many Right to Lifers who found it a reasonable approach if abortion rights were eliminated, which had to be done because it was clearly murder. This solution also has the advantage of keeping the issue under the purview of each individual state, for the ability of the Constitution to deal with this matter is limited, since most domestic relations matters

---

1   Sisson, Relinquished: The Politics of Adoption and the Privilege of American Motherhood, 7.

2   Quine, "Introduction: Adoption and Familial Complexity in the Hebrew Bible," 2.

3   Parker, "Absence of Adoption in the Hebrew Bible? Childist, Comparative, and Cross-Cultural Insights in Response to a Textual Conundrum," 12.

are reserved for state guidance, with the federal Congress having limited direct authority on matters of domestic relations, which is one reason both women's rights to vote, and abortion have generally been applied to the states, and to become a federal issue would require an amendment.[4]

The first state to pass adoption legislation was Massachusetts in 1851, when they passed the Adoption of Children Act, which established a legal parent-child relationship after adoption, and set the standard for other states to follow.[5] In order to try and add assistance in helping the state governments and families deal with this issue, the National Committee For Adoption was founded in 1980, and helped adopt means by which the U.S. Department of Health, Education, and Welfare (HEW) could assist in this regard. In 1994, the Uniform Adoption Act (UAAS) was passed by Congress, advising how to legislate good adoption policy and practices which has helped provide advice on a national level for all state agencies to follow.

The problem is that abortion is not a state issue, it is a vital national concern, and we must have a uniform policy that crosses state boundaries, just like we needed for voting and the issue of slavery, and that means we must deal with this either by passing an amendment, or returning *Roe v. Wade* to the law of the land. Recommending adoption as a solution has been seen by some other commentators as possibly arising from ulterior motives that cared little about the adoptive process. Dorothy Roberts, George A. Weiss University Professor of Law and Sociology, Civil Rights at the University of Pennsylvania Carey Law School, for example, took this view in another direction, and saw the use of adoption as a right-wing strategy of reproductive control that included not only abortion laws that compelled pregnant people to give birth, but then forced them to relinquish the babies for adoption as the answer to denying them access to abortion.[6] Sure, pacify your guilt complex for denying abortion by forcing adoption, and pretend that all participants will be satisfied with their outcome.

While both of these conclusions may have relevance to show how Republicans are trying to find a way to sleep at night after

4   Bevan, "Changing Laws and Culture to Reduce Barriers to Adoption," 8.
5   Pertman, Adoption Nation: How the Adoption Revolution is Transforming America, 21-22.
6   Roberts, "The Failure of Dobbs, The Entanglement of Abortion Bans, Criminalized Pregnancies, and Forced Family Separation," 175.

overturning *Roe v. Wade*, I don't agree that looking at adoption as a means to attenuate the problems that are associated with making abortion illegal is a viable option, even though it will theoretically supply some minimal aid to the problem. First of all, adoption simply cannot handle the number of unwanted births that will result, as I have already shown by there having been 3.65 billion abortions performed worldwide over the last 50 years. Adoption cannot handle this many children, and we will once again find infanticide and child abuse being utilized, which is totally unacceptable. The issue of adoption was discussed in Republican circles before the *Dobbs* decision was made, because during the arguments made during the trial, Justice Amy Coney Barrett asked the District Attorney of Mississippi during her cross-examination if the potential burdens that would be caused by overturning *Roe v. Wade* could be averted if more women gave their newborn children up for adoption.[7] I was surprised, embarrassed, and angered that this question was raised, for it indicated to me that the Justices actually believed that adoption was going to be a reasonable alternative to their making abortion illegal throughout the country, an indication to me that they were totally unaware of the number of abortions performed, both in America and across the world by that time. I say this because if they were aware of that statistic, and still asked the question, it shows how much they did not care whether adoption was an answer, or if they were unaware of this statistic, it shows that they simply didn't care about the issue, and relied on their reliance that a person's life began at conception because that is what the Catholic Pope determined.

Because the Justices raised the issue, I want to discuss the use of adoption in some detail, in order to explain why America will be overwhelmed by the two crimes of infanticide and child abuse if my amendment is not passed, and why I believe adoption will not make a significant difference in the severity of the problem. There is no question that if you deny abortion, you will find that adoption is the one available resource for mothers who do not want to raise their child once it is born, but while adoption is a legal, and ethical, pathway to alleviating some of the unwanted births, it cannot possibly lead to any prevention of significant numbers of children who will die

---

7   Sisson, Relinquished: The Politics of Adoption and the Privilege of American **Motherhood, 6.**

because they were born unwanted. Even today, with 50% of unwanted pregnancies aborted, it has not been seen as the preferred path available to stressed-out parents, and in this chapter, I will outline some of the reasons why I do not believe adoption is an effective alternative to allowing pregnant mothers who do not want to maintain the birth of an unwanted child.

Justice Alito claimed that a 2008 Centers for Disease Control and Prevention report indicated nearly 1 million women were seeking to adopt in 2002. Still, in my review of the information he referred to, the article indicated that the number of abortions reported by the CDC in 2002 was 854,000, and by the Guttmacher Institute was 1,293,000. Still, you didn't see that there were any statistics for attempts at adoption in that report at all, and during my research on adoption, I found no other references for such a statistic.[8] The statistics I did find indicated that in 2021, one in four children exiting foster care — around 53,300 kids in the United States — were adopted, and about 80% of these children were under age 11, and more than half — 52% — were between the ages of 1 and 5.[9] Foster care refers to children who were being raised mostly because of abuse and neglect, and the numbers increased from 273,500 in 1986 to 452,000 in 1993 because of tax benefits that began to be provided in 1996, while adoptions remained constant at about 50,000 per year.[10] That may seem like a large number, and an effective way to deal with the problem, but since during the peak years of abortion in the United States, over 1 million abortions were performed every year, 53,300 kids being adopted, and those being aided by foster care, would still leave the vast majority remaining in a toxic, potentially fatal, existence.

In addition to there being little chance that many of the mothers would choose to try and adopt their child, there would be untold numbers resorting to attempts at illegal abortion, resulting in innumerable numbers of death or illness to the mother, and even to the child who would likely now be a viable fetus, and a murder, rather than a feticide. In addition, the statistics of child abuse in families

---

8   Roberts, "The Failure of Dobbs, The Entanglement of Abortion Bans, Criminalized Pregnancies, and Forced Family Separation," 177; "Health, United States, 2008, With Special Features on the Health of Young Adults," 181.

9   Ibid.

10 Fagan, "Adoption: The Best Option," 2.

who adopt suggests that 10% of adopted children are diagnosed with complex trauma from past abuse, and about 27% show signs of new abuse or neglect.[11] I therefore insist that adoption cannot be a viable alternative to my proposed amendment, and if it is not approved, someone will have to figure out how else to deal with the massive supply of child abuse victims that will result from this dilemma.

I am not attempting to dissuade people from seeking to put their unwanted births up for adoption, for it is a well-accepted fact that, in the words of the Annie E. Casey Foundation, which is a private philanthropy group founded in 1948, and based in Baltimore, Maryland: "Adoption is a legal process that permanently transfers parental responsibility from a child's birth parents to their adoptive parents. After reunification, it is the next most secure permanency option for children in foster care."[12] Many families have had multiple gratifying adoptions, and the process can aid both the adopter, and the adoptee, to live a more fulfilling life than was forecast when the birth took place, but in the numbers we are talking of here, foster care is the only other option for large numbers of children offered by religious institutions or governmental agencies, and while they may be better than leaving children on the street to fend for themselves, these facilities simply cannot handle the large numbers of unwanted children that will be born in America if abortion is found to be illegal. Our country has the wealth to adopt the largest number of children, but we simply cannot handle a larger load than we have right now, and the history of how abandoned children have been treated for most of our recorded history makes our present situation a crisis in need of a passage of an amendment to allow unwanted, nonviable pregnancies to be aborted as a constitutional right.

The first thing to realize about adoption is that its history has not always been so beneficent as it appears in some of the articles promoted by anti-abortionists. Poverty and slavery led to a surplus of children available to be adopted in nineteenth-century America, but in the twentieth century there was an increased need of finding children to fill childless homes, as children were often orphaned from wars and economic hardship.[13] This led to adoptions being offered by people

---

11 "Adoption Abuse Statistics," 1-2.

12 "Adoption," 1.

13 Sisson, Relinquished: The Politics of Adoption and the Privilege of American Motherhood, 18-19.

like Beulah George "Georgia" Tann (1891-1950), who operated the Tennessee Children's Home Society, which became infamous for child trafficking, rather than legal adoption. Todd would often take children from homes to sell on the black market to wealthy families desperate for wanting a child, and willing to pay outrageous sums of money.[14] Although the state of Tennessee only allowed children to be adopted for a fee of $7 at the time, between 1940 and 1950, Tann was able to place children in New York and California for as much as $5,000, and in other states for $700-$750.[15] It is estimated that she eventually sold more than 5,000 children before her operation was discovered.[16] There is no question that in other parts of America, there were others like her doing the very same thing. Tann often paid the parents a small amount of money, but if she had any evidence of other crimes they were possibly guilty of, she would threaten to tell the police of their involvement if they didn't pay her entire fee. Today, a healthy child could cost adoptive parents as much as $10,000, and the dearth of children has caused adoptions to spread to countries across the world.[17]

International adoptions took place during World War I and II, but the practice didn't become systematic until mixed-race children began to be adopted during the Korean War (June 25, 1950-July 27, 1953), followed by large numbers of adoptions from China, and then Russia.[18] The first year the Immigration and Naturalization Service (INS) required data for this statistic was 1964, when 1,700 such children came into the country, and by 1984, the number was 9,500, and in 1998, it was 15,724, so there would be little effect on reducing the number of unwanted children if abortions are banned.[19] The number of international adoptions reached 12,700 in 2009, but the number dropped to 1,300 in 2023, and it is estimated that from the end of World War II to the legalization of abortion, about 4 million American infants were relinquished for adoption, and the prices paid

---

14 Ibid., 20.
15 "Georgia Tann," 1-2.
16 Ibid., 6.
17 Sisson, Relinquished: The Politics of Adoption and the Privilege of American Motherhood, 21.
18 Pertman, Adoption Nation: How the Adoption Revolution is Transforming America, 30.
19 Ibid., 31.

were astounding.[20] Known as the "Baby Scoop Era," it is estimated that 4 million children were placed for adoption during this era before changes were made against the lucrative practice.[21]

To see why an unlimited number of children are not going to likely be able to be adopted, one only has to see what the response of the United Nations was to this rise in adoption on a worldwide basis. On November 20, 1989, the General Assembly of the United Nations passed an act in the Convention on the Rights of the Child, and in the Preamble to that declaration, it was stated that: "Recognizing that the United Nations has, in the Universal Declaration of Human Rights and in the International Covenants on Human Rights, proclaimed and agreed that everyone is entitled to all the rights and freedoms set forth therein, without distinction of any kind, such as race, color, sex, language, religion, political or other opinion, national or social origin, property, birth or other status, a statement that clearly was intended to state a crass warning"[22] The Convention then went on to approve 54 different Articles, which, in essence, asserted that children should "not be adopted internationally when there is suitable care for them available within their own country."[23]

Wham! Wake up America! Although the United Nations did not define exactly what that other "suitable care" was, it is clear that they are not going to let your wealth fulfill the need for adopting more children, as this resolution was primarily created by the large number of foreign adoptees that were taken by Americans who found out that there were many children available for adoption in poverty stricken regions of the world for more reasonable prices. Following up this action, Gretchen Sisson, a Sociologist in the Department of Obstetrics, Gynecology, and Reproductive Sciences at the University of California, San Francisco, interviewed over 100 American women who had given their infants up for adoption between 2000 and 2010, and because of the problems she found that persisted for all of their lives, she stopped calling the process adoption, and instead referred to it as "relinquished."[24] She estimated that adoptions represented

---

20 Fleck, "U.S. Adoptions From Abroad Are Declining," 1.
21 "Baby Scoop Era," 1.
22 "Convention on the Rights of the Child," 2.
23 Ibid.
24 Sisson, Relinquished: The Politics of Adoption and the Privilege of American Motherhood, 26.

approximately 0.5% of all births from 1982-2014, which is close to what I estimated was the infanticide rate during the years *Roe v. Wade* was the law of the land, reducing the rate of infanticide throughout history from 10-15% of births.[25] I have repeatedly said in this book that we need women to have the right to abort unwanted, nonviable pregnancies in order to lower the rate of infanticide and child abuse increasing in those births, and that is not going to be attenuated by the number of adoptions that take place if the abortions are not approved.

There are few studies that have been done to truly assess the outcome of the value of adoption in women denied abortion, primarily because all the data that is collected cannot truly determine what caused the eventual outcomes to take place, and those outcomes have never been searched for. One study that was mentioned by Dorothy Roberts was "The Turnaway Study," which, in her words: "tracked one thousand women who sought abortions over ten years, found that the women who were denied abortion care suffered serious physical, emotional, and economic harm."[26] The problem is that this study, which was done at the University of California San Francisco, recruited 1000 women who had attempted to receive abortions at 30 facilities across the country, and were "turned away" because they had passed the gestational limit of the facility before they arrived for care. The details of how long it took for the patient to decide to have an abortion were not provided, but it is clear that these patients had undergone enormous stress from both trying to decide whether to have an abortion in the first place, and then being turned down once they thought they wanted an abortion. They then had to deliver the baby and decide how to manage their lives, and so collecting data on how they dealt with the problem obviously created a multitude of problems, which, in my professional opinion, would be impossible to blame simply on the fact that they were turned away.[27] It is sometimes very difficult to design a study that provides statistically significant information, and that is a problem that we have in trying to develop information of why child abuse is so prevalent throughout human history.

Dorothy Roberts, the George A. Weiss University Professor

---

25 Ibid., 31.
26 Roberts, "The Failure of Dobbs, The Entanglement of Abortion Bans, Criminalized Pregnancies, and Forced Family Separation," 178.
27 "The Turnaway Study," 1-10.

of Law & Sociology at the University of Pennsylvania, with joint appointments in the Departments of Africana Studies and Sociology and the Law School, where she also holds the title of Raymond Pace and Sadie Tanner Mossell Alexander Professor of Civil Rights, has discussed the failure of looking on abortion as a means to reduce the loss of the right to have the right to choose an abortion in the following manner, and I agree with her assessment:

> The vision of a well-functioning market for babies conveniently omitted the physical and mental costs of gestating a fetus and the ethical problem of overriding pregnant people's autonomy over their bodies. The Court considered only the burdens that arise after the compelled birth and not those that occur during the pregnancy. Moreover, the adoption market imagery falsely treats the decision to surrender the baby as if it were a freely made reproductive choice when, in reality, it was coerced by the inability to obtain an abortion."

I also agree with her assessment of President Bill Clinton's signing of the Adoption and Safe families act of 1997 to double the number of foster children adopted annually by 2002 as "falsely equating permanency with adoption," and failing to keep families together.[28] I do not see adoption as an acceptable alternative to a woman's right to choose to abort an unwanted pregnancy, so let me now move on to my proposal for a solution to this problem that will hopefully be a permanent solution.

---

28 Roberts, "The Failure of Dobbs, The Entanglement of Abortion Bans, Criminalized Pregnancies, and Forced Family Separation," 187.

Chapter VII
Proposal For A Twenty-Eighth Amendment

Amendment XXVIII

ABORTION

BE IT ENACTED BY THE SENATE AND HOUSE OF REPRESENTATIVES OF THE UNITED STATES OF AMERICA CONGRESS

SECTION 1

This Act shall be known as the Gestational Abortion Act Amendment. It sets forth the fundamental rights of individuals to make autonomous decisions about their own reproductive health, including the fundamental right of an individual who becomes pregnant to continue the pregnancy and give birth to a child, or to have an abortion if the fetus is determined to be nonviable by having a gestational period of less than 20 weeks. This assessment must be made by a licensed Health Care Professional. This Act restricts the ability of any State to deny, interfere with, or discriminate against this fundamental right of every American woman to terminate a nonviable, unwanted pregnancy. In so doing, this Act is setting the definition of the beginning of life in the fetus as taking place at 20-weeks-gestation. This definition will be reassessed every two years and adjusted if necessary by medical evidence of the ability to survive at lower gestation intervals.

SECTION 2

Abortion is part of essential health care, and is one of the safest medical procedures in the United States. An independent, comprehensive review of the state of science on the safety and quality of abortion services, published by the National Academies of Sciences, Engineering, and Medicine in 2018, found that abortion in the United States is safe and effective, and that the biggest threats to the quality of abortion services in the United States are State regulations that create barriers to care. These abortion-specific restrictions that conflict with medical standards, and are not supported by the recommendations and guidelines issued by leading reproductive health care professional organizations, including the American College of Obstetricians and Gynecologists, the Society of Family Planning, the National Abortion Federation, the World Health Organization, and others, will be ignored.

(1) International human rights law recognizes that access to abortion is intrinsically linked to the rights to life, health, equality and non-discrimination, privacy, and freedom from ill-treatment. United Nations (UN) human rights treaty monitoring bodies have found that legal abortion services, like other reproductive health care services, must be available, accessible, affordable, acceptable, and of good quality. UN human rights treaty bodies have likewise condemned medically unnecessary barriers to abortion services, including mandatory waiting periods, biased counseling requirements, and third-party authorization requirements.

(2) Core human rights treaties ratified by the United States protect access to abortion. For example, in 2018, the UN Human Rights Committee, which oversees implementation of the ICCPR, made clear that the right to life, enshrined in Article 6 of the ICCPR, at a minimum requires governments to provide safe, legal, and effective access to abortion where a person's life and health is at risk, or when carrying a pregnancy to term would cause substantial pain or suffering. The Committee stated that governments must not impose restrictions on abortion that subject women and girls to physical or mental pain or suffering, discriminate against them, arbitrarily interfere with their privacy, or place them at risk of undertaking unsafe abortions. Furthermore, the Committee stated that governments should remove existing barriers that deny effective access to safe and legal abortion, refrain from introducing new barriers to abortion, and prevent the stigmatization of those seeking abortion.

(3) UN independent human rights experts have expressed particular concern about barriers to abortion services in the United States. For example, at the conclusion of his 2017 visit to the United States, the UN Special Rapporteur on

extreme poverty and human rights noted concern that low-income women face legal and practical obstacles to exercising their constitutional right to access abortion services, trapping many women in cycles of poverty. Similarly, in May 2020, the UN Working Group on discrimination against women and girls, along with other human rights experts, expressed concern that some states had manipulated the COVID–19 crisis to restrict access to abortion, which the experts recognized as "the latest example illustrating a pattern of restrictions and retrogressions in access to legal abortion care across the country" and reminded U.S. authorities that abortion care constitutes essential health care that must remain available during and after the pandemic. They noted that barriers to abortion access exacerbate systemic inequalities and cause particular harm to marginalized communities, including low-income people, people of color, immigrants, people with disabilities, and LGBTQ people.

(4) Abortion-specific restrictions affect the cost and availability of abortion services, and the settings in which abortion services are delivered. People travel across State lines and otherwise engage in interstate commerce to access this essential medical care, and more would be forced to do so absent this Act. Likewise, health care providers travel across State lines and otherwise engage in interstate commerce to provide abortion services to patients, and more would be forced to do so absent this Act.

(5) Health care providers engage in a form of economic and commercial activity when they provide abortion services, and there is an interstate market for abortion services when states can determine the legality of abortion in their state alone. The issue of abortion legality should be a concern for the federal government to determine when and how an abortion can be performed, and it was recommended by the Supreme Court in Dobbs v. Jackson Women's Health Organization that this be done by passage of an amendment to the Constitution. This amendment is written to follow that recommendation.

(6) It is a federal responsibility to have this legislation because abortion restrictions substantially affect interstate commerce in numerous ways. For example, to provide abortion services, health care providers engage in interstate commerce to purchase medicine, medical equipment, and other necessary goods and services. To provide and assist others in providing abortion services, health care providers engage in interstate commerce to obtain and provide training. To provide abortion services, health care providers employ and obtain commercial services from doctors, nurses, and other personnel who engage in interstate commerce and travel across State lines.

(7) It is difficult and time and resource-consuming for clinics to challenge State laws that burden or impede abortion services. Litigation that blocks one abortion restriction may not prevent a State from adopting other similarly burdensome abortion restrictions or using different methods to burden or impede abortion services. There is a history and pattern of States passing successive and different laws that unduly burden abortion services. To correct that problem, an Amendment to the Constitution is an appropriate remedy.

(8) When a health care provider ceases providing abortion services as a result of burdensome and medically unnecessary regulations, it is often difficult or impossible for that health care provider to recommence providing those abortion services, and difficult or impossible for other health care providers to provide abortion services that restore or replace the ceased abortion services.

(9) Health care providers are subject to license laws in various jurisdictions, which are not affected by this Act except as provided in this Act.

(10) Congress has the authority to enact this Act to protect abortion services pursuant to—

(a) its powers under the commerce clause of section 8 of article I of the Constitution of the United States;

(b) its powers under section 5 of the Fourteenth Amendment

to the Constitution of the United States to enforce the provisions of section 1 of the Fourteenth Amendment; and

(c) its powers under the necessary and proper clause of section 8 of Article I of the Constitution of the United States.

(11) Congress has used its authority in the past to protect access to abortion services and health care providers' ability to provide abortion services. In the early 1990s, protests and blockades at health care facilities where abortion services were provided, and associated violence, increased dramatically and reached crisis level, requiring Congressional action. Congress passed the Freedom of Access to Clinic Entrances Act (Public Law 103–259; 108 Stat. 694) to address that situation and protect physical access to abortion services.

(12) Congressional action is necessary to put an end to harmful restrictions, to federally protect access to abortion services for everyone regardless of where they live, and to protect the ability of health care providers to provide these services in a safe and accessible manner.[1]

SECTION 3

Definitions

(1) "Abortion" means the act of using, prescribing, administering, procuring, or selling an instrument, medicine, drug, or any other substance, device, or means with the purpose to terminate the pregnancy of a woman. It may include aspiration, also called surgical or suction curettage, where the inside of the uterus is scraped out, or dilation and evacuation, and does not mean any of the following acts, if performed by a physician:

(a) A medical procedure performed with the intention to save the life or preserve the health of an unborn child.

(b) The removal of a dead unborn child or the inducement or delivery of the uterine contents in case of a positive

---

1   H. R. 3755

diagnosis, certified in writing in the woman's record, or is in the unavoidable and untreatable process of ending due to spontaneous miscarriage or incomplete abortion.

(c) The removal of an ectopic pregnancy.

(d) The use of methotrexate to treat an ectopic pregnancy.

(2) "Abortion provider" means a person who performs elective abortions.

(3) "Elective abortion" means an abortion other than those performed or induced in response to a medical emergency.

(4) "Medical emergency" means a condition in which an abortion is necessary to preserve the life of a pregnant woman whose life is endangered by a physical disorder, physical illness, or physical injury, including a life-endangering physical condition caused by or arising from the pregnancy itself.

(5) "Woman" means an individual whose biological sex is female, with a uterus, regardless of any general identity that the individual attempts to assert or claim.

(6) "Nonviable fetus" means a fetus whose gestational age is estimated in the professional judgment of the attending health care professional, based on the particular facts of the case, to be 20-weeks or less. This limitation will be reevaluated every two years to determine if medical advancements have progressed to a level that has lowered that number by the proven survival at a statistically significant level.

(7) "Viable fetus" means a fetus whose gestational age is estimated by a physician to be greater than 20 weeks if able to be determined, or greater than 24 weeks if unable to be definitively determined.

(8) "Possibly viable fetus" means a fetus between the gestational age of 20-24-weeks if reliability of determination is uncertain.

(9) "Health Care Professional" means a person who is licensed as

a physician, advanced practice registered nurse, or physician assistant, licensed under a State Medical Practice Act.

(10) "Gestational age" means the age of the unborn fetus as measured by the time elapsed since the first day of the last menstrual period as determined by a physician, and confirmed through the use of an ultrasound test of a quality generally used in existing medical practice.

(11) "Person" in the Constitution under this Amendment is intended to include an individual who has undergone a natural birth, as well as a viable fetus that is at a gestational age of at least 20-weeks, which has been determined to support the capability of life with artificial support in an intensive care unit, and then independent living upon survival, and eventual discharge from the hospital. At the present time, a fetus is presumed to be viable, and therefore a "person," at the age of 20-weeks gestation, but that designation will be reassessed every two years.

SECTION 4
Statute Of Limitations

(1) Filing Deadline

   (a) All legal claims under this amendment must be filed within two years from the date of occurrence of the event, or when the claimant should have become aware of the event.

   (b) The statute of limitation may be extended for fraudulent concealment of relevant facts, or physical or mental incapacity of the claimant.

SECTION 5
Nonviable Fetus Abortion

(1) Any fetus that is considered nonviable by a licensed physician, either because there is no audible or visible heartbeat, or because the pregnancy is less than 20 weeks in duration, may be terminated if the mother attests that she does not want to continue the pregnancy. Such certification

shall be submitted before the abortion is performed by a registered medical practitioner, and failure to comply with this requirement gives rise to a presumption that the abortion was unjustified.

SECTION 6

Possibly Viable Fetus Abortion

(1) A possibly viable abortion may be performed in pregnancies between 20-30-weeks in duration if there is substantial risk that continuance of the pregnancy would gravely impair the physical or mental health of the mother, or that the child would be born with grave physical or mental deficit, or that the pregnancy resulted from rape, incest, or other felonious intercourse, as attested to by a licensed physician.

(2) In determining whether the continuance of a pregnancy would involve risk of injury to health, account may be taken of the pregnant woman's actual or reasonably foreseeable environment.

SECTION 7

Viable Fetus Abortion

(1) A viable fetus abortion is defined as abortion of a fetus of greater than 30-weeks gestation, and may only be performed if there is substantial risk that continuance of the pregnancy would gravely impair the physical or mental health of the mother, or that the child would be born with grave physical or mental deficit, or that the pregnancy resulted from rape, incest, or other felonious intercourse, as attested to by a licensed physician.

(2) In determining whether the continuance of a pregnancy would involve risk of injury to health, account may be taken of the pregnant woman's actual or reasonably foreseeable environment.

SECTION 8

Conscientious Objection To Participation In Treatment

(1) No person shall be under any duty, whether by contract or by any statutory or other legal requirement, to participate in any treatment to which he has a conscientious objection. The burden of proof of conscientious objection shall rest on the person claiming to rely on it.

Chapter VIII
Conclusion

In case you have forgotten, in Chapter IV I discussed how the *Dobbs* Supreme Court case put us in a constitutional crisis. I asked you why we allow our Supreme Court to change our common law without any complaint that their action is unconstitutional. I said: "How? Why? I'll tell you why at the conclusion to this book, but let me first describe how we got here, and how we can correct the problem quickly." I then spent time describing what happened, and I have finally come to the end of the book where I must now summarize the how and why of what we must do to get out of this crisis. The short answer is simply that we cannot rely on the Supreme Court to determine whether women have the right under our Constitution to abort an unwanted, nonviable pregnancy, and we must approve a Twenty-Eighth Amendment to the Constitution providing women with the privacy right to choose abortion instead of giving birth to an unwanted, nonviable pregnancy. Now that we know that abortion is a safe and straightforward means to end an unwanted pregnancy, there is no reason to deny them that right unless life begins at conception, as the Catholic Pope says, and not at "quickening," as the American common law says. In the following pages, I will now expand my answer to prove to you that quickening is when life begins, and ask you to please help me be sure we get out the vote so my amendment proposal can be approved.

Before I explain my reasoning in more detail, I also want to emphasize that my concern for not allowing our country to become a Theocracy, instead of a Democracy, is not because I do not believe in the existence of the same God as Donald Trump does. This is the seventeenth book I have published, and most of them concern my analysis of monotheism as a faith that is followed by more than one-half of the world population today. All three monotheistic religions purport to believe in the same God, but their description of that God, and their recollection of what that God said and did, is markedly different from each other, which makes it evident that one's faith in His existence is dependent on one's interpretation of what happened over time, and not on any provable facts. I am personally convinced that there is only One Almighty God, but like all people who believe in God, I do this because I have faith that it is true, not because I can prove it is true. This is how monotheism has been accepted by more than one-half of the world population, who all have the same faith, but their understanding seldom agrees with that of other monotheists, even within the same religion. This discrepancy is both a blessing and a curse. It is, of course, a blessing because it has provided a brief opportunity for many of us to live a life and appreciate what it is to be aware of emotions like love, joy, and pride in being alive. We have comfort because we believe that there is a God who was responsible for all this, and we are assured that our benefit may even extend into the hereafter, which provides hope that our death will not be eternal. We also have a curse, however, for our Creation, in all three religions, tells us how we were made imperfect from the very start, as told in the Torah tale of Adam and Eve, who sinned by disobeying God's first order not to eat from the Tree of Knowledge of Good and Evil.[1] Christianity has referred to this failure as "The Fall," or "Original Sin," and it shows that we all have inherited this same imperfection as did their first son, Cain, who killed his first brother, Abel, because he was angry that God preferred his sacrifice, and from that time forward, all mankind has inherited the capacity to kill again. We may have been created in the image of God, *imago Dei,* but that portrayal is filled with many faults that God may, or may not, have.

Why do I bring up this seemingly horrible trait as the impetus for my faith in the One Almighty God? It is because I believe that the best thing all mankind has received from the blessing we first received is that we have also evolved for at least 300,000 years. Our capacity to use our brains has continued to improve, and we will hopefully learn from our prior errors to continually strive to improve in the years to come. I will do my part in this learning process by providing what I genuinely believe is a necessary vital next step toward reaching that goal by assuring that all future generations of mankind can improve the manner in which they take care of all their children, because in the past, we have failed to adequately provide that care to unwanted children. The history of mankind on earth is filled with evidence that 10-15% of unwanted children have been killed by one of their parents, and many more who survived were treated with child abuse, lived a miserable life, and suffered an early death. I discussed this in

---

1   Gen 2:16-17; 3:1-6.

my book, *Hardness of Heart, Hardness of Life: The Stain of Human Infanticide*, which was first published in 1999, after *Roe v. Wade* was passed. There was little interest in the book because safe abortion was suddenly available to all American parents who had an unwanted pregnancy, and few people cared about the past, and thought only about the present and the future. Throughout history, there was little that new mothers could do to safely end an unwanted pregnancy, but by the time *Roe v. Wade* was passed, a safe and effective method was available to assure that women could choose when to give birth, in order for them to provide the best type of care that will improve our genetic pool as we continue our evolutionary process.

Now that *Roe v. Wade* has been overturned, however, there is no way to safely and legally terminate unwanted pregnancies, and women are being forced to return to the statistics that have been present since life first began. This will result in the rates of infanticide and child abuse rising once again to levels they have always been, unless we pass the amendment I propose. We are being forced to undo a benefit that finally reduced the necessity of carrying every pregnancy to a term delivery, and we are told that all of this is because the Catholic Pope made the decision that life begins at conception, instead of the common law definition that it begins at quickening. This is despite the fact that all three of the monotheistic religions have their own holy books that detail the principles of their unique religion, but they still follow the story of the Torah for their origin of Creation, and understand that the first 10 generations of human life were abhorrent to God, Who then destroyed all living beings except for the family of Noah, and a breeding pair of every animal that was part of Creation, to eliminate all prior human life on earth, and start over again with Noah's offspring. This time, however, God decided to select a few Chosen People to be given special care, derived from a man named Abraham, who would be born 10 generations later. Abraham had two sons, Isaac from his wife Sarah, and Ishmael from his wife's maid Hagar, whom Sarah allowed Abraham to obtain a son, since she had been unable to become pregnant. Eventually, God allowed Sarah to give birth, and as the boys grew up, Sarah saw that Ishmael was endangering her son and made Abraham send him away. Abraham was distraught, but God told him that His Chosen People, who would be the Hebrews, would come from Isaac, and then from his son Jacob, but they would not come from Ishmael, so when Sarah later asked him to send his first illegitimate son away, Abraham agreed, and God told him that it was the right thing to do, and He would also make Ishmael's descendants great, as well.

When Christianity and Islam later developed, they wrote their own holy books, but continued to follow the histories contained in the Hebrew Bible. Christianity relied on its history being told in the New Testament, then referred to the Hebrew Bible as the Old Testament. The Jews who became Christians believed that Jesus Christ was born 27 generations later in the lineage of King David, and He was the Messiah who was promised by the Jewish Prophets. They accepted that the Jews were forsaken by God and punished with the Babylonian Exile because of their apostasy. God sent His Son, Jesus, to declare that those who believed in Him would become the true Chosen People. About 600 years later, the Arabs, who were descended from Ishmael, were told by their prophet Muhammad that they were God's Chosen People because the Christians believed in Jesus as a Son of God, which was an apostasy that God could not accept. That is how we now have three religions believing in the same God, although each of them has its own version of who the real Chosen People are. I'm not going to discuss the three monotheistic faiths any further in this book, but it is essential to understand that there is an inheritable tendency to kill in all three monotheistic religions of Judaism, Christianity, and Islam, and that they retained this tendency despite the moral commandments from God contained in the Ten Commandments that were delivered to the Hebrew people after the Exodus from Egypt on Mt. Sinai, with the Sixth Commandment being "You shall not murder."[2] The problem is that both the Jews and the Muslims live under a Theocracy, and we now have a President of the United States who wants to do the same thing in America. As a result, he decided that God did not believe in abortions, as declared by the Catholic Pope, and so he wants to change our county to become Great Again by making it a Theocracy. Fortunately, I am here to try and prevent that from happening, and I hope you will help me fulfill that purpose.

As we try to understand why so many unwanted children have been killed by their parents, we must also remember that the Catholic Popes who declared life began at conception were also the ones who

---

2   Exod 20:13; Deut 5:17.

started Crusades Holy Wars against the Muslims from 1096-1270 to determine whose God was more powerful, and in the process resulted in the deaths of 1-3 million people, including Christian and Muslim soldiers, civilians, and Jewish residents, who were hated by both sides in the wars.[3] Those wars have not abated, and continue today among Christians, Muslims, and Jews, so it is clear that Monotheism has not taught the human race much about the true nature of God, or how to live a life without murder. We also have not learned how to properly care for unwanted children, but we have seen that we can utilize abortion as a method to allow pregnancies that are unwanted and nonviable to be prevented from continuing their gestation, and select when children should be born. In this way, we can assure that the long period of time the human species takes to allow infants and children to be raised by their parents can be assured, and the billions of other births will never know the disasters that once faced them.

Now that we understand that our country is now in a critical part of our own history of strife because our Constitution is in danger of being shredded by a President and a Supreme Court that has given up the principle of Separation of Church and State, which has been the most important support structure that has made America a great symbol of Democracy. Freedom of religion is not only the right to practice the religion of your choice in America, it means that while you believe in any God you want, or no god at all, you must follow the precepts of the Constitution in all matters that are brought to your attention, and not the precepts of your religion. When it comes to abortion, the reason the *Dobbs* court overturned *Roe v. Wade* and *Casey* is that seven of the nine Justices were orthodox Catholics, and six closely followed the teaching of the Catholic Pope, and not the common law of the United States, which puts our Democracy in danger of being obliterated, and replaced by a Theocracy which follows morality as determined by the Catholic Church.

I ask all Catholics to please continue to believe in your God with all your heart, and the President of your choice, but please respect the Democracy in which you live in America, and do not allow abortion of unwanted, nonviable fetuses to be denied. Vote for Trump if you want him to be President, but also vote for the right of women to not give birth to an unwanted pregnancy for the sake of both the mother and the unwanted child.

---

3   "The Human Toll: How Many People Died in the Crusades," 1-11.

When I began to write this book, I thought that the claim I was making about the reason the three Supreme Court cases about abortion came to reveal divergent opinions on the constitutionality of the right of a woman to seek an abortion of an unwanted, nonviable pregnancy, was due to the fact that two of the Courts believed that life of the fetus began at "quickening," and that the common law in America agreed with that view, which made abortion before that time a right that was guaranteed by the Amendments to the Constitution. The third *Dobbs* Court was then formed by the Republicans with a majority of conservative Catholic Justices who believed in the teaching by modern Popes that life began at conception, and therefore all abortions were murder, and could not have been intended by the Founding Fathers, and so if they wanted abortion to be a right, it required that an Amendment be passed. I had never read of anyone else making this claim, but after researching and writing the book, and completing the final draft with a sigh of relief, I suddenly read that Amy Coney Barrett had written a book about *Roe v. Wade* entitled *Listening to the Law: Reflections on the Court and Constitution* that was to become available on September 7, and so I put my manuscript aside, and waited to read her story before sending a copy to my editor. I am now adding what I found in that book to the Conclusion, for it proves that I am correct.

When I heard Amy Coney Barrett wrote a book about the overturning of *Roe v. Wade*, I was about to send my completed manuscript in to the publisher for it to be prepared for publication, but I put it aside until I could be assured that my personal research was correct. No matter how much research you do, you always realize that there are things that you might have missed, and then worry that your research was not detailed enough. With Barrett, I realized that at the very start of the book when she mentioned that one of her seven children had Down's Syndrome, and two were adopted from slaves in Haiti, that I may have been too harsh on her vote in *Dobbs*.[4] Before I finished 20 pages, however, I realized that you can't always trust that what you read, for on page 20 she also said that "Once a judge is on the bench, she is a United States judge, not a Democrat or Republican official beholden to a particular administration or party," and I knew that she was not

---

4   Barrett, Listening to the Law: Reflections on the Court and Constitution, 2, 139.

telling the truth.[5] I also realized then that I would be writing in this book about the few people who hold the rarest position you could ever have in the United States government, for she mentioned that she was the 103rd Associate Justice of the Supreme Court, and President Trump is now the 47th President of the United States.[6] That realization made me whisper, "God give me strength," and as I rushed to finish this book, I found it hard to imagine one person actually holding the jobs of President and Chief Justice of the Supreme Court at different points of their life, yet I found out that William Howard Taft (1857-1930) actually had achieved that remarkable feat.[7] I greatly respect everyone who reaches those vital positions, but all human beings can sometimes be wrong, and I must call out this President, and these six Catholic Justices on the *Dobbs* Supreme Court, for being wrong to say the Constitution does not support abortion. Despite being highly respected and regarded, they are about as unpatriotic as you can be and not charged with a crime.

Unfortunately, Barrett never dealt with any of the issues that I found important, especially with respect to the number of conservative Catholic Justices on the *Dobbs* Supreme Court. Let me tell you what was not in Barrett's book: any discussion of why there were so many Catholic Justices, and whether they had any discussion of the definition of life at conception; anything about what role President Trump played in their decision to overturn *Roe v Wade*; anything about Robert Bork's theory of Originalism; anything about why the Chief Justice did not believe *Roe v. Wade* should be overturned; anything about what they thought of *Casey* not overturning *Roe v. Wade*; anything about what was going to happen when suddenly abortion was illegal after 3.65 billion abortions were performed in the last 50 years worldwide; anything about the topic of Theocracy; anything about First Amendment rights; anything about the frequency of infanticide of unwanted children; anything about the problem of child abuse in America; anything about . . . forget it, you get the point.

It is true that the Constitution of the United States does not mention the word "abortion," but it does make reference to the common law, and states in the Seventh Amendment that, "In Suits at common law,

---

5   Ibid., 20.

6   Ibid., 22.

7   Ibid., 91.

where the value in controversy shall exceed twenty dollars, the right of trial by jury shall be preserved."[8] This admission that the Founding Fathers were aware of the common law is to be expected because many of the members of the Constitutional Convention were English, and were well-aware of the writings of William Blackstone, the English jurist who was recognized as an expert in the development of English Law, and this was a clear reference to the English common law which was prevalent when the Constitution was written. Although the U. S. Constitution does not explicitly require that our judicial system operate under common law, and designates Congress to write the laws that would govern the country, the Constitution was still written under that tradition. Common law would remain a tradition for guidance when there was no specific legislative act written. In his *Dobbs* opinion, Justice Alito made reference to the common law, and even mentioned the fact that abortion under common law was felt to be a crime after the first movement of the fetus was felt in the womb, usually taking place between the 16th and 18th week of pregnancy, an issue I previously discussed in *Roe v. Wade* was the reason Blackmun accepted that definition.[9] Alito discarded the importance of the quickening rule, however, saying that "the rule was abandoned in the 19th century," which is an outright lie, for he clearly knew that *Roe v. Wade* discussed its importance, and accepted that it was legal in the 20th century, as did England and many other countries in the world.[10] What Alito was actually referring to here was that the rule was abandoned in the 19th century by the Catholic Church, when Pope Pius IX made the stunning majority opinion in his apostolic constitution, *Apostolicae Sedis*, in 1869 that there would no longer be a distinction between animated and unanimated fetuses, and that all abortions would be punished by immediate excommunication, because it was an act of murder. Justice Alito was intent on following the Catholic view of when life begins, totally ignoring the view of the scientific medical community and the judicial holdings throughout the rest of the world. The only place that it began to be abandoned in the 19th century was the Catholic Church. It is clear to me that all of Alito's conclusions on when life began came

8   Microsoft CoPilot (8/17/2025). Personal communication.

9   "Dobbs, State Health Officer of the Mississippi Department of Health, et. al. v. Jackson Women's Health Organization et al.," 24.

10   Ibid., 30.

from his Catholic education, ignoring the medical community and the judicial holdings throughout the rest of the world, which were wrong, and were why he believed the common law ended in the 19ᵗʰ century.

I say this knowing full-well that I will be incurring the wrath of president Trump, but I myself accept that America must indeed be Made Great Again, but only by returning to the plan of our Founding Fathers to make our country the beacon of Democracy, and not by following the teaching of the Catholic Pope, and turning our country into a Theocracy, or by paying homage to the public appeal of Donald Trump. I have no quarrel with Catholicism or the edicts put forth by the Pope, and I agree that those who believe in their religion must be loyal to the teaching of the Pope, who is given the authority to speak for God. In the courtroom, however, the loyalty of Justices must only be to the Constitution, and not to Papal edicts that go against the intent of our Constitution and our common law. If they cannot put aside the Pope's differing opinion on conception, they must recuse themselves from participating in the case. With abortion, this means they cannot vote on that issue, for as the American lawyer and legal analyst for CNN, Jeffrey Toobin, said: "There were two kinds of cases before the Supreme Court. There were abortion cases – and there were all the others."[11] Or so it seems. If the Supreme Court Justices continue to believe that life begins at conception and demand that it be made constitutional by an amendment, then they have to follow their own edict and present an amendment to change the common law. If their amendment fails, their opinion on overturning *Roe v. Wade* must be overturned, and they can change their quickening rule to 15 weeks, as Mississippi, and I will be satisfied.

The effect of the *Roe v. Wade* decision given by Justice Blackmun on January 21, 1973, was an incredibly important, and unexpected boost to women across the world, for it validated many of their claims that women had the right to choose whether to carry an unexpected, and unwanted, pregnancy to term under the U. S. Constitution. As Mary Ziegler, the Martin Luther King Jr. Professor of Law at the University of California, Davis, School of Law, wrote: "At the stroke of a pen, the vast majority of the nation's abortion laws were made unconstitutional," a landmark change for women that opened up

---

11 Toobin, The Nine: Inside the Secret World of the Supreme Court, 42.

a whole new era of progress for women's lib supporters.[12] While many men did not find this ruling so important, women across America acclaimed it to be equivalent to the Thirteenth Amendment, which was ratified on December 6, 1865, abolishing slavery, and the Nineteenth Amendment, which gave woman the right to vote when the amendment was passed by Congress on June 4, 1919, and then ratified on August 18, 1920, fourteen months and fourteen days later. Unfortunately, it took a Civil War to awaken Americans to the need to make all citizens aware of the need to abolish racial inequality, and it took 70 years for women to finally get the right to vote after the Suffrage movement began at the Seneca Falls Convention in 1848. *Roe v. Wade* immediately gave women the legal right to obtain an abortion, and the event, while welcomed by Democrats, infuriated Republicans who began a spirited campaign to overturn the decision, finally accomplishing it 49 years and 153 days later, forcing me to write an amendment proposal to make that right a permanent part of the Constitution.

Warren Burger and Harry Blackmun were on the Supreme Court together in the 1970 term, and that year, *Roe v. Wade* was chosen as the 18th case to be on the docket.[13] I discussed at length in Chapter III that the choice was Burger's alone to proceed with reviewing the case, and there is no evidence that he talked to Blackmun about it before making his decision. I also explained how the *Casey* case was vitally important to allowing *Roe v. Wade* to not be overturned, so that abortion remained legal for almost 50 years, allowing statistical proof of its safety and ability to lower the infanticide rate of unwanted children from 10-15% to below 1%. The *Dobbs* Supreme Court was put together by Republican Presidents, and first met during the 2023 term. The *Dobbs* case was the 1,392nd case docketed in the 2019 term, when John Roberts was Chief Justice.[14] This shows that Roberts was trying to get the case on the docket so that it could be tried while Trump was still President, but delays were unavoidable to format the Court with assured Catholic Justices, and unexpectedly, Trump lost his reelection bid. This shows that while Burger, in my opinion, was rash and wrong to docket the case when he did, the *Dobbs* case delay did

---

12 Ziegler, Roe: The History of a National Obsession, 10.
13 Microsoft CoPilot (9/13/2025). Personal Communication.
14 Ibid.

not allow Trump to be the acting President when it was decided, for he lost his bid for reelection, and both Chief Justices were disappointed.

Blackmun was the man who was chosen to write the opinion of *Roe v. Wade,* a Justice who had been appointed by a Republican President to help form a new conservative Supreme Court, but believed in a woman's right to choose whether to carry an unwanted pregnancy to term, and in so doing gave all the world an understanding of how important it was to allow safe abortion of unwanted pregnancies to be constitutionally protected up to the gestational age of 24-28 weeks. His decision to approve abortion eventually showed how safe the procedure was. The results over the ensuing years proved that "induced abortion is less dangerous than childbirth, colonoscopy, or even wisdom tooth extraction," according to Dr. Daniel Grossman, Professor in the Department of Obstetrics, Gynecology & Reproductive Sciences at the University of California, San Francisco.[15] Despite this recognition, it remains "far more stringently regulated than other health services," as aptly put by Deborah R. McFarlane and Wendy L. Hansen, two Professors of Political Science at the University of New Mexico who truly appreciate the difficult political environment surrounding the issue of abortion, for it was never accepted by Republicans, and its passage was to eventually be doomed from the start.[16] By finding a constitutional basis for the right of a woman to choose an abortion, however, Blackmun was able to provide statistical evidence of not only the safety of the procedure to abort an unwanted pregnancy, but evidence that the rate of infanticide of such children could drop from 10-15% of births that it had maintained throughout the history of mankind, to below 1% after *Roe v. Wade* was passed, a truly remarkable effect that we cannot afford to lose now that his decision has been overturned. Now that he has proven the procedure is safe and effective in reducing infanticide, it is time to make it a federally granted constitutional right.

Since I believe that Justice Alito failed to follow the principle of Separation of Church and State in his *Dobbs* decision to overturn the *Roe v. Wade* and *Casey* verdicts, and improperly defined the common law to now be that life begins at conception, I must now propose a

---

15 Microsoft CoPilot (9/17/2025). Personal Communication.
16 McFarlane and Hansen, Regulating Abortion: The Politics of US Abortion Policy, 13.

Constitutional Amendment that will allow for abortions to once again continue on women before the fetus is viable, which has been the common law in America from the time the Constitution was written. Originally referred to as "quickening," when the mother was able to feel movement of the fetus in her abdomen, it is now more accurately determined by clinical evidence of the survival of premature births by assisted methods of respiration and nutrition so that the 24-28-week period of gestation when quickening generally appeared can now be shown to take place at 20-week gestation, which is when my proposal has determined viability to begin. The irresponsible manner in which that benefit was overturned by *Dobbs* is a true travesty of justice, and I showed in this book why we must pass this amendment in order to prevent a rise in the rate of infanticide of unwanted children that has been ever-present in the history of mankind.

When the-wolf-is-at-the-door, as the idiom of imminent danger explains, to act in the manner that unwanted births have been treated in the past is understandable, if not excusable, and knowing that it is an inherited human trait is essential if we are going to try and attenuate the horrible history that is clearly evident in the historical record of mankind. If you are Catholic, I remind you of what Jesus Christ said to his Father when he was being crucified on the cross: "Father, forgive them; for they know not what they do."[17] If only the modern Catholic hierarchy were as realistic about the frailties that much of their flock has to deal with, my task would not be so difficult. But the modern Catholic Church has determined that life begins at conception, and they have the authority to make that decision because religion is based on faith, and not proof. Public polls, however, have shown that only about 12% of people accept this view, and I contend that a majority of Catholics do not believe that a nonviable fetus is truly a living person as defined by the Constitution. The common law across the world in countries that are primarily Catholic in population allows the abortion of nonviable fetuses, including Italy and Mexico, although the sovereign-city-state Vatican does not.

When you go to the polls to vote on the abortion amendment, I ask you, if you are Catholic, to please remember the request of the Lord you worship, and do not judge a woman until you have walked in the shoes she has to wear, and remember your other biblical passages. In

---

17 Luke 23:34. The Holy Bible, 733.

Luke 6:37, it is said: "Judge not and ye shall not be judged: condemn not, and ye shall not be condemned: forgive, and ye shall be forgiven,"[18] and in Ephesians 4:32: "And be ye kind one to another, tenderhearted, forgiving one another, even as God for Christ's sake hath forgiven you."[19] I understand that you are likely so abhorred by the taking of potential future life that you believe it should be a cardinal sin, but I only ask that you realize everyone does not have the same view of nonviable fetuses as the Pope does, and that includes many devout Catholics who simply disagree on this one important issue. The Pope believes in your soul even more than your body, for that is the part that reflects his image of God. Human beings have only one body, and God decided that the body would not be immortal because the Creation process was flawed, but your soul will still be immortal and live on after your body dies. There are times when a pregnant woman is better off not giving birth until times change, and if you don't know the circumstances, don't prejudge their decision, and allow them the right to follow the common law if they choose.

The investigative reporter Bob Woodward, who is best known for the book he wrote with Carl Bernstein, *All the President's Men*, about Richard Nixon's Watergate scandal, which won them a Pulitzer Prize in 1973, also wrote a book about the events leading up to the *Roe v. Wade* decision with the journalist Scott Armstrong, and in the Introduction to that book they noted how the Supreme Court for nearly 200 years had made its decisions in absolute secrecy, its deliberative process "hidden from public view."[20] The conference room where the nine Justices met to vote in these two Supreme Court cases was not the same one that the Supreme Court first met in, for the present structure was designed by Cass Gilbert (1859-1934), and had the cornerstone laid in 1932, with the first session taking place on October 7, 1935.[21] Both courthouses were oak-paneled, and had a 12-foot-long table covered in green felt under a splendid chandelier, which was surrounded by nine handsome high-backed green leather swivel chairs, each with a brass nameplate identifying its occupant for much

18 Luke 6:27. Ibid., 714.
19 Eph 4:32. Ibid., 815.
20 Woodward and Armstrong, The Justices Behind Roe v. Wade: The Inside Story, xv.
21 Microsoft CoPilot (5/18/2025). Personal Communication.

of that time.[22] During the deliberations in *Roe v. Wade*, Chief Justice Warren Burger sat at one end of the table, and the Senior Associate Justice William O. Douglas sat on the other, which meant that they faced each other as the other Justices opined their views, and argued why the case should be approved or denied. Tradition says that we often do not know much about what conversations take place, for it is the final opinion that matters, and is available for all to read and see how the Supreme Court functions. The appeal to better understand how these two cases came to such different decisions, however, and created so much interest in what happened, that more than the usual investigative reporting took place, leading to information about what went on, like in no other Supreme Court case to date. We know more about how each of these Supreme Court cases was adjudicated than ever before, with the amount of information available to be distributed by modern technology, and this has allowed me to discover how Blackmun and Alito came to their opinions.

In this book, I tried to honestly explain why each of these varying opinions was made, and why I think one was right, and one was wrong. I cannot decide for you when you vote on my amendment, but I hope you can see that the definition of viability of a life should not be made by religious views alone, but rather by the reality of what life entails for the majority of human beings. One cannot always be assured that their lives will not entail disastrous circumstances that cannot be avoided, and I contend that the decision a woman makes when she finds out that she is pregnant is one of those instances that the Constitution understood was a right she was allowed to make before the fetus became viable.

Harry Blackmun did not lead the discussion throughout the *Roe v. Wade* trial, and we have full transcripts of both trials readily available for everyone to follow online. Blackmun listened intently during the trial, I am sure, and I believe he spoke persuasively, for the vote to approve was not close, which indicates to me that his argument that the Constitution intended for women to have the right to end an unwanted, nonviable pregnancy persuaded many of the Justices to accept his view. In my opinion, Chief Justice Burger would have dissented if the vote was close, but because his vote did not matter,

---

22 Woodward and Armstrong, The Justices Behind Roe v. Wade: The Inside Story, 30.

he voted with the majority because he was the one to pick Blackmun to give the opinion, and felt obligated to go along with his decision. Woodward and Bernstein were correct in showing the grandeur of the room in which the case was discussed, and how the initial judicial decision was reached "hidden from public view," but with the details I have provided in this book, I believe that you can clearly see why the vote, although unexpected, was well-thought out, and supported by the evidence presented. The explosive interest in how abortion was first legalized, and then restricted once again, has led many investigative reporters to publish commentary and insight about the *Roe v. Wade* decision in more than 3,000 books, which showed up in the computer research program in my local library. You can research as thoroughly as I did, even more so if you want, but I contend that the recent publication of Amy Barrett's book should convince you that what I say is true. I haven't been able to read everyone of these treatises, but while the deliberative process may have been hidden from public view, the interest that was generated has opened up much of the secretive process to critical review, and I have presented the evidence I learned in my research of this book to convince you that the amendment I have written should, and must, be passed.

We live in an era of Google search and AI assistance, which has allowed educated people like me to do research on topics that would have taken much more time and much more training than is necessary today. I have enough legal training to understand what I am reading, given I graduated law school with High Honors, and I believe my discoveries in this case on the actions of both Justices who wrote the divergent opinions is a true reflection of their thought process, and will be confirmed by others in the years to come. Although my monotheistic preference is in Judaism, I have also written many books on Christianity and Islam. I believe I understand the true essence of all these religions, and my recommendations in this book are consistent with the teachings of the holy texts in each faith. If I can convince the voting public to pass my amendment because of what I found out, and in so doing, hopefully prevent the deaths of thousands of unwanted children, allowing women the right to choose whether to take their unwanted pregnancies to term, my efforts will be my reward, and I will be proud of what I've done. I hope many Pro-Life advocates will listen to my pleas and change their minds about the amendment before they vote, even though they may continue to believe in their hearts that life begins at conception. I simply want them to believe that not everyone who believes in God has the same particular religious belief, and they must live their lives in a manner they believe is the right thing to do, based upon the faith they have in the same One Almighty God. I also will feel secure in thanking you for helping to keep a nonviable fetus from having to suffer an interminable end to their life, because they were either killed by their parent, or suffered through a life with child abuse.

In Chapters II and III of this book, I described how *Roe v. Wade* and *Dobbs v. Jackson Women's Health Organization* were two Supreme Court cases that were both decided on faulty legal and social premises, and the end-result of their efforts was simply that the issue of whether a woman had the right to abort a nonviable fetus had to be determined by an amendment to the United States Constitution, rather than by judicial interpretation of the Constitution. This should come as no surprise, since both the slavery of mostly black individuals and the right of women to vote needed the passage of amendments to achieve that constitutional right, as Supreme Court cases in both of these issues came to a faulty decision. If personal rights such as these required an amendment, so be it with the personal right to choose whether to carry an unwanted pregnancy to term. The two Supreme Court decisions were separated by almost 50 years, but the time was not wasted. The lesson we learned from the legalization of abortion was that instead of unwanted children being born and then suffering an early death 10-15% of the time, that rate dropped to below 1%, and for the first time in the history of mankind. Progress was made in reducing this horrible statistic, and we now know that the statistic, which was present for thousands of years, can be corrected, and I have written this book to show you the evidence. Now that we have means of safe abortion, and 50% of unwanted pregnancies in the Western World have been aborted, we must pass my amendment to ensure that this benefit to mankind is not lost, and will continue into the distant future. In the past 50 years, there have been 3.65 billion abortions worldwide, and we cannot just stop the process and not create a disaster that is easily avoided.[23] We cannot let that happen, for it would be a moral failure on all of our parts if we do.

It is essential that everyone who is old enough to vote realizes how

---

23 Microsoft CoPilot (8/15/2025). "Abortions worldwide over the past 50 years."

vital this proven fact is, and understands that, like it or not, we cannot accept that if human life is sacred and deserving of being protected by rights given to all human beings, that ignorance of what will happen to unwanted babies is irrelevant because life begins at conception. We are not made perfect, and some of our nature must be kept in check by punishments of those whose nature is so dangerous that they endanger the lives of others around them. We should not force people to raise children they do not want, and so while adoption is a possible acceptable alternative in a small number of cases, it simply cannot handle the number of unwanted pregnancies that occur throughout the world. Society will be safer if those unwanted fetuses can be eliminated before they become viable and have to undergo a painful death. When the human egg and sperm first unite, and an embryo is conceived, it takes about 20 weeks before the fetus reaches a point where life can persist outside the womb with assistance, even though the natural process of maturation takes about eight months before the human fetus reaches the end-point of normal development. It would be wrong to abort fetuses who are viable unless the mother's life is in extreme and immediate danger, but it would be just as wrong to subject that unwanted fetus to a painful life, or possible early death, because of abuse.

Whether this process of our existence on earth was developed by natural evolution, or by Divine Creation, there is clearly a difference between a fertilized egg that reaches a state of being able to exist on its own, and one that may never be independently able to achieve the status of life, and the rules for whether abortion is legal or not should be based on that determination, and not on the religious belief that life begins at conception. I personally believe in the existence of a monotheistic God, but I also accept that the story of that God was first told in the Hebrew Torah, and then accepted in both the Christian New Testament, and the Muslim Qur'an, is now a belief that is held by more than 50% of the world population, but not because the story is factual, but because all adherents have faith that there is a God that generated our reality. That God, however, had no problem destroying all human life except for the family of Noah when He felt that His Creation was not to His liking. The human race is not perfect, as evidenced by the violence that has characterized all of our history, but the amendment I now propose, to abort unwanted nonviable fetuses, will do much to reduce the killing and abuse of millions of unwanted children at a time before they become a viable human being, capable of feeling pain or suffering. Freedom of religious belief is an accepted tenet of the U.S. Constitution, but so is separation of Church and State, which means we must not let our religious beliefs overpower our understanding of what the Founding Fathers meant the Federal government's powers to be.

The Constitution was set up to allow for states to retain many rights not specifically given to them by the Constitution, but like it or not, the legislative results in this country clearly show that many states do not agree with that right without limitation, and that is why I believe the amendment process is the correct way to do that, and I hope this book accomplishes that feat. The *Dobbs* case overturned *Roe v. Wade*, but the state of Mississippi allowed for abortion up to 15-weeks gestation, and it was Justice Alito, and not the state legislature, who said life begins at conception. Some legislatures have modified their views and passed more strict laws reflecting the *Dobbs* decision, but I contend that the legislatures have voted that way because they believed what the *Dobbs* Court ruled was valid common law, and not just a judicial ruling. They were wrong to think that way, for Justice Alito had no authority to make common law, only to interpret the Constitution, and he even said so in his opinion when he said that if abortion were to be approved, it had to be by an amendment to the Constitution. We must now proceed to vote for a reasonable amendment that is scientifically based and will protect the future of unwanted children by not forcing them to be born if they are going to be unwanted and unprotected. I have directed the writing of my book to the common people, and not the politicians running for office, and I am confident that my amendment proposal will be passed. If it is not, then we must overturn the *Dobbs* case and return to *Roe v. Wade* as law, while a new amendment can be proposed.

Because Supreme Court Justices serve for life, they have an enormous effect on the way in which our Constitution in the United States is interpreted, but this case shows how dangerous that power can be. We cannot always rely on the infallibility of the Supreme Court, as we saw with the issue of slavery and the right of women to vote. We are at the same crossroad today, and we either must pass the amendment I propose or overturn the *Dobbs* verdict. I prefer the amendment to be passed, for I believe it is what 3/4 of Americans want, but if Trump's power is significant enough to prevent passage, I will fight to overturn *Dobbs*.

Our Founding Fathers, in my opinion, wanted us to expand our Constitution with the use of amendments. Despite the fact that they could only get ten approved initially, it took seventeen more to reach the range of liberties we have today. Two of those amendments were passed to provide freedom from slavery and the right of women to vote, and it is time to now pass the Twenty-Eighth Amendment to finally give women the right to have an unwanted, nonviable pregnancy terminated. The foresight of our Founding Fathers is very clear in the issue I am discussing in this book, and we can find a happy medium for both the rights of each state to retain the power to use their population choices in a manner that will fulfill both national and state interests at the same time. Is 3/4 majority the right requirement for something as important as the right of a woman to decide to carry her pregnancy to term? I personally believe it is because of the success it has had since its inception, but I am sure there will be disagreement on that issue, along with many others, as well. We are dealing with a very sensitive topic here, and so controversy over whatever happens should be expected, but I do not think we should modify what has worked to date, and I contend that this means Catholic Justices who do not swear to not follow Papal beliefs, and rely on Constitutional interpretation alone, should recuse themselves on cases involving abortion. Despite the fact that there have been roughly twelve thousand amendments proposed in Congress since our government began, I still believe we can reach our goal if I can get every man and woman who are married, or hope to have children one day whether they are married or not, vote together on the day the ballot is available, and take your friends and neighbors with you to assure my proposal will pass.[24]

Without getting into a heated debate about what Democracy means, I believe that the United States Constitution has both defined and carried out the most democratic system of government that has ever existed in civilization to date, and that its system of amendments to correct any deficits to the changing times is the best method to maintain that ideal. While I disagree greatly with many of Alito's views in the *Dobbs* opinion, I primarily claim that only one is a fatal

---

24 Barrett, Listening to the Law: Reflections on the Court and Constitution, 150.

flaw, and that is his refusal to separate the principles of Church and State. His reasoning is clearly based on his religious beliefs, and not in the writing of the Constitution. His refusing to separate the principles of Church and State while deliberating in the courtroom is setting a dangerous precedent, and it is following the same practice President Donald Trump is displaying in the Oval Office. One of the crucial teachings of the Constitution has been the principle of separation of Church and State, and that is a critical element that must not be forgotten. We cannot let our personal understanding of God, or our disbelief in God, affect how our personal rights are determined, Whoever, or Whatever, that God is. Yes, we have had two World Wars, and we pray there will not be another, but if there is a God, those wars were still played out, and we must do our best to deal with this problem as if God is an uninterested spectator, letting the chips fall where they may. Justice Alito is going to remain on the Supreme Court for the rest of his life unless he decides to retire. I ask him to please look into his heart and his mind, and decide whether he can truly reflect the desires of our Founding Fathers without remaining loyal and obedient to the Pope, who reflects the teaching of the Catholic Church.

Postscript

During my research for this book, I read much material written by feminists who felt the need to claim that overturning the *Roe v. Wade* verdict was nothing more than further evidence of the so-called natural order "where women and black people are inferior to white men, and where LGBTIQ people simply should not exist," as claimed by Siân Norris, an investigative journalist who specializes in investigative reporting on women's rights.[1] Norris considered the overturning of *Roe v. Wade* the result of a far-right conspiracy "that pins women to reproductive labour and puts their bodies under male control."[2] She does not comment on how some people, not on the far-right, consider abortion to be murder, like many devout Catholics do, or how some people who believe in, and understand, the Constitution of the United States consider that, like the right to vote, abortion should be legalized in the country only by an amendment, rather than a Supreme Court decision. She claims she is only giving an "overview of the fascist thought architecture that wants to restore a natural order of white male supremacy," but makes no mention of the difference between feticide and infanticide, or the fact that before safe abortion was available, 10-15% of unwanted babies born were eventually killed by their parents, often the mother.[3] Like many other investigative journalists, her investigations are often guided by personal interests, rather than a quest for the truth, and I hope that I will not be charged with that closed-minded approach by what I said in this book, and how I said it.

I agree that there is no question that most of civilization was guided by what is today considered a sexist agenda, and this includes religions, as well as social structures, whose past history did not see equality between the sexes. I do not want to be seen as denying that women have undergone a long history of degradation by a male-dominated world, but we are talking of thousands of years of that behavior dating back not only to the writing of the Hebrew Bible, but the beginning of *Homo Sapiens* on earth. Feminists, in general, while biased towards the long-ignored equal rights of women, have been an important

---

1   Norris, Bodies Under Siege: How the Far-Right Attack on Reproductive Rights Went Global, 5.

2   Ibid.

3   Ibid., 9.

public source of information since the National Organization for Women (NOW) was founded in i966 by Betty Freidan (1921-2006), who wrote *The Feminine Mystique* in 1963, and Pauly Murray (1910-1985), a black feminist who was born to North Carolina slaves. They were the ones who framed abortion as a right for women and began a campaign to repeal abortion laws.[4] Their formation followed the Civil Rights Act of 1964, and its initial focus was on the *Equal Employment Opportunity Commission (EEOC),* which was the federal agency charged with enforcing that act. Their membership grew to over 500,000, and they were active in their efforts to convince the Supreme Court to pass the *Roe v. Wade* decision, and I congratulate them for all they have done. What's important now, however, is to pass the amendment I have written that will not only improve women's rights, but will concentrate our attention on the rights, and needs, of the children of America in general, and in particular to those born unwanted, and suffering their entire lives because there was no way to allow them to wait until they were wanted before they were born. We are not talking about sexism, even though it is only a woman who can biologically give birth. We now have the ability to make real progress in that desperate area of need, and I hope that it will soon be a constitutional law by amendment and will not be seen as an issue involving only women, but rather all mankind.

In this book, I have tried to present an argument that will educate the public to understand why we need to pass an amendment that will be acceptable to people who consider abortion murder, because it is feticide, and not murder, if done before the fetus is viable. If I fail, and we force women to have all unwanted pregnancies, we will create a murder rate in this country that is not morally acceptable under any theory at all. We must find a way to include the right of a woman to choose whether to deliver an unwanted pregnancy or not in our Constitution, and just like the Bill of Rights, we need to do it with an amendment, and not a Supreme Court decision. I am hopeful that this book will help convince enough Americans to change their views on abortion as being equivalent to murder. I realize that my task may seem like those lines from the song "The Impossible Dream (The Quest)", written by Joe Darion (1911-2001) (lyrics) and Mitch Leigh (1928-

---

4   Ziegler, Dollars for Life; The Anti-Abortion Movement and the Fall of the Republican Establishment, 6-7.

2014) (music) for the 1965 Broadway musical *Man of La Mancha*, where Don Quixote sings: "To dream the impossible dream, To fight the unbeatable foe..." but sometimes the end justifies the means, and I must do what I gotta do.

> A philosopher once said to a fish, "The purpose of life is to reason and become wise."
> The fish answered, "The purpose of life is to swim and catch flies."
> The philosopher muttered, "Poor fish."
> Back came a whisper, "Poor philosopher."[5]

Live and let live. There are enough important issues to die for, so don't make mountains out of mole hills, and follow JFK's advice – not to ask what your country can do for you, ask what you can do for your country.

It is simple: Live and let live, but not if it is an unwanted and nonviable fetus.

---

5   Moorhead, The Meaning of Life, 24.

Bibliography

Articles

"A Brief History of Abortion – From Ancient Egyptian Herbs to Fighting Stigma Today," <https://the conversationtoday.com/a-brief-history-of-abortion-from-ancient-egyptian-herbs-to-fighting-stigma-today-213033> (2/17/2025), 1-4.

"A Thousand Infants Overlain," British Medical Journal 1 (1895): 36.

"Abortion Act, Roe v. Wade, 410 U.S. 113 (1973)," <https://en.wikipedia.org/wiki/Abortion_Act_1967> (11/30/2024), 1-6.

"Abortion in Russia," <https://en.wikipedia.org/wiki/Abortion_in_Russia> (3/3/2025), 1-7.

"Abortions Worldwide This Year," <https://www.worldometers.info/abortions/> (3/25/2025), 1-2.

"Adoption," <https://www.aecf.org/topics/adoption?msclkid=8e563a0562ba1c35112a5d9351900e22&utm_source=bing&utm_medium=cpc&utm_campaign=Adoption+-+Topics&utm_term=adopting+resources&utm_content=Adoption+Resources> (1/26/2025), 1-20.

"Adoption Abuse Statistics," 1-2. <https://gitnux.org/adoption-abusse-statistics, (5/17/2025), 1-12.

Aird, John S., "China's War on Children," American Enterprise (March/April 1996):58-61.

"American Medical Association," <https://en.wikipedia.org/wiki/American_Medical_Association> (9/9/2025), 1-18.

"Amicus Curiae Brief in Whole Woman's Health," Whose Choice Is It?: Abortion, Medicine, and the Law, edit. David F. Walbert and J. Douglas Butler, Chicago: ABA Publishing, 2021, 173-189.

Aramesh, Kiarash, "Shiite Perspective on the Moral Status of the Early Human Embryo," T & T Clark Reader in Abortion and Religion: Jewish, Christian, and Muslim Perspectives, edit. Rebecca Todd Peters and Margaret C. Kamitsuka, London: T&T Clark, 2023, 299-304.

"Articles of /Confederation," <https://www.archives.gov/milestone-document/articles-of-confederation> (3/6/2025), 1-9.

Asch, Stuart S., "Crib Deaths: Their Possible Relationship to Post-Partum Depression and Infanticide," Journal of the Mount Sinai Hospital 35 (1968): 214-220.

"Baby Scoop Era," <https://en.wikipedia.org/w/index.php?title+Baby_Scoop_Era&form=MGOAV3> (2/24/2025), 1-7.

Baird, David, "Introduction," Abortion: Medical Progress and Social

Implications, Ciba Foundation Symposium 115, edit. Ruth Porter and Maeve O'Connor, London: Pitman, 1985, 1-3.

Balkin, Jack M., "Abortion, Partisan Entrenchment, and the Republican Party," Roe v. Dobbs: The Past, Present, and Future of a Constitutional Right to Abortion, edit. Lee C. Bollinger and Geoffrey R. Stone, New York: Oxford University Press, 2024, 81-100.

Balkin, Jack M., "Jack M. Balkin (judgment of the Court)," What Roe v. Wade Should Have Said: The Nation's Top Legal Experts Rewrite America's Most Controversial Decision, edit. Jack M. Balkin, New York: New York University Press, 2005, 31-62.

Balkin, Jack M., "Roe v. Wade, *An Engine of Controversy*," What Roe v. Wade Should Have Said: The Nation's Top Legal Experts Rewrite America's Most Controversial Decision, edit. Jack M. Balkin, New York: New York University Press, 2005, 3-62.

Barnes, Rhae Lynn, & Clinton, Catherine, "Introduction," Roe v. Wade Fifty Years After, edit. Rhae Lynn Barnes & Catherine Clinton, Athens, GA: The University of Georgia Press, 2024, 1-49.

"The Belmont Report," 3. <https://www.hhs.gov/ohrp/sites/default/files/the-belmont-report-508c-pdf> (2/8/2025), 1-10.

Bernat, James L., "Arguments Supporting Neurologic Criteria to Determine Death," Death Determination by Neurologic Criteria: Areas of Consensus and Controversy, edit. Ariane Lewis and James L. Bernat, Cham, CH: Springer, 2023, 11-26.

Bernat, James L., and Lewis, Ariane, "Historical Introduction," Death Determination by Neurologic Criteria: Areas of Consensus and Controversy, edit. Ariane Lewis and James L. Bernat, Cham, CH: Springer, 2023, 1-7.

Bevan, Cassie Statuto, "Changing Laws and Culture to Reduce Barriers to Adoption," Adoption Factbook III, edit. Connaught Mashner, National Council for Adoption, 1999, 7-11.

"Bigelow v. Virginia," <https://tile.Joc.gov/storage-services/service/11/usrep/usrep4211/usrep421809/usrep421809.pdf> (3/23/2025), 1-28.

Biggers, John D., "Generation of the Human Life Cycle," Abortion and the Status of the Fetus, edit. William B. Bondeson, H. Tristram Engelhardt, Jr., Stuart F. Spicker, and Daniel H. Winship, Dordrecht, Holland: D. Reidel Publishing Company, 1984, 31-53.

Bollinger, Lee C., and Stone, Geoffrey R., "Opening Dialogue," Roe v. Dobbs: The Past, Present, and Future of a Constitutional Right to Abortion, edit. Lee C. Bollinger and Geoffrey R. Stone, New York: Oxford University Press, 2024, xv-xxiv.

Bomboy, Scott, "A Short List of Overturned Supreme Court Landmark Cases," <https://constitutioncenter.org/blog/a-short-list-of-overturned-supreme-court-landmark-decisions> (2/2/2025), 1-10.

Brennan, Karen, and Milne, Emma, "100 Years of Infanticide: The Law in Context," 100 years of the Infanticide Act: Legacy, Impact and Future Directions, edit. Karen Brennan and Emma Milne, Oxford: Hart, 2023, 1-46.

Bridge, Dave, Pushback: The Political Fallout of Unpopular Supreme Court Decisions, Columbia, MO: University of Missouri Press, 2024.

Bridges, Khiara M., "The *Dobbs* Gambit, Gaslighting at the Highest Level," Roe v. Dobbs: The Past, Present, and Future of a Constitutional Right to Abortion, edit. Lee C. Bollinger and Geoffrey R. Stone, New York: Oxford University Press, 2024, 120-128.

"The Burger Court Opinion Writing Database," 1-38. <http:// supremecourtopinions.wustl.edu/files/opinion_pdfs/1971/70-18.pdf> (6/28/2025), 1-38.

"By The Numbers: Americans opine on the direction of the Catholic church," <https:///www.msn.com/en-us/video/other/by-the-numbers-americans-opine-on-the-direction-of-the-catholic-church/vi-AA1Ev6FN? ocid=msedgntp&pc=DCTS&cvid=46eebc0955224617b743984de344bab 9&ei=60#details> (5/11/2025), 1-4.

Campbell, Alastir V., "Viability and the Moral Status of the Fetus," Abortion: Medical Progress and Social Implications, Ciba Foundation Symposium 115, edit. Ruth Porter and Maeve O'Connor, London: Pitman, 1985, 228-243.

Charalambous, Peter, Romero, Laura, and Kim, Soo Rin, "Trump has tapped an unprecedented 13 billionaires for his administration. Here's who they are," <https://abcnews.go.com/US/Trump-tapped-unprecedented-13-billionaires-top-administration-roles/story?id=116872968> (1/25/2025), 1-12.

Cellania, Miss, "The Historical Horror of Childbirth," <https://www. mentalfloss.com/ 50513/historical horror-childbirth> (12/10/2024), 1-5.

Center for American Progress, "Increasing politicization of the Supreme Court Is a Danger to the Nation's Democratic Principles," The Politicization of the Supreme Court, edit. Eamon Doyle, New York: Greenhaven Publishing, 2022, 31-39.

Chemerinsky, Erwin, "Justice Blackmun Got It Right in *Roe v. Wade*," Roe v. Dobbs: The Past, Present, and Future of a Constitutional Right to Abortion, edit. Lee C. Bollinger and Geoffrey R. Stone, New York: Oxford University Press, 2024, 67-77.

"Civil War Casualties," <https://www.battlefields.org/learn/articles/civil-war-casualties> (4/17/2025), 1-10.

"Cloning," <https://animalbiotech.ucdavis.edu/cloning> (6/18/25), 1-7.

"Cloning Fact Sheet," <https://www.genome.gov/about-genomics/fact-sheets/Cloning-Fact-Sheet> (6/18/2025), 1-2.

Cohen, I. Glenn, "Reproductive Technologies and Embryo Destruction after *Dobbs*," Roe v. Dobbs: The Past, Present, and Future of a Constitutional Right to Abortion, edit. Lee C. Bollinger and Geoffrey R. Stone, New York: Oxford University Press, 2024, 281-298.

Committee on Oversight and Reform, "A State of Crisis: Examining the Urgent Need to Protect and Expand Abortion Rights and Access," Abortion Rights, Access, and Legislative Response, edit. Jorge P. Sandford, New York: Cnova, 2022, 1-102.

"Constitution of the United States," <https://en.wikipedia.org/wiki/Constitution_of_the_ United_States> (11/26/2024), 1-31.

"Constitutional Amendment Processes in the 50 States," <https://statecourtreport.org/our-work/analysis-opinion/constitutional-amendment-processes-50-states> (8/31/2025), 1-9.

"Constitutional Convention. Notes Taken in the Federal Convention, [1–26 June 1787]," <https://founders.archives.gov/documents/Hamilton/01-04-02-0093> (5/22/2025), 1-12.

"Convention on the Rights of the Child," < https://www.ohchr.org/en/instruments-mechanisms/ instruments/convention-rights-child> (1/26/2025).

"Countries Where Abortion is Illegal, 2025," <https://worldpopulationreview.com/country-rankings/countries-where-abortion-is-illegal> (6/21/2025), 1-4.

"Cruzan v. Director, Missouri Department of Health," 2-4. https://en.wikipedia.org/wiki/Cruzan_v._Director,_Missouri_Department_of_Health> (5/31/2025), 1-8.

"CRUZAN, BY HER PARENTS AND CO-GUARDIANS, CRUZAN ET UX. v. DIRECTOR, MISSOURI DEPARTMENT OF HEALTH, ET AL" <https://www.globalhealthrights.org/wp-content/uploads/2013/01/SC-1990-Cruzan-v-Director-Missouri-Department-of-Health.pdf> (7?8/2025), 1-53.

Damme, Catherine, "Infanticide: The Worth of an Infant Under Law," Medical History, 22 (1978): 1-24.

Da Silva Carvalho, Adriano, "The Bible and Abortion: Exodus 21:22-23 in the Septuagint and Other Opinions." International Journal of Philosophy, 2023, 11(1):6-10.

Dayton, Cornelia Hughes, "Taking the Trade: Abortion and Gender Relations in an Eighteenth-Century New England Village," The William and Mary Quarterly, Vol. 48, No. 1 (Jan., 1991), pp. 19-49 (31 pages).

"Death of Sarah Grosvenor," <https://en.wikipedia.org/wiki/Death_of_Sarah_Grosvenor> (6/25/2025), 1-3.

"Decades of progress in reducing child deaths and stillbirths under threat, warns the United Nations," <https://www.unicef.org/press-releases/decades-progress-reducing-child-deaths-and-stillbirths-under-threat-warns-united> (5/8/2025), 1-10.

"Defining Death, A Report on the Medical, Legal and Ethical Issues in the Determination of Death (excerpt)," Exploring the Philosophy of Death and Dying: Classical and Contemporary Perspectives, edit. Michael Cholbi and Travis Timmeman, New York: Routledge, 2021, 3-9.

DeMause, Lloyd, "The History of Child Assault," Journal of Psychohistory, 18 (1990):1-29.

"Did Colonial America have abortions? Yes, but . . .," <https://wng.org/sift/did-colonial-america-have-abortions-yes-but-1617409251> (3/29/2025), 1-10.

"Didache, The Teaching of the Twelve Apostles" <https://legacyicons.com/content/didache.pdf> (2/9/2025), 1-17.

"Dobbs v. Jackson Women's Health Organization," <www.britannica.com/topic/Dobbs-v-Womens- Health-Organization> (11/15/2024), 1-13.

"Dobbs v. Jackson Women's Health Organization (2022)," <https://constitutioncenter.org/the-constituion/supreme-court-case-library/dobbs-v-jackson-womens-health-organization> (2/18/2025), 1-41.

"Dobbs, State Health Officer of the Mississippi Department of Health, et. al. v. Jackson Women's Health Organization et al.," <https://d3i6fh83elv35t.cloudfront.net/static/ 2022/06/19-1392_6j37-2.pdf> (11/13/2024), 1-213.

"Doe v. Bolton," https://en.wikipedia.org/wiki/Doe_v._Bolton (4/19/2025), 1-5.

"Does Isaiah 7:14 Refer to as Virgin?" <https://hermeneutics.stackexchange.com/questions/17042/does- isaiah-714-refer-to-a-virgin> (8/3/2025), 1-20.

"Dolly, Cloned Sheep," <https://www.britannica.com/topic/Dolly-cloned-sheep> (9/14/2025), 1-4.

"Dolly (sheep)," <https://en.wikipedia.org/wiki/Dolly_(sheep)> (2/23/2025), 10-19.

Dry, Murray, "The Debate Over the Ratification of the Constitution: The Federalists v. The Anti-Federalists," From Reflection and Choice: The Political Philosophy of the *Federalist Papers* and the Ratification Debate, edit. Will R. Jordan, Macon, GA: Mercer University Press, 2020, 26-47.

Eberl, Jason T., "Aquinas's Account of Human Embryogenesis and Recent Interpretations," T&T Clark Reader in Abortion and Religion: Jewish, Christian, and Muslim Perspectives, edit. Rebecca Todd Peters and Margaret C. Kamitsuka, London: T&T Clark, 2023, 238-244.

"Ebers Papyrus," <https://en.wikipedia.org/wiki/Ebers_Papyrus>uropebaby," <https://www.uab.edu/news/health/item/12427-uab-hospital-delivers-record-breaking-premature-baby> (12/17/2024), 1-13.

"Ecclesiastes," <https://en.wikipedia.org/wiki/Ecclesiastes>, (8/3/2025), 1-12.

Edwards, R. G., "The Pre-implantation and Implanting Human Embryo," Embryonic Medicine and Therapy, edit. Eric Jauniaux, Eytan R. Barnea, and R. G. Edwards, New York: Oxford University Press, 1997, 3-31.

"Eisenstadt v. Baird," <https://en.wikipedia.org/wiki/Eisenstadt_v._Baird> (1/9/2025). 1-4.

Emery, John L., "Child Abuse, Sudden Infant Death Syndrome, and Unexpected Infant Death," American Journal of Disease of Children 147 (1993):1097-1100.

Engelhardt, Jr., H. Tristram, "Introduction," Abortion and the Status of the Fetus, edit. William B. Bondeson, H. Tristram Engelhardt, Jr., Stuart F. Spicker, and Daniel H. Winship, Dordrecht, Holland: D. Reidel Publishing Company, 1984, xi-xxxii.

"Europe Divided Over Robot 'Personhood,'"< https://www.politico. eu/article/europe-divided-over-robot-ai-artificial-intelligence-personhood/> (2/25/2025), 1-10.

Fagan, Patrick F., "Adoption: The Best Option," 2. Adoption Factbook III, edit. Connaught Mashner, National Council for Adoption, 1999, 2-6.

Feldman, David M., "Abortion: The Jewish View," T&T Clark Reader in Abortion and Religion: Jewish, Christian, and Muslim Perspectives, edit. Rebecca Todd Peters and Margaret C. Kamitsuka, London: T&T Clark, 2023, 201-206.

Fildes, Valerie A., Breasts, Bottles, and Babies, Edinburgh: Edinburgh University Press, 1986.

Filshie, G. Marcus, "Termination of Pregnancy," Handbook of Family Planning, edit. Nancy Loudon, Edinburgh: Churchill Livingstone, 1985, 234-249.

"First Abortion Conference in the U.S.," <https://today in clh.com/ levent=first=abortion-conference-in-the-u-s>, (1/8/2025), 1-2.

"First Amendment to the United States Constitution," 2. <https:// en.wikipedia.org/wiki/First_Amendment_to_the_United_States_ Constitution> (4/18/2025), 1-59.

Fisher, Russell S., "Criminal Abortion," 3. Abortion in America: Medical, Psychiatric, Legal, Anthropological, and Religious Consideration, edit. Harold Rosen, Boston: Beacon Press, 1954, 1967, 3-11.

Fleck, Anna, "U.S. Adoptions From Abroad Are Declining," <https://www. statista.com/chart/33552/number-of-children-adopted-in-the-us-from-abroad/> (1/26/2025), 1-8.

Ford, Norman, "The Human Embryo as Person in Catholic Teaching," T&T Clark Reader in Abortion and Religion: Jewish, Christian, and Muslim

Perspectives, edit. Rebecca Todd Peters and Margaret C. Kamitsuka, London: T&T Clark, 2023, 231-237.

Franklin, Cary, and Siegel, Reva, "Equality Emerges as a Ground for Abortion Rights in and after *Dobbs*", Roe v. Dobbs: The Past, Present, and Future of a Constitutional Right to Abortion, edit. Lee C. Bollinger and Geoffrey R. Stone, New York: Oxford University Press, 2024, 22-48.

"French Colonization of the Americas," https://en.wikipedia.org/wiki/French_colonization_of_the_Americas>(5/12/2025), 1-13.

"Full Text of the United States Constitution with All 27 Amendments," <https://constitutionus.com/constitution/full-text/>, (8/25/2025), 1-24

Garroway, Kristine Henriksen, "Claiming the Unclaimed: The Role of Feet in Adoption and Levirate Marriage," Adoption in the Hebrew Bible, edit. Ekaterina E. Kozlova and Cat Quine, London: T&T Clark, 2024, 76-95.

Gargiulo, Michele, "Japan Has Created the First Artificial Womb," <https://michelegargiulo.com/japan-artifical-womb-embryos-outside-body> (9/15/2025), 1-8.

"Georgia Tann," <https://en.wikipedia.org/wiki/Georgia_Tann> (1/26/2025), 1-10.

Gilmore, Cody, "What It Is to Die," Exploring the Philosophy of Death and Dying: Classical and Contemporary Perspectives, edit. Michael Cholbi and Travis Timmeman, New York: Routledge, 2021, 28-37.

Ginsburg, Tom, "American Exceptionalism and the Comparative Constitutional Law of Abortion," A Requiem for *Roe:* When Property Has No Privacy, Roe v. Dobbs: The Past, Present, and Future of a Constitutional Right to Abortion, edit. Lee C. Bollinger and Geoffrey R. Stone, New York: Oxford University Press, 2024, 259-277.

Glantz, Leonard, "Is the Fetus a Person? A Lawyer's View," Abortion and the Status of the Fetus, edit. William B. Bondeson, H. Tristram Engelhardt, Jr., Stuart F. Spicker, and Daniel H. Winship, Dordrecht, Holland: D. Reidel Publishing Company, 1984, 107-117.

Glennie, Madison, Milwit, Lily, and Zuckerbrod, Julie, "The World's Abortion Laws," Whose Choice Is It?: Abortion, Medicine, and the Law, edit. David F. Walbert and J. Douglas Butler, Chicago: ABA Publishing, 2021, 1-75.

"Global Catholic population rising as number of priests, religious falls," <https://www.vaticanchurch/news/2023-10/fides-catholic-church-statistics-world- mission-sunday.html> (12/19/2024), 1-3.

"The Global Religious Landscape," <https://www.pewforum-org/2012/12/18/global-religious-landscape-exec/>(04/17/2019), 1-3.

Goodwin, Michele Bratcher, A Requiem for *Roe:* When Property Has No

Privacy, <u>Roe v. Dobbs: The Past, Present, and Future of a Constitutional Right to Abortion</u>, edit. Lee C. Bollinger and Geoffrey R. Stone, New York: Oxford University Press, 2024, 190-202.

Gordon, Linda, <u>How Contraception and Abortion God Divorced, A Requiem for *Roe:* When Property Has No Privacy, Roe v. Dobbs: The Past, Present, and Future of a Constitutional Right to Abortion</u>, edit. Lee C. Bollinger and Geoffrey R. Stone, New York: Oxford University Press, 2024, 215-226.

Graetz, Michael J., and Greenhouse, Linda, <u>The Burger Court and the Rise of the Judicial Right</u>, New York: Simon & Schuster, 2016.

Greenhouse, Linda, <u>Becoming Justice Blackmun: Harry Blackmun's Supreme Court Journey</u>, New York: Henry Holt and Company, LLC., 2005.

Greenhouse, Linda, and Siegel, Reva, "Foreword," <u>Before Roe v. Wade: Voices That Shaped the Abortion Debate Before the Supreme Court's Ruling</u>, edit. Linda Greenhouse and Reva Siegel, New York: Kaplan Publishing, 2010, ix-xv.

Greenwald, Gary I., & Greenwald, Maria White, "Medicolegal Progress in Inquests of Felonious Deaths: Westminster, 1761-1866," <u>Journal of Legal Medicine</u> 2 (1981): 193-264.

Grimes, David A., "Provision of Abortion Services in the United States," <u>Abortion: Medical Progress and Social Implications</u>, Ciba Foundation Symposium 115, edit. Ruth Porter and Maeve O'Connor, London: Pitman, 1985, 26-31.

Grimes, David A., and Schulz, Kenneth F., "The Comparative Safety of Second-trimester Abortion Methods," <u>Abortion: Medical Progress and Social Implications</u>, Ciba Foundation Symposium 115, edit. Ruth Porter and Maeve O'Connor, London: Pitman, 1985, 83-101.

Hale, Ellen, "The Brutality of Growth Control," <u>Detroit News and Free Press</u>, (July 10, 1994), 1A.

"Harry Blackmun," <https:/en.wikipedia.org/kristofHarry_Blackmun> (11/28/2024), 1-8.

"Health, United States, 2008, With Special Features on the Health of Young Adults," <u><https://www.cdc.gov/nchs/data/hus/hus08.pdf></u> (7/19/2025), 1-603.

Helmholz, "Infanticide in the Province of Canterbury During the 15th Century," <u>History of Childhood Quarterly: Journal of Psychohistory</u> 2 (1974):379-390.

"History of Abortion," <u><https://en.wikipedia.org/wiki/History_of_abortion></u> (7/24/2025), 1-34.

"History of Christian Thought on Abortion," <u><https://en.wikipedia.org/wiki/History_of_Christian_thought_on_abortion></u> (2/17/2025), 1-9.

"Homicides Among Infants in the United States, 2917-2020," National Vital

Statistics Reports, CDC, <https://www.cdc.gov/nchs/products/index.htm> (11/20/2024), 1-10.

"The Hope of Salvation for Infants Who Die Without Being Baptised," <https://www.vatican.va/roman_curia/congregations/cfaith/cti_cocuments/rc_con_cfaith_doc_20070419_un-baptized-infantis_en.html> (8/3/3025), 1-35.

Horan, Dennis J., and Balch, Thomas J., "*Roe v. Wade*: No Justification in History, Law, or Logic," Abortion and the Constitution: Reversing *Roe v. Wade* Through the Courts, Dennis J. Horan, Edward R. Grant, Paige C. Cunningham, Washington, D.C.: Georgetown University Press, 1987, 57-88.

"Horatio Storer," 1. <https://en.wikipedia.org/wiki/Horatio_Storer> (9/1/2025), 1-5.

Horwitz, Daniel, "Changed by the Court: The Evolving Jurisprudence of Justice Blackmun and the Supreme Court, <https://www.harvardmagazine.com/2002/20/changed-by-the-court-htm/> (5/25/2025), 1-7.

"How Have US Fertility and Birth Rates Changed Over Time? ' <https://usafacts.org/articles/how-have-us-fertility–and-birth-rates-changed-over-time/> (9/5/2025), 1-10.

"How Many Democrats, Republicans are there in RI? Here's the Voter Breakdown," < https://www. providencejournal.com/story/news/politics/2024/07/21/how-many-registered-voters-are-there-in-ri-heres-the-breakdown/74491303007/> (7/22/2025), 1-2.

"H. R. 3755," <https://www.congress.gov/bill/117th-congress/house-bill/3755/text> (8/5/2025), 1-12.

"The Human Toll: How Many People Died in the Crusades," <https://www.medievelchronicles.com/the_crusades/the-human-toll-how-many-people-died-in-the-crusades/> (8/16/2025), 1-11.

"Humane Vitae, Encyclical Letter of the Supreme Pontiff Paul VI (July 29, 1968)." Before Roe v. Wade: Voices That Shaped the Abortion Debate Before the Supreme Court's Ruling, edit. Linda Greenhouse and Reva Siegel, New York: Kaplan Publishing, 2010, 71-77.

Huq, Aziz Z., and Wexler, Rebecca, "*Dobbs* and our Privacies," A Requiem for *Roe:* When Property Has No Privacy, Roe v. Dobbs: The Past, Present, and Future of a Constitutional Right to Abortion, edit. Lee C. Bollinger and Geoffrey R. Stone, New York: Oxford University Press, 2024, 299-317.

"Infanticide," <https://en.wikipedia.org/wiki/Infanticide> (12/25/2024), 1-40.

"Infanticide Act," <https://en.wikipedia.org/wiki/Infanticide_Act> (4/10/2025), 1-3.

"Introduction" The Politicization of the Supreme Court, edit. Eamon Doyle, New York: Greenhaven Publishing 2022, 7-10.

"Islam and Abortions," <https://en.wikipedia.org/wiki/Islam_and_abortion> (6/28/2025), 1-11.

"IVF Eggs and Ebryos to Live Birth-Rates," <https://extendedfertility.com/ivf-eggs-and-embryos-to-live-birth-rates/?form=MG0AV3> (2/23/2025), 1-6.

Jason, Janine, Gilliland, Jeanne C., & Tyler, Carl W. Jr., "Homicide As a Cause of Pediatric Mortality in the United States, Pediatrics 72 (1983): 191-197.

"Jesus in Islam," <https://en.wikipedia.org/wiki/Jesus_in_Islam" (9/1/2025), 1-31.

Josephus, "Against Apion," The Complete Works of Josephus, transl. Wm. Whiston, Grand Rapids, MI: Kregel Publications, 1981, 6-7-636.

"John Roberts," <https://en.wikipedia.org/wiki/John_Roberts> (2/14/2025), 1-37.

Kim, Daniel T., Curlin, Farr A., Wolenberg, Kelly M., and Sulmasy, Daniel P., "Back to the Future: The Ama and Religion, 1961-1974, *Academic Medicine* Vol. 89, No. 12, Dec., 2014, pgs 1603-1609.

Kitchen, William H., Richards, Annel L., Ford, Geoffrey W., Ryan, Margaret M., and Lissenden, Jean V., " Live-born Infants of 24-28 Weeks' Gestation: Survival and Sequelae at Two Years of Age," Abortion: Medical Progress and Social Implications, Ciba Foundation Symposium 115, edit. Ruth Porter and Maeve O'Connor, London: Pitman, 1985, 122-135.

Klabusich, Katie, "Abortion is as Old as Pregnancy: 4,000 Years of Reproductive Rights History," <https://truthout.org/articles/abortion-is-as-old-as-pregnancy-4-000-years-of-reproductive-rights-history/> (12/10/2024, 1-7.

Koh, Harold Hongiu, "The Justice Harry A. Blackmun Oral History Project," <https://tile.loc.gov/storage-services/service/mss/mss84430dig/mss84430dig/1429/02/142902.pdf> (8/1/2025) 1-442.

Kristof, Nicholas D., "Stark Data on Women: 100 Million Are Missing," New York Times November 5 (1991): C1.

Lee, Patrick, and George, Robert P., "The Wrong of Abortion," Bioethics: An Anthology, Fourth Edition, edit. Udo Schüklenk and Peter Singer, Hoboken, NJ: John Wiley & Sons, Inc., 2022, 42-53.

Lee, Rex, E., "Forward," Abortion and the Constitution: Reversing *Roe v. Wade* Through the Courts edit. Dennis J. Horan, Edward R. Grant, Paige C. Cunningham, Washington D.C.: Georgetown University Press, 1977, xiii-xvi.

"Lewish F. Powell, Jr.," < https://en.wikipedia.org/wiki/Lewis_F._Powell_Memorandum_1971> (3/6/20/2025) 1-12.

"Lincoln and the U.S. Constitution", <https://www.nps.gov/liho/learn/historyculture/constitution.htm> (5/20/2025), 1-5.

Lizza, John P., "Defining Death in a Technological World," Exploring the Philosophy of Death and Dying: Classical and Contemporary Perspectives, edit. Michael Cholbi and Travis Timmeman, New York: Routledge, 2021, 10-18.

"MAHMOUD ET AL. V. TAYLOR ET AL. CERTIORIA TO THE UNITED STATES COURT OF APPEALS FOR THE FOURTH CIRCUIT," <https://www.supremecourt.gov/opinions/24pdf/24-24-297_supremecourt.gov/opinions/24pdf/ 24-297_4f14.pdf> (7/1/2025), 1-135.

Maimonides, "The Book of Judges," Sanhedrin, Treatise One, 12.3, The Code of Maimonides Volume III, 1-35.

Marietta, Morgank, "Introduction: The 2021-2022 Term at the Supreme Court," SCOTUS 2022: Major Decisions and Developments of the US Supreme Court, edit. Morgan Marietta Cham, Cham, SW: Palgrave Macmillan, 2023, 1-28.

Marquis, Don, Why Abortion is Immoral," Bioethics: An Anthology, Fourth Edition, edit. Udo Schüklenk and Peter Singer, Hoboken, NJ: John Wiley & Sons, 2022, 54-66.

Matijček, Z. Dytrych, Z. And Schüller, "Follow-up Study of Children Born to Women Denied Abortion," Abortion: Medical Progress and Social Implications, Ciba Foundation Symposium 115, edit. Ruth Porter and Maeve O'Connor, London: Pitman, 1985, 136-149.

McConnell, Michael W., "Some Realism about Precedent in the Wake of *Dobbs*," Roe v. Dobbs: The Past, Present, and Future of a Constitutional Right to Abortion, edit. Lee C. Bollinger and Geoffrey R. Stone, New York: Oxford University Press, 2024, 101=116.

Milner, Larry S., "The Constitutionality of Medical Malpractice Legislative Reform: A National Survey," Loyola University of Chicago Law Journal, 18 (1987): 1053-1984.

"Minor v. Happersett,: <https://en.wikipedia.org/wiki/Minor_v._Happersett> (2/16/2025), 1-5.

Mitchell, Jonathan F., "Why was *Roe v. Wade* Wrong?" Roe v. Dobbs: The Past, Present, and Future of a Constitutional Right to Abortion edit. Lee C. Bollinger and Geoffrey R. Stone, New York: Oxford University Press, 2024, 51-66.

Mo, "At What Point Can a Fetus Survive Outside the Womb?" <https://wellwisp.com/at-what-point-can-a-fetus-survive-outside-the-womb?> (1/28/2025), 1-9.

"A Mouse Embryo Has Been Grown in an Artificial Womb - Humans Could be Next," <https://www.technologyreview.com/2021/03/17/1020969/mouse-embryo-grown-in-a_jar-humans-next>(12/4/2024), 1-11.

"Murder of George Tiller," <https://en.wikipedia.org/wiki/Murder_of_George_Tiller#Perpetrator> (1/15/2025), 1-18.

Murray, Melissa, and Shaw, Katherine, "*Dobb's* Democratic Deficits," Roe v. Dobbs: The Past, Present, and Future of a Constitutional Right to Abortion, edit. Lee C. Bollinger and Geoffrey R. Stone, New York: Oxford University Press, 2024, 158-171.

Nair-Collins, Michael, "We Die When Entropy Overwhelms Homeostasis," Exploring the Philosophy of Death and Dying: Classical and Contemporary Perspectives, edit. Michael Cholbi and Travis Timmerman, New York: Routledge, 2921, 19-27.

"Ninth Amendment," <https://www.law.cornell.edu/constitution/ninth_amendment> (2/16/2025), 1-4.

"Nineteenth Amendment to the United States Constitution," <https://en.wikipedia.org/wiki/Nineteenth_Amendment_to_the_United_States_Constitution, (11/26/2024), 1-30.

"Northwest Territory," <https://en.wikipedia.org/wiki/Northwest_Territory> (6/1/2025), 1-20.

"Number of abortion-related deaths reported in the U.S. from 1973-2021," <https://www.statista.com/statistics/658555/number-of-abortion-deaths-us/> (4/14/2025), 1-5.

"Number of U.S. Supreme Court Cases Decided by Year," <https://en.wikipedia.org/wiki/Number_of_U.S._Supreme_Court_Cases_decided_by_year> (3/9/2025), 1-10.

"Oaths of Office," <https://www.supremecourt.gov/about/oathsofoffice.aspx> (5?18/2025), 1-3.

"Originalism," <https://en.wikipedia.org/wiki/Originalism> (2/18/2025), 1-9.

Paintin, David B., "Legal Abortion in England and Wales," Abortion: Medical Progress and Social Implications, Ciba Foundation Symposium 115, edit. Ruth Porter and Maeve O'Connor, London: Pitman, 1985, 4-20.

Parker, Julie Faith, "Absence of Adoption in the Hebrew Bible?" Childist, Comparative, and Cross-Cultural Insights in Response to a Textual Conundrum," Adoption in the Hebrew Bible, edit. Ekaterina E. Kozlova and Cat Quine, London: T&T Clark, 2024, 12-28.

Partridge, John Colin, "Definitions of Viability and Their Meaning for

Neonatal Care," <u>Abortion Care as Moral Work: Ethical Considerations of Maternal and Fetal Bodies</u>, edit. Johanna Schoen, New Brunswick, NJ: Rutgers University Press, 2022, 170-176.

Payne, Russell, "What's the Point of Having Congress,?: Even Some Conservatives Now Say it's a Constitutional Crisis," <u><https://www.salon.com/2025/02/05/whats-the-point-of-having-congress-even-conservatives-worry-about-musks-illegal/></u> (3/2/2025), 1-10.

Peters, Rebecca Todd and Kamitska, Margaret C., "Introduction," <u>T & T Clark Reader in Abortion and Religion: Jewish, Christian, and Muslim Perspectives</u>, edit. Rebecca Todd Peters and Margaret C. Kamitsuka, London: T&T Clark, 2023, 1-17.

Pew Research Center, "The United States Has Become More Politically Polarized," <u>The Politicization of the Supreme Court</u>, edit. Eamon Doyle, New York: Greenhaven Publishing, 2022, 11-18.

Pfeifer, Michael Pearce, "Abandoning Error: Self-Correction by the Supreme Court," <u>Abortion and the Constitution: Reversing *Roe v. Wade* Through the Courts</u>, edit. Dennis J. Horan, Edward R. Grant, Paige C. Cunningham, Washington, D.C.: Georgetown University Press, 3-22.

Phillips, Kimberly, "Abortion in Colonial America: A Time of Herbal Remedies and Accepted Actions,"<u><https://today.uconn.edu/2022/08/abortion-in-colonial-america-a-time-of-herbal-remedies-and-accepted-actions/#></u> (3/29/2025), 1-16.

Philo, "The Special Laws, III." <u>The Works of Philo</u>, transl. C. D. Younge, Carol Stream, IL: Hendrickson Publishers, 1995, 594-615.

"Planned Parenthood v. Casey," <u><https://en.wikipedia.org/Planned_Parenthood_v._Casey></u> (2/21/2025), 1-17.

"Planned Parenthood of Southeastern Pa. v. Casey, 505 U.S. 833 (1992)," <u><https://copilot.Microsoft.com/PhBjRBV8poGuhlaak7fc4d></u> (2/21/2025), 1-79.

"Pope Sixtus VI," <u><https://en.wikipedia.org/wiki/Pope_Sixtus></u> (1/28/2025), 1-9.

"Preamble to the United States Constitution," <u><https://en.wikipedia.org/wiki/Preamble_to_the_United_States_Constitution,></u> (11/29/2024), 1-20.

"The Project Gutenberg eBook of Medicine in Eight Books," <u><https://www.gutenberg.org/cache/epub/64207/pg64207-images.html></u> (6/7/2025), 1-390.

"Pythagoras's Philosophy and Immortality of the Soul," <u><https://Philosophies of life.org/Pythagoras- philosophy-and-immortality-of-the-soul/></u> (6/20/2025), 1-14.

Quine, Cat, "Introduction: Adoption and Familial Complexity in the Hebrew

Bible," <u>Adoption in the Hebrew Bible</u> edit. Ekaterina E. Kozlova and Cat Quine, London: T&T Clark, 2024, 1-8.

"R v. Morgentaler," <u><https://en.wikipedia.org/wiki/R_v_Morgentaler></u> (1/18/2025), 1-7.

Radbill, Samuel X., "Children in a World of Violence: A History of Child Abuse," <u>The Battered Child</u>, edit. Ray E. Helfer & Ruth S. Kempe, Chicago: University of Chicago Press, 1987, 3-22.

Re, Richard M., "Should Gradualism Have Prevailed in Dobbs?" <u>Roe v. Dobbs: The Past, Present, and Future of a Constitutional Right to Abortion</u>, edit. Lee C. Bollinger and Geoffrey R. Stone, New York: Oxford University Press, 2024, 140-157.

Reed, Anna, "A Future from the Past: Self-Managed Abortion with Ancient Care and Modern Medicine," Whose Choice Is It?: Abortion, Medicine, and the Law, edited. David F. Walbert and J. Douglas Butler, Chicago: ABA Publishing, 2021, 231-281.

"Religion in Mississippi," <u><https://uscanadainfo.com/religion-in-mississippi/></u> (6/16/2025), 1-7.

"Republicans Just Can't Stop Calling for Civil War," <u><https://thehill.com/opinion/campaign/4187490-republicans-just-cant-stop-calling-for-civil-war></u> (5/15/2025), 1-13.

"Research on the Fetus," <u><https://scholarworks.indianapolis.iu.edu/server/api/core/bitstreams/b837d2c4-ffd9-449e-a2fb-370dbb91874b/content></u> (2/8/2025), 1-11.

Riddle, John M., "Women's Knowledge of Abortifacients from Antiquity to the Present," <u>Whose Choice Is It?: Abortion, Medicine, and the Law</u>, edit. David F. Walbert and J. Douglas Butler, Chicago: ABA Publishing, 2021, 207-229.

Roberts, Dorothy, "The Failure of *Dobbs*, The Entanglement of Abortion Bans, Criminalized Pregnancies, and Forced Family Separation," <u>Roe v. Dobbs: The Past, Present, and Future of a Constitutional Right to Abortion</u>, edit. Lee C. Bollinger and Geoffrey R. Stone, New York: Oxford University Press, 2024, 175-189.

"Roe v. Wade, 410 U.S. 113 (1973)," <u><https://supreme.justia.com/cases/federal/us/410/113/></u> (11/13/2024), 1-36.

"*Roe v. Wade* (film)," <u><https://en.wikipedia.org/wiki/Roe_v._Wade_(film)></u> (5/9/2025), 1-5.

Rosen, Harold, "Anno Domini 1967: The Year of the State Abortion Bill," <u>Abortion in America: Medical, Psychiatric, Legal, Anthropological, and Religious Consideration</u>, edit. Harold Rosen, Boston: Beacon Press, 1954, 1967, xv-xix.

Saunders, Edward, "Neonaticides Following 'Secret' Pregnancies: Seven Case Reports," <u>Public Health Reports</u> 104 (1989): 368-372.

Savitt, Todd I., "Smothering & Overlaying of Virginal Slave Children: A Suggested Explanation," <u>Bulletin of the History of Medicine</u> 49 (1975): 400-404.

Scott, P.D., "The Psychiatrist's Viewpoint," <u>The Maltreatment of Children,</u> edit. Selwyn M. Smith, Baltimore: University Park Press, 1978, 175-204.

Selia, Shelley, "The Meaning of Viability in Abortion Care," <u>Abortion Care as Moral Work: Ethical Considerations of Maternal and Fetal Bodies</u>, edit. Johanna Schoen, New Brunswick, NJ: Rutgers University Press, 2022, 105-109.

Sachar and Zubrzycki, Carllean, "Informational Privacy After Dobbs," 75 Ala L. Rev 1-3 (2023), <https://hls.harvard.edu/bibliography/informational-privacy-after-dobbs/> (3/25/2025), 1-3.

Shannon, Thomas A., "Abortion: A Challenge for Ethics and Medical Policy," <u>Abortion and the Status of the Fetus</u>, edit. William Bondeson, H. Tristram Engelhardt Jr., Stuart F. Spicker, and Daniel H. Winship, Dordrecht: D. Reidel Publishing Company, 1984, 3-14.

Shaw, Margery W. and Damme, Catherine, "Legal Status of the Fetus," <u>Genetics and the Law</u>, edit. Aubrey Milunsky and George J. Annas, New York: Plenum Press, 1976, 2-37.

Soupart, Pierre, "Present and Possible Future Research in the Use of Human Embryos," <u>Abortion and the Status of the Fetus</u>, edit. William Bondeson, H. Tristam Engelhardt Jr., Stuart F. Spicker, and Daniel H. Winship, Dordrecht: D. Reidel Publishing Company, 1984, 67-104.

"Statue of Liberty," <https://enwikipedia.org'widi/statue_of_Liberty> (4/5/2025), 1-35.

Stewart, Katherine, "Fx's Jane Roe Deathbed Confession Reveals the Abortion Lie at the Heart of the Religious Right," <https://www.nbcnews.com/think/opinion/fx-s-Jane-Roe-deathbed-confession-reveals-abortion-lie-heart-nena1214381> (2/19/2025), 1-5.

Strauss, David A., "Liberal Critics of Roe," <u>Roe v. Dobbs: The Past, Present, and Future of a Constitutional Right to Abortion</u>, edit. Lee C. Bollinger and Geoffrey R. Stone, New York: Oxford University Press, 2024, 3-21.

Sunstein, Cass R., "*Dobbs* and the Travails of Due Process Traditionalism," <u>Roe v. Dobbs: The Past, Present, and Future of a Constitutional Right to Abortion</u>, edit. Lee C. Bollinger and Geoffrey R. Stone, New York: Oxford University Press, 2024, 130-139.

"Text of Lincoln's Speech," <https://www.owleyes.org/text/gettysburg-address/read/text-of-lincolns-speech>(3/23/2025), 1-3.

"Thirteen Colonies" <https://en.wikipedia.org/wiki/thirteen-colonies> (6/20/2025), 1-19.

Thomson, Judith Jarvis, "A Defense of Abortion," Bioethics: An Anthology, Fourth Edition, edit. Udo Schüklenk and Peter Singer, Hoboken, NJ: John Wiley & Sons, 2022, 16-41.

Thomson-DeVeauz, Amelia, "When Abortion Was Only Legal in 6 States," <https://fivethirtyeight.com/features/when-abortion-was-only-legal-in-6-states> (11/26/2024), 1-2.

"Timeline of Reproductive Rights Legislation," <https://en.wikipedia.org/wiki/timeline_of_reproductive_rights_legislation> (3/6/2025), 1-53.

Tooley, Michael, "Abortion and Infanticide," Bioethics: An Anthology, Fourth Edition, edit. Udo Schüklenk and Peter Singer, Hoboken, NJ: John Wiley & Sons, 2022, 15-30.

"Transcript of First Oral Argument in *Roe v. Wade 410 U.S. 113 (1973)*" <https://aul.org/wp-content/uploads/2021/05/68497248-Transcript-Roe-v-Wade-1st-Oral-Dec-13-1971.pdf> (6/10/2025), 1-25.

"Transcript of Rearguement in *Roe v. Wade, 410 U. S. (1973)*," <https://aul.org/wp-content/uploads/2021/05/68497271-Transcript-Roe-v-Wade-Re-Argument-Oct-1972.pdf>, (4/19/2025), 1-25.

Tribe, Laurence A., "Finding Abortion Rights in the Constitution," Whose Choice Is It?: Abortion, Medicine, and the Law, edit. David F. Walbert and J. Douglas Butler, Chicago: ABA Publishing, 2021, 471-509.

"Trump reveals his top pick for the new Pope - himself," <https://www.independent.co.uk/news/world/americas/us-politics/trump-wants-to-be-pope-b2742082.html> (9/8/2025), 1-5.

"The Turnaway Study," <https://www.ansirh.org/research/ongoing/turnaway-study> (2/6/2025), 1-18.

"Uniform Determination of Death Act," <https://en.wikipedia.org/wiki/Uniform_Determination_of_Death_Act> (2/1/2025), 1–3._

"Unintended Pregnancy and Abortion Worldwide," <https://www.guttmacher.org/fact-sheet-induced-abortion-worldwide> (12/27/2024), 1-7.

"United States v. Vuitch," <https://en.wikipedia.org/wiki/United_States_v._Vuitch,> (1/9/2025), 1-98.

"U.S. Dictionary," <https://usdictionary.com/idioms/whats-good-for-the-goose/> (8/22/2025), 1-10.

"Va. Pharmacy B/ v/ Va. Consumer Council," <https://casetext.com/case/virginia-state-board-of-pharmacy-v-Virginia-citizens-consumer-council-inc> (3/23/2025), 1-37.

"Vatican City," <https://en.wikipedia.org/wiki/Vatican_City> (9/12/2025), 1-31.

"W. Clement Stone Quotes," <https://www.azquotes.com/ author/14190_W._Clement_Stone> (6/27/2025), 1-11.

Walbert, David F., "Politics, Religion, and Abortion in the United States," Whose Choice Is It?: Abortion, Medicine, and the Law edit. David F. Walbert and J. Douglas Butler, Chicago: ABA Publishing, 2021, 191-205.

Walters, Leroy, "The Fetus in Ethical and Public Policy Discussion From 1973 to the Present," Abortion and the Status of the Fetus, edit. William Bondeson, H. Tristram Engelhardt Jr., Stuart F. Spicker, and Daniel H. Winship, Dordrecht: D. Reidel Publishing Company, 1984, 15-30.

Ward, Roy Bowen, "The Use of the Bible in the Abortion Debate," T&T Clark Reader in Abortion and Religion: Jewish, Christian, and Muslim Perspectives, edit. Rebecca Todd Peters and Margaret C. Kamitsuka, London: T&T Clark, 2023, 245-252.

Weddington, Sarah Ragle, "The Woman's Right of Privacy," Abortion: A Reader, edit. Lloyd Steffen, Cleveland: The Pilgrim Press, 1996, 25-34.

Weiner, Gary, "Introduction," Personhood, edit. Gary Weiner, New York: Greenhaven Publishing, 2022, 14-19.

Weiss, Deborah Cassens, "Supreme Court Justices Recused Themselves 1890 Times in Most Recent Term," <https:/www.abajournal.com/news/ article_supreme_court_justices_recused_themselves_180_times_in_ most_recent_term/> (/8/2025), 1-2.

"What Was the Population of Ancient Greece," <https://greekreporter. com/2025/01/18/ population-ancient-greece-demographics/> (7/22/2025), 1-8.

"Where Do Americans Stand on Abortion," <https://news.gallup.com/ poll/321143/americans-stand-abortion.aspx> (2/27/2025), 1-5.

Williamson, Laila, "Infanticide: An Anthropological Analysis," Infanticide & The Value of Life, edit. Marvin Kohl, Buffalo: Prometheus Books, 1978, 115-129.

Wise, Steven M., "Animals Deserve to be Recognized as Persons," Personhood, edit. Gary Wiener, New York: Greenhouse Publishing, 2022, 29-42.

"The World's Abortion Laws," <https://reproductiverights.org/maps/world-abortion-laws/> (5/3/2025), 1-24.

Ziegler, Mary, "The Anti-Abortion Movement and the Punishment Perogative," Roe v. Dobbs: The Past, Present, and Future of a Constitutional Right to Abortion, edit. Lee C. Bollinger and Geoffrey R. Stone, New York: Oxford University Press, 2024, 227-240.

Ziegler, Mary, "Dobbs v. Jackson Women's Health Organization on Abortion," SCOTUS 2022: Major Decisions and Developments of the US Supreme Court, edit. Morgan Marietta, Cham, SW: Palgrave Macmillan, 2023, 29-38.

Bibliography

Books

Abortion: A Reader, edit. Lloyd Steffen, Cleveland: The Pilgrim Press, 1996.

Abortion and the Constitution: Reversing *Roe v. Wade* Through the Courts, edit. Dennis J. Horan, Edward R. Grant, Paige C. Cunningham, Washington, D.C.: Georgetown University Press, 1987.

Abortion and the Status of the Fetus, edit. William Bondeston, H. Tristram Engelhardt, Jr., Stuart F. Spicker, and Daniel H. Winship, Dordrecht: D. Reidel Publishing Company, 1984.

Abortion in America: Medical, Psychiatric, Legal, Anthropological, and Religious Consideration, edit. Harold Rosen, Boston: Beacon Press, 1954, 1967.

Abortion: Medical Progress and Social Implications, Ciba Foundation Symposium 115, edit. Ruth Porter and Maeve O'Connor, London: Pitman, 1985.

Abortion Care as Moral Work: Ethical Considerations of Maternal and Fetal Bodies, edit. Johanna Schoen, New Brunswick, NJ: Rutgers Press, 2022.

Abortion Rights, Access, and Legislative Response, edit. Jorge P. Sandford, New York: Snova, 2022.

Adoption in the Hebrew Bible, edit. Ekaterina E. Koslova and Cat Quine, London: T&T Clark, 2024.

Aristotle, Politics, The Basic Works of Aristotle, edit. Richard McKeon, New York: Random House, 1941.

Barrett, Amy Coney, Listening to the Law: Reflections on the Court and Constitution, New York: Sentinel, 2025.

The Battered Child,, edit. Ray E. Helfer & Ruth S. Kempe, Chicago: University of Chicago Press, 1987.

Becker, Amanda, You Must Stand Up: The Fight for Abortion Rights in Post-*Dobbs* America, New York: Bloomsbury Publishing, 2024.

Before Roe v. Wade: Voices That Shaped the Abortion Debate Before the Supreme Court's Ruling, edit. Linda Greenhouse and Reva Siegel, New York: Kaplan Publishing, 2010.

Bioethics: An Anthology, Fourth Edition, edit. Udo Schüklenk and Peter Singer, Hoboken, NJ: John Wiley & Sons, 2022.

Biskupic, Joan, Nine Black Robes: Inside the Supreme Court's Drive to the Right and Its Historic Consequences, New York: William Morrow, 2023.

Braine, Naomi, Abortion Beyond the Law: Building a Global Feminist Movement for Self-Managed Abortion, London: Verso, 2023.

Caron, Simone M., Who Chooses?: American Reproductive History Since 1930, Gainesville, FL: University Press of Florida, 2008.

Cienappo, Jonathan, <u>Against Constitutional Originalism: A Historical Critique</u>, New Haven: Yale University Press, 2024.

Coby John Patrick, <u>The Constitutional Convention of 1787: Constructing the American Republic</u>, New York: W. W. Norton & Company, 2018.

<u>The Complete Works of Josephus</u>, transl. Wm. Whiston, Grand Rapids: Kregel Publications, 1981.

Congreve, William, <u>Love for Love</u>, Lincoln, NB: University of Nebraska Press, 1966.

Crowther, Kathleen M., <u>Policing Pregnant Bodies: From Ancient Greece to Post-Roe America</u>, Baltimore: Johns Hopkins University Press, 2023.

<u>Death Determination by Neurologic Criteria: Areas of Consensus and Controversy</u> edit. Ariane Lews and James L. Bernat, Cham, CH: Springer, 2023.

DeFrain, John, Taylor, Jacque, & Ernst, Linda, <u>Coping With Sudden Infant Death</u>, Idaho Falls, ID: Lexington Books, 1982.

Dias, Elizabeth, and Lerer, Lisa, <u>The Fall of Roe: The Rise of a New America</u>, New York: Flatiron Books, 2024.

Dyer, Frederick N., <u>Champion of Women and the Unborn: Horatio Robinson Storer, M.D.</u>, Canton, MA: Science History Publications, 1999.

<u>Embryonic Medicine and Therapy</u>, edit. Eric Jauniaux, Eytan R. Barnea, and R. G. Edwards, New York: Oxford University Press, 1997.

Epicurus, Sextus, <u>Outlines of Pyrrhonism</u>, transl. R. G. Bury, London: William Heinemann, Ltd., 1933.

Epstein, Lee, Segal, Jeffrey A., Spaeth, Harold J., and Walker, Thomas G., <u>The Supreme Court Compendium: Data, Decisions and Developments, Second Edition</u>, Washington D.C.: Congressional Quarterly, Inc., 1996.

<u>Exploring the Philosophy of Death and Dying: Classical and Contemporary Perspectives</u>, edit. Michael Cholbi and Travis Timmeman, New York: Routledge, 2021.

Faux, Marian, <u>Roe v. Wade: The Untold Story of the Landmark Supreme Court Decision That Made Abortion Legal</u>, New York: Macmillan Publishing Company, 1988.

<u>Fighting Mad: Resisting the End of *Roe v. Wade*</u>, edit. Krystale E. Littlejohn and Ricke Solinger, Oakland: University of California Press, 2024.

Freidenfelds, Lara, <u>The Myth of the Perfect Pregnancy: A History of Miscarriage in America</u>, New York: Oxford University Press, 2020.

<u>From Reflection and Choice: The Political Philosophy of the *Federalist Papers* and the Ratification Debate</u>, edit. Will R. Jordan, Macon, GA: Mercer University Press, 2020.

Genetics and the Law, edit. Aubrey Milunsky and George J. Annas, New York: Plenum Press, 1976.

Gillis, Chester, Roman Catholicism in America, New York: Columbia University Press, 1999.

Graff, Garrett, M., Watergate: A New History, New York: Avid Reader Press, 2022.

Gunkel, David J., Person, Thing, Robot: A Moral and Legal Ontology for the 21st Century and Beyond, Cambridge, MA: The MIT Press, 2023.

Hamilton, Alexander, Jay, John, & Madison, James, The Federalist Papers and the Constitution of the United States: The Principles of the American Government, New York: Racehorse Publishing, 2016.

Harari, Yuval Noah, Nexus: A Brief History of Information Networks From the Stone Age to AI, New York: Random House, 2024.

Hattery, Angela, and Smith, Earl, The Social Dynamics of Family Violence, Boulder: Westview Press, 2012.

Hesiod, Theogony, transl. Apostolas N. Athanaskis, Baltimore: Johns Hopkins Press, 1983.

The Holy Bible, King James Version, E. B. Trent and Company, 1962.

The Holy Qur'an, Text, Translation and Commentary A. Yusuf Ali, Brentwood MD: Amana Corp., 1983.

Hoover, J. E., Uniform Crime Reports - 1966, Washington, D.C.: Government Printing Office, 1966.

Huser, Roger John, The Crime of Abortion in Canon Law: An Historical Synopsis and Commentary, Washington, D.C.: The Catholic University of America Press, 1942.

The Jewish Study Bible, Jewish Publication Society, TANAKH Translation, edit. Adele Berlin and Marc Zvi Brettler, New York: Oxford University Press, 2004.

Kapparis, Konstantinos A., Abortion in the Ancient World, London: Duckworth, 2002.

Kolbert, Kathryn, & Kaay, Julie F., Controlling Women: What We Must do Now to Save Reproductive Freedom, New York: Hachette Book Group, Inc., 2021.

Lavin, Talia, Wild Faith: How the Christian Right is Taking Over America, New York: LegacyLitBooks, 2024.

Lea, Henry Charles, History of Auricular Confession and Indulgences in the Latin Church, Philadelphia: Lea Brothers, 1986.

Manninen, Bertha Alvarez, <u>Pro-Life, Pro-Choice: Shared Values in the Abortion Debate,</u> Nashville: Vanderbilt University Press, 2014.

Martinson, Floyd M., <u>Growing Up in Norway, 800-1990,</u> Carbondale, IL: Southern Illinois University Press, 1992.

McBride, Dorthy E., and Keys, Jennifer L., <u>Abortion in the United States: A Reference Handbook,,</u> Santa Barbara, CA: ABC-Clio, 20218.

McFarlane, Deborah R. and Hansen, Wendy L., <u>Regulating Abortion: The Politics of US Abortion Policy,</u> Baltimore: Johns Hopkins University Press, 2024.

Milner, Larry S., <u>Hardness of Heart/Hardness of Life: The Stain of Human Infanticide,</u> Jacksonville, FL: Mazo Publishers, 1998, 2023.

Milner, Larry S., <u>Hebraic Influences on Greek Civilization: Was Achilles a Jew?,</u> Jacksonville, FL: Mazo Publishers, 2025.

Milner, Larry S., <u>Shattered Faith: The Life of Abraham,</u> Jacksonville, FL: Mazo Publishers, 2021.

Milner, Larry S., <u>The Three Lives of Sigmund Freud: Evidence of an Important Identity Crisis, Volumes I, II, III,</u> Jacksonville, FL: Mazo Publishers, 2024.

Mohr, James C., <u>Abortion in America: The Origins and Evolution of National Policy, 1800-1900,</u> New York: Oxford University Press, 1978.

Montgomery, Heather, <u>Violence: A History of Child Abuse,</u> Cambridge, UK: Polity Press, 2004.

Moorhead, Hugh S., <u>The Meaning of Life,</u> Chicago: Chicago Review Press, 1988.

Mooney, Carla, <u>Overturned: The Constitutional Right to Abortion,</u> San Diego: Reference Point Press, 2023.

Motz, Anna, <u>If Love Could Kill: The Myths and Truths of Women Who Commit Violence,</u> New York: Alfred A. Knopf, 2024.

Murkof, Heidi, <u>What to Expect When You're Expecting,</u> New York: Workman Publishing, 2022.

Norris, Silan, <u>Bodies Under Siege: How the Far-Right Attack on Reproductive Rights Went Global,</u> London: Verse, 2023.

O'Connor, Anne, <u>Child Murderess and Dead Child Traditions, A Comparative Study,</u> Helsinski: Acaemia Scientiarium, Fennica, 1991.

Olasky, Marvin and Savas, Leah, <u>The Story of Abortion in America: A Street-Level History, 1652-2022,</u> Wheaton, IL: Crossway, 2023.

Pertman, Adam, <u>Adoption Nation: How the Adoption Revolution is Transforming America,,</u> New York: Basic Books, 2000.

Plato, <u>The Republic,</u> transl. Allan Bloom, Basic Books, 1968.

The Politicization of the Supreme Court, edit. Eamon Doyle, New York: Greenhaven Publishing, 2022.

Prager, Joshua, The Family Roe: An American Story, New York: W. W. Norton & Company, 2021.

Raring, Richard H., Crib Death, Hicksville, NY: Exposition Press, 1975.

Reagan, Leslie J., When Abortion Was a Crime: Women, Medicine and the Law in the United States, 1867- 1973, Oakland: University of California Press, 1997.

Roe v. Dobbs: The Past, Present, and Future of a Constitutional Right to Abortion, edit. Lee C. Bollinger and Geoffrey R. Stone, New York: Oxford University Press, 2024.

Roe v. Wade Fifty Years After, edit. Rhae Lynn Barnes & Catherine Clinton, Athens, GA: The University of Georgia Press, 2024.

SCOTUS 2022: Major Decisions and Developments of the US Supreme Court, edit. Morgan Marietta, Cham, SW: Palgrave Macmillan, 2023.

Shabar, Shulamith, Childhood in the Middle Ages, London: Routledge, 1999.

Singer, Elyse Ona, Lawful Sins: Abortion Rights and Reproductive Governance in Mexico, Stanford, CA: Stanford University Press, 2022.

Sisson, Gretchen, Relinquished: The Politics of Adoption and the Privilege of American Motherhood, New York: St. Martin's Press, 2024.

Skousen, Paul B., The Federalist Papers Made Easier: The Complete and Original Text Subdivided and Annotated for Easier Understanding, Salt Lake City: Izzard Ink, 2022.

Storer, Horatio Robinson, The Causation, Course, and Treatment of Reflex Insanity in Women, Boston: Lee and Shepard, 1871.

Storer, Horatio Robinson, On Criminal Abortion in America, Philadelphia: Lippincott, 1860.

Storer, Horatio R. and Heard, Franklin Fiske, Criminal Abortion: Its Nature, Its Evidence, and Its Law, Boston: Little, Brown, and Company, 1868.

T&T Clark Reader in Abortion and Religion: Jewish, Christian, and Muslim Perspectives, edit. Rebecca Todd Peters, and Margaret C. Kamistuka, T&T Clark, 2023.

Toobin, Jeffrey, The Nine: Inside the Secret World of the Supreme Court, New York: Anchor Books, 2008.

Veatch, Robert M., and Ross, Lainie F., Defining Death: The Case for Choice, Washington, DC: Georgetown University Press, 2016.

Waldman, Michael, The Supermajority: How the Supreme Court Divided America, New York: Simon & Schuster, 2023.

Weddington, Sarah, A Question of Choice, New York: G. P. Putnam's Sons, 1992.

Wenz, Peter S., Abortion Rights as Religious Freedom, Philadelphia: Temple University Press, 1992.

What Roe v. Wade Should Have Said: The Nation's Top Legal Experts Rewrite America's Most Controversial   Decision, edit. Jack M. Balkin, New York: New York University Press, 2005.

Whose Choice Is It?: Abortion, Medicine, and the Law, edit. David F. Walbert and J. Douglas Butler, Chicago: ABA Publishing, 2021.

Woodward, Bob and Armstrong, Scott, The Brethren: Inside the Supreme Court, New York: Simon & Schuster, 1979.

Woodward, Bob and Armstrong, Scott, The Justices Behind Roe v. Wade: The Inside Story, New York: Simon & Schuster, 1979, 2021.

The Works of Philo, transl. C. D. Yonge, Carol Stream, IL: Hendrickson Publishers, 1995.

100 years of the Infanticide Act: Legacy, Impact and Future Directions, edit. Karen Brennan and Emma Milne, Oxford: Hart, 2023.

Zenicka-Goetz, Magdalena and Highfield, Roger, The Dance of Life: The New Science of How a Single Cell Becomes a Human Being, New York: Basic Books, 2020.

Ziegler, Mary, Abortion and the Law in America: Roe v. Wade to the Present, Cambridge, UK: Cambridge University Press, 2020.

Ziegler, Mary, Dollars for Life; The Anti-Abortion Movement and the Fall of the Republican Establishment, New Haven: Yale University Press, 2022.

Ziegler, Mary, Roe: The History of a National Obsession, New Haven, Yale University Press, 2023.

Index

www.ingramcontent.com/pod-product-compliance
Lightning Source LLC
Chambersburg PA
CBHW062159270326
41930CB00009B/1589